Authorship and Copyright

Authorship and Copyright

David Saunders

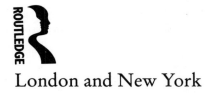

London and New York

First published 1992
by Routledge
11 New Fetter Lane, London EC4P 4EE

Simultaneously published in the USA and Canada
by Routledge
a division of Routledge, Chapman & Hall, Inc.
29 West 35th Street, New York, NY 10001

As the author of *Authorship and Copyright* I hereby assert
generally my moral right to be identified as its author
whenever it is commercially published in the United
Kingdom.

Typeset in 10 on 12pt Garamond by
Ponting–Green Publishing Services, Sunninghill, Berks
Printed in Great Britain by
T J Press (Padstow) Ltd, Padstow, Cornwall.

British Library Cataloguing in Publication Data
Saunders, David
  Authorship and Copyright
  I. Title
  344.10648209

Library of Congress Cataloging in Publication Data
Saunders, David
  Authorship and Copyright / David Saunders.
     p.   cm.
  Includes bibliographical references and index.
  1. Copyright – History.   2. Law and literature – History.   3.
Authors – Legal status, laws, etc. – History.   4. Authorship –
History.   I. Title.
K4140.S28   1992
346.04'82–dc20
[342.6482]   91–43745

ISBN 0–415–04158–9

Contents

Preface

This is a work of history that reconnects a phenomenon of print literate cultures – authorship – to its legal conditions, and a legal phenomenon – ownership of copyright – to its historical and cultural conditions. It is a project at the threshold where two different styles of reasoning – call them aesthetic and legal, or philosophical and governmental, or theoretical and positive – have long confronted one another. In treating authorship as a legal status, I might therefore be seen as having opted for a merely technical domain of social existence rather than the high ground of moral and aesthetic culture. Perhaps so. However, this does not stop me suggesting that copyright lawyers and historians should have a better sense of aesthetics. This suggestion is not made in order to assert some fundamental value. The point is to bring to light the impact of a particular ethos – that of the *whole* or *integral* person – on law concerning authorship. This ethos is one whose spheres of operation have long since extended beyond the realm of poets on mountains or artists in garrets. Scratch a well-trained executive of today and find that concern with achieving a balanced life, an equilibrium of imagination and realism that, historically, has been the mark which distinguishes . . . the product of the aesthetic education. These are days in which we can all attend a seminar on personal growth and integrity. This whole or – in its more definitive appellation – aesthetic persona, together with the legal personality or status associated with the ownership of copyright, are the principal forms of personhood whose history is addressed in the pages that follow. This is, therefore, a work about some actual forms of personhood, not about all possible ones.

While committed to historical description, the book is intended also as a contribution to the 'history of the present'. In the context of current American, British, Canadian and Australian debates on the future directions of the humanities, it might be that the boundary between the cultural and the legal or governmental spheres will blur, a circumstance apt for hybrid and impure researches such as this. In a different direction, pressures for reform of legal studies are apparent, particularly where strictly profession-oriented curricula in the law schools leave graduates open to the charge of being highly trained but barely cultured. Those who make this charge might welcome a comparative history that explores a form of property important in the modern economy – copyright – not only in its Anglo-American regimes but also in the continental regimes of the *droit d'auteur* or author's right in which the distinctive form of the *droit moral* or moral right has emerged, albeit more recently than is usually supposed. Putting the legal historical record straight with respect to these different legal systems permits a surer footing when, as now, there is activity at the international level. When the US Congress acknowledges a form of accommodation with the *droit moral* by passing the Berne Convention Implementation Act of 1989, and the United Kingdom and Canadian Parliaments acknowledge it through provisions of the UK Copyright, Designs and Patents Act of 1988 and the Canadian Copyright Amendment Act of the same year, there is point in having some grasp of the comparative history of copyright and the *droit moral* and their cultural circumstances.

This study is intended also to illustrate what a practical and pluralist form of literary and cultural studies might look like – not least as an alternative to the post-structuralist ascendancy in literary and cultural theory. Crudely put, this means a return to historical information. In a recent review of a work on English Renaissance literary culture, the reviewer – let him go unnamed – laments that in schools and departments of English 'instructors are oppressing their students with facts'. This statement is indicative of a cultural milieu in which authorities defend that special species of learned ignorance whereby the discipline of English has aimed to detach its students from facts and technical competence the better to concentrate on an aesthetic refashioning of their personality. In this milieu, the emergence of the literary author has been taken to exemplify how aesthetic self-production is achieved: hence the importance accorded to a Romantic theme – the 'birth' of the author. The presumed mundanity of legal matters allowed practical conditions of authorship such as ownership of copyright to be reduced to small change, regardless of the fact that in the actual world of book publishing they were big money.

More recently, in what has seemed a powerful theory-based breakthrough, a post-structuralist (or deconstructionist) account of authorship has popularised a counter-theme – the 'death' of the author. This second account offers a critique of the author as origin and end of meaning, and presents itself as an emancipation – there are tones of an epochal shift in cultural politics – from the individualised authorial subject of Romanticism. The precondition of all possible forms of personhood (and meanings) is now to be 'language', 'discourse' or 'writing'. Yet once again the status of institutional conditions – including legal arrangements – is trivialised, this time by an enthusiastic dismissal of positive fact as a discursive fiction arbitrarily imposed on linguistic possibility. From the more historical and practical perspective of this book, however, the antagonism of the author's birth and author's death brigades is not fundamental. In the name of resistance to and emancipation from positive institutions and knowledge, each risks that loss of contact with historical specificity which comes when we neglect the actual forms of agency. Both accounts of authorship are in this regard unhelpful. By contrast, my conviction is that once we are into the technicalities of positive law, we cannot be entirely stupid.

Whatever my personal commitment to the present research, this work could not have been written without the collaborative ambience of the Division of Humanities at Griffith University. The opportunity of participating in team-based teaching and research, together with the financial and secretarial support of the Division, have made the book possible. I want to record a particular debt to Ian Hunter and Dugald Williamson, my co-authors in *On Pornography: Literature, Sexuality and Obscenity Law*, the writing of which taught me many lessons that are both explicit and implicit in the present work. My thanks go also to Jeffrey Minson, Peter Anderson and Wayne Hudson. These colleagues will, I hope, recognise here one particular outcome of a shared intellectual project. More anonymously but no less warmly, I acknowledge the work of the legal writers and historians on whom I have depended, sometimes to a great extent. To its credit, knowingly or unknowingly, their work proceeded without concern for the distinctive imperatives of contemporary literary and cultural theory. I hope to have given the work of these writers a relevance to certain current debates in literary and cultural studies which they did not seek but with which, I trust, they would not be entirely unpleased. Elements of the present argument derive from studies I have published in *Critical Inquiry*, *English Literary History* and *New Formations*; I thank these journals for giving me their permission to elaborate on those earlier formulations.

D.S.

Introduction

Authorship has proven a magnetic topic for literary and cultural studies. For their practitioners, the treatment accorded the issue of authorship has become an index of the current state of literary and cultural theory, to be regretted or applauded, resisted or embraced. Yet it is the measure of an abstraction from institutional realities that so much garrulous debate about authorship has proceeded in ignorance of and with indifference to the actual legal conditions in which some individuals who write have come to occupy definite legal statuses. This silence in the face of the law is also a sign of aesthetic culture's historical capacity to have its devotees withdraw themselves from concern with positive institutions and knowledge in order to pursue the goal of personal self-refinement. This neglect of or withdrawal from an interest in the legal dependency of the cultural sphere no doubt encourages lawyers to turn an equally blind eye on the cultural dependencies of law. It also suggests why, despite its centrality as a philosophical topic, authorship as a legal institution awaits a comprehensive history. No matter how historical their aspiration, Romantic historicist and post-structuralist accounts of authorship both persist with a quasi-philosophical project, the former to establish the author as the necessary consciousness of history, the latter as the necessary preliminary for the dissolution of that consciousness into its real – that is, non-conscious – linguistic and textual determinations.

The problem with these philosophical 'histories' is that they impose necessity and direction on the contingency of things. In a classic study of the birth of the modern author such as Ian Watt's (1957) *The Rise of the Novel*, the emergence of a law of copyright is noted, but only to be located among the several historical phenomena – Protestantism, capitalism, philosophical realism, individualism, the displacement of patronage by the professionalisation of writers, the collapse of the classic genre system, the abandoning of the conventions of the romance, the 'rise of the novel' – that are shown as finding their necessary synthesis in the emerging historical consciousness of the writers of the early modern novel. As if this convenient convergence did not go far enough, Watt's epigone, McKeon (1987), brings the scientific and typographical revolutions within the same dialectic of subjectivity and its material determinations, identified respectively with literary forms ('generic transformation') and social change – the breaking of the traditional nexus of social status and economic class position by the rise of a new entrepreneurial stratum (of which Daniel Defoe was an exemplary manifestation). We seem to see an epoch-making threshold. In such accounts, in fact, a familiar dialectic is at work, drawing the many threads together as the necessary movement of 'history', balancing the growth of individual or collective consciousness and the advance of material history. These twin forces, it would seem, then find their destined reconciliation in the exemplary figure of the author – typically Defoe – through whom 'history' moves into the modern age and 'man' escapes the bounds of localised conventionality to grasp his own historical reality as universal subject. This scheme has done no little damage. Above all, it leads us to impose a philosophical direction on a patchwork of diverse and contingent historical phenomena. What are the consequences of this 'historicist' approach for histories of authorship and copyright? As one element of the manifold purportedly directed by the march of 'history' towards the modern synthesis, copyright is admitted to that march. But the admission price is high – nothing less than subordination to the invisible force and irresistible principle of the dialectic, the law's role being simply to play out its allotted part in the scenography of 'man's' inevitable completion in (literary) culture. In the historicist account, it was always to be the role of copyright to support the persona that came to be enshrined in Romantic aesthetics.

It is not entirely unfortunate, then, that under the assault of a loose coalition of theoretical forces – linguistic, rhetorical, post-Marxian, psychoanalytic, feminist – the empire of Romantic historicism and the birth of the author has ceded ground to post-structuralism and the death of the author. The latter approach identifies the individual authorial consciousness of history as no more than a linguistic illusion, a discursive fiction prematurely imposed upon the flux of language. In relation to copyright law, this illusion takes the form of the emergence of the 'author as proprietor' (Rose 1988). However, thanks to the momentous advance of literary theory, we are told that this gross historical error is now seen for what it was, an illusion first staged but then upstaged by 'writing'. It was never the author who made sense but the non-conscious forces of the language system. This post-structuralist account of authorship, with its corollary that language (and images) are by their nature beyond ownership, has exercised its effect on at least one sector of artistic practice, that of 'appropriation' art – the making of an art on art that flaunts the fact of its unauthorised citation of other works. It is not clear what this supposedly more critical account of authorship has to offer historians of copyright. A quasi-philosophical necessity remains: the figure of the author has become the necessary preliminary to the eclipse of consciousness where previously it was the place in which that consciousness had risen. In this new schema, the law's role is to appear but only in order to disappear, a mere ancillary to the more fundamental process whereby the author as subject of consciousness is dispersed by the determining transgressivity of language or writing.

Because Romanticism and post-structuralism (or deconstruction) form anything but a simple opposition, my antinomy of 'Romantic historicist' and 'post-structuralist' accounts of authorship requires comment. While I shall use this antinomy as a coordinating and classificatory device, I do not mean to imply that Romanticism and post-structuralism are two massive and coherent entities of thought standing in a singular relation of opposition one to the other. The Romantic historicism to which I refer is not the sum total of that complex and internally diverse array of cultural phenomena and personalities denoted by the term Romanticism. If for the purposes of the argument I set my account of authorship and copyright against the historicist account, I none the less reserve the right elsewhere to admire an achievement of Romanticism such as the German historical school of law associated with Savigny.

A similarly modulating comment applies to my use of 'post-structuralism' as the other term of my schematic pair. Without adding to the mountain of expositions already written on post-structuralism (and deconstruction), I shall simply offer three sets of remarks on this matter: they concern the internal diversity of post-structuralism; the problem of its 'turn to language'; and an indication of what the present study might have drawn from the broader post-structuralist project. On the first two of these I shall be brief.

On the question of authorship, it seems to me, authorities such as Roland Barthes, Jacques Derrida and Michel Foucault have not spoken with a single voice. Although an impression has formed that they have all equally embraced the image of 'transgressive' language as 'author', this impression is false. For Foucault in particular, as I will argue in chapter 9, there was no lasting commitment to a notion of language or writing as the antecedent condition of all social being. This is not to say that – among the epigones – extravagant formulations of the discursive 'death' of the author were not proposed. On the contrary, we have grown familiar with the figure of the author no longer as the origin of the work but as the imaginary discursive effect thrown up by discourse. We are familiar too – and sometimes not a little weary – with the 'critical politics' that has been assumed to flow from this turn to language. It is as if we were asked to believe that an adequate historical account of copyright law could be written entirely in terms of linguistic profusion, textual subversion and unbounded plasticity of being – all the time confronted with the assertion that we cannot get beyond the bounds of language. Post-structuralism in this style is just a clever logicist game of unsettling sets of established terms by claiming to uncover their purported aporias and logical contradictions. This game, moreover, is caught up in a pressure to be emancipatory (or emancipated), as if in a caricature of Frankfurt School political analysis every history of copyright law was required to be a critique of society or every account of the English common law had to be written in terms of indigenous 'resistances'. Historical description is disabled when all phenomena have to be treated within some version of the exhaustive antinomy of domination and subversion, blame and praise.

However, the work of Derrida and Foucault – in part at least – calls for a quite different comment. Few have done more than them to thematise difference and discontinuity. Importantly, they have also begun the task of demonstrating that difference is more than just a literary feature. They give a firm lesson in why and how to turn from the generalities of philosophical history towards a less transcendental but more practical account of human attributes. In the present study, where the attributes in question are those attaching to certain legal and aesthetic personalities, there will be more than one occasion for applying this lesson, even though it is true to say that neither Derrida nor Foucault have done more than gesture towards a concrete history of copyright. In this respect, my debt to them is more an atmospheric relation than a specific borrowing. That said, I suspect the present argument will be seen by some to embrace a positivism and an institutionalism not entirely welcome in post-structuralist literary, cultural and – to judge by Carty (1990) and Kramer (1991) – legal theory. For these post-structuralist persons, to specify a positivity is to run the risk of imposing fixity, normativity and a dominant meaning; for the present study, however, the aim is to do justice to the historical positivity of certain legal-cultural arrangements relating to authorship. The picture is one of a patchwork, not a triumphal road. What has counted as a right in one legal environment or jurisdiction has not always so counted in another. This, of course, is the problem for any too-philosophical address to rights and attributes at some universal level.

It should now be clear what I have in view in saying that this book pursues a historical and theoretical alternative to both the Romantic historicist and the post-structuralist templates for conceiving of modern forms of authorship. The alternative consists above all in writing a history that remains within the purview of positive law and actual legal systems. There are three main coordinates for such a history. The first is provided by an important body of cultural historiography oriented not to philosophical subjectivity but to a specific communications technology: print literacy. Although authorship as a specific topic is not fully dealt with by the book historians – Davis (1975), Febvre and Martin (1976), Eisenstein (1979), Chartier (1987) – their various explorations of print and its implications for the interests and attributes of writers and readers light a path. To cite one instance, Elizabeth Eisenstein treats the attributes of the early modern author neither as the inevitable outcome of the dialectical reconciliation of consciousness and material forces nor as the dispersal of consciousness by its non-conscious determinations in language, labour or whatever. Instead what she describes is a new cultural milieu, the unforeseen outcome of a variety of alterations occasioned in pre-modern institutions and conducts by the spread of print:

From the very first, authorship was closely linked to the new technology.
. . . The romantic figure of the aristocratic or patrician patron has tended to
obscure the more plebeian and prosaic early capitalist entrepreneur who
hired scholars, translators, editors and compilers when not serving in these
capacities himself. Partly because copyists had, after all, never paid those
whose works they copied, partly because new books were a small portion
of the early book trade, and partly because divisions of literary labour
remained blurred, the author retained a quasi-amateur status until the
eighteenth century. During this interval printers served as patrons for
authors, and sought patronage, privileges, and favours from official
quarters as well. This was the era when men of letters and learning were
likely to be familiar with print technology and commercial trade routes in
a manner that later observers overlook.

(Eisenstein 1979: 153–4)

Like any actual cultural milieu, this one is irreducible to 'consciousness' or
'language'. A lower-level analysis is preferred. In the early modern printing-
shop, the treatment of intellectual property as common property, the reprint
industry and the amateur status of authors carry over from the culture of hand-
copying. Other features – the hiring of scholars as journeymen, the fluid
distribution of technical capacities, the closeness of intellectual and entrepreneurial activities – arise with print technology. The development of the
technical capacity for mass mechanical copying is central to Eisenstein's
account. It was through the printed book that writing and writers became
connected to a system of literary production and markets of a different order
and kind from that associated with the clerically controlled activity of hand-
copying. In this new and uncertain milieu, new divisions of literate labour and
new types of economic and moral activity also arose, organised to varying
extents by new forms of legal regulation. As to the person of the author, this
was not so easily differentiated from that of the artisanal book producer. Nor
was there some predestined or necessary boundary – let alone a guarantee of
future reconciliation at some higher level of being – between a writer's
material and ideal concerns.

The second main coordinate of my alternative account of authorship is
furnished by a historical anthropology of personhood that is sufficiently
pluralist to be immune to the unifying pressure of philosophical histories. A
perspective of this sort is outlined in the work of Marcel Mauss and Max
Weber and in the late writings of Michel Foucault. In a variety of ways, they
show that forms of personhood are not inevitable outcomes of some fundamental global process. Rather, they are purpose-built for their particular
environments. Forms of personhood depend on the definite arrays of
instituted statuses and attributes, rights and duties that organise the practical
deportment of individuals and groups. An advantage of this anthropological
perspective – to be explored more fully in chapter 1 – is that it distinguishes

persons and *individuals*. This might recall the legal truism that not all individuals are legal persons, while not all legal persons – corporate bodies for example – are human individuals. Applied to the legal and the aesthetic personalities of individuals who write, this distinction cuts across that Romantic habit of mind which equates the person with the expression of individuality. By adopting this anthropological concern with differentiating types of person and establishing the specific circumstances of their emergence and functioning, we can focus more attention on the statuses and attributes that constitute a given form of personhood. Considered in this light, the statuses and attributes of legal personality are seen to be inseparable from the definite yet limited parameters of particular legal systems. They do not float free in some undifferentiated space of consciousness or language.

My third coordinate for an alternative to philosophical histories of authorship and copyright involves according a determining role to positive law. In the first instance – to perpetuate the classical distinction between it and natural law – positive law is law made by particular custom or enactment. It thus refers positively to the laws as they actually have been, not normatively to what they might or should have been. For the German social theorist, Niklas Luhmann, this distinction raises the question of the preconditions under which a 'society can run the risk of making its law positive', the course of action that has been followed in our modern western states:

> For us, the foundations of law can no longer be located in a supreme natural law that exists objectively and through its objective truth is permanently binding. The stability and validity of the law no longer rests upon a higher and more stable order, but instead upon a principle of variation: it is the very alterability of law that is the foundation for its stability and validity.
>
> (Luhmann 1982: 94)

The 'very alterability' of positive law – its inseparability from the fact of historical variation – is a bulwark against higher-level explanations of particular bodies of law. To treat the law of copyright as positive law is to recognise it as an independent and variable phenomenon of culture, and to address the historical particularity of its objects and means. Not every culture has had a legal system or print literacy, let alone something so specialised as a law of copyright.

However, 'positive' also carries an anti-philosophical charge. It signals a willingness to conceive of copyright law as contingent upon certain jurisdictions and their instruments, rather than as determined or directed by some fundamental logic or necessary process in culture. To proceed from the actuality of the positive law of copyright to the cultural phenomenon of authorship should also help avoid the subordination of the law to philosophical schemata that is a characteristic feature of both Romantic historicist or post-structuralist accounts. In practice, this means allowing historical examples to do the work of arguing that the writer's legal person and its attributes were determined by statutes executed and cases decided – and by legal doctrine – not by consciousness or its linguistic simulacrum.

These three coordinates – the good example of the book historians, the historical anthropology of personhood and the determining powers of positive law – have a common motif: the technical and technological character of authorial personality as it has been recognised in law. However, given the historically and jurisdictionally variable nature of this personality, in developing an account of copyright law and authorship that is historically rather than conceptually grounded I shall deploy my coordinates as the circumstance dictates. In some instances the three overlap, as in Eisenstein's (1979) demonstration that protection of literary works by copyright presumed a technical capacity to stabilise the relation between a particular author or printer and a particular text, a condition which could not be routinely met prior to the typographic fixity that print made possible. The lesson is this: far from being an essential attribute of all (fully developed) human beings, the capacity to conduct oneself as responsible for one's written work was contingent upon the availability of print technology. Moreover, like any other cultural attribute, the sense of personal responsibility for one's literary compositions had to be acquired – much in the same way as late twentieth-century westerners have acquired a reluctance and incapacity to spit in public. And when this ethical capacity for responsibility was acquired, it was not a sign that consciousness (or its illusion) had decisively advanced 'man' into the 'modern'; it was a contingent outcome of the new cultural environment of print communications technology, a complex environment in which early modern English law, drawing on available legal instruments, began to regulate the relations of commerce, government and cultural activity in an entirely characteristic way: by constructing a piecemeal array of different rights and remedies – attributes of legal personalities – that the law ascribed to individuals as their means of entering into specific kinds of cultural activity and commercial relationship.

As I shall approach them, the law of copyright and the very different form of law concerned with authors' rights – the European *droit moral* – will no longer find themselves subordinated to whatever currently purports to be the fundamental principle of 'man's' cultural development. These forms of law will be studied as historical positivities, to be described in their own terms. By showing the legal sphere a measure of respect as an independent phenomenon, a more pluralist and pragmatic form of literary and cultural studies might encourage legal researchers to explore the overlaps that have occurred between the legal and the cultural spheres. This would help break the complicity between legal research which studies nothing but the law and cultural critique which claims to know the truth of everything. As for literary and cultural studies, the point will be to do some actual historical work, to give some positive information and to learn some law – without assuming any universal vantage point, be it 'consciousness' or 'discourse', from which all the different spheres of life could be inspected and judged.

As should now be clear, I shall not treat authorship as a unified phenom-enon of culture that emerged in a single historical or theoretical space, that is, as if it fell within a single framework of explanation. The delineation of legal and aesthetic personalities and the manners of their occupation by individuals who write and publish obeyed no single logic or necessity. Given these precepts, my major objective is to propose a comparative framework for micro-histories of the different legal-cultural environments described below. In constructing this framework, I have relied on the existing histories. At every turn, however, I have resisted that untamed cultural historicism which has imagined an essential continuity of aesthetic and legal development from ancient Welsh bards to modern copyright holders (Wincor 1962) or from Roman bibliopoles to bearers of a *droit moral* (Dock 1962, 1963). Chrono-logically and thematically, I have therefore limited myself principally to the legal relations of print authorship and publication in the eighteenth and nineteenth centuries. Yet even these narrower limits do not reveal (or construct) a unified epoch. Within the span of the eighteenth and nineteenth centuries, different legal norms emerged in different geopolitical and juridical circumstances. In copyright regimes the general object has been to provide a remedy against unauthorised reproduction of a protected commodity; in *droit moral* regimes, to protect the integrity of an authorial personality. Observing these chronological limits and concentrating on the issues raised in law by print production and dissemination has none the less allowed an adequate demonstration of the complex relations that have obtained between legal and aesthetic personalities. It has also demonstrated the fact of juris-dictional difference between different national regimes.

Anonymous regulatory systems are not conventionally the heroes of cultural history, although what Marxian discourse once did for the mode of production and post-structuralism still does for the language system perhaps leaves room for hope (even though in both those cases it was a matter of constructing precisely the form of universal subject and philosophical necessity that I wish to avoid). Moreover, having recently completed a (co-authored) history of obscenity law, I hesitate to claim for copyright the ambivalent *frissons* of that topic. Nor does copyright history have a crowd-drawing equivalent – except perhaps for the heady days of 1774 when the House of Lords decided *Donaldson* v. *Beckett* – of the mid-twentieth-century literary show trials and *causes célèbres* of Anglo-American obscenity law. Yet there are indices of the importance of our present topic. If in England by the turn of the nineteenth century there had been just one Obscene Publications Act – that of 1857 – by contrast, as the 1878 Royal Commission on Copyright reported, there were 'the provisions of fourteen Acts of Parliament, which relate in whole or in part to different branches of the subject and . . . common law principles, nowhere stated in any definite or authoritative way, but implied in a considerable number of reported cases scattered over the law reports'. And not for nothing does the copyright clause in section 8 of article 1 of the United States Constitution contain the only use of the term 'right' in the Constitution proper. Along with the freedoms of speech and press, copyright functions as a key mechanism for the dissemination of public knowledge. From the viewpoint of historical description, however, it might be advantageous that – unlike obscenity law – the law of copyright and its history do not offer so easy an opportunity to claim to speak with the voice of right, of universal history. Indeed, given the profound historical tension between legal-governmental and philosophical-aesthetic spheres and the orientation of Romantic historicist and post-structuralist approaches to authorship, simply to describe in positive terms the legal relations of authorial personality will be to engage in polemic.

Chapter 1

Preliminaries: positivities and polemics

I

The starting point is to recognise the independent and purposive character of legal persons. In 1710, what has been called the world's first copyright act was passed by the British Parliament. It has become known as the Statute of Anne. With this Act, writers acquired a statutory capacity to exclude others from the right to reproduce copies of the work and to publish and circulate these copies in a market. However, the writer was not the only individual with access to this right; printers, publishers, in fact anyone who bought, inherited or otherwise acquired a copyright now occupied the same legal status and bore the same legal personality. The right brought into statutory existence in 1710 was the perfectly alienable right – it could be sold and traded – to engage in certain economic exchanges based on the mechanical duplicates of a work. As a trade regulation statute, the Act of 1710 neither assumed nor required any equivalence between the person of the copyright holder and the moral or aesthetic personality of the writer; rather, it delineated and attributed the legal capacity to own copyright in a manner designed for the regulation of a specific economic activity – the making of and trading in a printed commodity.

Described in these terms, the first copyright act was neither a successful nor a failed attempt to recognise a writer's subjectivity in a written work or to give legal recognition to an inalienable human right inherent in the writer. Indeed, some writers of the times found the idea of an equivalence between their moral authority and a pecuniary interest repugnant. But then it was not the purpose of the Statute of Anne to establish any such equivalence. By allowing anyone, whether or not a member of the Stationers' Company to hold copyright – provided they complied with the formalities set out in the Act – the purpose of the legislation was to break the Company's 150-year-old monopoly on the publishing of books in England.[1] This step – deregulatory but also inaugurating a new threshold of regulation – was taken at a time when the technology of print and the development of new markets for books had transformed the once protective functions of the Stationers' traditional monopoly into an unacceptable constraint on an expanding book trade. There is an immediate lesson to be drawn. It makes no sense to view the statutory law of copyright, in this its founding instance, as if it should or could have been the pliable instrument through which history writes subjectivity into economic interests and economic interests into subjectivity. It was a positive legal device invented within a particular jurisdiction to solve a specific set of trade problems by drawing on available legal instruments. The construction of rights, liabilities and conditions provided for in the Statute of Anne was piecemeal. The durations of copyrights were differentially defined, all existing copyrights being vested in the present owners for a period of twenty-one years from 10 April 1710 (the day the law came into effect); for new publications the period of the exclusive right to produce copies was fourteen years, although in the circumstance that the author of the work was still living at the end of this period, there was a possibility of a second fourteen-year term. By the early eighteenth century, the possibility was thus emerging whereby copyright law began to personify certain print-literate capacities and products by attaching them to a purpose-built legal personality: the author as bearer of a claimable – but entirely assignable – exclusive right to the economic exploitation of his or her work.

At the same time, other aspects of book production and distribution were legally personified – not by statute but by judicial decision – in a quite different way and for a quite different purpose. This development involved the creation of another new legal personality: the obscene libeller, one who had the capacity to be held criminally liable for the corruption of public morality by virtue of issuing an obscene libel. In 1727 an individual was for the first time convicted of the crime of obscene publication. In both the Statute of Anne and the judicial creation of this new criminal offence, the outcomes proved durable. On the one hand, the 'English lawyer maintained a remarkably consistent view of copyright as a right to stop the making of copies, despite the extension of that right from 1709, when all it covered was books and sheet music, to the first great consolidation of copyright in 1911, by which time the law could be seen to protect such diverse objects as photographs, sculptures, gramophone records and telegram codes' (Phillips 1986: 104). On the other hand, the crime of obscene libel was to endure in English law for 232 years from its creation in *Rex* v. *Curll* in 1727 until the Obscene Publications Act of 1959. Thus, as legal persons, individuals who wrote acquired in 1710 the capacity to own copyright and in 1727 the capacity to be held criminally responsible for publishing an obscene libel. Yet the writer as owner of copyright and the writer as locus of criminal liability are legal persons that stand in no necessary relation one to another. If in chronological terms these legal persons so nearly coincide, this is contingent upon specific circumstances: economic power plays (the book trade and new commercial interests), technological possibilities (print production and a growing distribution capacity), cultural shifts (growth of discursive literacy and emergence of new audiences with new interests in and uses for printed works), and the political rationality of governmental action at the time.

In 1727 Edmund Curll was finally sentenced by the Court of King's Bench for having published *Venus in the Cloister; or, the Nun in her Smock*, together with certain other works. When Curll became the first individual to be ascribed this new form of liability – this new legal personality – it was not as an author but as the printer and publisher of a work which, previously judged anodyne, now found itself in circumstances such that he gained a place in legal history. The conduct of Curll's case does not suggest crude repression of an authorial subject by the law. The judges wrestled with contradictory precedents in deciding whether an immoral work was the concern of the common law courts – rather than a sin to be dealt with in the ecclesiastical courts – and whether a 'libel' that harms no one in particular could constitute a crime. The Attorney General, prosecuting, asked the judges to distinguish between a private immoral act and one that is public, and that therefore affects all the King's subjects; he drew an evidently persuasive analogy in asserting that 'particular acts of fornication are not punishable in the Temporal Courts, and bawdy houses are'. What is crucial is the manner in which the judges drew distinctions that established the public character of a written and printed publication. According to one judge, '[t]he Spiritual Courts punish only personal spiritual defamation by words; if it is reduced to *writing*, it is a temporal offence'. And Justice Reynolds commented: 'This is surely worse than *Sir Charles Sedley*'s case [Sedley had been indicted in 1663 for going naked on a balcony and causing a disturbance by pissing on the crowd below], who only exposed himself to the people then present, who might choose whether they would look upon him or not; *whereas this book goes all over the kingdom*' (*Rex* v. *Curll*: 850–1; emphasis added).*[2] What pushed Curll's action across the threshold from sin to crime was the judges' sense of the unprecedented scope of moral dissemination conferred by a new communications technology: that of the printed book circulating through the book trade network.

What, then, of the emergence of a statutory law of copyright? With the Act of 1710, as I have already suggested, the English legal apparatus was not attempting to recognise the presence of the writer's subjectivity in the work but regulating a novel and unstable sphere of cultural, commercial and technical activity by delineating and attributing a right to trade in mechanical duplicates of the work. As with the criminal liability for obscenity, it is important to register the fact that the law's interest attached not to the act of writing but to that of publication and sale. In relation to obscene publication, we are wrong to presume that the law treats these different activities as equivalent, as if the prosecution of the latter was a convenient way to repress the former. In other words, the law does not assume that the person expressed

* For the reference to this and other cases cited, see the Index of cases, p. 261.

in the work is necessarily identical with the person liable for the crime of obscene publication. In constructing this new crime, the common law altered the threshold between sin and crime, establishing a mechanism for attributing criminal responsibility quite independently of any attribution of moral or aesthetic responsibility for the work. In relation to copyright, one of our tasks will be to trace the manifestation of an analogous distinction in the sphere of literary property.

First, however, is it possible to clarify the relation of these two legal personalities – as obscene libeller and owner of copyright – to the writer's subjectivity? A certain habit of mind remains attached to the notion of an essential person, one which in terms of the history of authorship would typically be moral or aesthetic, the locus of a subjectivity deeper and more general than mere institutional constructs such as the juridical persons of copyright holder or obscene libeller. Unlike them, so it might seem, this subjectivity would not depend on attributes formed in a technical apparatus resting on executed statutes and judicial determinations. The writer's legal personalities appear extrinsic constructs, complex artefacts perhaps but finally incidental to the intrinsic personality reflected or recovered in the writing. Surely there has to be a fundamental personality, the person itself, that constitutes the necessary ground of legal personalities, the anchorage on which they ultimately depend. And so we might habitually assume that legal personality itself ought ideally to equate or approximate to subjectivity.

There is, however, an important historical sense in which the Act of 1710 could not assume a relation of equivalence between the legal person of the copyright owner and the moral or aesthetic person of the writer. The capacity to be morally responsible for one's writings is not an attribute of all human beings. The notion that a literary work is the expression of its author's moral or aesthetic personality – and not, say, a correct imitation of the best rhetorical model or a calculation as to what will sell – is inseparable from the specific cultural conditions and practices in which writers came to acquire an interest in and a capacity for having such a personality. Before a system of law could be asked to distinguish literary writing as expressive of its creator's moral or aesthetic persona, literary writers first had to acquire an expressible interiority and literary writing had to become a specialist ethical activity. These are among the special acquisitions of Romantic culture. As such, however, they long postdate the Statute of Anne. At the time of that statute, it was not an aesthetic concern with the dialectical balancing of a 'complete' self but the austere Puritan ethic of conscience that organised a moral persona for an individual such as Daniel Defoe, a very different yet no less intense form of inwardness based on rigorous devotional techniques and specific literate abilities (Saunders and Hunter 1991). We begin to see two important truths: not only are the pertinent forms of legal status or person historically variable; so too is the ethical subject that has been taken to be their ground or anchorage. The balance of this opening chapter is therefore expended on providing support to these propositions and on specifying in more detail the line of approach I have adopted in the present study.

II

If legal personality is taken to depend on the individual writer's 'inner' personality, what do we make of the fact that what has counted as inner personality is historically variable, whether the intensely didactic interiority of the Puritan subject or the intensely aesthetic interiority of the Romantic subject? Confronted by these different forms of inwardness, whoever wishes to assert a necessary grounding of legal personality in some deeper subjectivity than a legal system must first decide which of these two inwardnesses, the Puritan or the Romantic, is to be that ground. Or, given the fact of historical variation, would it not be better not to impose a principle of necessity on the historical and cultural diversity of forms of personhood that individuals have happened to bear?

It would also help if, analytically and descriptively, we differentiated *person* from *individual*. The French anthropologist Marcel Mauss (1985) draws the following distinction: whereas individuals are biological and psychological beings, persons represent the definite complexes of instituted statuses and attributes that have provided the means of actually conducting oneself and one's relations with others. Mauss' distinction rests on evidence drawn from societies in which not all individuals are or have persons. Moreover, those individuals who are or have persons do not necessarily bear this personhood in what modern westerners would recognise as an individual manner – that is, entirely within themselves. The forms of having or being a person have sometimes been invested in trans-individual institutions such as name systems or mask-wearing rituals in which the rights, duties or other attributes that constituted personhood were attached not to an individual but to the name or mask. In some societies, names or masks were fewer in number than were individuals; nameless or maskless individuals were individuals without persons.

The first relatively even distribution of persons to individuals came, Mauss argues, with the establishment of the rights ascribed to all those individuals who were citizens under the laws of Rome. However, the form of personhood that has emerged in the west is one that Mauss identifies as a special case in a number of respects. Moral and legal in nature, it has been extended to almost every individual member of our societies. It is also a special case in so far as a very large proportion of individuals – no longer just a few specialists in Stoic castes and Christian monastic orders – have come to acquire the ethical ability of locating a moral personality within their self. The fact that certain forms of personhood have been internalised is, however, a matter of historical contingency, important in a practical sense but not a fundamental difference. Mauss is thus quite clear that the identification or equivalence of the individual with an internalised moral persona is not the essential form of human subjectivity nor the sign of a recovery of fundamental human being. It is, as Mauss puts it, an arrangement 'only for us, among us', distinguished by its rarity and 'delicacy', not by its universal truth and necessity. Moreover, this form of personhood belongs to a particular cultural, religious and legal-administrative history in which there has occurred a wide distribution of an interest in having an inner moral persona and in which there have been the technical conditions for internalising a moral conscience and acquiring a consciousness of self. Such attributes, according to Mauss, were developed by the Stoics but among them remained limited to a cult practice. A wider dissemination of this moral persona was achieved among the Puritan sects. Mauss' lesson on the independence of the moral persona from the individual suggests one way in which to lift the heavy philosophical pressure to reconcile the writer's legal and aesthetic personalities in an organic relation. This lesson consists in learning to see the aesthetic persona as a definite but limited mode of personhood, one that has been internalised by certain members of the population along the same lines as – but until now, perhaps, with a narrower distribution than – the moral conscience.

If these historical and anthropological distinctions are valid, the legal and aesthetic personalities stand in no general relation one to the other. No claim can be made that one of them is, as it were, the person itself. These points can be underscored by reference to the concept of *Lebensführung* or 'conduct of life' that Wilhelm Hennis (1988) has reconstructed as Max Weber's central theme.[3] It is a matter of the formation of 'personalities' appropriate to particular life orders (*Lebensordnung*) or 'spheres of existence'. 'Conduct of life' names the specific ethical techniques and practical means whereby these personalities are methodically and reliably organised – like habits, they are not acquired merely by thinking. The most famous of these Weberian personalities is the Puritan, the typical denizen of that ethos which emerged in the particular life order associated with the radical Protestant sects. Others are the German peasant personality in the East German agrarian-economic system, the persona of the scientist within his or her professional vocation, and the persona of the English common lawyers that shaped and was shaped by the professional, client-oriented milieu of the Inns of Court, so unlike the academic persona of the continental lawyers formed in the European university law school (Weber 1968: 785–8).

Adapting Mauss' typology and Weber's concepts to the discussion of the history of authorship and copyright we can, first, differentiate the attributes of the authorial persona – a specific ensemble of instituted rights and liabilities, capacities and virtues – from the individual who writes. Second, we can identify the aesthetic persona with a particular historical ethos or sphere of existence, and thus distinguish it from an expression of human subjectivity in some general sense. Like other forms of person, the aesthetic personality is thus neither in accord with nor at the expense of a natural way of being human. It is an artefact too specialised to be counted as 'the subject' (or 'the person'). And, third, we can thus begin to rethink the vexed concepts of subject and subjectivity in a similarly historical and anthropological fashion. This could mean no longer taking them as the fundamental form of being human but, much more precisely, as the *manner* in which individuals bear the persons ascribed to them.[4] This is to echo Foucault's (1985: 26) concern in his studies of the 'practices of the self' in late Antiquity with the specific 'manner in which one ought to form oneself as an ethical subject acting in reference to the prescriptive elements that make up the [moral] code'. We have noted, for instance, the manner in which Weber's Puritan internalised in the form of an ever-watchful inner conscience the public norm embodied in the predestinarian doctrine or code, rather than externalising that norm in religious ceremonies and images or, for that matter, in a legal system. The manner of bearing one's person depends on a diversity of factors, and has no general or necessary form. It is not determined by some general process or logic in 'man's' cultural development. No form of having or being a person, says Mauss, is to be considered 'in any way primitive'. And in Weber's terms, the question is not how well a particular personality equates with the truth of human experience or subjectivity in general, but how one gets individuals willing and competent to bear that personality which fits the circumstances of a given sphere of existence.

   The point is therefore to construct a historical and practical account of cultural attributes such as the ability to sustain a moral responsibility for what one has written or the capacity to own a right of copyright, an account which shows the actual 'conducts of life' involved and the technical conditions for producing and deploying them. After all, ideas – even the idea of necessity – are not of themselves actionable. They guarantee nothing by way of actual competence (but they presume it). This is a point to keep in view when, for instance, we encounter attempts to bring economic theory to bear on actual conduct in the intellectual property field. To reconcile the gap between the forms of an ideal economy and the norms of conduct of actual populations, the best the theorist usually comes up with is an appeal to a psychology that oscillates between a normative science of subjectivity and a positive anthropology of actual conducts. We thus read: 'Property rights serve to internalise externalities and can influence the behaviour of participants in the economy by acting as a system of incentive, reward and efficiency control. ... As justification [of property rights] in the area of patent law, for example, reference has always more or less intuitively been made, among other things, to a "reward and incentive theory", although these considerations could not have been influenced by property rights theory' (Lehmann 1985: 530). Indeed they could not, while theory remains disinterested in the historical means of forming personal attributes, not least the human dispositions needed for a given economy to succeed.

   The problem of ahistorical approaches to the historical relations of authorship and copyright could be indicated if we asked what common 'reward and incentive' could bridge the different cultural circumstances of the 1710 'Act for the Encouragement of Learning, by vesting the Copies of printed Books in the Authors or Purchasers of such Copies', the declaration in paragraph 8 of article 1 of the United States Constitution that Congress shall have the power to 'promote the Progress of Science and useful Arts, by securing for limited Times to Authors and Inventors the exclusive Right to their respective Writings and Discoveries', and today's expanding universe of intellectual property rights that has been described as resembling a 'game of conceptual Pac Man in which everything in sight is being gobbled up' (Lange 1981: 156). The problem requires that we face – and discard – the metaphysical assumption that all the forms of legal and other personhood ascribed to individuals in their passage through social institutions have a common ground or essence. Failure to do so has a clear consequence: legal personality is made to depend on a purportedly more fundamental form of personhood and, in this way, loses its independence and historical specificity.

III

Legal attributes are delineated and ascribed in the legal sphere. To accord this point is to free a space for description of legal persons as historical positivities. Something of what is at stake can be discerned from the following commentary on a problem encountered during preliminary work on the Berne Convention of 1887:

> The title of the Convention is 'The Berne Convention for the protection of literary and artistic works'. However, as a statement of the purpose of the Convention, this is amplified by the preamble and article 1. The first states that the countries of the Union, 'being equally animated by the desire to protect, in as effective and uniform manner as possible, the rights of authors in their literary and artistic works, ... have agreed as follows', while the second states that the countries to which the Convention applies have agreed to constitute 'a Union for the protection of the rights of authors in their literary and artistic works'. 'Rights of authors' is a literal translation of the expression 'des droits des auteurs' which is used in the French text. The latter was inserted by the 1885 Conference, in place of the expression used in the earlier drafts, 'des droits d'auteur', which in French had the simple connotation of a monetary royalty due to the author (in English there would appear to be no material difference between the expressions 'the rights of authors' and 'the rights of the author'). Does the expression 'the rights of authors' as it appears in the present text [of the Berne Convention] presuppose any particular juridical conception of the nature of authors' rights? This question arose in the 1885 Conference in relation to the title of the Convention, where the French delegates proposed that this be entitled

'Draft Convention concerning the creation of a general union for the protection of literary and artistic property'. The reason for this proposal arose out of their dislike of the term '*des droits d'auteur*' which was used in the 1884 text, and which had, in French, the restricted meaning explained above. However, the German delegation, in turn, took objection to the term 'literary and artistic property' on the ground that this was a different juridical conception from that of '*Urheberrecht*' as it had been developed in German law, and that its adoption in the proposed convention would therefore put German participation in doubt. As a result, the Swiss delegation proposed the neutral expression 'protection of literary and artistic works', which had already been used in a number of other bilateral conventions, and this was accepted by the Commission in its final report to the Conference.

(Ricketson 1987: 154–5)

For the practical purposes of the international law of copyright – to which I return in chapter 7 – this solution poses no problem. It relies on the technical device of 'national treatment' – each member country of the Berne Union uses the means available in its own laws to meet the standards of protection required by the treaty and, therefore, is not required to recognise one particular juridical conception as the universal ground of the rights in question. But the incident is exemplary: in the specific context of developing an international treaty to protect the rights of authors across different national territories, a section was drawn across a number of independent jurisdictions within each of which the legal personality and status of authors had emerged as a particular configuration of attributes. In defining the precise object of the treaty, the geopolitical fact of discontinuities between the different national jurisdictions was unavoidable. The *sui generis* character of copyright categories rendered them untranslatable into the German or French systems of protection.

The way in which the Commission proceeded underscores the positivity of legal personality. Positivity is perhaps too grand a word, but it describes the quality of a cultural phenomenon sufficiently particular and independent to merit description in its own terms, rather than in terms of some supposedly more fundamental reality. In seeking to define the powers of protection in as 'uniform a manner as possible', the Commission did not seek out some fundamental common substance underlying the English law of 'copyright', the French '*propriété littéraire et artistique*' and the German '*Urheberrecht*'. In legal terms there was none. To have retired to read *The Rise of the Novel* or 'The death of the author' would have changed nothing, the Commission still being left to confront the fact that English, French and German laws were historically different one from another. And Swiss neutrality is a practical device not a metaphysical solution. Thus the Commission elaborated a formula agreeable to the different delegations, one that was workable through the relativising instrument of 'national treatment'. As Sam Ricketson comments: 'In a substantive sense, there was not in 1885 (nor is there now) any exact equivalence between the terms "*la propriété littéraire et artistique*", "*das Urheberrecht*" and "copyright"'; what the Convention represents is a 'hybrid view of authors' rights which is peculiar to itself and the result of many influences' (1987: 155–6). In one respect it is a matter of terminology. Yet something more than terminology is suggested by the fact that there was no question of unearthing the fundamental person of all possible authors and proceeding from this archaeological discovery to the universal definition for adoption by the Convention. With this example, the point of my two previous sections might be somewhat clearer: it is a matter of setting limits to projections of philosophical notions of subject, individual and person, on to the history of authorship and copyright. A Kantian claim to have recovered the universal ground or primary causation of all actual forms of personhood or, for that matter, of authorship would have been of no use to a multinational Commission faced with the task of harmonising different national legal traditions each of which had elaborated its particular manner of handling printed books and their authors. The tradition of 'copyright' had developed in England, the *Urheberrecht* in Germany and the *propriété littéraire et artistique* in France and that was that. There was and is no way of by-passing the fact of historical difference; unless, that is, one is not concerned with actual laws but on the utopian route to nowhere in particular.

In addition to setting limits to discussion of authorship in terms such as the dialectic of the real and the ideal or the formation of the human subject, the example of how Berne Convention conferences in the 1880s resolved national variations illustrates another important fact. The history of authorship is inseparable from differences within the legal sphere. Legal personality displays an internal diversity according to the historical architecture and purpose of the law in question. We have already noted the historical and conceptual discontinuity between the legal personality of the copyright owner and that of the one criminally liable for an obscene publication. It is also a matter of procedural differences. The procedures for determining responsibility for and entitlement to copyright ownership are quite distinct from those for determining criminal liability for obscene publication. A copyright can be easily assigned; divestment of criminal responsibility is somewhat harder.

Historical diversities and internal discontinuities make the legal sphere a good obstacle to any global theory concerning authorship. They also suggest why, given its purposive character, legal personality is not and does not need to be all of a piece. As an attribute of a legal personality, ownership of a copyright is inseparable from a particular purpose or purposes; in this respect, as a personifying or person-forming mechanism, the law of copyright is not bound by the philosophical ideal of an absolute or unified right. Yet, as we shall see, in less positive accounts of authorship it is in the name of just such an ideal that copyright law is charged with the narrowness of its concerns and the piecemeal nature of the rights, remedies and objects of protection that have come to be bundled under its provisions.

The *sui generis* character of English copyright categories rendered them untranslatable into the German or French systems of legal protection. This was not due to a resistance inherent in language; rather, it indicated that copyright's central categories – 'author', 'originality' and 'literary work' – were determinate and specialised elements of one part of the English legal system's historical architecture. It is a commonplace that legal wording is not what the general reader of English is used to, and it is sometimes held that this results from an act of wilful obscurantism by lawyers. It would perhaps be less fanciful to relate this state of affairs to the historical contingency whereby – unlike the moral and, increasingly, the aesthetic systems – the legal system has not been internalised by the majority of citizens. Legal expertise, we might say, happens to have remained on the outside.

Modern copyright categories provide an instance of this highly specified character. The British Copyright Act of 1956 defines 'author' only in relation to the protection of copyright in photographs; here, according to section 48(1), the author is the owner of the material on which the photograph was made at the time it was taken. In the 1988 UK Copyright, Designs and Patents Act, section 9(1) defines an 'author' in relation to a 'work' as the person who creates it. Section 9(2) specifies who is to be considered the author in the case of a sound recording, film, broadcast, cable programme and typographical arrangement of a published edition (in this last case, the 'authorial' person is the publisher). Section 9(3) specifies that the author 'shall be taken to be the person by whom the arrangements necessary for the work are undertaken', this being in relation to a literary, dramatic, musical or artistic work which is computer generated. But no general principles are stated as to who is to be taken as the author of a literary, dramatic, musical or artistic work because, whatever post-structuralists might assert, the British Parliament 'did not consider it to be a difficult task to identify the author in the case of those works' (Flint, Thorne and Williams 1989: 21). For copyright protection to be accorded, and for an 'author' to be legally recognisable, determinate criteria must be met. Thus in sections 153–6 of the 1988 Act it is a matter of the place of first publication or, in the case of broadcasts or cable programmes, the place from which the broadcast was made or the cable programme sent. Protection as an 'author' is available only to 'qualifying persons'. A 'qualifying person' is one who, at the material time, is 'a British subject or a British protected person' within the meaning of the British Nationality Act 1981 (section 154(1)(a)), an individual domiciled in the United Kingdom, or 'a body incorporated under the law of a part of the United Kingdom or of another country to which the relevant provisions of this Part extend'.

Without unduly extending these examples of how the current British statute specifies authorial attributes, it is worth commenting briefly on the treatment of the categories of 'originality' and 'literary work' within the terms of copyright law. To qualify for copyright protection a work must be 'original'. For a work to be original it need not demonstrate novelty: 'Originality is not to be equated with the creation of something which had not hitherto existed; it is the word used to describe the causal relationship between an author [who or which must be a 'qualified person'] and the material form in which a work is embodied' (Whale and Phillips 1983: 39). This relationship need be no more than the minimum of labour that distinguishes a writing from a copying; no profound originary mental state is required. Originality, in this sense, is not a quality located in the work itself, as was made clear in the classic 1936 dictum of Judge Learned Hand:

> Borrowed the work must indeed not be, for a plagiarist is not himself *pro tanto* an 'author'; but if by some magic a man who had never known it were to compose anew Keats's 'Ode on a Grecian Urn', he would be an 'author' and . . . others might not copy that poem, though they might of course copy Keats's.
>
> (*Sheldon* v. *Metro-Goldwyn Pictures Corporation*: 669)

Half a century on, in a current handbook of intellectual property law, the conundrum has a new airing:

> A work which actually incorporates large tracts of another's work – even without a vestige of consent – can still be regarded as original to its author. The consequence of this is that if a skilful author goes through a John Fowles novel, rewrites passages of prose and dialogue which he considers aesthetically ill-conceived, and then publishes his work as an improved edition, he will undoubtedly be successfully sued for copyright infringement by John Fowles; but if that august writer were so impressed by the rewriting that he wished to publish the revised version himself, he could not do so without infringing copyright in a book the vast bulk of which was, in truth, 'unoriginal' to the revising author since it had been written by [Fowles] himself.
>
> (Phillips 1986: 115)

Originality thus defined requires no particular aesthetic merit or creativity. Copyright can subsist in a compilation of factual information or 'in the abridgement of another work, where the abridgement itself involves skill or labour, even though no original thought in terms of the content has been added' (Flint 1990: 22). Hence the well-known lists of protected original works including football pools coupons, street directories, mathematical tables, stock exchange quotations and so on.

Similar qualifications concern the category of 'literary work', demonstrating that 'when Parliament chose the word "literary" it was not searching for a laudatory epithet as in "literary masterpiece"' (Phillips 1986: 118).

Computer programmes are now accorded protection as literary works, joining the historical examples of such 'literary works' as examination questions, instructions on the use of herbicide and letters to newspapers, not to mention railway timetables and exhaust pipe specifications, trade catalogues and lists of foxhounds. At the lower quantitative threshold, however, there remains an untried doubt as to whether a work consisting of a single word could claim 'originality' and thus the protection of the law.

Three observations on the technical character of these copyright categories are appropriate. First, by its conceptual specificity – the definite conditions determining what is entitled to protection, for how long, and where – the legal calculus of copyright underlines the historical positivity of the legal personification of the author within the copyright regime. However determinate their character, the provisions of copyright have also been historically variable. As demonstrated by a long series of copyright-reform campaigns, ranging from that conducted by the eighteenth-century London book trade cartel for a perpetual copyright to those in the nineteenth century for international copyright protection in American territory for English authors and in the late twentieth century for legislation to protect the *droit moral* of authors in copyright countries, these provisions can always be imagined – and sometimes made to become – different. Second, the highly specified character of these legal categories does not constitute a general problem. It is not as though the law would be improved if legal definitions were extended to embrace all possibilities. On the contrary, these limits are the practical precondition of legal decision-making, of reaching a final word and a binding decision at the end of the proper processes of legal judgment. In another sphere of intellectual activity matters are different. Thus in literary or philosophical hermeneutics, it has been said, there is no 'last word ... [o]r else, if there is any, we call that violence' (Ricoeur 1973: 110). Third, the intelligibility of these delimited categories is inseparable from the law of copyright's particular object – the regulation of printed books as traded commodities. Different jurisdictions have had different objects; copyright 'protects a work because it can be copied with undesirable results, while [European] civil law protects an author because he has a moral entitlement to control and exploit the product of his intellectual labour' (Phillips 1986: 104). This historical distinction between a legal regime – copyright – directed to the protection of a property and a regime – the *droit moral* – directed to the protection of a personality will be a constant point of reference. For the present, we can state this: while in a general sense every print culture has had some sort of law to deal with the production and circulation of printed books, the categories of the law of copyright are jurisdictionally specific.

Differences have also marked the enforcement of the law. For instance – and to anticipate the discussion of nineteenth-century copyright practices in chapter 5 – Simon Nowell-Smith (1968: 67–8) draws attention to the use of the formula 'All rights reserved', recalling that in 1878 the London publishing house of Macmillan had offered a German publisher translation rights to their English Men of Letters series. The Germans responded by claiming that Macmillan had no such rights to offer, having failed to comply with the formal requirement under the British Act of 1852 that a notice reserving translation rights be printed on the title page of the original edition. In the United States, the relevant statute required 'All rights reserved' to be printed 'below the notice of copyright entry', that is – according to the trade convention – on the title-verso page. Nowell-Smith comments: 'So a publisher if he was to conform strictly to the laws of both countries must in theory put the words "All rights reserved" . . . on his British title-page and on his American title-verso. No wonder from time to time publishers nodded.' The task is to learn which print cultures have had which legal regulatory systems, remembering that each system has personified the 'author' in a particular manner. Such differences may have material effects. The same individual may at one and the same time but in different national jurisdictions be the bearer of non-congruent or even incompatible attributes or rights. Even within the sphere of his or her legal existence, the individual who writes may be more than one person.

IV

As an alternative to subject-centred histories, we can arrive at the history of authorship through the personalities formed in the different legal systems. Following a similar path, it also becomes possible to recognise the aesthetic persona as a positivity now in the ascendant. The rise of aesthetics and, in particular, of the image of the 'whole' or 'complete' person, exerts a pressure on a copyright tradition that has never depended on what are taken to be the attributes of the individual subject and whose historical object has never been the subjectivity of writers. The pressure is rendered more acute by the fact that Romantic aesthetics carries its own powerful model of cultural history. The model promises 'man's' advance from the loss of an original unity, followed by division and alienation from nature, self and world; however, this presently divided state of being is but a stage in the advance towards a future healing of this division when the fundamental antagonisms – body and mind, desire and morality, history and consciousness, self and society, practice and theory – are dialectically reconciled. Thanks to culture or, in the Marxian sequel, labour, human subjectivity recovers from its objectification and the fullness of human being is ours again.

In its several inflections, this has been a potent image of human development, individual and social. Paraphrasing Kant, a current ethnographer of cultures signals the scale of the claims made by aesthetics:

What is at stake in aesthetic discourse, and in the attempted imposition of a definition of the genuinely human, is nothing less than the *monopoly of humanity*. Art is called upon to mark the difference between humans and non-humans: artistic experience, a free imitation of natural creations, *natura naturans*, whereby the artist (and through him, the beholder) affirms his transcendence of *natura naturata* by producing a 'second nature' subject only to the laws of creative genius, is the closest approach to the divine experience of *intuitus originarius*, the creative perception which freely engenders its own object without recognising any rules or constraints other than its own.

(Bourdieu 1984: 491)

As a sociologist, Pierre Bourdieu circumscribes this transcendental claim by relocating it squarely within the division of intellectual labour that Kant (1979) draws in *The Conflict of the Faculties*: 'scholars' – whether 'incorporated' (in the university guild) or 'independent' – are distinguished from mere 'men of letters' ('businessmen and technicians of scholarship'), priests, judges and doctors, all of whom purvey the knowledge acquired at the university to their particular clienteles – 'the people, which is composed of ignoramuses'. Kant further distinguishes the temporally dominant 'higher' faculties of the university – law, medicine and theology – from the temporally dominated but spiritually dominant 'lower' faculty – that of philosophy – which even though (or because) it lacks temporal power is 'independent of the orders of government' and knows only its own law, that of reason. In this sense the philosopher is said to be entitled to exercise his power in an ideal and total freedom (Bourdieu 1984: 599n). Kant's picture is one of certain human beings – the philosophers – quite other than the institutionally bespoke and compromised men of letters, lawyers, doctors and theologians who, in the end, are mere officials bound by their offices and in no way 'independent of the orders of government'.

Such formulations are all too familiar, as are the antinomies between the free and the bound, the universal and the particular, the necessary and the contingent, the philosophical and the governmental. These antinomies return when, in the late eighteenth century, Friedrich Schiller elaborates his scheme for an 'aesthetic education' depicted in terms of a dialectical neutralising of his over-specialised and divided attributes that would allow 'man' again to realise his full potentialities. The Kantian hierarchy is set in motion by what is taken to be the fundamental process of the aesthetic dialectic:

[The aesthetic disposition] which contains within it the whole of human nature, must necessarily contain within it *in potentia* every individual manifestation of it too. . . . Precisely on this account, because it takes under its protection no single one of man's faculties to the exclusion of the others, it favours each and all of them without distinction; and it favours no single one more than another for the simple reason that it is the ground of possibility of them all. Every other way of exercising its functions endows the psyche with some special aptitude – but only at the cost of some special limitation; the aesthetic alone leads to the absence of all limitation. Every other state into which we can enter refers us back to a preceding one, and requires for its termination a subsequent one; the aesthetic alone is a whole in itself, since it comprises within itself all the conditions of both its origin and its continuance.

(Schiller 1967 [1795]: 151)

If these formulations remain recognisable to us as the ideal of the whole person, so too does the mythopoeic 'history' that accompanies the scheme of aesthetic education:

It was civilization itself which inflicted this wound upon modern man. Once the increase of empirical knowledge, and more exact modes of thought, made sharper divisions between the sciences inevitable, and once the increasingly complex machinery of State necessitated a more rigorous separation of ranks and occupations, then the inner unity of human nature was severed too, and a disastrous conflict set its harmonious powers at variance. The intuitive and the speculative understanding now withdrew in hostility to take up positions in their respective fields, whose frontiers they now began to guard with jealous mistrust; and with this confining of our activity to a particular sphere we have given ourselves a master within, who not infrequently ends by suppressing the rest of our potentialities.

(33–5)

The aesthetic 'alone leads to the absence of all limitation'. In their glossary to his letters *On the Aesthetic Education of Man*, Wilkinson and Willoughby note that Schiller's definition of 'aesthetic' owes something to Kant's attempts to differentiate art from existing branches of philosophy such as logic, ethics and metaphysics with which it had traditionally been associated. However, Schiller's achievement was to distinguish 'between different ways of being related to things, or different modes of awareness, and not between different branches of philosophy'. His usage of 'aesthetic', they continue, refers to 'a distinctive modality of the *whole* being' (304).

We are at home with arguments that assume a division and recommend a healing balance between the rational or technical side of our being and the imaginative or feeling side. What is more, we are familiar with the assertion that law and government are too functional and mechanical, that they lack the organic wholeness of authentic human being. It is as though we had all learned Schiller's lesson. Yet his scheme of aesthetic education was designed for a tiny few in a position to devote themselves to its demanding self-discipline; somehow it has come to have a vastly broader dissemination. Thousands in western cultures have internalised the aesthetic technique of self and, in the name of their own and society's wholeness, have developed aesthetic interests and capacities, not least the developed capacity for being against almost anything. But why does aesthetically derived cultural criticism, theory and history adopt so superordinate a stance towards positive law, indeed towards positive forms of knowledge or institutions, such as legal personality? The key lies in the commitment to the aesthetic as the point of reconciliation of all divisions (or, as Marx was to put it in *Capital*, the 'synthesis of many determinations'). In Schiller's words:

> Herein, then, resides the real secret of the master in any art: that he can make his form consume his material; and the more pretentious, the more seductive this material is in itself, the more it seeks to impose itself upon us, the more high-handedly it thrusts itself forward with effects of its own, or the more the beholder is inclined to get directly involved with it, then the more triumphant the art which forces it back and asserts its own kind of domination over him. The psyche of the listener or spectator must remain completely free or inviolate; it must go forth from the magic circle of the artist pure and perfect as it came from the hands of the Creator. The most frivolous theme must be so treated that it leaves us ready to proceed directly from it to some matter of the utmost import; the most serious material must be so treated that we remain capable of exchanging it forthwith for the lightest play.
>
> (Schiller 1967 [1795]: 155–7)

The practical artefact of aesthetic education is a highly engineered and stylised social persona whose special capacity is to balance 'opposites' within itself. It is not hard to imagine how distinctive the individual would be who had mastered this persona with its self-monitoring, self-questioning, self-distancing, self-reconciliation. But, by virtue of its social and cultural distinction, the aesthetic persona shows itself more a rare artefact than a universal subject.

Relating the aesthetic persona to the writings of Schiller is all very well, but this does not sufficiently signal the historical scale and gravity of the phenomenon. For Philip Kain (1982), the Hegelian and Marxian theories of labour as the fundamental process of 'man's' self-realisation are nothing other than improvisations on Schiller's aesthetic conception of art as a self-realising activity pursued outside the normal forms of production. Stephen Gaukroger (1986) too refers Marx's theory of labour – the future overcoming of labour's present alienation and, with this, the overcoming of all alienations – to Schiller's model of aesthetic activity and its elaboration in German Romanticism. The aesthetic was a new conception of human development in terms of an inner striving to realise oneself against all outside forces. Anticipated in Spinoza and Leibniz, this dynamic replaced a static identification of human being as identical with a pre-given consciousness, the goal of this inner striving being the completing of 'man's' presently incomplete being through the dialectical transcendence of the fundamental antinomies. Marx's contribution was to substitute labour for the aesthetic activity which, in Schiller, is the privileged vehicle for the complete development of 'man's' capacities. Gaukroger observes the striking resemblance between Marx's fourfold classification of forms of alienation (from the products of one's labour, from the activity of labour, from man's species-being, and finally, the alienation of man from other men) and Schiller's depiction of the four consequences of the inception of the division of labour following society's fall from the ideal wholeness of life in ancient Greece: enjoyment is divorced from labour; occupations no longer develop the individual's being but impose their over-specialised and technical imprint on him; ranks and occupations are separated; and the state and its laws become alien to the citizens. With the division of labour, activity becomes sheer toil and results in a fragmentation rather than an integration of being. 'Man's' activity must therefore be transformed, and the means of transformation will be aesthetic activity. As Gaukroger puts it: 'The idea of Man being constituted through his activity, of the activity being turned against him, and finally of his overcoming this estrangement so that his activity becomes his own again, is a strikingly simple and powerful image' (1986: 308).

It is indeed a powerful image. So much so that well-meaning literary critics such as William Wimsatt and Cleanth Brooks (1957) can claim that those of their fellow citizens who do not have access to aesthetic experience are 'uneducated'. Within the field of literary studies, the urge to speak in the name of 'man's' aesthetic wholeness has marginalised philological researches in the style of T.W. Baldwin's (1944) painstaking reconstruction of the rhetorical milieu in which Shakespeare was formed. In its emphasis on the historical particularity of a cultural milieu, such research has fallen foul of aesthetic criticism from the psychology of I.A. Richards (1949) who argues a universal response to Shakespeare to post-structuralist dialectics that would connect the Tudor dramaturge's artefacts to subjectivity, language, the unconscious, sexuality or whatever. A recent contribution thus begins:

> I am eating fish and chips in Stratford-upon-Avon. . . . A major concern of this essay lies in the encounter of Nature and Culture. Stratford, both a natural and a cultural centre of England seems to offer a particularly fruitful location in this respect. Here a river (Nature) joins a canal (Culture) in a setting where one kind of Englishness (the Royal Shakespeare Theatre) confronts another (a fish-and-chip shop) in the sale of quintessential English goods. Here, certainly, one Stratford appears to engage with its opposite. My capacity to ingest both fails to allay a sense of broad and potent distinctions.

> (Hawkes 1986:1)

Without entirely denying the aesthetic game, in the end the display of a well-trained dialectical persona is uninformative. So how did so specialised an ethos come to enjoy so wide a dissemination? Elements of an answer are found in studies of the ingress of aesthetic education into public schooling where, as the discipline of English and operating through a system of pedagogic supervision instituted by nineteenth-century administrative reforms of the popular classroom for the purposes of moral education, it has worked on students' personality formation (Hunter 1988).

In parts of the legal sphere too, for instance in obscenity law, the aesthetic stance has become the dominant regulatory standard. A work of art, it is said, can never be merely erotic, that is, merely tied to the instrumental purpose of arousing prurient interest or encouraging an autoerotic use of the material. This is because in the work of art depiction of sex will always be integrated into a more complex aesthetic whole, thereby achieving the reconciliation of sexual desire and moral seriousness. But has the rise of the aesthetic ethos in any way affected the law of copyright? Certainly an 'authorial' rationale has emerged that claims to be the essential ground of copyright. This is the idealising claim challenged by Jane Ginsburg (1990b: 1866–7), who points to the 'misguided – and increasingly untenable – attempt in United States copyright law to impose a unitary, personality-based concept of copyright'. Correctly noting that this concept is a relatively recent product of the late nineteenth century, she argues that it 'continues – often subconsciously, but certainly pervasively – to inform our ideas about copyright today, too often to the exclusion of competing models of copyright'. The competing models include a 'sweat of the brow' rationale historically associated with the protection of 'personality-deprived' works of information, those in which the law has traditionally protected the investment of labour and resources. Ginsburg's pluralism allows for more than one rationale: despite the 'surface coherence' imposed by the personality model, in historical and doctrinal terms copyright protects not only the 'authorial presence within the work' but also capital value. Thus the 'error of our modern doctrine lies in its implicit, but unexamined, claim that a personality-based approach to copyright law has completely displaced the sweat/investment model. Recognition of our dual bases for copyright would squarely confront the interests at issue in a rapidly growing sector of publishing activity' (1990b: 1870). The failure to recognise more than one rationale that has accompanied the historical law of copyright is, perhaps, in part a consequence of the rise of the personality concept.[5] By contrast, as we shall see, in European doctrine on the rights of authors a provision like the French *droit moral* arguably entails a legal personality identical to the aesthetic personality. As such it represents a limiting case for an argument on the non-congruence of legal and aesthetic personalities.

Assessed by the aesthetic criterion as an expression of the potential wholeness of being, the positive law of copyright does not do well. Its limited functions and highly specified categories appear as if in need of fundamental rectification. It is then no surprise that aesthetically grounded histories of authorship have attempted just such a rectifying and rewriting on the positive law of copyright. In their Romantic historicist version, these histories treat the existing forms of law as inadequate to the emergent consciousness of authors; in their post-structuralist version, they treat copyright law as a limiting factor, a legal buttressing of the fiction of the proprietary author said to have been imposed on the infinite possibility of language.

V

To discuss the law of copyright in terms of its limited object – the regulation of printed books as traded commodities – is to confront the claim of aesthetics as the general theory of human development through culture. This theory purportedly sees beyond the legally buttressed crudities of identity, property and individual authorship. The challenge of the present project is therefore to describe the historical forms of the law without trying to open them to the infinite or connect them to the totality of human development. That is what the aesthetic histories of copyright do, in one way or another.

In the first instance, I am helped by the fact that the historical record reveals a diversity of rationales for the grant of copyright. In *Roper* v. *Streeter* (1672) the court recognised investment and expense as justifying a claim to a property in a copyright; in *The Company of Stationers* v. *Seymour* (1677) the plaintiff's case – an unsuccessful claim that supplementing an existing work created a new work and thus a new property – was argued on the grounds of industry and labour and judged on its merits. In these early cases, legal protection was sought as the means to ensure a fair return on expenditure of money, skill and time; it was not a matter of recognising the public utility of the act of publication or the originality and personality embodied in the work. However, in *Gyles* v. *Wilcox*, a 1740 case heard in Chancery, the court added the exercise of personal judgement to the admissible grounds for a grant of protection, finding that '[t]o make an Abridgment is a Work of Judgment; and the Question in the present Case is, whether the Book that is now before the Court is an Abridgment or not'. If a personal theme is discernible in these early decisions, it is inseparable from the concept of a right of property, incorporeal perhaps, but always a property, as articulated in *Millar* v. *Taylor*, a leading English case decided in 1769:

> It is a personal, incorporeal property, saleable and profitable; it has *indicia certa*: for, though the sentiments and doctrine may be called ideal, yet when the same are communicated to the sight and understanding of every man, by the medium of printing, the work becomes a distinguishable subject of property, and not totally destitute of corporeal qualities.
>
> (*Millar* v. *Taylor*: 221–2)

Nothing here suggests the emergence of the authorial personality as a preordained value to be protected independently of the property right. This different rationale will emerge only a century and more later, and then not in English law.

To the extent that the early copyright cases can be said to have been determined by a 'theory', that theory is usually identified with the Lockean theme of 'man' as the one who owns his property by virtue of a natural right attaching to the fruits of labour. In his *Second Treatise of Civil Government*, Locke argues that

> every Man has a *Property* in his own *Person*. This no Body has any Right to but himself. The *Labour* of his Body, and the *Work* of his Hands, we may say, are properly his. Whatsoever then he removes out of the State that Nature hath provided, and left it in, he hath mixed his *Labour* with, and joyned to it something that is his own, and thereby makes it his *Property*.
>
> (1960 [1690]: 305–6)

By conceptualising 'man' as a naturally possessive subject prior even to his entry into social relations as a member of a citizenry of free and private property owners, Locke's aim was to confirm a natural relation of property as the foundation for the notion of right in general. This assertion of 'man's' natural proprietorial right was one element of a resistance to the notion of absolute monarchy, to 'rights' artificially created by royal will and, therefore, to the institution of royal grant of privilege. However, Locke's view of law was unremittingly negative: never an institution grounded in either reason or conscience, law was for Locke the instrumental means to punish those who contravened the 'natural' order of property. Property, not law, guarantees that 'man' will be respected in his freedom.

Of itself, Locke's principle is incapable of generating a specific law of literary property; however, subsequent commentators made the figure of the proprietary author a locus of his principle of the right of property. In Locke's own times, the guild of London printers and booksellers assumed and, when challenged, argued in court and in petitions to Parliament that a legally obtained copyright was protected by an absolute and perpetual right of property arising from an author's labour. Three centuries later, however, some writers doubt the applicability of Lockean notions to copyright. For Stephen Breyer (1970: 289) the difficulty with Locke's theory is that it 'neither explains *why* property ought to be created on this basis nor does it describe our actual practice.... Nor does the fact that the book is the author's *creation* seem a sufficient reason for making it his *property*.' And he adds: 'We do not normally create or modify property rights solely on the basis of labour expended.'[6] Be that as it may, the Lockean doctrine of property furnished copyright doctrine with a ground in natural right that could justify admitting the author – or the printer-bookseller to whom he or she assigned the work for publication – as the legal owner of a property in the work.

Applied to property in copyright, the Lockean scheme rests on the idea of the work's distinctiveness as the fruit of an individual's labour, not on some notion of the integrity of his or her personality. This distinctiveness allows the work to be protected by its lawful proprietor's exclusive right over the production of copies. It might seem that when originality became the criterion for determining the distinctiveness of the product, the law of copyright necessarily anticipated the protection of authorial personality, that is, of a right that is not in essence economic. In fact it is only later, and after considerable work by courts and by theorists in continental jurisdictions, that a regime of law will emerge whose express object is the subjectivity of the author present in the work. As the French jurist Marcel Plaisant put it in describing the *droit moral* or right of personality:

> Above and beyond the pecuniary and patrimonial right, we understand that the author exercises a lofty sovereignty over his work, such that when it is damaged he is injured. Publication is envisaged as a phenomenon that extends the personality of the author and thus exposes him to further injuries because the surface of his vulnerability has been enlarged.
>
> (Plaisant and Pichot 1934: 50–1)

At stake is the protection of a sphere of personality that is taken to lie beyond the material domain of property and thus to persist regardless of whether or not the property in the work has passed to someone other than its creator. For Plaisant, 'Creation entails enduring relations of filiation' between author and work. These are relations that can never be broken because the work is an inalienable extension of the author's person, part of his or her integrity as a human being. With the proprietorial person of copyright, this is simply not an available option. To underscore 'just how striking a provision this really is', Boyle (1988: 629) asks: 'Could we imagine giving a plumber control over the pipes she installs even after the work is paid for, or a cabinet maker the right to veto the conversion of her writing desk into a television cabinet?'

There is no reason to assume that with its installation in continental jurisdictions, the aesthetic persona has reached the limits of its dissemination. In the common-law countries, it is true, not all the rights that are recognised and protected rest on the fact of possession. For example, an array of tort law provides remedies against civil injuries such as defamation, misrepresentation, trespass and breach of confidence. There is also the right of privacy on which, late in the nineteenth century, the Americans Samuel Warren and Louis Brandeis published their famous paper. In outlining the theoretical grounds for this new right to an 'inviolate personality', they turned to court decisions under the law of copyright to argue that the 'principle which protects personal writings and all other personal productions, not against theft and physical appropriation but against publication in any form, is in reality not the principle of private property, but that of an inviolate personality' (Warren and Brandeis 1890: 205). Something is stirring here in the direction of a right of personality that is not of an economic nature. But, at least in that last decade of the nineteenth century, the boundary was anything but clear: 'The right of property in its widest sense, including all rights and privileges, and hence embracing the rights to an inviolate personality, affords alone that broad basis upon which the protection which the individual demands can be rested' (1890: 211).

VI

Thus far the object has been to introduce the historical diversity and institutional positivity of the legal statuses or persons occupied by authors. To this end, some initial indications have been given not only of the varied rationales that have emerged within the sphere of copyright law but also of the historical particularity of different jurisdictions. Most important has been the attempt to proceed without forcing the varied conditions and forms of law about authorship into a single mould, as if a fundamental relation of equivalence and dependency existed between legal personality and the attributes of the individual subject. Drawing a lesson from the historical anthropology of personhood allowed us to distinguish persons from individuals. Adopting this lesson helps free the legal person from any mortgage or subordination to the notion of the subject form. Approached in like manner, the aesthetic persona shows itself to be historically contingent on the system of aesthetic education and, in this sense, no less technical than legal personality. The aesthetic persona is thus incapable of being the necessary foundation or anchorage of legal personality. Released from the pressure of this or that philosophical scheme, we begin to see that legal personality is formed neither by the rise of the subject of consciousness nor by its dissolution by non-conscious forces. On the contrary, it is the positive creation of legal systems on whose categories and procedures it depends.

These legal systems have been open to technological factors, commercial pressures, philosophical arguments, ethical norms, special knowledges, aesthetic practices, political rationalities, cultural interests and so on. This is not to imply that legal personalities and statuses dissolve into (or are subverted by) extra-legal determinations, conscious or otherwise. Rather, it is a reason for thinking in terms of historically and geopolitically specific 'legal-cultural sets', grids of relations that have cross-cut and organised the legal and cultural fields. There is a model for a descriptive schema of this sort in what – albeit in a quite different connection – Michel Foucault (1980: 194) terms a *dispositif*: a diversely constituted machinery of 'discourses, institutions, architectural arrangements, regulations, laws, administrative measures, scientific statements, philosophic propositions, morality, philanthropy'. By analogy, we might imagine the *dispositif* or legal-cultural set of early modern English copyright as a fluid yet problem-oriented mix of legal institutions and statuses, techniques of reasoning, literate abilities, Lockean theory, investments, book-trade practices, an expanding print communications technology, the growing governmental sphere, the whole arrangement distinctly operative yet having no singular constitutive subject and responding to no singular process of cultural development. Like a *dispositif*, a legal-cultural set is conceived as a mixture not a compound, a fluid arrangement but one that resists unitary explanation in terms of the usual sociological structures or cultural historical processes.

The following chapters sketch a variety of legal-cultural sets: early modern England, France from the *ancien régime* to the late nineteenth century when the *droit moral* was emerging as a coherent body of case law and theory, nineteenth-century Germany, England and the United States and, finally, the new international environment of which the Berne Convention for the Protection of Literary and Artistic Works is the enduring monument. While they contain the occasional polemic, chapters 2 to 7 are primarily descriptive, albeit in the space available they are indicative not exhaustive. Specialist studies have been devoted to matters that these chapters can only touch on. Elizabeth Armstrong (1990), for example, devotes an entire monograph to the book privilege system in France between 1498 and 1526, while Stig Stromholm (1966) devotes a multi-volume research to reconstructing the history of the *droit moral* in the law of France, Germany and the Scandinavian countries. My aim too is comparative, the better to demonstrate the historical diversity of legal arrangements respecting authorship, a diversity that cannot be properly contained within the one framework of explanation. In the two final chapters, I draw out certain implications for legal and for literary and cultural studies.

Despite my emphasis on historical differences and cultural discontinuities, some themes persist and certain personages recur. There is also an unelaborated subtext. To this subtext is related my decision to offer not an aesthetic account of authorship's legal history but an account of literary authorship as it looks from the legal field. At one level this is a choice between two different views or perspectives. But it is not just a matter of imagery. It is also a decision between two different and perhaps incommensurate modes of conducting oneself as an intellectual. We are familiar with the aesthetic intellectual persona that defines itself in opposition to all positive norms, legal and bureaucratic, moral and sexual. In this sense aesthetics is a practice of subjecting positive norms to critique in the name of a more complete and fundamental humanity. The aesthetic persona sets its own purported wholeness or integrity against the alleged incompleteness or one-sidedness of positive institutions such as law and government. These it takes as the merely mechanical side of the organic whole. This familiar representation generates an occasional riposte, as in Weber's (1968: 1404) telling reminder that the 'idea that the bureaucrat is absorbed in subaltern routine and that only the "director" performs the interesting, intellectually demanding tasks is a preconceived notion of the literati and only possible in a country which has no insight into the manner in which its affairs and the working of its officialdom are conducted'.

Something of what is at issue – and a pointer to my unelaborated subtext – can be found in Foucault's (1979a, 1981) discussions of the rise of 'governmentality' and in accounts of early modern state formation by Gerhard Oestreich (1982) and Reinhart Koselleck (1988). Albeit with different emphases, these studies let us see the historical emergence in the sixteenth and seventeenth centuries of a particular cultural threshold. On the one side of this threshold, law became positive and legal intellectuals directed their interests and competences away from absolutes and into the pragmatic projects of the government of states. On the other side of the threshold, philosophical intellectuals – later exemplified by Kant's scholar-philosopher 'independent of the orders of government' and by the aesthetic persona – directed a deeply sceptical moral critique at the orders of positive law and government from which they developed the ability to disengage themselves. It should be clear on which side of this enduring threshold the present study is located.

Chapter 2

Early modern law of copyright in England: statutes, courts and book cultures

I

A recent literary historian of copyright observes that prior to the eighteenth century a book could be legally printed only if it had received the approval of the crown censor and been entered at Stationers' Hall – that is, in the Register Books of the Worshipful Company of the Masters and Keepers or Wardens and Commonalty of the Mystery or Art of Stationers in the City of London. And he is moved to indignation by the fact that the practices of the time were not what they should have been:

> Once entered and printed ... *perpetual* rights under common law were vested in the bookseller or printer who made the entry, and any un-registered manuscript or book that fell into the hands of a member of the Company could be claimed by him as his property by entering and printing. This kind of legalized piracy seems to have troubled almost no one ... the majority [of authors] do not seem to have conceived of their work as property of which they were the legal owners.
>
> (Kernan 1987: 98–9)

Such a reaction to this 'legalized piracy' rests on an unexamined assumption that writers – by the fact of writing – are rendered capable of assuming a proprietorial interest in and responsibility for what they write, even if such a capacity went unrecognised by the legal rules and commercial practices of the times. But what if writers had to *acquire* this interest and responsibility? And what if there has been no one way of *becoming* responsible for what one writes? After all, the Romantic writer's aesthetic responsibility is not the moral responsibility of the Puritan writers in early modern England. And what if the Romantic author was not the magnetic pole to which all earlier legal arrangements were pointed whether they knew it or not? In dealing with the circumstances of early modern copyright, perhaps we are dealing not with a mere stage in an inevitable advance towards more modern and complete forms of authorial and legal personality but with a specific set of arrange-ments having their contemporary logic, one that was in some respects significantly discontinuous with later logics for the protection of authors and their works.

To appreciate the circumstances of the times, we need some idea of how legal business was conducted. For instance, where case law is concerned, it was common to litigate the same issue in different courts at the same time. This poses problems for legal historians because it means that a reduction of litigation in one site might not signal the ending of a matter but its pursuit elsewhere (Baker 1978: 3–4). Nor is it just that the system of courts was used differently in those days; there was no system of courts in the modern sense. True, the appellate jurisdiction of the House of Lords – where the bedrock copyright case of *Donaldson* v. *Beckett* would be judged in 1774 – dated from the seventeenth century, but the activities of the House as the final court of appeal were minimal, averaging six cases per year and even these, until 1779, remained a mystery since they were protected by parliamentary privilege *against* being reported, the business of the House being confidential (Dawson 1968: 89). In short, there was no 'clear and unchallengeable hierarchy of courts':

> The pattern was far more confused in the eighteenth century [than today], and it was by no means easy to say that decisions were 'binding' solely by reason of the sources from which they emanated. The complexity which resulted from the coexistence of three jurisdictions in Common Law [the Court of Exchequer, the Court of King's Bench and the Court of Common Pleas], a jurisdiction in Equity [the Court of Chancery] which often diverged from that of the Common Law, and of the two superior courts in the Exchequer Chamber and the House of Lords, made it extremely difficult to distinguish degrees of authority; and this complexity was not thoroughly reformed, though there had been several previous modifications, until 1876 [when the Judicature Acts established a single hierarchy of courts].
>
> (Allen 1964: 220)

What is more, a legal opinion furnished by the 'Law Lords' to the House of Lords sitting as the highest court of appeal was not binding but advisory only, since it could be rejected by a majority of the peers – as was to occur in *Donaldson* v. *Beckett*. Consequently it was the decisions in the Exchequer Chamber that in practice 'represented the cream of judicial deliberation' (1964: 221). Alongside these royal courts there were local courts and jurisdictions, including that of the Stationers' Company, one of the metropolitan local courts which did not depend on Westminster (Brooks 1986: 34–5); none the less, as the records show, Company officials could settle disputes between members, hear complaints against members and even imprison recalcitrant members of the guild.

Nor was there a singular official system of reporting. The consequences can be gauged from Sir Harbottle Grimstone's 1657 'Address to the Students of the Common Laws of England':

A multitude of flying reports have of late surreptitiously crept forth. .... We have been entertained with barren and unwanted products, *infelix lolium et steriles avenae*, which not only tends to the depraving of the first grounds and reason of our students at the Common Law and the young Practitioners thereof, who by such false lights are misled, ... but also to the contempt of our common Law itself and divers of our former grave and learned Justices and Professors thereof, whose honoured and reverend names have in some of the said books been abused and invocated to patronise the indigested crudities of those plagiaries; the wisdom, gravity and justice of our present justices not deeming or deigning them the least approbation in any of their courts.

(in Allen 1964: 227)

Since they could be written and published by anyone, these 'flying reports' – also known as 'scrambling reports' – were refused by the courts if judges were so minded. The distinctive common law doctrine of *stare decisis* or binding precedent presumes that certain decisions have authority as law, but in the absence of official law reports, how was a given decision to be considered legal authority? Here too it is only with nineteenth-century reforms and the appearance of a system of official law reports that legal authority and a doctrine of precedent gain a systematic basis. *Burrow's Reports* are considered among the most diligent of eighteenth-century reporting, yet even Sir George Burrow could editorially 'correct' his report of *Donaldson* v. *Beckett* so as to make the votes by the Law Lords in the House appear to be in keeping with the arguments put by each judge.[1] So what were the contemporary alternatives? Michael Harris has argued that in publications such as the *Proceedings in the King's Commission of the Peace, Oyer and Terminer, and Gaol Delivery of Newgate* there was no clear boundary of taste and readership distribution between 'law report' and 'pornography':

The more serious the crime the more likely it was to fill a substantial amount of space [in the *Proceedings*]. However, on occasion it seems reasonable to suppose that a long account of a trial was related as much for its appeal to the general reader as to the legal substance. This seems to be indicated in the case of Edmund Curll. The circumstances were trivial enough but the presence of such a notorious public figure in court would have added spice to the report.

(Harris 1982: 11)

What law report today would carry advertisements for our equivalent of Curll's publication *Onania; or, the heinous Sin of Self pollution*? However clear it might have become for us, there was at that time no firm distinction between law reports and novels. If from the mid-eighteenth century the

'*Proceedings* were becoming primarily a legal text' (Harris 1982: 26), this mutation in print literate tastes and distributions was contingent on changing circumstances, including the improving status of the court shorthand writers, the increasing specialisation and autonomy of the legal process, and the differentiation of the role of bookseller and printer. However, as if in keeping with the notion of *dispositif*, Harris (1982: 28n) refers to the particular architectural arrangement whereby the 'mingling within Westminster Hall of booksellers' stalls and courts in session provides an apposite illustration of the close relationship between the [book] trade and the law'.

Where legislative procedure is concerned, early modern England risks seeming no less strange to us. For instance, in relation to private bill procedure, anything like an efficient management of legislation is confronted by the fact that there were as many as nineteen stages through which the bill had to pass. What is more, Commons committees on petitions and bills after a second reading could have fifty or more members. Giving these and other details of contemporary law-making practice, Sheila Lambert (1971: 98) notes also that in the later eighteenth century, 'routine business, whether public or private, was transacted round the speaker's chair, while the rest of the House chatted and moved about to speak to friends'. If the years 1710 to 1727 saw the emergence of more modern elements such as the establishment of a statutory protection for copyright, these were still the times when the public hangman burned condemned books and Queen Anne used her numinous powers – she was the last sovereign to have the 'royal touch' – to cure scrofula (Starkey 1977: 208, 219). Within the legal sphere more generally, traditional relations based on status and tenures persisted even as contractual relationships developed. Notwithstanding this diversity, it remained essential to adhere punctiliously to the archaic niceties, forms and technicalities of the law. These were the times when the English common law was being celebrated – for instance in the *Commentaries on the Laws of England* published by Sir William Blackstone in 1765–9 – as an indigenous glory of the British nation and bulwark against foreign law, just as British sovereign rule was a bulwark against foreign tyranny (Cairns 1984).

Cultural arrangements were no more unified and coherent. Limiting ourselves to a directly relevant matter – the state of the book trade – we need to recognise that '[books] may be the most interesting product of the book trade, but to those whose livelihoods depended on it, this was not so'. Explaining this historical conundrum, John Feather (1980a) shifts the focus from texts and ideas to the architecture of the trade and its distribution network. Particularly outside London, the booksellers

sold far more than blank and printed paper. They were deeply involved in the sale of duty stamps; many indeed were holders of the crown offices of distributors and sub-distributors of stamps. We find many booksellers who were patent medicine vendors, grocers, and insurance agents. Bibliography which concentrates only on books will not even pose the question 'Why should this have been so?', yet in the answer to that question lies the key to an understanding of the economic structure of the book trade, and of its role in English provincial life before the transformation of the distributive trades by the transport revolution of the mid-nineteenth century.

(Feather 1980a: 7)

The motley of commodities using the conduits of the book trade indicates the manner in which the products of authorship actually moved around the country and were bought by booksellers and readers. It is a reminder, in other words, that books – and with them the very possibility of a literary history – depended on an actual distribution system. No wonder Feather states his regret that Anglo-American bibliography has been 'swamped by textual scholarship' to the extent of neglecting 'the trade through which the books were marketed'(1980a: 3, 6).[2] The distributive mechanisms – legal provisions among them – are not incidental and extrinsic to the cultural phenomenon of authorship. They define its very scale.

Although there was no fundamental change in the machine technology of printing, the cultural technology of print literacy was less than stable. We have noted Eisenstein's description of the fluid divisions of literary labour in the early modern printshop. The same historian records the uneven impact of print on different readerships, such that even the 'family circle . . . became the target of a complicated literary cross-fire' as tastes within the household grew more specialised (Eisenstein 1979: 133). New audience types emerged, beyond the old clerical monopoly on literate abilities and cultural and moral concerns and with interests beyond the system of classical genres – of which a writer such as Alexander Pope was still a representative. The print literate audience was enlarged but also increasingly differentiated in the complex environment where print communications technology acquired that un-precedented breadth of dissemination – the ability to have a book go 'all over the kingdom' – that in 1727 occasioned the criminalisation of obscene publication as a threat to public morality. And as the career of a figure such as Sir Robert Harley shows, the political stratum too began to use the print media for the purpose of political address to an electorate that by the time of Queen Anne included approximately one in five of the adult male population.

To return to the book trade, the Copyright Act of 1710 is a sign not only of print technology's capacity to increase the rate of production of copies of a book but also of the profitability that generates disputes, litigation and lawyers. Of itself, however, print guaranteed neither literacy nor profit. People actually need a reason – such as was provided, for instance, by Protestantism – to learn to read and write in the first place. As Natalie Zemon Davis (1975: 214) puts it, 'reading from printed books does not silence oral culture. It can give people something fresh to talk about. Learning from printed books does not suddenly replace learning by doing. It can provide people with new ways to relate their doings to authority, new and old.' In other words, practical lives are not directed by a singular cultural logic or historical necessity of which print literacy and literary interests were an automatic function. The relations of printing and conduct were less straightforward. On the one hand, print literacy could 'destroy traditional monopolies on knowledge and authorship'; on the other hand, it could set up a 'new two-way relationship between an author and his anonymous audience' (1975: 216).

The foregoing indicates something of the contingency and diversity of the early modern legal-cultural environment. It was not a planned environment. Nor – to extrapolate from the arguments of Eisenstein, Davis and Feather – is it now reducible to a singular principle or process such as the Romantic historicist process of an emerging consciousness that moves in step with the purported phases of historical and cultural development. Rather, it was a matter of circumstances in which certain traditional forms of agency and institutions, dating from Tudor legislation and prerogative, were approaching the end of their effective life even as new forms of agency emerged. The Stationers' controls – external and internal – were strained by the emergence of an increasingly autonomous and dispersed book-trade network and by a factionalising of the guild around the diverging interests of the printers on the one hand and the booksellers on the other. These were becoming different trades or livelihoods with different conditions and requirements: controls on training and apprenticeship were more important for the printers than for the booksellers, whereas control of copyrights was more important for the latter. This new division of labour marks an important reconfiguration of the English book trade, but one in which the role of the author was not a leading one. In practice, control over the stages of the normal publication process – purchase of the manuscript (in the case of a new and previously unpublished work), arranging for printing, folding and binding of the printed sheets, distribution and selling – increasingly fell within the ambit of the booksellers' system and network. It was the bookselling faction that took steps to organise against piratical printers by forming commercial combines or 'congers', outside the organisational framework of the Stationers' Company, to protect their property in copyrights (Blagden 1960: 165).

We are now in a position to consider the cultural and legal circumstances prior to the Statute of Anne in 1710, and to explore this first copyright act. I shall then outline the eighteenth-century 'battle' of the booksellers that led to the notable cases of *Millar* v. *Taylor* in 1769 and *Donaldson* v. *Beckett* in 1774.[3]

II

In 1987, under the auspices of the American University in Washington, a modern judicial test was staged of the evidence available for establishing the historical Shakespeare's claim to authorship of 'Shakespeare'. Presenting the case for the Stratford Shakespeare before Justices Brennan, Blackmun and Stevens of the United States Supreme Court, James Boyle (1988: 627) argued that 'the Shakespeare debate has much to tell us about attitudes to textual indeterminacy and to the Romantic picture of the author on which so much of our interpretive tradition – both constitutional and literary – depends'. However, in his view, arguments advanced for the authorship of 'Shakespeare' either by Shakespeare or by the Earl of Oxford, like arguments over the 'original intent' of the framers of the US Constitution, are 'almost entirely without merit as investigations into historical fact' (1988: 627). This is because the general adoption of 'Romantic conceptions of authorship' has meant that the historical differences between the sixteenth century and ours become inadmissible as soon as they threaten those conceptions:

> How terrible it would be then, to find that the greatest author of all was a professional playwright who knocked out scripts for money, and made canny investments of the proceeds. How bizarre it would be if, while showing great concern over the management of his real estate, Shakespeare did not protest pirated, corrupt, or unauthorized versions of his work. . . . And if we do not stress the importance of culture and context to the formation of the Romantic author's work, still less do we even entertain the notion that she could possibly have taken any of her work from the work of others. The Romantic author may violate the norms of sexuality, decorum, and social propriety, but never the norms of literary property. How horrific then, to think that the greatest author of them all would 'borrow' freely from the works of his contemporaries.
>
> (Boyle 1988: 629–30)

This apposite warning is directed against those who would write literary history – or that of authorship – backwards from the Romantic present.[4]

The appropriate tone is set by Gary Taylor's finely circumstantial account – even if he later exhausts himself in his own version of reflexivity – of how Shakespeare *became* a published author. Taylor (1990: 30) recalls that 'Shakespeare was apparently not popular enough to be pirated'. This explains why Pollard (1920) and others have recourse to speculation on the matter of Shakespeare and the pirates. By the eighteenth century, however, as Taylor's 'cultural history' describes, the picture was very different, thanks in large part to the publisher Jacob Tonson – 'not a producer but a consumer of theatre; not a writer but a reader; not a Cavalier but a Whig; not a courtier but an entrepreneur [who] became for the first half of the eighteenth century what Davenant had been to the second half of the seventeenth: both maker and epitome of a new Shakespeare' (Taylor 1990: 53). Known as 'Chief Merchant to the Muses', this entrepreneur printer and bookseller had been among those who petitioned Parliament in the period prior to the Copyright Act of 1710 for statutory protection to be granted to the property they held in copyrights.

The legal arrangements that emerged in the eighteenth century were evidently to his and his family's liking and profit:

> Ninety-three years after Shakespeare's death Tonson had a monopoly on publication of his plays; the House of Tonson kept its stock [of copyrights] in Shakespeare until 1772, when the grandson of Jacob Tonson's nephew died and the family copyrights were auctioned. The Tonsons were sole or part publishers of all the great Shakespeare editions of the first two-thirds of the eighteenth century: Rowe's (1709), Pope's (1725), Theobald's (1733), Warburton's (1747), Johnson's (1765), and Capell's (1768). The Tonsons decided who would edit Shakespeare in the period that cast the mould of all future editions of his work.
>
> (Taylor 1990: 70)

The selection of these several editors was based on a commercial calculation, the Tonson practice being to seek editors 'for the market value of their reputations, which made their names as important to the reading public as Shakespeare's'. Let us resist anachronistic indignation at this particular configuration of economic and cultural power and, instead, accept the fact of this fluid distribution of literate functions and capacities which – and this will be a lesson of the present study – are only contingently embodied in the person of the author as this is defined (if it is defined) in a given legal-cultural milieu. Nor do we need to follow Taylor's theme that privileges performance over print – 'The stage sank as the bookshop rose' – in order to appreciate his account of the construction of 'Shakespeare' as the exemplary genius that pre-Romantic taste and criticism were to make him. Because Shakespeare stole from authors whom the cultivated of the eighteenth century did not read, it was possible for them to imagine him as the great original. Responding to Edward Young's (1968 [1759]: 573) formulation that Jonson 'is as much an Imitator, as Shakespeare is an Original', Taylor (1990: 141) proposes that where Jonson stole 'conspicuously' – he recorded his sources – Shakespeare stole 'surreptitiously'; and he comments: 'The proprietorial concept of authorial copyright, the criminalisation of literary expropriation, the entre-preneurial cult of originality – all were harnessed, like so much else, to the bandwagon of Shakespeare's reputation'.

Let us therefore return to the specific instance of the publication in folio in 1616 of the *Workes of Benjamin Jonson*, the first printed book of dramatic works in English. Joseph Loewenstein (1985) depicts this print reclassification of playwright into author as an inevitable process operating at both the individual and the social levels. It is a matter of the 'expansion in which Jonson's career is a crucial stage' of the general cultural advance towards full authorship from pre-authorial circumstances where '[o]n the margins of dramatic representation – in introductions and epilogues – the Elizabethan play is regularly represented by the speaking actor as "ours", the possession and, indeed, the product of the actors'. If mentioned at all, the playwright was 'almost never "the Author" or "the Playwright"; he was "our poet", an adjunct to the proprietary group of performers. While playwrights almost always wrote the prologues to their scripts, the marketplace was such that authorial assertions of preeminent domain were all but unthinkable' (Loewenstein 1985: 102). Only as a corporate possession did the work acquire attributes of exclusivity: performance rights, reproduction of the manuscript or its sale to a printer, this latter perhaps occurring at the point when audiences were falling away. The move to print and stabilise the play responded also to the threat of piracy. To forestall a piracy a company such as Henslowe's would register a title at Stationers' Hall to secure the exclusive right to copy, even if they had no immediate intention of printing, in order to block some printshop's pirate edition.[5] Once the practice of registering or selling plays for printing became established, 'an economic value relatively autonomous from either the author's scribal labour or the stationer's reproductive and disseminative labour began to inhere in scripts' (1985: 106). The historical information on these mechanisms is useful. However, as soon as Loewenstein moves to distinguish between the author's 'creative' and 'scribal' labours, his account begins to oscillate in that entirely characteristic dialectical way between ideal and material determinants – between Jonson's Sidneian defences of poesy and his 'nascent awareness of the new value that was beginning to accrue to dramaturgy' (1985: 106). This is the familiar formula of the aesthetic reconciliation of the growth of consciousness and the movement of history, a formula repeated time and again by literary and aesthetic historians of copyright, whether in relation to Tudor dramatists such as Jonson – who predictably 'presents himself as a man *ambiguously* engaged with the literary marketplace' (1985: 109; emphasis added) – or Puritan novelists such as Defoe.

Jonson's proto-authorial 'career' Loewenstein treats unquestioningly in terms of an 'advance' for culture as a whole. Is there an alternative to this over-orchestration of historical circumstances into a general movement of history? At least for Shakespeare a special circumstance applies – his status as a proprietor of the company he wrote for. In this instance, the status of proprietary author emerged not from history's recognition of truly 'creative' labour but from a chance joint occupancy of the statuses of company boss and scribe, one individual of two persons. Yet in general it is anything but easy to take our distance from the Romantic image and the historicist account of authorship, even when considering legal-cultural arrangements that obtained before Romanticism set the terms for later approaches. The promise of synthesis and harmony between individual consciousness and historical advance, between ideas and their material conditions, the goal of a complete development of human capacities, the notion that 'literary' writing is a more complete form of being literate than any other because it provides the means for 'man' to become and express his whole person – these Romantic leitmotifs are too pervasive to be easily jettisoned. Not that we need to jettison them entirely. The point is to recognise their historicity – they are the components of one particular cultural milieu and one particular manner of personification or self-formation, not the foundation or destiny of all. If no such limit is set, all earlier (and perhaps all actual) publishing arrangements will be deemed incomplete, sub-authorial. At best, like Jonson's publication of the *Workes* as described by Loewenstein, they will merely mark a staging post on the necessary path to 'man's' cultural completion (which is said to have its exemplary realisation in the Romantic persona of the expressive author). At worst, institutional conditions such as legal arrangements will be deemed impediments to the dialectical advance of consciousness and history, a reification of the rational, mechanical and material side of the dialectic. Untempered by imagination and desire, the legal forms will be depicted as norms that commodify literary creativity.

This same schema is routinely imposed on pre-Romantic institutions such as rhetoric, the ideal of imitation, and patronage. On these matters I shall limit myself to a few revisionist pointers in the style of Walter Ong's invitation to consider Shakespeare as an 'expert re-tooler of other men's thoughts' who was formed in a very specific rhetorical ethos that depended on a certain system of linguistic training:

> The indelible marks of the system on Shakespeare, for example [are] often observable in his most effective and moving and seemingly unaffectedly 'natural' writing. Since Latin, with a dash of Greek, was virtually the only school subject, studied daily all day long for a period of seven to ten years, it is little wonder that skill in the language occasioned skill in the vernaculars. Perhaps never before or after was training in language skills so vigorous in England as in Tudor times.
>
> (Ong 1971: 59)

This was the training that produced a cultural persona with the competence required for survival in that 'court society' described as a 'stock exchange' of reputations by Norbert Elias (1983: 93–5) who refers to the 'specific form of rationality that became second nature to the members of this society, that they exercised with effortless elegance and which, indeed, like the specific control of affects which its exercise demanded, was an indispensable instrument in the competition for status and prestige'. The court persona, says Elias, 'springs from a quite specific structure of social existence'. However one-sided and non-dialectical the courtier's preoccupation with 'externalities' and technique might seem from the aesthetic perspective, the court persona was a creation appropriate to a milieu in which 'conversation with the king himself [Henry VIII in this particular instance] must have been like small talk with Stalin' (Greenblatt 1980: 136–7).

A commonplace of Renaissance poetics held that poetry and painting imitated nature. Orgel (1981: 485) confirms that imitation meant imitation of traditional models, as Scaliger had pointedly remarked in observing that we can best imitate nature by imitating Virgil. The rhetorical compositional doctrine of latinate imitation is a particular bugbear to Romantic assumptions concerning the fundamental values of originality and imagination in authentic literary creation. It might seem that a doctrine of imitation implies a practice of copying or plagiarism, fitting only for a 'stage' of cultural development that has not yet recognised the values of individual originality – protected by a properly author-centric law of copyright. However, as White (1965) demonstrates, imitation and plagiarism or copying were far from identical in practice.[6] It is as helpful to consider plagiarism and copying in relation to distributional factors as it is to align them with early modern theories of composition and criticism, that is, theories in circulation in the period from the seventeenth century to Johnson, which embraces the Statute of Anne, the 'battle' of the booksellers and the crucial decisions in *Millar* v. *Taylor* and *Donaldson* v. *Beckett*. What did early modern readers actually want to read? What were they willing to spend on? Where there was demand and therefore a potential profit, piracy if not plagiarism – the passing-off of another's work as one's own – found a concrete *raison d'être*. The distinction between piracy and plagiarism has been variously drawn. In the case of imitation of a successfully marketed commodity, the pirate's interest is to reproduce the work for sale with all due credit explicitly given to the author, since the latter's name is a selling point. The plagiarist, by contrast, disguises the authorship of the work. Broadly speaking, piracy is what publishers do to one another, while plagiarism is a similar act between authors. According to Taylor (1990: 140–1), however, in *The Dunciad* Pope 'in effect equated the piracy of unscrupulous publishers (like Edmund Curll who infringed other booksellers' copyrights) and the piracy of unscrupulous authors (like Theobald and Cibber, who pinched material from other writers)'. And as Taylor goes on to show, plagiarism too has also been variously judged: in the eighteenth century one effect of the rising 'entrepreneurial cult of originality' was to damage the reputation of authors – including Milton and Sterne – accused of plagiarism.

A distributional factor attaches also to the distinction between a work written for a particular patron and works published for unknown, diverse and dispersed audiences. In the latter category we find that best-selling book – best-selling because it met multiple interests – *Robinson Crusoe*. John Feather (1988a: 15) argues that, in the age of print, book production by patronage was no longer viable: 'To produce a single copy of a printed book is a commercial and technological nonsense; to produce 500, however, or even 150, requires a distribution and marketing system which the patrons simply did not have.' Moreover, as Feather goes on to indicate, in the shift from the patronage to the commercial payment of authors, it was precisely those categories of publication which were most in demand and thus most profitable – almanacs, practical manuals, collections of stories and other such works directed at a popular market – that a distinguished patron would be least likely and willing to lend his or her name to. Nevertheless, we should not assume that a patronal regime such as supported authors into the seventeenth century was necessarily restrictive while, by contrast, a market regime is free. In relation to political patronage in Stuart times, Linda Peck (1981) has identified various positive outcomes of the patronal support of authors. What is more, as argued by Alain Viala (1985) in relation to the French literary field in the seventeenth century, for a writer who moved from patron to patron, the necessary survival skill was 'polygraphic', a rhetorical and clientelist ability to change one's style to suit the particular patronal imperative. By contrast, in a free market such as emerged in the nineteenth-century United States, homogeneous taste not variety and innovation may be the order of the day. The system of patronage and the market system do not, in other words, correlate in any necessary way with particular modes of literary composition. Here as elsewhere, the historicist error is to impose a singular articulation on quite different sets of phenomena.

Nor should we forget an important moral determinant: in the mid-seventeenth century, '[i]f men write books . . . it was not for money' (Bennett 1970: 3). In addition, well into that century there is still a circulation of copies in manuscript. To cite just one example, in 1618 Richard Rogers' *The Practice of Christianitie* was printed. Of the time fourteen years earlier when it had been hand-copied for circulation to the author's circle of friends, Rogers wrote that he had not 'any least cogitation of permitting it to come into print':

> But finding of late that I could not call in the copies I had given and lent abroad, and fearing lest some (which is a common practice in these days) might have thrust it forth with wrong to me . . . I gave way (not without much conflict and doubting) to the publication thereof.
>
> (in Bennett 1970: 9)

Far from being an inevitable stage in the cultural development of 'man', the move into print is simply a 'practice in these days'. Nevertheless, as the book historians have shown, the historical emergence of print technology transformed the social dissemination of 'writing' and the personal capacities associated with its uses. Unlike manuscript dissemination, print tended to create a socially dispersed or, in other words, a non-aristocratic audience; in fact, this was the 'stigma of print' (J. Saunders 1951; May 1980). Not that this type of sensitivity afflicted early modern figures such as Edmund Curll or John Dunton, Curll's bookseller-printer-writer-publicist contemporary – or for that matter Alexander Pope.[7] Dunton's 'cogitations', for instance, aimed at getting into print as fast and in as large a run as possible. As his biographer reports, Dunton's sales figures were extraordinary. In 1693, a 'death-bed' account (of disputed authenticity) – *The Second Spira* – sold 30,000 copies in six weeks and ran through thirteen editions in two years, while in 1708 his most successful work was *The Hazard of a Death-Bed-Repentance*, a 'reply to Dr White Kennet's sermon preached at a funeral of the Duke of Devonshire':

> As an added attraction, Dunton promised on the title-page an essay called 'Conjugal Perjury, or an Essay on Whoredom'. 'Conjugal Perjury' was one of many essays which Dunton announced on his title-pages but failed to bring into print. Nevertheless, three genuine editions of *The Hazard* were soon sold, as well as three pirated editions. Two months later, Dunton offered *The Hazard of a Death-Bed-Repentance, Further Argued*, which included his essay on whoredom, but not the 'Secret History of the Author's Failings, or D . . . . . at Confession', which he promised on the title-page.
>
> (Parks 1976: 163)

A printed work of this sort constitutes a cultural phenomenon quite other than a manuscript circulated to a circle of friends. It is on a par with Dunton's finest entrepreneurial achievement as writer-publisher: the 'querist' method, on which he built his newspaper *The Athenian Mercury*. Entered in the register and licensed by the Stationers as *The Athenian Gazette* [it became the *Mercury* after just one number], *resolving weekly all the most nice and curious Questions proposed by the Ingenious*, this publication was the first to develop the interactive technique, the readers being invited to submit their questions for answer and publication by the 'Athenian Academy'. This they could do thanks to the General Penny Post that allowed questions to reach the editor at Smith's Coffee House in Stocks Market in the Poultry at London. At least one (early anti-bureaucratic) reader wanted to know if the publication was in league with the Post Office. Other 'querists' displayed higher concerns, wanting to know where the waters went after the Flood and whether the 'sky is a substance and may be felt'; still others asked why 'a Horse with a round Fundament emits a square Excrement', why 'Scripture forbids the wearing of Linsy-Woolsy' and revealed endless other devotional and sexual curiosities to which answers were passionately sought. The commercial success of *The Athenian Mercury* attracted interlopers and imitators, including the equally entrepreneurial and devout Daniel Defoe who, like Dunton and Curll, would borrow without scruple in order to produce copy that was wanted and would sell. Piracy – like plagiarism – is an index of the current distribution of literate abilities and the configuration of tastes.

III

In early modern England, the principal agent in the copyright field was not an individual but a corporate entity: the Stationers' Company.[8] It is in the records of the Company that the term 'copy right' appears for the first time in 1701. As to its legal status, this 'copy right' was not a common-law right, but a 'right' grounded solely on the by-laws which the Company was empowered to make under the Charter of Incorporation granted by Queen Mary in 1557 allowing printers, bookbinders and booksellers to form themselves into a recognised guild of traders. The only form of copyright that the legislators of 1710 knew was this stationers' copy right, a device formed in and by the book trade for the express purpose of protecting individual stationers' ownership of the right to print copies of works whose titles had been registered with the Company. Independently of this guild provision, however, the institution of crown printing patents bestowed monopoly rights to print certain classes of books for a given period of time, usually measured in multiples of seven years. Thus the King's Printer held the exclusive and profitable right of printing 'prerogative books', a category that included Acts of Parliament, law books, books of the Church of England, almanacs and grammars. Printing patents were granted by royal grace and favour, without consistent application of a general principle, to individual printers (whether or not members of the Stationers' Company) and, on rare occasions, to writers. As in the drawn-out struggle over the right to publish law books, the ensuing monopolies were much disputed, not least because from Tudor times it was from highly profitable categories of publication such as almanacs and grammars – along with the law books – that non-patent holders found themselves excluded. Along with these two different forms of right, a third type of arrangement emerged in relation to books published without the Stationers' registration; not necessarily pirated editions of protected works, these works could later enter the 'legitimate' circuit if a member of the Company bought or was assigned the 'right' from the original publisher.

For one and a half centuries prior to 1710, the Stationers' guild ordinance protected publishing interests. Reviewing the conflicting opinions on the relation between entrance in the Register and establishment of copyright, L. Ray Patterson (1968: 63) is pragmatic: 'The two conclusions that entrance was essential to copyright and that copyright could be acquired by publication alone could both be wrong, because they proceed from the assumption that the ownership of copy and copyright were synonymous.' Given ownership of copy by purchase from the writer of a work or from another owner, the stationer made a practical calculation as to whether it was worth paying the fee to register the fact of his ownership. Some works promised not to be of sufficient market value to justify the fee and effort of registration. However, the fact of registration was part of the machinery whereby a stationer could attempt to protect his property against piracy – piracy being a greater risk in relation to books having a high market value.

What, then, guaranteed protection of an owner's exclusive right to produce copies if it was neither ownership nor entrance in the register? For Patterson the only guarantee of protection for published works was the licence to print from the wardens of the Stationers' Company. He thus rejects the views that copyright flowed from the fact of publication or that registration was the source of the exclusive right, arguing instead that the function of registration was to safeguard copyright by furnishing evidence of the property. Registration was not in itself a necessary condition for legal publication. Just as the essential element of a patent was the royal permission to exclude others from printing copies of the work or works in question, so for the Stationers' copyright the permission from the wardens of the Company was the crucial component, entrance in the register being only the evidence of the grant of permission.

The right was a mechanism in a set of business practices, not an expression of regard for authors' creativity. In the early modern environment the right to publish – as defined by the Stationers' Company rules – was one which could be bought, willed, jointly owned, pledged as security and so on. Above all, this property was perpetual, and tailored to the practical interests and circumstances of the printers and booksellers, not to those of the author. For Patterson, this was not necessarily a disadvantage. The Stationers' copyright was a right to produce and trade in copies and no more; it did not blur the fundamental boundary that he discerns between the divergent interests of publisher and author. Yet the 1710 Act was to do precisely this when it established a statutory copyright, transposing a device purpose-built by and for stationers into the device that has subsequently been used to protect not only the publisher's but also the author's interests.

Within the established practices of early modern publishing, a key legal component attaching to the printer-bookseller's initial purchase of a manuscript was the conveyance of property in the work to the purchaser. This involved the author's entry into a negative covenant or agreement not to object to the publishing of the work. The positive right – the right to publish copies – was limited to members of the Stationers' Company. As such, the copyright derived from a legal capacity of the Company and was simply not available as a right that the author could hold or contract to accord to another. Milton's 1667 conveyance of *Paradise Lost* to the stationer Samuel Simmons is usually cited as an instance of the conveyancing procedure:

> And the said John Milton . . . doth covenant with the said Samll. Symons . . . that hee . . . shall at all tymes hereafter have, hold, and enjoy the same [All that Booke, Copy or manuscript of a Poem intituled Paradise lost], and all Impressions thereof accordingly, without lett or hinderance of him, the said Jo. Milton, . . . And that the said Jo. Milton, . . . shall not print or cause to be printed, or sell, dispose, or publish, the said Booke or Manuscript, or any other Booke or Manuscript of the same tenor, or subject, without the consent of the said Samll. Symons.
>
> (in Patterson 1968: 74)

The capacity to enter into a negative covenant of this sort is not the stuff of which the Romantic notion of the author is made. In the *Encyclopedia of Literary and Typographical Anecdote*, Timperley (1977 [1842]: 544) comments that this particular conveyance is one of the earliest authenticated instances of 'copy-money' paid by prior agreement for a new work. And, turning to the fact that with time, this agreement had come to be seen as the classic instance of the abuse of authors, Timperley recalls that 'the first impression of the poem does not seem to have been fully sold off before the expiration of seven years, nor till the bookseller had given it five new title-pages by way of wets [*sic*] to the public appetite'. Seen in this light, 'the transaction will appear quite concordant with the natural course of things at the period'.

In fact Patterson (1968: 66) cites evidence that 'the relations between the stationers and authors were cooperative rather than competitive'. On occasions, however, he veers away from historical evidence to the philosophical prejudice of an author-centric perspective, from where he sees 'creative rights' despite their invisibility in positive law. This leads to the paradoxical outcome just noted: the Act of 1710, in which for the first time it would become possible for an author to be the holder of a copyright in the work, becomes for Patterson the point at which English copyright law goes astray. What should have been a law protecting the rights of authors was, he argues, simply the perpetuation in statutory form of the interests of publishers. But there is a problem in requiring a complex legal-cultural set to respond to a singular principle of cultural development. In fact, in occasional circumstances, an author could become a right holder. This was the case of George Wither to whom in 1623 the King granted an exclusive patent for printing his own *Hymns and Songs of the Church* and for their insertion into copies of the Psalm Books, the property in which had previously rested in the hands of the Stationers' Company; this unusual arrangement generated enough friction for Wither to compose a pair of contrasting character sketches of the 'Honest Stationer' and the 'Mere Stationer' (Birrell 1899: 78–90).

There is a second sense in which early modern copyright was something quite other than a principled recognition of an authorial right. What had emerged was, rather, a dual process of registration by the Stationers' Company and licensing by the royal censor. The 'private' business of the Company was conveniently complicit with the 'public' business of the state, and copyright protection was linked to press control. As Feather (1983: 187) puts it, 'the trade was no more anxious than the politicians to have a completely free press, but its reason was different: not the protection of the state, but the protection of investments, especially investments in copies'. Feather's assessment refers to circumstances immediately prior to 1710 and the Statute of Anne. In 1694, the Commons' failure to renew the 1662 Printing Act not only ended pre-publication checking and censorship of printed works, it also removed the only legal basis for copyright protection, the 1662 Act having given statutory recognition to the Stationers' traditional monopoly and the administrative device of registration of title at Stationers' Hall.

In 1637, a decree of the Court of Star Chamber codified laws relating to book licensing. Among its thirty-three clauses is the provision that every printer of a book 'shall set his own name, as also the name of the author, there unto, upon pain of forfeiture of the books, the defacement of the press and corporal punishment'. The object of this provision was not, of course, to protect the attribution of the work to its author, but to assist the policing of the press. A House of Commons order of January 1642 made a similar move. The divergent yet overlapping functions of censorship and copyright administration involved a piecemeal division of labour between licensees and registrars. The Star Chamber decree of 1637 specifies that law books will be licensed by certain judges, history books by the Secretaries of State, heraldry and titles of honour by the Earl Marshall, and all other books – physic or poetry, divinity or philosophy – by the Archbishop of Canterbury or the Bishop of London. Within the Universities of Oxford and Cambridge, the Chancellors or Vice Chancellors were to license books but not books of the common law and affairs of State. Once licensed, the work was duly entered in the register books of the Company of Stationers. In all of this we should remember that early modern England had neither a professional magistracy nor a regular police force – hence the significance of Fielding's initiatives later in the eighteenth century in relation to procedural reforms of the magistrates courts and the Bow Street Runners. Instead, there was Newgate and the pillory. The array of early modern censorship and copyright devices should be seen in this context – not forgetting the aftermath of the Civil War, the Restoration and the Revolution of 1688.[9]

IV

Without renewing the historical link of copyright with censorship, the Act of 1710 provided 'a spring-board from which professional authors could assert their power' (Feather 1980b: 37). However, before exploring the establishment under English law of a statutory copyright, we should establish the precise mode of reference to this legislation. Feather correctly recommends that we refer to the Act of 1710 not 1709, given that the first reading was on 11 January 1710, royal assent being granted on 4 April and the law coming into force six days later. The confusion is caused by the fact that most of the Bill's passage through Parliament is recorded in the *Journals* of the Commons and the Lords under the legal year 1709, which ended on 25 March 1710.

The Act of 1710 – the Statute of Anne – emerged from fifteen years of agitation following the final lapsing of the 1662 Printing Act in 1694. The post-1694 regulatory vacuum might be compared to the situation that was to emerge a century later, in Revolutionary France, although in the latter case all protections of literary property were expressly removed not by a failure to legislate but by legislation promulgated in the name of an ultra-principled adherence to the Enlightenment ideal of free access of all to all knowledge, a circumstance to which I return in chapter 3. Between 1695 and 1707 there were ten unsuccessful attempts at legislation restoring either press licensing or copyright registration or both. These attempts ranged from a 1695 Bill which would have reinstated government press controls but abolished copyright registration to more sophisticated moves in 1704 and 1707.[10] Defoe appears in Feather's account of the action leading up to the Copyright Act of 1710, but not as the prototype of the modern author in whom consciousness and the movement of history are synthesised. Feather's Defoe is the agent of a specific political interest: Sir Robert Harley's moderate Toryism that sought, without recourse to control through licensing, a means of rendering the press responsible at a time when news was ceasing to be entirely under state control. As Feather (1980b: 23) notes, Harley was 'the first major politician ever to be exposed to a more or less free press at a time of great political discord. The decade which preceded the Copyright Act was the decade in which the first successful daily newspaper appeared, and in which Daniel Defoe established himself as the first great journalist.' In these novel circumstances Defoe figures as the author-client of the 1704 Harleian pamphlet, *An Essay on the Regulation of the Press*,[11] which rejects a full-blown licensing system but recommends legislation that, in relation to the transcendent matters of church and state, would require the author's name to appear as a statement of origin on all title-pages, along with the names of the printer and the bookseller. Such a law would 'put a Stop to a certain sort of Thieving which is now in full practice in *England*, and which no law extends to punish, viz. some Printers and Booksellers print copies none of their own'. An author's name on the title-page would facilitate the apprehension of offenders not only against public order but also against the private property rights of copy holders.

A second but quite different rationale also specified a role for authors in the publication process. The booksellers' strategy of arguing that authors' interests were booksellers' interests first appeared in a 1707 petition to the Commons by a group of the most prominent London booksellers, Tonson included. As Feather puts it, in arguing that 'literary property' should be secured to the writer, to his assignee or to the purchaser of the copy, the booksellers managed to 'give prominence to the protection of authors without undermining their own positions' (1980b: 30). The 1707 petition had its issue in a Bill on copyright that received a second reading in the Commons but was then abandoned. However, its argumentation sets the scene for the successful passage of the 1710 Copyright Act with its provision 'for the Encouragement of Learned Men to Compose and Write useful Books'. This active petitioning was doubtless given added urgency by the administrative uncertainty introduced into both governmental and book-market spheres by the 1707 Act of Union with Scotland, not least because the Scottish 'intelligentsia' was as modernising as the English 'Augustans' were conservative (Weinbrot 1978).[12]

Four petitions were advanced by interested parties once the Bill was before the Parliament in January 1710. One of these petitions – *More reasons humbly offered to the Honourable House of Commons, for the Bill for Encouraging*

Learning, and for securing property of copies of books to the rightful owners thereof – requests Parliament to legislate to protect the concept of perpetual copyright, arguing that in its absence those booksellers who legally buy their copies are ruined by the pirates who do not, and that in this way the publication of learned works with slow sales will be discouraged. Feather also discerns the indelible influence of the booksellers on amendments accepted in the committee stages of the Bill (it was a ministerial or Public Bill, not a Private Bill initiated by petition), the consequence of which was to reduce the emphasis on author's rights in the original draft of the Bill. From the original preamble, the Commons in Committee made two important excisions. First, they omitted references to books as authors' 'undoubted property' – albeit *also* the rightful property of 'such persons to whom Such Authors for good Considerations have lawfully transferred their Right and title therein' – and to the respect held for such property in 'all Civilised Nations'. A second omission of a draft provision concerned the author's capacity to claim copyright

> where any Author shall hereafter Compose or write any book or books and shall reserve to himself ye Copy or Copies of Such book or Books Share or Shares thereof Or any Bookseller printer or other person who hath already purchased or acquired or shall hereafter purchase or acquire ye Copy or Copies of any Book or Books Share or Shares thereof in order to print or reprint ye same that in any or either of these cases.

According to Feather (1980b: 36) the notion that an author might 'reserve to himself' the whole or some part of the copyright was anathema to the trade: 'They [the booksellers] saw the Bill as being for their protection, not for the protection of authors and certainly not to encourage authors to enjoy the profits of their work after publication.'

The preamble to the Act of 1710 furnishes an exposition of the circumstance which necessitated the new law, together with a statement of its purposes:

> Whereas, Printers, Booksellers and other persons have of late frequently taken the Liberty of Printing, Reprinting, and Publishing, or causing to be Printed, Reprinted, and Published Books, and other writings, without the Consent of the Authors or Proprietors of such Books and Writings, to their very great Detriment, and too often the Ruin of them and their Families. . . .

> For Preventing therefore such Practices for the Future, and for the Encouragement of Learned Men to Compose and Write useful Books; may it please your Majesty. . . .

Then follow the principal provisions of the Act. These include the fixing of a time limit defining the duration of the exclusive rights of the author or assignee in the copy. All existing copyrights are vested in their present owners for a period of twenty-one years from 10 April 1710, the date of the law's coming into effect. For new works, the period of exclusive right is set at fourteen years, with the possibility of a second fourteen-year term of protection, provided that the original owner of the copyright is still alive. To qualify for such protection, a formal procedure of registration must be complied with: the copy must be entered in the 'Register Book of the Company of Stationers, in such manner as hath been usual'. In addition, a regulatory pricing mechanism is envisaged in the provision, retrospective to 25 March 1710, whereby complaints can be levied against those who 'set a Price upon, or Sell, or Expose to Sale, any Book or Books at such Price or Rate as shall be Conceived by any Person or Persons to be High or Unreasonable'.

While the booksellers had wanted no time limit imposed on what they considered their perpetual property rights in the 'copy' purchased from authors and other copyright holders, on the central matter their victory was complete: they now held a statutory right to copyright, and no longer relied purely on judges' decisions and common-law custom. Moreover, the Act also provided statutory backing for civil suits against those who infringed copyright. But the issue is not quite so simple. The Act is vague as to precisely what it is that is being protected – there is no definition of 'literary property' – although as Feather (1988a: 76) observes, such an omission was 'a direct consequence of the Act's origins in the inner circles of the London book trade, where men like Tonson and Baldwin knew exactly what rights and copies were, and had no need of a law to define them'. However, the issue of the legal status of the work at the end of the statutory period of copyright is left unclear. Did any right at all continue to subsist, and if so, in what form? The problem was to become acute after 1738, the year in which the renewed new copyrights of 1710 began to expire. Nevertheless, with the Act of 1710 an overriding statutory-governmental regime was for the first time imposed across the whole print-publishing field. Whatever else it did or did not do, the 1710 Act thus signalled an end to the exercise of royal privilege as a significant device.

In opening the legal status of copyright owner to non-members of the Stationers' Company and setting a term to the duration of copyright, the Act has something of the anti-trust spirit that in 1720 saw the Bubble Act pass into law. As the statutory marker of a new commercial regime, the Act points towards the ending of archaic guild constraints on the publication and distribution of commodities; Mayo (1962) confirms its expansionary effects. This tendency notwithstanding, the Act gives legal force to many of the Stationers' existing practices, and makes entry in their Register the key formality and administrative device in the policing of copyright.

With the Act of 1710, the three forms of copyright move towards their clear definition: first, the new statutory copyright, entirely the creature of the legislature but overriding – at least in principle – the other two forms; second, the Stationers' copyright, the creature of the Company's by-laws and trade practices; third, by implication, a residual 'common-law' copyright, distinct from the other two forms in being a traditional right recognised by the common-law courts. Most of the elements of copyright discourse are assembled by 1710. The future balancing of personalist and instrumentalist rationales in a form of statute-based social contract between author, copyright owner and public is foreshadowed in the confirmation and defence of the copyright holder's property right in a qualified form that meets the public policy purpose of the state: to provide 'for the Encouragement of Learned Men to Compose and Write Useful Books'. And there is also the pointer to the uneasy split in the personalist rationale between author and publisher as the person to which right of ownership of the property attaches. But it is not a sign of the alienation of the human subject in commodity production that the Statute of Anne concerns itself with the book as a mechanically replicable commodity, nor does this indicate a failure of the law to see the human subject in its (potential) fullness as embodied in the authorial persona. Such legislation cannot be explained in terms of the movement of history towards its rendezvous with authorial consciousness; on the contrary, it represents a specific legal construction of certain legal-cultural attributes occasioned by a new communications technology and an expanding demand for certain types of reading. Nor can the Act be detached from all circumstances bar the economic ones in the manner that allows Posner to write that the 'first copyright law in England was passed at the beginning of the eighteenth century and *might have been passed earlier* if books had not been so expensive and if printing had not been licensed' (1988: 351; emphasis added). As if – but for certain circumstances – a cultural phenomenon as complex and contingent as this would have followed the singular path of economic rationality and necessity.

The Act of 1710 is not purely a legal phenomenon. It is coloured by private and public interests, commercial and national 'policies'. Here we might recall that regulatory devices might not be of a legal nature at all. Thus it was not through law but as a historical work practice that in the early eighteenth century 'it became an established rule for dramatic authors to have the profits of the third, sixth and ninth nights for their benefit' (Timperley 1972 [1842]: 623). And even in publishing the law might not be everything. Prescott (1989: 453) suspects that 'for the most part, the [London] publishers did not really mind if they had protection or not', adding that they 'probably didn't need it'. In support of this contention, he claims that except for some proceedings in Chancery and some rare actions founded on royal grants of monopoly, it is hard to find 'a single case before the Statute of Anne where anyone, pauper or plutocrat, was sued for copyright infringement at common law at all' (1989: 453). If – as was the case – the Stationers promoted the Act of 1710, their reason was related to geopolitical circumstance: the 1707 Union with Scotland. 'The real motive behind the first Copyright Act, therefore, seems to have been an attempt to *export* copyright control to a region of Great Britain where the Stationers' Company's writ did not run' (1989: 455). And indeed it was to be the 'distant pirates', as Feather (1988a) terms the Scottish (and Irish) publishers with access to the provincial English markets, who were to challenge the London monopoly during the course of the century.

In any case the booksellers' ploy succeeded. This is Feather's assessment of the Act. Bonham-Carter (1978: 16), however, is among those Romantics who see in it the definitive move in favour of authors that they are looking for: '[the Act] established the author's right to his own property'. L. Ray Patterson (1968: 145) shares Feather's judgement, and draws attention to the fact that the term 'author' appears in the Statute 'alternatively with the terms "purchaser of copy", "proprietor of copy" or "assignee"'. The only right conferred on 'authors' but not available to any 'purchaser of copy' was the right to renew the copyright:

> Authorship came of age in eighteenth-century England as a respectable profession, and it would be fitting to think that the first English copyright statute was enacted in 1709 to benefit such authors as Pope, Swift, Addison, Steele and Richardson. Fitting perhaps, but hardly accurate. The facts are less romantic. The Statute of Anne (8 Anne c. 19.) was [not] intended primarily to benefit authors. It was a trade-regulation statute enacted to bring order to the chaos created in the book trade by the final lapse in 1694 of its predecessor, the Licensing Act of 1612, and to prevent a continuation of the booksellers' monopoly.
>
> (Patterson 1968: 143)

The 'negative' assessments of the Copyright Act of 1710 by Patterson and Feather are scarcely new. Almost a century ago, Augustine Birrell argued that 'this perfidious measure' had 'complicated, and, indeed, butchered' the question of literary property in England:

> [The Copyright Act] was originally, such is the tradition, drafted by Dr Swift solely in the interests of authors and booksellers, who, ever since the abolition of the Star Chamber and the subsequent expiration, in 1679, of the Licensing Acts, found themselves much put about for summary remedies against piratical printers, who, when pursued through all the forms of actions in the King's or Queen's Bench, were accustomed, like John Bunyan's inimitable and immortal Mr Badman, 'to break', or if they did not break, then, if I may use language which has not the warrant of Bunyan, 'to bolt'. Swift's draft Bill, like Cranmer's rough draft of the Articles of our Faith, has unfortunately disappeared, but that it was rudely treated in Committee is certain, though all we know now is the measure as it received the Royal Assent and remained upon the Statute Book of the Realm until repealed in 1842.
>
> (Birrell 1899: 19–20)

Birrell's principal complaint is that the 1710 Act removed from 'the British author' the entitlement to a perpetual property in his or her published work. In this – good Darwinian or Spenserian that he was – Birrell finds 'evolution artificially arrested' (1899: 22).

V

The early modern debate on literary property – conducted in the manner of a 'battle' – centred on the issue of *perpetual* property.[13] At stake was the notion of an author's perpetual right in the disposal of his or her unpublished manuscript. This right was the so-called common-law copyright, existing independently of statute law and the stationers' copyright. It was in fact the London book monopolists who most vehemently asserted this 'natural' right of authors, and who litigated to this effect. After all, once assigned by the writer to the bookseller – and assignment of manuscript and all rights therein continued as the standard practice in the trade – the copyright or right to print and publish the manuscript belonged for ever to the bookseller, to use, sell or bequeath as most convenient. In practice the booksellers did not use the statutory penalties provided by the 1710 Act, but instead 'fell in love with the High Court of Chancery, and sought injunctions to restrain the publication of the books of which they alleged themselves to be the proprietors' (Birrell 1899: 101). For their part, the lawyers in Chancery seem to have dealt with copyright cases within the traditional terms of English property law. Although the central question was the perpetual right of the author to a property in the work, in general it was not authors that were the litigants when disputes in fact arose.

From Birrell (1899) to Rose (1988), the story of the 'battle of the booksellers' from 1710 to 1774 has often been told. Faced with the statutory curtailment of a perpetual property in copyright, the copyright-holding booksellers invented the theme that there had always been an author's copyright in common law. It was this 'property' that authors had always sold and assigned to the booksellers, confirming the conveyance by a covenant not to impede the bookseller's exercise of his exclusive right to produce copies of the work. In this story, the author's purported common-law right became the key element of the traditional order of the book trade.

Donaldson v. *Beckett*, decided in the House of Lords in 1774, will mark the failure of the monopolist booksellers' stratagem. However, in *Donaldson* v. *Beckett*, the monopoly of the London establishment booksellers was finally broken by other booksellers, not by campaigning authors. Yet in the process copyright came – by force of the restatement of the theme – to be thought of as an author's right. The notion that an author's rights in his or her work were protected in common law – the question was not in fact tried in a common-law court until 1760 – flowed neither from consciousness nor from some power in 'writing'; it emerged uncertainly, and piecemeal, from certain sites of legal decision-making, in particular the Court of Chancery.

Strictly speaking, it is not the law that decides and acts in legal matters any more than it is 'man' or 'consciousness', 'history' or 'language' or 'the subject'. These terms do not refer to agents with the definite means and competence to define and recognise an authorial right, let alone to reach a socially binding decision in a dispute over literary property. For an example of a competent agent we can turn to a complex organisational and discursive entity such as the Court of Chancery, whose means of action included the injunctions that this court had the power to grant. The injunction, like the Court of Chancery itself, is an entity internal to the legal field. It was usually granted for the specific purpose of preserving a property in dispute – for instance by restraining a publication by one whose right to produce copies is challenged by one who *prima facie* holds the exclusive copyright to the work in question – pending a determination in a court of law.

It is an object of the present study not to trivialise the institutional means – as distinct from the meanings – of authorship. Among other institutions, the Court of Chancery played its part in the history of authorship in England. With the abolition in 1641 of the Star Chamber – the locale of criminal proceedings against the powerful under the Tudors and of abuses of royal power under the Stuarts – the policing of publishing tended to remain with Chancery and the Chancellors. In 1720 *Burnett* v. *Chetwood* was heard by Lord Macclesfield. Chetwood had without authorisation translated into English and published the noted theologian Thomas Burnett's Latin text, *Archaeologia Sacra*. Although the plaintiff's claim that his copyright had been infringed was not upheld, Burnett obtained an injunction against the publisher of the English version. Of interest is Lord Macclesfield's comment that the *Archaeologia Sacra* contained ideas which should be 'concealed from the vulgar in the Latin language, in which language it could not do much hurt, the learned being better able to judge of it'. As the source of authority for this assertion concerning the variable abilities and susceptibilities of different contemporary readerships, the Chancellor asserts Chancery's 'superintendency over all books . . . [in order to] restrain in a summary way the printing or publishing any that contained reflexions on religion and morality' (*Burnett* v. *Chetwood*: 1009). This claim was made at a time when – as in Curll's sentencing for obscene libel in 1727 – the common-law courts too were acquiring a new competence to deal with certain aspects of print literate culture.

The legal device most frequently deployed in copyright disputes was the Chancery injunction. A characteristic instance is the suit brought by William Taylor against Thomas Cox in 1719. Taylor had entered his claim to the whole of the copyright of *The Life and Strange Surprising Adventures of Robinson Crusoe, of York, Mariner* in the register of the Stationers' Company on 23 April that year. Prior to the Chancery suit, Taylor had threatened legal action against Cox in the *St James's Post* on 7 August, concerning the latter's pirated and 'abrig'd' and 'more portable' version of Defoe's book (Rogers 1979: 4–10). It is also characteristic that the move in Chancery functioned above all as a threat, and in fact came to nothing. Why was the injunction an appropriate means for the defence of copyright claims? In essence, the advantage of proceeding in Chancery was that it provided an effective and immediate restraint on rival publishers without requiring a thorough testing of the issue in a court of law. Like other proceedings in the court of equity, the point of the injunction was to restrain an action which the common law would have deemed an injury and a violation, had the matter been tried there. To apply for an injunction in Chancery, it was necessary to file a bill, and then to move – supported by an affidavit as to the legal purchase or acquisition of the property in the copyright – for an interim injunction pending the hearing of the case. Injunctions were usually granted until trial if a *prima facie* case existed; at the trial, the interim injunction would either be dissolved or made perpetual. It was, says Birrell (1899: 101), 'a formidable species of artillery to set a-roaring'. Chancery judges had a tendency to grant interim injunctions to those claiming ownership of copyright. Birrell cites the case of a member of the Stationers' Company who claimed to own *The Pilgrim's Progress* 'because, forsooth, it was one of the books he bought at the sale of stock of a retiring stationer' (1899: 102). On this basis he was granted the injunction he sought against a rival printer. In principle, the Chancery injunction was given to assist a common law right; if the existence of such a right had been in any doubt, the proper course was not to grant the injunction and to have the matter tried as a question of law in a common-law court. However, Chancery judges granted injunctions to booksellers who alleged themselves to be proprietors of copyright even where – under the Statute of Anne – the copyright had expired, and by this action the judges gave tacit support to the argument that a common-law author's copyright did indeed exist. The Court of Chancery thus helped booksellers to maintain their traditional monopoly regardless of the limitations formally imposed by the Act of 1710, even if the issuing of an injunction did not constitute legal authority in a common-law case.

Within the jurisdiction of Chancery too there were diverse types of copyright claim, as Lord Chief Justice de Grey indicated in 1774 when, in *Donaldson* v. *Beckett*, he reviewed decisions that had been made in equity:

> The causes which have come before the court of Chancery since the statute, I find to be 17 in number. Of these eight were founded on the statute right; in two or three, the question was, whether the book was a fair abridgment; and all the rest were injunctions granted *ex parte*, upon filing the bill, with an affidavit annexed. In these cases the defendant is not so much as heard; and can I imagine, that so many illustrious men, who presided in the court of Chancery, would, without a single argument, have determined so great

and copious a question, and which has taken up so much of your lordships' time? In fact, none of them wished to have it said he had formed any opinion on the subject.

(in Cobbett 1813: 989–90)

In the absence of reports it is impossible to know if cases heard prior to the 1731 deadline for ending statutory protection for 'old books' – *Knaplock* v. *Curll* and *Tonson* v. *Clifton* both in 1722 – were based on the Act of 1710. However, Patterson (1968) confirms that there are sufficient cases about which there is no question to show that the Chancellor did not consider himself bound by the statute. These include *Motte* v. *Falkner* in 1735 (where an injunction was granted to restrain a publication of *Miscellanies* of Swift and Pope first published in 1701–2 and 1708), and *Tonson* v. *Walker* in 1739. Birrell cites *Tonson and another* v. *Walker* as one example among others of this independent Chancery style of action. Lord Chancellor Hardwicke granted an injunction to Jacob Tonson to restrain the defendant from publication of an edition of *Paradise Lost*. Tonson claimed his title from Simmons – through the contract by which seventy-two years earlier, in 1667, Milton had conveyed the property to Simmons – and produced that original assignment to uphold his claim. However, the report does not indicate whether the assignment from Simmons to Tonson was tendered in evidence. *Paradise Lost* was first published in 1667; as such, it was clearly and unambiguously an 'old book' as defined by the Statute of Anne. As if in disregard of the terms of the statute, Tonson was granted the injunction that he sought, thus maintaining his monopoly on the publication of precisely the sort of work – Milton's – that other newer and non-London booksellers wanted to publish. A second case involving the same plaintiff, defendant and work came to Chancery thirteen years later. Lord Hardwicke followed the established procedure by granting the injunction until the hearing date, but anticipated that at the hearing he could refer the question of whether there was a common-law copyright independent of the statute to another court. The work in question contained not only Milton's text but also a life of the poet and a set of notes on the poem, these latter coming within the terms of the 1710 Statute. The injunction sought to restrain the defendant from publishing Milton's poem, or the Life of Milton, or Dr Newton's notes. As Patterson (1968: 164) observes, the relief sought was accorded but 'the Chancellor relied on the Statute of Anne, which was directly contra to the aims of the booksellers'.

From mid-century in courts other than Chancery – despite petitions to Parliament and pamphlets to the public – judicial support for the London booksellers' interests began to fade. Instituted in the Scottish Court of Sessions in 1743 by seventeen London booksellers seeking penalties, damages and injunctions against twenty-four Scottish booksellers, *Millar* v. *Kincaid* was finally decided in 1750 in the House of Lords, the plaintiffs' action being rejected on a variety of technical grounds. In the period of this long and complex suit – with its element of confrontation between metropolitan and provincial interests – in 1748 the Scottish Court of Sessions judged in *Midwinter* v. *Hamilton* that only if a work met the registration requirements of the Act of 1710 was it protected. What is more, even a correctly registered work would not be protected beyond the statutory term of years. As in the United States in the following century, this judicial conduct might not have been entirely unrelated to the fact that a thriving local reprint industry had grown up based on English editions yet, to an extent, beyond the London booksellers' control.

Like *Millar* v. *Kincaid*, *Tonson* v. *Collins* suggests the complexity of copyright litigation at the time. This 1758 suit concerned the unauthorised sale of *Spectators* first published in 1711. The bookseller plaintiffs went twice to the Court of King's Bench and also appealed to the Exchequer Chamber before their action was dismissed on the grounds of collusion. *Tonson* v. *Collins* is notable, however, for the fact that the issue of the author's customary common-law right was finally tried in a common-law court. The case for the right was put by counsel for the London publishing establishment who advanced a dual argument: first, the author's right to the profits of his or her work; second, the recognition of this right at common law:

> While a work is in manuscript, the author has entire dominion over it. . . .
> If, instead of copying by clerks, an author prints for the use of his friends,
> he gives them no right over the copies. Proceed one step further: If he
> published by subscription and no books are delivered but to subscribers,
> they have no right over the copies, but only to use them. This leads us to a
> general publication: there also every purchaser has a right to use but
> nothing further. The profits of the sale must go to somebody. The printer
> and other mechanic artists concerned in the impression are paid for their
> parts: the author who is the first mover ought in justice to be paid too.
>
> (*Tonson* v. *Collins*: 169–70)

For the defendant, the case was argued on the ground of the limited monopoly accorded by the Act of 1710. In fact the issue of the author's right was not decided, although in the second hearing Blackstone, for the plaintiff, returned to that issue: 'I contend that by law, (independent of Stat. 8 Anne) every author hath in himself the sole exclusive right of multiplying the copies of his literary productions; which right is, by assignment, now vested in the plaintiffs' (*Tonson* v. *Collins*: 180). In response, counsel for the defendant allowed that 'the author has a property in his sentiments till he publishes them':

> He may keep them in his closet; he may give them away; if stolen from him,
> he has a remedy; he may sell them to a bookseller, and give him a title to

publish them. But from the moment of publication, they are thrown into a state of universal communion.

(Tonson v. Collins: 185)

The issue of the property right attaching to authorship was thus argued in the name of a customary right which had not previously found explicit expression in positive law. Argument for the existence of such a right in common law was supported either by appeals to precedents and established practices or by assertions of principle, such that it began to seem that if the common law did not now recognise the author's right, a fundamental break with native tradition would occur.

To an extent, this customary proprietary 'author' was a new discursive effect of the reiteration of the booksellers' argument disseminated in pamphlets, petitions and, from *Tonson* v. *Collins*, in court. But law does not reduce to discourse; non-discursive actions and practices too were part of this legal-cultural environment. Thus, at the time of *Tonson* v. *Collins*, the London booksellers combined to establish a fighting fund to meet the costs of prosecuting any bookseller trading in books the copyright of which was claimed by the monopolists. Provincial booksellers were promised that the copyright holders would purchase any pirated editions in the stock of those joining the fund. However, booksellers refusing to enter the agreement would not be allowed to enter the trade sales where, as Collins (1927) describes, copyright (or shares therein) were bought and sold.

Even in Chancery cases some judicial opinion shifted away from author and monopoly and towards the statute. In 1765, in *Osborne* v. *Donaldson* and *Millar* v. *Donaldson* injunctions obtained by authors' assignees were dissolved, Lord Northington stating that it was

> a new question (none of the cases being precedents in point, being orders made before the expiration of the fourteen years given by the statute). That it was a point of so much difficulty and consequence, that he should not determine it at the hearing, but should send it to law for the opinion of the judges. . . . He desired to be understood as giving no opinion on the subject, but observed that it might be dangerous to determine that the author has a perpetual property in his books, for such a property would give him not only a right to publish, but to suppress too.

(Osborne v. Donaldson: 924)

In his *History of British Publishing* Feather (1988a: 80–3) directs our attention to the pattern of competition within the book trade between London publishers and Scottish reprinters and, in particular, to the role of the Edinburgh reprinter-bookseller, Alexander Donaldson. Having made 'a reasonable fortune as a pirate' and with his reprints widely available in English provincial markets, Donaldson found that the improved distribution system and collaborative arrangements that the London trade had developed with its provincial counterparts was beginning to damage his business. His response was to open a bookshop in London. As Feather observes, while this was not illegal, 'what was blatantly and provocatively illegal was that he sold there his own reprints, under the noses of the very booksellers who claimed to own the rights in the copies'. When on expiry of its statutory twenty-eight-year copyright he reprinted and sold an edition of James Thomson's *Seasons*, Donaldson was sued for breach of common-law rights of property by the owner of the Thomson copyright, the London bookseller Andrew Millar, with the support of the London trade. Because the reprinting had occurred in Scotland, the charge was heard in the Scottish Court of Sessions. While under English law the courts had tended to accept that on the basis of his labour the author had a common-law right of property in the resultant work, matters were different in the Scottish jurisdiction:

> The Scottish courts had never been entirely happy in dealing with copyright cases. A number of such cases had been heard in the Court of Sessions in the 1750s and 1760s, but no coherent body of practice had emerged. In general the Scots judges had ruled against perpetual copyright, because there was an underlying feeling that Scots law did not recognise the existence of copyright at all. The problem was that the Roman basis of Scots law did not admit of the concept of 'incorporeal' property: to be a legal entity, a property had to have real, or physical, existence. Thus although a book or a manuscript was certainly a piece of property, Scots lawyers were generally very doubtful whether the same could be said of the text.
>
> (Feather 1988a: 81)

On this ground the plaintiff, Donaldson, argued that there was no case to answer and, after reviewing such precedents as there were, the court agreed. It was then that Millar shifted his attack to the London sale and its purported illegality, starting the series of decisions that was to end with the 1774 decision of the House of Lords in *Donaldson* v. *Beckett* where, once again, the persistence of Alexander Donaldson would be rewarded by a favourable judgment.

Prior to that, however, in 1769 – and although the case did not involve a living author – in *Millar* v. *Taylor* the four judges of the King's Bench finally delivered opinions concerning the common-law copyright of the author. The issue was presented in terms of the authorial right as the fundamental ground of the right or property sold or assigned in perpetuity to the bookseller. By a majority of three to one, the judges found that copyright – as a form of property – indeed had a perpetual existence. In this instance the same Andrew Millar had sued an outsider, Robert Taylor, for having published and offered for sale copies of Thomson's *Seasons*. Millar had purchased the copyright from the author in 1729, had the right assigned to himself and registered at Stationers' Hall. Of course, when Taylor published his edition in 1763 the protection granted by the Statute of Anne had expired. As Mr Justice Willes observed, the author's title to the copy depends upon two questions: 'Whether the copy of a book, or literary composition, belongs to the author by the common law', and 'Whether the common-law right of authors to the copies of their own works is taken away by 8 Ann. c.19' (*Millar* v. *Taylor*: 206). The majority spoke in forthright terms, with Mr Justice Aston typical in this regard: '[F]or, I confess, I do not know, nor can I comprehend any property more emphatically a man's own, nay, more incapable of being mistaken, than his literary works' (224). Such a view was said to stand 'upon every principle of reason, natural justice, morality and common law, upon the evidence of the long received opinion of this property, appearing in ancient proceedings, and in law cases' (228–9). As one of the majority who found for the author's common-law right, Lord Mansfield recalled the fact of four decisions in Chancery in which the unauthorised publication of unpublished manuscripts was the object of injunctions and drew the following distinctions between pre- and post-publication:

> The common law, as to the copy before publication, can not be found in custom. Before 1732 the case of a piracy before publication never existed: it never was put, or supposed. There is not a syllable about it to be met with any where. The regulations, the ordinances, the Acts of Parliament, the cases in Westminster Hall, all relate to the copy of books after publication by the authors. Since 1732 there is not a word to be traced about it, except from the four cases in Chancery.
>
> (*Millar* v. *Taylor*: 252)

Having found no support in custom and precedent, Lord Mansfield swings to a Lockean path to ground the pre-publication right in a natural right in the property that one's labour has created:

> [I]t is just, that an author should reap the pecuniary profit of his own ingenuity and labour. It is just, that another should not use his name without his consent. It is fit that he should judge when to publish, or whether he will ever publish. It is fit he should not only choose the time, but the manner of publication; how many; what volume; what print. It is fit, he should choose to whose care he will trust the accuracy and correctness of the impression; in whose honesty he will confide, not to foist in additions: with other reasonings of the same effect.
>
> (*Millar* v. *Taylor*: 252)

The effect of this discourse on behalf of the author was to provide an unshakeable ground for the claim advanced by the monopolist booksellers. The judgment implies their 'correctness' and 'honesty' and, by implication, the lack of these qualities in the enterprise of an outsider such as Taylor. If the pre-publication right is admitted, then, in Lord Mansfield's words, 'the same reasons hold after the author has published'.

The London booksellers were thus confirmed under English common law as the proper guardians – through legal purchase or assignment – of the fruits of authorial labour, a ground quite independent of the Act of 1710: 'The 8th of Queen Anne is no answer. We are considering the common law upon principles before and independent of that Act' (*Millar* v. *Taylor*: 252). Consequently, far from finding the Chancery injunctions in any way questionable, Lord Mansfield takes them as authority on the matter of the authorial right:

> The judicial opinions of those eminent lawyers and great men who granted or continued injunctions, in cases after publication, not within 8 Queen Anne; uncontradicted by any book, judgment, or saying; must weigh in any question of law; much more, in a question of mere theory and speculation as to what is agreeable or repugnant to natural principles. I look upon these injunctions, as equal to any final decree.
>
> (*Millar* v. *Taylor*: 253)

And, drawing to his conclusion, Lord Mansfield confirmed: 'I always thought the objection from the Act of Parliament the most plausible. But upon consideration it is, I think, impossible to imply this Act into an abolition of the common law right, if it did exist, or into a declaration "that no such right ever existed"' (*Millar* v. *Taylor*: 253). However, Mr Justice Yates' dissenting opinion was that the only copyright was the one available under the Statute once a work is published, although prior to that point: 'every man has a right to keep his own sentiments, if he pleases: he has certainly a right to judge whether he will make them public or commit them only to the sight of his friends' (*Millar* v. *Taylor*: 242). Once again, the fact of print publication and dissemination becomes a critical issue for the court, as does the definition of property – Yates argued that 'the property here is all ideal: a set of ideas which have no bounds or marks whatever, nothing that is capable of a visible possession, nothing that can sustain any one of the qualities or incidents of property' (233). The fact of Yates' dissent – on the issue of copyright – is notable. In the thirty years of Lord Mansfield's presidency of the court, only twenty dissenting opinions are recorded. And in the decade 1756 to 1765 there was no decision that was not unanimous (Fifoot 1936). In 1770 Millar's Chancery injunction was duly granted even though – as Birrell (1899: 113) has it – Millar himself in the meantime 'vexatiously died'. As for Mr Justice Yates, he was doubtless solaced by the reversal of *Millar* v. *Taylor* when *Donaldson* v. *Beckett* was decided by the Lords in 1774.

VI

In 1774, *Donaldson* v. *Beckett* (it had been *Beckett* v. *Donaldson* at the trial in Westminster Hall) was heard on appeal to the House of Lords. Spectators had to be turned away, and there was extensive coverage in the press in London and in Scotland. Such interest is perhaps a sign that no one knew which argument would prevail – and a reminder to us not to write with the anachronistic benefit of hindsight. Once again, metropolitan monopolists and provincial 'pirates' were in conflict, the latter again represented by Alexander Donaldson, the Edinburgh publisher and reprinter who continued to fight his cause through the British courts (Forbes-Gray 1926). After the case of *Millar* v. *Taylor*, the copyright – such as it was now recognised in common law – to Thomson's *Seasons* had been acquired by a partnership of printer-booksellers, among them the Beckett who obtained an injunction in the court of Chancery against Alexander and John Donaldson who had published an 'unauthorised' edition of the work. Donaldson's appeal to the Lords was thus the occasion, once again, where rival editions of James Thomson's *Seasons* – a work first published in the 1720s – were pitted one against the other. Once again the argument that the author's labour created a literary property to be held – like any other property – in perpetuity by its lawful assignee confronted the argument that a literary work, once published, constituted no such property. And once again the authority of common law and custom was set against the authority of Queen Anne's Statute of 1710. And once again no author was active in the litigation, Thomson having died in 1748. Thank God, one wants to say, that the law – in this instance the House of Lords as the highest court of appeal – has the last word.

The Lords voted twenty-two for the outsider, Donaldson, against eleven for the Londoner, Beckett. The Lords' decision meant above all else that the rights protected under the Act of 1710 ceased to exist once the term of protection decided by the legislature expired. At that point the once protected work entered what is now termed the public domain. With this decision, the authority of the statutory copyright was confirmed in principle. In this respect, it was a defeat for that common law in which, as Blackstone intones, the 'goodness of a custom depends upon its having been used time out of mind, or, in the solemnity of our legal phrase, time whereof the memory of man runneth not to the contrary'. If with the majority finding in *Millar* v. *Taylor* the common law had installed a natural law rationale for the protection of copyright as recognition of the author's right of possession through labour, then *Donaldson* v. *Beckett* turns the earlier ruling on its head, defining copyright as a right of property deriving from the statutory grant.

The whole debate on literary property – its possibility and its impossibility, its sacredness and utility, its injustice and its problems – was rehearsed yet again in 1774, following the decades of polemic and law suits, during which the forces of eloquence had been deployed to defend literary property by all possible means, from carefully wrought distinctions between literary compositions and clocks (Bishop Warburton) to classifications which set literary property alongside such undoubted properties as 'items seized from an alien enemy' and 'items found in the sea' (Blackstone). If *Donaldson* v. *Beckett* is a concluding moment in this struggle, there none the less remains a measure of doubt as to the conduct of the twelve Law Lords – Lord Mansfield had heard the previous trial and so by delicacy remained silent in the Lords, the convention being that in such a circumstance he would not support his own judgment – in considering the five questions put to them so that they should advise the House and clarify the facts of the law. The questions were: first, whether at common law the author had sole right of first printing and publication, and could thus bring an action against any person who printed, published and sold the work without consent; second, whether, if the author had this right originally, the law was that upon publication the right was lost and so any person could then reprint and sell the work; third, whether, if there had been such an action at common law, it was abrogated or taken away by the Statute of Anne, such that the only lawful remedies available to an author were those provided by that statute; fourth, whether the author or his assigns had the exclusive right of printing and publication in perpetuity; and fifth, whether such a right was taken away by the Statute of Anne.

To judge from the pages of *Burrow's Reports*, the clarificatory advice was not without its own complexities. On the first question only one voice was against, and on the second question, four. In each case, Blackstone was with the majority, and it is known that Mansfield – although expressing no opinion – was of similar mind. On the third question – whether the statute precluded all remedies except those provided by the Act of 1710 – Blackstone was in the minority of five who held that such was not the case. Clearly, if Lord Mansfield had expressed the view that he was known to share with the author of the *Commentaries*, the balance of advice on this key question would have been different. Moreover, on closer inspection, of the six judges who were of the opinion that the Statute of Anne had taken away the common-law right of the author, there was only one whose view was that the author did not have the sole right of first publication and could not maintain an action in law against a person who published the work without authorisation. Two judges held that, although the author had the right at common law, he could not maintain an action, unless the work had been taken from him by fraud or force, while a fourth judge held that, although an author had the sole right of first publication and could maintain an action in the case of an infringement, the moment he published the work he also abandoned this right. As a result, only two of the judges in fact considered the key point: did the Statute of Anne abrogate a previously existing right? The remaining four did not agree that there was such a right.

The majority of peers in the House, it would seem, listened less to the distinctions drawn by the judges in their reasoning than to their own general predisposition against monopolies. The tenor of the majority opinion in the House can be gauged from the discourse of Lord Camden, who played a large part in the debate:

In short, the more your lordships examine the matter, the more you will find that these rights are founded upon the charter of the Stationers' Company and the royal prerogative; but what has this to do with the common law right? for never, my lords, forget the import of that term. Remember always that the common law right now claimed at your bar is the right of a private man to print his works for ever, independent of the crown, the company and all mankind. In the year 1681 we find a bye-law for the protection of their own company and their copy-rights, which then consisted of all the literature of the kingdom; for they had contrived to get all the copies into their own hands. In a few years afterwards the Revolution was established, then vanished prerogative, then all the bye-laws of the Stationers' Company were at an end; every restraint fell from off the press and the whole common law of England walked at large. During the succeeding fourteen or sixteen years, no action was brought, no injunction obtained, although no illegal force prevented it; a strong proof that at that time there was no idea of a common law claim. So little did they then dream of establishing a perpetuity in their copies, that the holders of them finding no prerogative security, no privilege, no licensing act, no Star Chamber decree to protect their claim, in the year 1708 came up to parliament in the form of petitioners with tears in their eyes, hopeless and forlorn; they brought with them their wives and children to excite compassion, and induce parliament to grant them a statutory security. They obtained the Act. And again and again sought for a further legislative security.

(Cobbett 1813: 994)

Lord Camden's motion to reverse was seconded by the Lord Chancellor, Lord Apsley, and the decree of the Court of Chancery was thus reversed in Alexander Donaldson's favour.

Following their defeat, the London booksellers immediately petitioned the Commons for leave to bring in a Bill for the relief of booksellers. The arguments in this 1774 Bill were much the same as before: extension of the statutory protection periods, and reassertion of a common-law right of authors that was customarily assigned in perpetuity to the purchasing bookseller. It is interesting to note that during debate in the Commons, Mr Burke cited Blackstone's arrangements for the copyright of his *Commentaries on the Laws of England*. Having published and registered the work at Stationers' Hall, Blackstone sold the copyright to the bookseller Thomas Cadell for £4,000. This assignment of the copyright was confirmed fourteen years later when, as allowed under the Act of 1710, Blackstone assigned a further fourteen-year copyright in the work (including corrections and alterations) to the same bookseller. Yet the assignment was made 'forever', in the customary term that the jurist had in no way resisted. The principle of perpetual copyright had been endorsed not only by Blackstone's own practice as author, but also in his argument as counsel for Tonson in the second trial of *Tonson* v. *Collins* and for Millar in *Millar* v. *Taylor*, and in his discussion of literary property in the second volume of the *Commentaries*. So much for the principle; the money, the manoeuvres and the mentality of the trade can be gauged from the testimony submitted at the committee stage by a London bookseller, William Johnston, who claimed absolute and perpetual copyright of Steele's *Tatler*, Camden's *Britannia*, the works of Dryden, Locke and Bunyan's *Pilgrim's Progress*. The last of these he owned by assignment by the executors of a previous owner, and the Dryden copyright he had purchased at Tonson's sale. In addition, he claimed to own many part shares in other works. He also continued to view a Chancery injunction as the best device for the protection of his properties in copyright (Birrell 1899: 131–4). The Bill had a third reading in the Commons but was rejected when it passed to the Lords.

Donaldson v. *Beckett* is the bedrock judicial decision in the English law of copyright, but its effects flowed on from London in 1774 into debates in the United States where, as we shall see in chapter 6, the issue of common law or statutory copyright was mapped onto the coordinates of state or federal law. Yet in the United Kingdom, if we accept the word of an 1813 *Address to the Parliament of Great Britain on the Claims of Authors to their own Copy-Right*, in the book trade the copyrights of Shakespeare were still being bought and sold at that time (Duppa 1813: 19–23). A profoundly familiar, long-standing and profitable practice is not so easily dismantled, neither for legal writers nor for the trade. And as for the author whose natural right to property the booksellers had so constantly invoked during the century and which had seemed to be confirmed in *Millar* v. *Taylor* until reversed in *Donaldson* v. *Beckett*, with the Copyright Act of 1814 the author's lifetime became the measure on which the period of copyright protection was based, alongside the older calculation based on the date of publication. Of course, compared to a perpetual right, no limited term, however long, is long enough. Like Balzac in France, Southey and Wordsworth, Coleridge and Scott were still lamenting the loss of their 'perpetual' right.

VII

To complete this sketch of the early modern copyright field in England, let us glance at the print-literate culture of the times, a culture where writing 'is become a very considerable Branch of the English Commerce. The Book-sellers are the Master Manufacturers or Employers. The several Writers, Authors, Copyers, Sub-Writers and all other Operators with Pen and Ink are the workmen employed by the said Master Manufacturers' (in Watt 1963: 55). This was the assessment of one particular Operator with Pen and Ink, the contemporarily notorious but subsequently canonised, aestheticised and dialecticised Daniel Defoe. However, since we have just reviewed *Millar* v.

Taylor and *Donaldson* v. *Beckett*, it is appropriate to consider the career of another denizen of early-modern print literacy, James Thomson, whose *Seasons* was the work in question in both those cases. Its publication reveals a feature worthy of note: the practice of constantly expanding a published text for the purpose of further 'pecuniary profits', as Lord Mansfield termed them.[14] 'Winter' grew longer between its first and second editions in 1726; after 'Summer' in 1727, 'Spring' appeared in 1728 together with the 'Proposals for printing by subscription *The Four Seasons*, with a hymn on their succession'. The subscription edition of 1730 was then augmented by the inclusion of the 'Hymn' and 'Autumn'. Thomson sold the copyrights for 'Summer', 'Autumn' and 'Winter', and for the 'Hymn', to John Millan in 1729; however, he retained control of the profits from the subscription edition for the complete work. In 1730, as we have noted, Thomson sold 'Spring' to Andrew Millar on condition that he the author might 'proceed to finish the printing of the said Poem called Spring once and no more in quarto as the same is now printing (and not otherwise) to go with other poems of the said James Thomson by way of Subscription to make a quarto Volume' (Thomson 1958: 70). This allowed both Millan and Millar to publish separate octavo editions selling at a lower price than Thomson's own edition, but neither could compete with the complete and augmented 1730 edition. Under the Statute of Anne, copyright expired in 1744 and so Millar published another version 1,064 lines longer than the 1730 complete edition.

Reviewing this episode, Howard (1965: 134) identifies the *Seasons* as an instance of 'composition by extension and compilation ... motivated by monetary rewards' but also calculated in terms of current book trade practice and copyright law. However, because it was 'more quickly assembled – little time was wasted in searching for a rhyme or polishing the form – prose became an even easier method through which an author might earn his bread' (1965: 135), and Howard cites the Pope–Swift *Miscellanies* as an example of this compositional-marketing technique whereby adding or 'improving' material could generate a new edition and thus an additional payment to the author and an additional property to the assignee of the copyright. In the course of the eighteenth century, calls were made for legislative action to oblige publishers of 'improved editions' to print the 'improvements' separately. These remained no more than threats, but they signal the persisting difficulty for copyright law of determining just when a work is a new and original work, with a material integrity that clearly marks it off from all other works. Three points can be noted.

First, this 'assemblage' mode of composition and the calculative authorial persona that goes with it was that of Defoe too, not only in *Robinson Crusoe* but also in a work like *The Storm; or, a Collection of the most Remarkable Casualties and Disasters Which Happened in the Late Dreadful Tempest, Both by Sea and Land* (1704). Here, as 'The Age's Humble Servant', Defoe collects providential deliverances, reports of lost shipping, the number of trees uprooted on estates, a discourse on the origin of winds, complaints of profiteering by roofing repairers, anecdotes of women blown out of their clothes and a pastoral dialogue on the seasons. This miscellany was a mix designed to appeal, within the covers of the one work, to a variety of audiences newly connected to the expanding book trade network (Saunders and Hunter 1991). Second – and to maintain the pressure on ahistorical post-structuralist accounts of early modern print-literate practices – we should learn to suspect immediately any move to displace intelligent and intelligible pecuniary and legal purposes by explanations in terms of 'writing' that 'transgresses', as in Lennard Davis' (1983) account of Defoe's compositional practice in terms of an emancipatory 'news/novel discourse'. Well perhaps so for some critics' purposes, but this rewriting of literary history is at the expense of Defoe's demographic sense and his marketing skill; he was, after all, probably not disinterested in the fact that the non-conformist readership of his times numbered some two million (Keeble 1987: 136–8).

The third point is somewhat lengthier. The writing and marketing technique of compilation poses a question not only for literary history but also for law – a very practical question: what is a book? In chapter 4 I shall consider Kant's answer to his own question: 'Was ist ein Büch?'; for the present, let us stay with that aesthetic conception of the book as an achieved unity of form and content, one that is said to be ideally realised in literary and artistic compositions – and only there. The aesthetic habit is to elevate this unity of form and content to a universal value, as if it is in this literary unity that 'man' finds his most complete expression. However, pursuing early modern practices of composition, Howard (1965: 402–17) discovers a quite different genealogy for the 'unified' work. One element of the genealogy is the historical difficulty of selling 'whole' works – as Fielding comments in *Joseph Andrews*, 'the heavy, unread, folio lump which long had dozed on the dusty shelf, piecemealed into numbers, runs nimbly through the nation'. More interesting, however, is a historical statement of concern to achieve a unity that is anything but a dialectical balancing of form and content. Rather, it is a practical pedagogical purpose that Ephraim Chambers pursued, as he described it in the Preface to his 1728 *Cyclopaedia*: ' . . . so to dispose such a multitude of materials, as not to make a confused heap of incoherent Parts, but one consistent whole' (in Howard 1965: 407). Chambers thus considered:

> the several matters, not only in themselves, but relatively, or as they respect each other: both to treat them as so many wholes, and as so many parts of some greater whole; their connexion with which to be pointed out by a reference. So that by a course of references, from generals to particulars; from premises, to conclusions; from cause, to effect, and vice-versa, i.e. from more, to less complex, and from less, to more; a communication might be opened between the several parts of the work; and the several articles be,

in some measure, replaced in their natural order of science, out of which the old alphabetical order had removed them.

(in Howard 1965: 408)

At issue for Chambers – the Scottish piracy of whose *Cyclopaedia* was to occasion the 1747 suit taken out in the Edinburgh Court of Sessions by Daniel Midwinter and the other London booksellers who had published the first edition of Chambers' work in 1728 – was the relation between the unity of knowledge and the image of a society unified by reason and science, the cultivation of these latter being a proper national concern. But there was also a more practical aspect. Chambers was 'partly motivated by the anxiety Leibniz expressed in 1680, when he spoke of that "horrible mass of books which keeps on growing", so that it would soon be a disgrace rather than an honour to be an author' (Yeo 1991: 27). Thus Chambers formed the plan for an encyclopaedia that would achieve a 'reduction of the body of learning'. What is envisaged in Chambers' project has nothing to do with the Romantic notion of the unity of the authorial personality; it has everything to do with a rhetoric, the artefact of which is a unified and bounded object: the book. In the 1738 edition of the *Cyclopaedia* there is an entry for *Book* – according to Howard the first in any English dictionary – in which Chambers criticises the dispersed and non-unified character of the contemporary book, in other words, the type of book produced by the technique of composition by continual extension and augmentation.

As we have seen in relation to Thomson's poem, this mode of composing by extension did not trouble only Chambers; it also troubled a copyright law whose grant of protection depended upon the capacity for a clear and definite recognition of a work's distinctiveness and originality as a writing that was not – substantially – a copying. This capacity was put at risk by the practice of augmentation. Perhaps we should therefore not be too surprised at Chambers' self-disinculpation in the entry on 'Plagiary' in the 1741 edition of the *Cyclopaedia*. After a 'philological' note on 'author theft: or the practice of purloining other people's works, and putting them off for a man's own', Chambers turns to what is his own case:

> Dictionary-writers, at least such as meddle with arts and sciences, seem in this case to be exempted from the common laws of meum and tuum; they do not pretend to set upon their own bottom, nor to treat the reader at their own cost. Their works are supposed, in great measure, compositions of other people; and whatever they take from others, they do it avowedly. In effect, their quality gives them a title to appropriate every thing that may be for their purpose, wherever they find it, and they do not otherwise than as the bee does for the public service.
>
> Their occupation is not pillaging, but collecting contributions; and if you ask them their authority, they will produce you the practice of their predecessors of all ages and nations.

However, it was not one 'employed by the Master Manufacturer' nor a rhetorically organised encyclopaedist, but yet another authorial persona who was about to emerge as the one who claimed he most fully and expressively wrote and published as himself. In 1759 in the subsequently famous 'Conjectures on original composition' – taken up more in Germany and France than in Britain – Edward Young elaborated his precept that the original work is one which expresses the individuality of its author. 'Born originals', he asks, 'how comes it that we die copies?' (1968 [1759]: 561). The villain of the piece is that 'meddling ape imitation [which] blots out nature's mark of separation, cancels her kind intention, destroys all mental individuality', with the result that 'a hundred books, at bottom, are but one'. Shakespeare, as we have noted, was held to be the exemplary 'Original', the one who 'mingled no water with his wine' (1968 [1759]: 573). We are familiar with the literary critical tradition which – as in Mann (1939), although even here there is a more anthropological reference to building up an 'attitude' – treats this phenomenon in terms of a watershed in intellectual history. There are a number of historical, anthropological and theoretical reasons for preferring an alternative approach.

In historical terms, an emerging group of 'literary' writers had to *acquire* an expressible interiority, such that a certain mode of printed work could be recognised and experienced as both 'mine' and 'me'. In a parallel fashion, an emerging category of 'literary' writing in print – it constituted a small fraction of the business of the publishing trade and of the concerns of copyright law – had to *become* a specialised ethical and aesthetic activity using print. A new manner of relating to one's self had itself to *establish* a manner of relating to print replication and dissemination. That these things came to pass is no doubt among the achievements of Romanticism, its highly particular historical artefacts. For all its intense inwardness – the biblical imperative to 'know thyself' is translated into the command to 'contract full intimacy with the stranger within thee' (Young 1968 [1759]: 564) – the 'self' of which the work comes to be conceptualised as an 'original' expression was nothing less than a new form of ethical-literate persona, one that those rare individuals who published and 'lived' in print might come to possess, provided they could follow Young's Latin and French citations and allusions. The aspiring 'author' is coached through the options: from 'too great indulgence of genius', writes Young, 'return we now to that too great suppression of it, which is detrimental to composition, and endeavour to rescue the writer, as well as the man' (1968 [1759]: 560). It is perhaps not too difficult to see why this balancing act succeeded as an ethical model in German literate coteries. This special exercise in literate self-fashioning does not so much flow out of the dialectic; rather, the dialectic flows out of this and similar ethical exercises. 'Originality' does not mark the spot where subjectivity at last enters the picture as a fundamental recovery of full (or fuller) authorial being, once the conventionalities of rhetorical culture had been subverted and outflanked.

But let me be quite clear: this refusal to ascribe the 'self' expressed in 'original composition' to the writer's subjectivity as such is not a way of debunking it as an illusion; it is a first step to seeing it as an exacting activity. In theoretical terms – and holding to the structure of the argument anticipated in chapter 1 – to begin to see this 'self' as a specific form of personhood is a guarantee against subordinating legal to aesthetic personality. The law of copyright did not change – or become defective – once the aesthetic persona and the expressive Romantic author joined the repertoire of available forms of life. The success or failure of that law is not gauged in terms of a capacity to recognise human subjectivity in printed commodities. That is not its object. If we can detach ourselves from the philosophical habit of mind that imagines a singular subjectivity underlying these two different kinds of personhood, we might be better placed to ask what were the actual means whereby individuals (and, in the case of legal personality, non-individuals) came to possess or bear them.

Chapter 3

France: from royal privilege to the *droit moral*

I

Eighteenth-century English provisions for the protection of literary property were an indigenous happening, springing from within a particular history. In turning now to the arrangements which emerged in France (and, in chapter 4, in Germany), the fact of historical and geopolitical differences will serve as a bulwark against the philosophical and theoretical urge to see through the specifics of actual legal-cultural arrangements to some purportedly more fundamental process of development or point of unity. The point remains: different legal systems have come to construct the legal personality or status of author in different ways. There is no surprise here, once it is recognised that the authorial statuses in question have been constructed at different times, in different circumstances and for different purposes. In this chapter, a central issue will be the legal treatment of this status under the *ancien régime* and at the time of the Revolution. I shall also note certain pointers to the emergence in France of the regime of the *droit moral*. From then onwards, much of my energy will be expended on the distinction between Anglo-American copyright and continental *droit moral* or rights of personality. This is the distinction between the set of attributes constituting the proprietorial status of copyright owner – a status occupied by authors or by their assigns, individual or corporate – and the quite different set of attributes constituting the author's status as a protected personality taken to have its inalienable extension and expression in the work of literary and artistic creation. On principle this second set of attributes can thus attach only to a human individual.

There is some point in loosely characterising the environments in which these different forms of legal personality have emerged in terms of different models of state formation. In Britain and the American territories a private, commerce-led expansion was accompanied by a primarily commercial and contract-oriented law; in central Europe (notably in Prussia) expansion was of a more public, state-led character, with codified statute law of central importance. Between the British type of loose commercial and capitalistic network driven by private commercial interests and the Prussian type of unitary network of state agencies – bureaucracy, army, university and government-controlled press – lies a mixed mode of commercialism and statism that could be said to characterise the historical environment in France. Of course, the relatively independent and specialised character of legal institutions concerned with literary property eludes reduction to a fundamental mode of state formation. None the less, the distinction between the contractual-commercial English and the statutory-bureaucratic Prussian models is sufficiently embedded in historical reality to remind us that the legal environments of literary culture have not shared identical geopolitical circumstances.

II

The notion of a distinctive French 'tradition' has encouraged a view of French law as author-centric from the very start, favouring the individual creator over the interest of the public. And indeed in the French Parliament's debate on the law of 3 July 1985 on Authors' Rights and Neighbouring Rights, M. Richard, the *rapporteur* in the National Assembly, invoked 'the longstanding tradition which makes the author's right, a right which is a moral as well as a property right, the guarantee of independence for authors of intellectual works'. In the context of debate on a Bill which significantly curtails the protection of the personal or private interests of authors, this allusion to a personalist authorial tradition no doubt had its particular rhetorical function.[1] We also find legal writers tracing back to the Revolution the 'principle that an exclusive right is conferred on authors on the ground that their property is the most justified because it flows from their intellectual creation' (Colombet 1988: 8).

Literary historians too have constructed, retrospectively, a seemingly unified French tradition of recognising the personal rights of authors. A recent study of the 'birth' of the author (the metaphor is a sign that the argument will follow the Romantic historicist model) locates the point of origin of the recognition of personal rights – of property and of personality – even before the Revolutionary period. In his account of the emergence of the 'first literary field', that of seventeenth-century France, Alain Viala (1985) postulates a 'literary property' that could exist in the emergent historical consciousness of authors even though no sign of it appeared in positive written law. This is a dismissive attitude towards positive law, but it allows the historian to argue the existence of an authorial right despite the fact that none was registered in the *lex* (or written law):

[I]n all matters concerning the law, it is necessary to distinguish between subjective law, or *jus*, which pertains to mentalities and practices, and written objective law, or *lex*. The real state of the rights of authors can only be understood through the analysis of the relations between *jus* and *lex*. Thus, in the classical period [of French literature], subjective rights predominated, often out of step with, or even contradictory to, the written laws.

(Viala 1985: 85–6)

Thus, although 'no law explicitly says that the author is owner of his text', usage is claimed to confirm that 'the *jus* of literary property existed from the moment when print was disseminated, and began to pass into the *lex*' (1985: 96). In questioning such a claim, it is not a matter of denying the efficacy of *jus* and legal and cultural practices or the historical priority that such practices might have in relation to *lex* and positive law. Rather, for reasons elaborated in chapter 8, we should be cautious about claims to perceive a pre-legal practice in which the 'true' relation of work to author is anticipated or already realised, in accord with the purportedly necessary direction of cultural (and therefore legal) development.

Fortunately, revisionist research occasioned by the bicentenary of the French Revolution has questioned the received notion that from its inception French law was organised by the principle of a personal right of the author. In fact, revision of the historical record was adumbrated in Stig Stromholm's *Le droit moral de l'auteur en droit allemand, français et scandinave* (1966), a study which establishes the terms for a historical description of what has emerged as the *droit moral*, the non-economic right of personality. As Stromholm recognises, the challenge in writing cultural and legal history is to avoid anachronistically imputing a philosophical necessity – a 'fundamental idea' – to the diverse array of elements out of which a particular synthesis happened to emerge:

The most elementary but also the most dangerous anachronism threatening studies of the general intellectual grounds of the genesis of the *droit moral* is to start from a conception often adopted in modern doctrine, according to which the protection granted to authors' personal interests takes the form of a uniform subjective right. If we look at things from the viewpoint of the interests concerned – and there is reason to believe that the juridical regime of the *droit moral* was created to protect certain definite interests – the unity of the three principal prerogatives is far from manifest. It is only at a fairly high level of abstraction that one could advance the proposition: 'the *droit moral* protects the personality of the author'. *As soon as we come down to the level of practical applications this unity disappears, giving way to more confused and diverse realities.* It is clearly at this level that we should approach the ideas which dominate the antecedents of the *droit moral*. The unity of this right is the result of a nineteenth-century search for doctrinal synthesis. ... We cannot assume *a priori* that the rights of publication, of respect for the integrity of the work, and of paternity or attribution present themselves as aspects of one fundamental idea before this synthesis was completed.

(Stromholm 1966: 34; emphasis added)

Replacing an anachronistic philosophical unity by a new attention to 'more confused and diverse realities' is the precondition for recovering both the historical specificity and the analytical flexibility lost when Romantic historicism sets the terms.

Stromholm also recognises that however familiar it might have subsequently become to those in *droit moral* regimes, the idea that one's original verses are an inalienable part of one's very person was not a self-evident candidate to become a rule of French or German positive law. If the activity of aesthetic creation came to be juridified in a way that distinguished it from those other human activities where the product of labour is not construed as an inalienable part of the maker's personality, this is a contingent outcome of particular circumstances, not a matter of historical inevitability. As Stromholm argues, this special treatment of literary creation and authors in certain jurisdictions 'seems so natural to us that we run the risk of forgetting that in no sense does it constitute a logical necessity. It is, rather, marked by historical relativity: indeed, *it is the juridical expression of a certain conception of art*' (1966: 37). This aesthetic conception is not necessarily very old, despite its being called a 'spiritual bond', an 'emanation of the spirit' or some other such appellation. Moreover, before the idea of the work as an emanation of the spirit or an embodiment of the person of its author could acquire legal recognition, definite conditions had to be met. Before achieving an existence as a legal norm, an extra-legal idea such as this had to acquire 'a minimum of universality' (1966: 38). Somehow the idea of the essential unity of work and authorial personality had to acquire the social and institutional 'gravity' that – in some but not all jurisdictions – was to persuade law-makers to protect interests which not only were not material and economic but also were confined to a highly specialised minority pursuing a rare activity in a cultivated milieu. In short, much separated the aesthetic notion of the literary work as indissolubly bound to its author's person from the notion of the work as a raw material supplied by what Defoe would have termed an Operator with Pen and Ink to the Master Manufacturer for printing, distribution and sale.

Perhaps we should be grateful that not every idea circulating among aesthetes transmutes into a legal norm. Specifically legal conditions also have to be met, whether general jurisprudential values or particular technical capacities. Protection of an author's non-economic rights of personality would thus be difficult to imagine 'in the framework of a legal system which was not largely founded on individualistic principles and on a respect for the human person in general':

Where creditors can reduce the debtor and his family to servitude and where the adage *pacta sunt servanda* [treaties must be performed] is applied with absolutely no allowance for considerations of humanity, the author will gain nothing by calling his work 'my spiritual child'. If the work has a venal value, it belongs to the investor; if it has been sold, it belongs to the buyer.

(Stromholm 1966: 39)

In such circumstances, the exchange of payment for a manuscript, and the latter's conveyance, would settle everything. To apprehend the new form represented by the *droit moral*, 'positive law had first to be *sufficiently equipped, from a technical point of view*, to translate into specific or general rules the protection of the interests concerned' (1966: 39). This condition is said to apply with particular force in circumstances where – as with the *droit moral* in France – it was in the courts rather than the legislature that appropriate rules were developed.

Stromholm's outline of the historical and institutional conditions for the legal recognition of the *droit moral* is not exhaustive. Cultural and ethical conditions must be taken into account, for instance those in which literary writers came to *acquire* a capacity to assume responsibility for their writings. Nevertheless, by signalling the fact of multiple preconditions for the legal protection of an authorial personality having its inalienable being in original literary works, Stromholm establishes the historical importance of what actually happened in the sphere of positive law. As he puts it, we can scarcely doubt that 'intellectual creators would, in any case, have a limited satisfaction in knowing that natural law offered them remedies which the courts could not but refuse!' (1966: 32). Along with this invitation to take a practical and historical view of the emergence of the *droit moral*, Stromholm also warns against presuming that its tributary elements – rights of divulgation, paternity, withdrawal and integrity – existed from the beginning as a unified structure. Instead, he draws attention to the slow and uncertain work of synthesis undertaken by French courts and theorists in the nineteenth century. The contrast with the metaphysical approach of Romantic historicism could not be clearer, for instance with Marie-Claude Dock's (1962: 52) claim that despite the lack of evidence of positive legislation recognising an individual right of authors under ancient Roman law such a right existed as a 'right *in abstract*'. Historicism typically proposes a continuous and necessary evolution. During the *ancien régime* – when 'author's right was not the object of any ruling' – the historian can thus none the less see through to the 'sense of intuitive justice [which] drew attention to the situation of those who, through their intellectual works, created new values' (1962: 77). Rather than the historical explanation of the phenomenon, such accounts are themselves part of what has to be explained.

III

The quintessentially personalist orientation of the *droit moral* was neither part of French law from the start nor an inevitable development within it. For all its air of fundamental principle, as a historical phenomenon the *droit moral* was formed piecemeal, from the decisions of French courts and from the work of academic theorists. Like any other legal norm, it has a determinate deployment within given jurisdictions. If protection of the *droit moral* has become a distinctive feature of French law, this is therefore not the sign that French law has finally become adequate to the nature of literary authorship; it is the sign of the manner in which one is an author under French law. Yet the urge to construct an ideally author-centric tradition for France is strong, particularly if that tradition is set in opposition to the commercial concerns of the Anglo-American law of copyright. In fact, the individualistic *droit moral* and its protection of an author's moral or non-pecuniary rights was a late nineteenth-century development. Moreover, it was not without a German influence. As to what preceded it, this was anything but the pure product of an immemorial personalist principle.

In her study of the first French printed book trade in the years 1498 to 1526, Elizabeth Armstrong (1990) shows that the legal device known as the book-privilege – first recorded in Wurzburg in 1479 and Venice in 1486 – was a familiar if not universal element of French publishing practice by the second decade of the sixteenth century. The concept of the privilege is clear: it was the legal instrument of a commercial concession granted by the king, on application to the royal chancery or other sovereign court or competent authority; by means of a grant of privilege, a printer or an author obtained permission to be or to decide the sole authorised publisher of the work. The rationale for the grant of privilege was economic, its purpose being to help ensure an equitable return on the costs of printing, production and, in the case of first-time printed books, the purchase of the manuscript. Contrary to the received idea, Armstrong reports that in this period 'privileges did not form part of any system of censorship. . . .: the choice lay with authors and publishers of new works whether to apply for them or not' (1990: 207). The privilege provided the grantee with some protection and legal bargaining power against an unauthorised reprinter. The protection was far from absolute. It was normally available only to works being published for the first time or to existing works that had been substantially amended or extended, for instance by the addition of a 'repertoire' or index. As to the duration of protection, in the period to 1526 no perpetual privileges were granted and only two ten-year ones, the norm being no more than two or three years (1990: 118). And of course the protection was limited territorially to the area of the granting power's jurisdiction. The use of the device was also limited, only 5.25 per cent of the 7,719 titles printed in the period are known to have carried the protection of privilege (1990: 78). Thus unlike in Tudor England there was no generalised recourse to the granting of royal printing monopolies.

From the seventeenth century, however, the royal authorities used grace and favour grants of privilege to control the contents of works and to regulate the commerce of the book market. More fully than in England, the privilege was the device that ordered the relations of crown, authorship and readership, there being no single centralising agency with an independence equivalent to that of the Stationers' Company through which permissions to print had to flow. Nor was there any statutory equivalent in France of the Act of 1710 which, in England, largely curtailed the remnants – in the form of the printing patent – of royal grants of privilege relating to publishing rights. None the less, in both France and England, the institution of the printing privilege marks recognition of a commercial principle that is also a legal norm: remuneration for labour expended. Applied to literary labour and its distinctive product, however, this norm did not flow easily from traditional thinking; it had to be slowly incorporated into the legal framework, 'a difficult and painful intellectual process which little by little taught European jurists what "construction" to put on something so alien to their roman-law system of categories as a right in intangible objects' (Stromholm 1983: 7–8).

Viala stays with the established history (Pottinger 1952; Dock 1963) of book-privileges in France. He argues that it remained undecided whether writing and publication constituted a profession of virtue – hence the usual anti-mercantile reading of Boileau's precept concerning well-known authors 'Qui ... font d'un art divin un métier mercenaire' – or whether it had the virtue of a profession paying enough to live on. He also shows the literary field as the site of various exchanges between royal and 'social' patronage, between traditional ethical values and emerging commercial interests. In pre-Revolution France, it seems, writers could acquire a socially recognised status or intellectual capital by negotiating the boundaries between imitation and homage, rewriting and plagiarism in a way that allowed the doctrine of imitation to co-exist with a sharp sense of the wrong of plagiarism. Viala notes the fittingly named Monsieur de Richesource, author of the theory of *plagianisme* expounded in *Le Masque des orateurs, ou manière de déguiser toute sorte de composition* (1667), a compositional manual on the techniques of rewriting existing texts in a socially acceptable manner. The rhetorical art of 'travestying' – or trans-vesting – existing texts was a legitimate means of producing 'new masterpieces', but mere copying was treated as a 'larceny' (Viala 1985: 91).

If *plagianisme* was a particular theory of originality accompanying a certain mode of composition and rejecting plagiarism, the book-privilege system itself presumed no particular theory of literary composition, being concerned with the regulation of piracy. Just because a theory emerges in the literary field, not all else follows. The law does not inevitably change even if that theory becomes a matter of general literary preoccupation. Nor, however, are all sanctions – for instance those against plagiarism – legal sanctions. Literary counter-attack and social reputation are also regulatory factors.

Whatever his aim, Viala's account is as much prescriptive as descriptive: it asserts that literary property rights were both affirmed and practised by the 'classical age', that is, under Louis XIV. In support, he refers to a miscellany of legal-cultural practices which resemble those of Stuart and early modern England but without the specific institution of the Stationers' copyright. He does not surprise us when he radicalises the distinction between the printer-bookseller's *privilège de librairie* and the *privilège d'auteur* into a matter of principle. Yet such a distinction is a matter of practical administration, part of a piecemeal shift from an environment in which most works printed were those of long dead authors or of anonymous collective authorities to one in which works of living writers provided the bulk of material for publication in print. In the former, the commercial monopoly could be unproblematically granted to the investor-printer. In the latter, a dilemma arose concerning the status of the privilege bearer: it was a status that could be occupied not only by the printer-bookseller but also by the writer and his or her heirs.

Two further comments are appropriate. The first concerns the argument from cultural practice not positive law. With the assertion that an economic property right already attached to the status of author in the classical epoch, Viala's wish is not to be too tightly bound by the fact that 'no law of then explicitly states that the author is the owner of his text'. The best he can do is to insist that 'usage and administrative texts prove that the *jus* of literary property came into being with the spread of print, and began to pass into the *lex*' (Viala 1985: 96). Yet if it was 'usage' to recognise a property right of authors, it was also 'usage' to assign this 'right' to the printer-bookseller. Second, when so sharp a distinction is drawn between the interests and rights of the author and those of the 'publisher', we anachronistically impose a division of labour now Romantically valorised in favour of the author. We project on to those earlier arrangements what has become for us a funda-mental disjunction between the interests of the bookseller (commodity-based, mercantile, alienating of aesthetic expressivity) and the interests of writers (expressive of the individual and transcending commodification). Yet this Romantic division of labour is not the universal goal of all 'developed' legal systems; it is the outcome of our particular cultural history. To the extent that the authorial right is treated as already formed and present (albeit latent) in the earlier literary practice, the complex doctrinal and judicial labour of constructing an authorial right is trivialised.

To give a less dichotomous picture would mean abandoning the dialectical schema of historicist accounts of the birth of the author and with it the discursive figures favoured by Viala: the 'birth' of the 'modern' from the dying order of the old; the clamping of historical particulars into universal bipolarities such as power and freedom, as when church and state are said – in a manner disconfirmed by Armstrong's findings on the book-privilege system – to have 'exercised censorship on art from the very start of artistic production' (1990: 116); and, above all, the unified and necessary movement of cultural development, a 'progress of literary property' (1990: 101), in which the law's historical independence and positivity are dissolved into the more fundamental imperative attributed to the rise of aesthetic personality and the authorial nature of literary creation. Nevertheless,Viala provides an informative guide to *ancien régime* literary and legal practices, including the privilege system as managed by the Royal Administration of the Book Trade. The problem lies in his attempt always to see through actual practices such as the granting of privileges to printer-booksellers to what are taken to be the emergent elements of a more complete cultural form, that of authorial rights in the modern style.

Parallels with English publishing history are evident, not least in the emerging competition between metropolitan monopolists and provincial entrepreneurs. But the geopolitical circumstances were different. Late in the day – and not only in relation to book publishing – reforms of the existing system were entertained and, in some cases, enacted in the last years of the absolutist regime. Royal edicts of 1777 and 1778 made printing privileges – rights of reproduction – available to both authors and printers. Indeed, the author's privilege became perpetual; acquired by the publisher, however, it lasted only for the term of the author's life.[2] An exclusive literary property right of authors was propounded by printer-booksellers in terms reminiscent of the campaigns waged by the London monopolists in the name of the author's property in common law. In France as in England, a rhetoric of the author's right in literary property was a routine instrument of publishers' interests. Until its final years, however, the regime itself did not promote the vesting of this exclusive right with the author. Unlike the English Parliament in 1710, it gave broad support to the metropolitan interests, the traditional holders of the reproduction right and agents of the state censor. This policy, together with the State's incorporation of the Academies and extension of patronage with the aim of rendering authors dependent upon its grants, allows Viala to claim that 'Absolutism undertook to turn the writer into one of the cogs in its machine and thus to combat his autonomy' (1985: 103).[3] A less negative assessment of absolutist projects is possible; it is unlikely, however, in an aesthetic or Romantic historicist perspective. The *ancien régime* had once been an exemplary absolutist court-society (Elias 1983) – an authoritarian monarchy exercising a direct control through a personal system of royal privileges whereby offices, rights and properties were distributed in exchange for support. By the 1770s, however, the government was confronted by an array of rational and reformist pressures, not least for a more productive administration of material and human resources at a time of fiscal crisis induced by military and debt expenditure; this, in 1760, accounted for a very large proportion of the national budget.

Improved administration presumed improvements in the civil sector, and a bureaucracy to manage them. That reform of the tangle of existing customary laws was under way in the 1770s with the aim of defining a clear and desirable public order in a legal code is one indication that the absolutist monarchy – driven by some enlightened ministers – was significantly reformist. Another such indication is the fact that the Revolutionary government did not enlarge the bureaucratic machinery which it inherited. It is outside my present concern to explore how the French monarchy's late reformist tendencies (and ploys) were constrained by the sedimented interests of traditional property holders – including holders of property in literary works – which rule by privilege had established. The edicts of 1777 and 1778 – the preamble to the former contains an explicit exposition of the rights of authors and, unlike the Statute of Anne, the edicts grant exclusive and perpetual rights to authors – belong in this context of an incomplete reform of the system of property relations.

Let us now look more closely at how the system of book-privileges organised the French book trade for a century and a half prior to the Revolution, granting different types of exclusive right according to the circumstances which happened to obtain.[4] The scope of a privilege, its duration, its mode of issue and registration could all vary. *Privilèges généraux* gave exclusive title to a whole class of works. At the other extreme, the *permissions tacites* used from the early eighteenth century were only *imprimaturs* or permissions to print, not the source of exclusivity; as such they could be granted outside the usual vetting procedures. This does not mean they were of trivial importance: the final ten volumes of Diderot's *Encyclopédie* and Montesquieu's *L'esprit des lois* appeared with the legal status of *permissions tacites*. As for the *privilèges de sceaux*, these created an exclusive right issued and recorded by the King in Council, the Chancellor and the Court of Châtelet; these were distinct from the *simples tolérances* which could be issued orally by the 'police' and involved no formality of registration.

The system of privileges endured as a coalition of interests between censors and traders – the royal government and the printer-bookseller associates of the Communauté des Imprimeurs et Libraires de Paris. The cement of this coalition was the reliable power of exclusion, both of counter-orthodoxy and of non-establishment Parisian and provincial printers and booksellers.[5] Again there is a partial parallel with English law in the fact of a monopolist control of the book market by the Communauté des Imprimeurs et Libraires and the Commonalty of Stationers. However, where the Stationers had their own copyright and resisted the granting of privileges to non-members of the Company, the *imprimeurs* and *libraires* were more complicit partisans of royal privileges. At least, that is, as long as the privilege was understood as royal acknowledgement of an anterior property in a work held as a right by the printer or bookseller by purchase or acquisition from its author or owner. But like any monopoly, particularly when granted arbitrarily and exercised unevenly, the system of privileges generated problems and polemics. A predictable issue of perpetual dispute was that of the term of protection granted by the *privilège en librairie* or booksellers' privilege. In principle the exclusive right was limited to a period of years deemed sufficient to allow recouping of the investment costs of producing the work, in the order of three to ten years. In practice, the privilege was used in a manner designed to keep already protected and published works out of the public domain for ever. Automatically renewed, a *privilège en librairie* became private patrimony like any other item of property.

For its whole duration, the French book-privilege system was marked by a persisting oscillation between two conceptions of the privilege: first, as an exercise of the royal grace to create an exclusive right for a specified period of time such that expiry of the privilege was expiry of the right; and second, as royal recognition of a pre-existing right whose source was the agreement between the writer and the printer-bookseller that the latter should print and publish the manuscript sold for that purpose. In short, was the royal privilege constitutive or declaratory of the property right? These positions were articulated in disputes on particular cases or, more generally, on book trade policy. In practice, the muddle of *ancien régime* administration was usually the order of the day, tolerating renewals which rendered meaningless the idea of the privilege as an exclusive right granted only for a limited term. The principal argument advanced by the Paris monopolists to justify automatic extension of privileges rested on the concept of the privilege as a royal recognition of the property right held by the *imprimeur* or *libraire*, a concept that implicitly denied royal grace as the source of property rights and not a simple administrative confirmation of a legal attribute independent of royal law-making (Birn 1971: 160). This contradiction remained unresolved, but as a working system with whose tricks the participants were familiar, privileges neither knew nor needed grand doctrinal theory.

On this unstable basis the privilege system developed from inception in the sixteenth century to the six rulings of 30 August 1777 which 'overturned the fundamental commercial principles upon which the French book trade had rested' (Birn 1971: 131). The key agent in that trade, the Communauté des Imprimeurs et Libraires de Paris, was established in 1618 and formed a 'patriciate closely linked with the regime' (1971: 135). Working routinely with the Chancellor's office where manuscripts were checked and privileges issued, the Paris Communauté was the beneficiary both of police actions against provincial presses – these actions continued into the 1770s – and of legal procedures such as the issue of royal letters patent by which, in 1701, provincial magistrates were forbidden to issue *permissions* to local printers and booksellers, such authority being restricted to the office of the Garde des Sceaux (Keeper of the Seals). Yet a status quo was never absolutely settled, despite attempts to establish a comprehensive *règlement* or administrative ruling for the book trade. In 1744 the Council of State set out in 123 articles a scheme to administer the whole national territory: the *Code du libraire*. The

Code – based on a set of regulations formulated in 1723 to regulate the bookselling and printing trades in Paris – was administration in the comprehensive style of absolutist government. It covered the system of *privilèges* and *permissions*, the running of the Communauté, press censorship procedures, the rights of authors and the definition of who could engage in the trade, down to such details as the role of *colporteurs* or itinerant traders. Just as the Statute of Anne did not define the rights it created and administered, the *Code du libraire* did not define 'privileges'. Nor did it establish definitive criteria for their renewal and extension. Yet it assumed that all books printed in France would be sanctioned by either a *permission de sceau* or a *privilège exclusif*. Books printed without such authorisation were deemed *contrefaçons* or counterfeit and pirated editions.

If the *Code* provided a legal buttressing for established practices of the major parties in the trade, the edicts of 1777 and 1778 represent a more ambivalent initiative. With them, the French crown ended the booksellers' legal capacity to claim perpetual property in a work. There was a certain logic in this new arrangement for existing privileges: only where a work had been extended by at least one quarter of the original length could a claim to prolong or renew an existing right be entertained. On the other hand, where the work remained in the hands of its author or the author's heirs, a privilege of indefinite term was established. A distinction thus emerged between a privilege held by a printer-bookseller and a privilege held by an author.[6] This was the first specific recognition of a legal personality for authors – and their heirs – in French positive law.

This reform was in part a response to the 1776 *Mémoire à consulter. Pour les libraires & imprimeurs de Lyon, Rouen, Toulouse & Nimes. Concernant les privilèges de librairie & continuations d'iceux*. The *Mémoire*, which followed a 1774 appeal by provincial printers and booksellers to the Royal Council, appeared in the same year that Turgot – Controller General of finances from 1774–6 – sought with Condorcet's assistance to put his free-trade theories into practice by suppressing all monopolies and corporations. However, just as the Stationers survived the Statute of Monopolies of 1623, so the Paris Communauté endured. It was the ministry that fell. Birn (1971: 159) describes the *Mémoire* as 'the most thorough *cahier de doléances* ever composed by the publishers of the country, and summing up a century of pain, frustration, and mistreatment'. Its object was 'to secure in legislation the abolition of automatic prolongations of *privilèges* and to place in the public domain all once-published books, including those which originally had been printed abroad'. These claims were advanced on the grounds that the Parisian monopolists both breached the law of nature by constraining the free circulation of the content of works and derogated from the exercise of royal prerogative. Hence the provincials' evidently successful ploy of signalling to the Royal Council that 'the capacity exclusively to print and sell a published book is born with the *Privilège* alone and not with the acquisition of the

Manuscript, since the Author himself has no title to this right, unless he obtains it from the Government' (in Birn 1971: 160).

In the style of *ancien régime* manoeuvring, the edicts were neither issued as royal letters patent nor sent to the Parliament for registration. What is more, the fact that the government sought from Séguier, the Advocate General, a further statement of position on the printing privileges suggests that the authorities themselves did not consider the edicts definitive. Séguier's report – it is dismissively treated by Birn although he characterises it as the 'last major theoretical analysis of the *privilèges en librairie* under the *Ancien Régime*' (1971: 101) – itself exemplifies the co-presence of reformist and conservative positions, balancing between progressive ministers and a Parliament aligned with the old monopoly order. As spokesperson of the government, Séguier's duty was to respect the royal grace; on the other hand, as a law officer, he could not deny the legitimate property right deriving from the purchase or assignment of the manuscript. It is not so much temporising – as Birn implies – as a difficult straddling of two political rationalities that is manifest in the Advocate General's discourse when an absolutist regime of prerogative and traditional monopolies is confronted by the claims of a free market. However, for Birn, with Malesherbes' appointment as chief of the Bureau de la Librairie 'the book trade entered a new era':

> During Malesherbes' thirteen-year stint the department expanded in size and scope, and the director assumed the awesome responsibility of deciding most of the ideological ground rules for dissemination of the Enlightenment in France. ... [D]etermined to protect writers and his censors from reactionary forces at Court, in the Church, and in Parlement, Malesherbes epitomised courage, delicacy, and skill in the handling of his assignment. He despised the *privilège* system; his sympathies lay with authors and non-favoured publishers.
>
> (Birn 1971: 147)

Malesherbes is an exemplary denizen of the fracturing environment of an *ancien régime* where modernising 'governmental' ministers confronted the traditional interests of privilege and property. He devised an extended use of the *permissions tacites* – already deployed to elude press censorship – to elude the restraints of the traditional privilege system as well. Because these restraints had fallen as much on the actual expansion of the book trade as on freedom of individual expression, they would have registered as an impediment to government in the view of an administrator who could recognise, as did Malesherbes, that 'what the orators of Rome and Athens were in the midst of a people assembled, men of letters are in the midst of a people dispersed'.

It remains important not to impose on the historical contingency of legal-cultural arrangements a neat opposition of (progressive) author-centred ideal and (regressive) trade-centred practice. We might then be less dismayed that an Enlightenment intellectual such as Denis Diderot defended the monopolists' claims than is Birn (1971: 152–3), whose attempts to 'disinculpate' the author of the 1767 *Lettre historique et politique sur le commerce de la librairie* end in nonsense: 'To give Diderot his due, however, it appears most likely that when he spoke up in favour of protecting the literary property of publishers, he had the rights of authors primarily in mind'. Such is the risk of unexamined commitment to author-centrism.

The juridical and administrative co-ordinates of the legal-cultural environment under the late *ancien régime* balanced a reformist governmental rationality against the established practice and principle of monarchical grace and favour. This balancing finds further expression in the compound 1764 document entitled *Représentations & observations en forme de mémoire sur l'état ancien & actuel de la librairie & particulièrement sur la propriété des privilèges, &c., présentées à M. de Sartine par les Syndics & Adjoints, & en marge les observations que M. Marin a faites sur chaque article, d'après les notes instructives que je lui ai remises par ordre du magistrat*. This document was presented to Sartine, the new head of the Bureau de la Librairie, by Le Breton, Syndic or chief of the Paris printers and booksellers. In these *Représentations*, Diderot's letter was augmented by a gloss prepared by François Marin, Secretary General of the Bureau. What Marin seizes upon is the fundamental contradiction between the monopolists' claim to property rights held in perpetuity and the intercessory principle of royal prerogative. To accede to the former would be to curtail the effective exercise of that prerogative and, more seriously, to admit that 'the privileged booksellers form a little republic independent of all authority' (in Birn 1971: 154). Asserting the primacy of the royal privilege over the 'republican' claim of perpetual monopoly, Marin underscored the limited duration of the exclusive right established by the monarch's act of grace. The Secretary General's notes show the royal administration moving against the monopoly, but it is not clear that this move is directed towards the interest of authors. As Birn remarks, Joseph d'Hemery (the inspector in charge of policing books and Marin's supervisor) found the 'proprietorship mentality was stimulating the greed of authors and publishers alike' (1971: 155). In a way typical of the ambivalent political rationality of the regime, Marin's gloss reaffirms the royal privilege as the sole source of exclusive rights while also attempting to enhance the book trade by curtailing the monopoly powers of the Paris Communauté. It is almost as if the regime of rule by privilege was oriented less towards an exclusivity of rights than towards a public interest – in the form of a more open market.

The edicts of 30 August 1777 emerged from this unstable background, occasioned by the *Mémoire* of the printers and booksellers of Lyon, Rouen, Toulouse, Marseille and Nimes. That *Mémoire* too was directed at a restoration of the principle of royal grace, not at the recognition of authors' rights: 'The exclusive capacity to print and to sell a published book originates with the *Privilège* alone and not with the acquisition of a property in the

Manuscript, since the Author himself holds this right by no title other than what he obtains from the Government.' Nevertheless, as already noted, the royal *arrêts* defined an authorial interest distinct from any that a printer and bookseller could hold, granting authors and their heirs an indefinite privilege, together with a capacity to have their works printed, published and distributed without surrendering that privilege. If an authorial status was emerging, its source was royal grace and its object was better policing.

This *ancien régime* network of power and property relations does not fit neatly into an aesthetic schema where the persona of the Romantic author provides the singular goal to which all earlier forms of authorship had to lead. Birn's essay on the system of *privilèges en librairie* is vitiated by this species of Romantic historicism. If a given royal decision can be construed to favour authors, it is treated as *ipso facto* positive and in accord with the necessary direction of cultural development. Thus, with the 1777 edicts, '[i]n one instance at least, the *Ancien Régime* saw how imperative it was to adapt an institution to social needs. . . . It was the decadent, crumbling monarchy that recognized the proprietary claims of authors to the product of their genius or their folly' (Birn 1971: 168). As suggested in relation to Viala, such author-centric historicism does a double disservice: first, in the name of a 'funda-mental' principle of cultural development, it imposes a philosophical unity on the diversity of legal-cultural arrangements; second, it encourages a serious underestimation of the uncertainty and contingency of the more author-centric legal environment which was slowly to form in the late nineteenth century.

This anachronism is not limited to literary historians and bibliographers. When they happen to think about the history of authorship, legal writers too have fallen back into an ideal 'tradition' in which the 'author is protected as author' (Desbois 1978: 538). As evidence for this allegedly enduring tradition, a gallery of canonical figures has emerged, including the *avocat* Marion in the 1586 *Muret* case, the *Leschassier* case of 1617, and the *La Fontaine* case of 1761. We find the terms of Marion's much-cited plea of 1586 – as creation belongs to God, so 'the author of a book is the absolute master thereof' – set alongside a reference to works which 'are so intimately incorporated in the person of the author whose whole genius they express . . . that to disrespect them is to harm the man himself in his pride as an artist, it is to injure him, to deprive him of the one attribute that no one has the right to dispose of without his permission and which the man himself in his pride as an artist, cannot entirely alienate: the creation of his mind' (in Edelman 1987b: 563). In assembling these formulations from 1586 and 1987 into their 'astonishing continuity', Bernard Edelman gives an exemplary demonstration of how the author-centric tradition is retrospectively constructed. An extended look at Marion's discourse allows a more nuanced reading of the case – it involved the publication by the bookseller Nivelle of an edition of Seneca by Marc-Antoine Muret without the latter's authorisation. Having remarked that 'the author of a book is the absolute master' of it, Marion went on to add: *'and, as such, can freely dispose of it,* whether keeping it forever private in his hand, as a slave, or liberating it, granting to the work common liberty' (in Dock 1963: 78–9; emphasis added). In terms less demiurgic than juridical, Marion pleaded his case before the Parliament, depicting publication as an equitable and binding agreement between writer and public, the one granting access in return for the other's recognition that the author is the master of his creation. Muret's wish was therefore to be respected as part of this valid agreement. Philological study could explore the relation of the metaphorics deployed by Marion and Renaissance notions of *ars, ingenium* and *poeta creator* (Kant-orowicz 1961) but I shall limit myself to one pragmatic point: Marion's is yet another statement of the customary 'right' to assign property in the work to the printer-bookseller who would reproduce the copies. It confirms a structure of legal and commercial relations similar to that which in the Statute of Anne is signalled by the fact that the term 'author' appears always in conjunction with the alternatives 'purchaser of copy', 'proprietor of copy', 'bookseller' or 'assignee'.

In France as in England, there were cases of authors (or their heirs) being granted an exclusive privilege. In 1761 La Fontaine's maiden granddaughters obtained from Malesherbes a permit to publish an edition of their great-grandfather's *Fables.* On the grounds that the *Fables* had fallen into the public domain with the expiry of the original privilege – which La Fontaine had sold and assigned – Malesherbes used his office to issue the author's heirs with a *permission* to bring out an edition. Doubtless because of the protest by the Communauté printers and booksellers at what they regarded as an arbitrary grant of privilege to an unprivileged publisher, Malesherbes was at pains to clarify the nature of his action: 'What I granted to the grand-daughters of La Fontaine who were dying of hunger was not a *privilège* but a mere permit for the *Fables of La Fontaine'* (in Birn 1971: 151). On this occasion the will of the royal council prevailed against the outrage of the Communauté who, moreover, had to register the *permission.* From an author-centric perspective, however, Malesherbes becomes an emergent figure pointing in the direction of man's cultural development and speaking with the voice of history, while the La Fontaine *permission* becomes an act of prescient administration, anticipating the Revolutionary truth.[7]

IV

An author-centric character has traditionally been attributed to the legislative texts of the Revolutionary period – specifically the decrees of 1791, 1792 and 1793. Giving chapter and verse, Jane Ginsburg leaves little room to doubt that this attribution is ill-founded. On the contrary, '[a]uthors are not securely at the core of the new [Revolutionary] literary property regime; rather, the public plays a major role' (Ginsburg 1990a: 1006). If correct, this radical revision of the traditional account will have the effect of relocating the emergence of personalist and authorial notions well into the nineteenth century. This is another step in debunking the assumption that it was always to be the role of law to give social form and expression to the authorial personality enshrined in the Romantic aesthetic.

The Revolutionary decrees followed the failure in January 1790 of a Bill for a law relating to sedition and to the regulation of the book trade, presented to the National Assembly by the Abbé Sieyès for the Committee of the Constitution (Hesse 1990: 118–24). The Bill pleased no one and was never voted on. It sustained attacks from those opposed to all and any form of regulation; from those opposed to any private property in ideas and their expression in books; and from those seeking retention of the Paris printers and booksellers' traditional right of perpetual property annulled by the royal decrees of 1777. As if this was not enough, Sieyès' proposal was also attacked by the supporters of a qualified property right who wanted protection to be limited to ten years after the death of the author.[8] In the administrative vacuum created by the abolition in 1789 of all existing privileges – it was less a deregulation of publishing than an 'unregulation' – there was deep uncertainty. By 1791, when the Paris guild of printers and booksellers was abolished by the National Assembly, we find a Paris police commissioner writing: 'There is no author who will consecrate his efforts to the instruction of his century if pirating is made legal' (in Hesse 1990: 118). This policeman's remark sets the scene for a revision of the traditional account.

By returning to the texts of the decrees of 1791, 1792 and 1793, Ginsburg has rediscovered that for the Revolutionary law-makers public interest criteria were predominant. She removes the misconception which has sedimented around the discourse of Le Chapelier, the *rapporteur* for the 1791 decree, a discourse that has done repeated service for those asserting the decree's author-centric character. In the words of the *rapporteur*, 'the most sacred, the most legitimate, the most unassailable, . . . the most personal of all properties, is the work which is the fruit of a writer's thoughts'. However, in reconstructing the circumstances of this piece of law-making whose objects were to circumscribe the traditional monopoly of the Comédie Française to produce theatrical works and to extend the public domain by establishing the right of any citizen to run a theatre and produce a work, we see that Le Chapelier's precept related only to unpublished works. His principal concern was to assert full public access to published works. Once a work is published, he argued, 'in the nature of things everything is finished for the author and the publisher when the public has in this way acquired the work'. The juridical principle for Le Chapelier is the public right. Any grant of authors' or publishers' rights is a specific exception to this principle. The emphasis is clear: any citizen has the right to be a producer of theatrical works, a status previously restricted to the Comédie Française.[9] The logic of the legislation is one of anti-exclusivity: to break the royal theatre's monopoly was to annul an exclusive right created by royal prerogative. Restored to its context, Le Chapelier's talk of the 'most sacred ... and most personal of all properties' no longer contradicts the order of precedence in the 1791 text. Article I establishes the right of all citizens to erect a theatre and therein to produce dramatic works of all kinds; article II declares that works of authors who have been dead for over five years are public property. It is only in article III that authors' rights are envisaged, and this by making performances of the works of living authors conditional upon their written consent.

A year later – not a short time in Revolutionary politics – the National Assembly passed a decree to protect the interests of the authors of dramatic works but subject to regulation by formalities to which compliance must be made. Ginsburg (1990a: 1008) again circumscribes the notion that the Revolutionary decrees were primarily author-centric, noting that 'the actual articles of the decree make the dramatist's public performance rights appear even more vulnerable than under the 1791 decree', the author being required to notify the public at the time of the publication that the performance right is reserved, a notice to this effect having to be printed at the head of the text and deposited with a notary. The object of this second decree is also to guarantee the public interest.

It is in keeping with this public access and instrumentalist orientation that the decree of 1 September 1793 moved the carriage of literary property issues from the Committee on the Constitution to the Committee on Public Instruction, it being no longer a matter of property rights. The *rapporteur* for the 1793 decree, Lakanal, thus addressed the National Assembly as spokes-person on public education. Analysing his discourse, Ginsburg argues – against some of the major authorities – that Lakanal's approach is not grounded in the concept of authorial property or personality:

> Unlike *ancien régime* advocates of literary property, Lakanal did not assert [with Diderot] that 'the author is the master of his work or no one in society is master of his property'. Indeed, unlike Le Chapelier, Lakanal did not even affirm 'the most sacred, ... the most personal of properties'. Rather he proclaimed that this right is '[o]f all rights the least subject to criticism, a right whose increase can neither harm republican equality, nor offend liberty'. The rhetoric here displays a looking-over-the-shoulder quality inconsistent with a firm conviction of the centrality of authors' personal claims.
>
> (Ginsburg 1990a: 1009)

The position staked out by Lakanal involved balancing the public interest as propounded by the government and the interests of authors and printer-booksellers. Were we to follow nineteenth-century commentators cited by Ginsburg rather than twentieth-century theorists committed to the authorial personality model, we would see that with the Revolutionary decrees 'nothing has changed either in ideas or in legislation: the word *property*, it is true, has replaced *privilege*, but this property is still but a charitable grant from society' (Laboulaye 1858). Given their relative proximity to the Revolutionary legislation and their immunity to the anachronism whereby subsequent commentary has aestheticised and personalised the Revolutionary decrees in particular and French law more generally, nineteenth-century commentators such as Renouard (1838–9) and Laboulaye (1858) simply do not know the aesthetic purism which Desbois (1978: 538) projects onto the French past: 'The author is protected as an author, in his status as a creator, because a bond unites him to the object of his creation.' And he continues: 'In the French tradition, Parliament has repudiated the utilitarian concept of protecting works of authorship in order to stimulate literary and artistic activity.' To put the historical record straight we need less philosophically bound revisions. Pursuing this goal, Ginsburg also levels the traditionally absolute opposition between a utilitarian and public-centred Anglo-American copyright regime and, on the other hand, a personalist author-centred French regime taking its origin from the Revolutionary decrees or even earlier.

Perhaps the Revolutionary decrees would have less easily served as the ideal point of origin for this French 'tradition' if their material effect on the French publishing trade had been better known. Their effect was catastrophic. As Carla Hesse has shown, the legislative reforms which dismantled the old monopoly and deregulated the book market were pursued with no anticipation of their practical and economic consequences:

> [T]he law of 1793 had rendered book publishing commercially unviable. The limiting of private copying claims to ten years after the author's death reduced the commercial value of a copyright to a single edition. Pirating was rampant because there was no effective mechanism to prevent it after the suppression of the National Administration of the Book Trade. But most important was the problem of competing editions of works in the public domain, because such editions made up the majority of book commerce. The lack of a national administration and of a compulsory system of registration of works in print, meant that there was no effective mechanism for regulating competition, even by the publishing community itself. The fundamental dilemma of commercial publishing under the Republic was that commerce in the printed word had been rendered 'too free' to be capable of fulfilling Brissot's revolutionary dream of 'spreading light in every direction' – at least through the medium of the printed book. Books require protection in order to exist.
>
> (Hesse 1989a: 20–1)

The Paris booksellers had specialised in the *grande édition*, the finely produced multi-volume work involving large investments. Post-Revolution circumstances saw the *grande édition* displaced by journalistic and ephemeral publications for immediate consumption. And if any major publication threatened to register a sales success, anyone could now print it, the

Declaration of the Rights of Man and of the Citizen having specified that all citizens can 'speak, write and print freely'. As Hesse (1989b) tells it, when the 1793 decree placed the whole corpus of already published literature in the public domain, the unplanned outcome of the total abolition of the Royal Administration of the Book Trade and its inspectorate, of the trade regulatory powers of the Paris Communauté and of all existing privileges was to drive the now unregulated trade into violent recession. The irony of Revolutionary publishing lies in the disjunction between the Enlightenment principle of emancipating human reason from all existing institutional constraints and the administrative reality which emerged from the 'emancipation' of the book trade.[10]

This is a telling reminder of the complex set of factors involved in any legal-cultural set. In the case of late eighteenth-century France, fiscal crisis, a state of war, the prohibition of exports (including books) to any hostile nation, internal uprisings in the French provinces, and the Revolutionary abolition of existing bureaucracies and police mechanisms formed the context in which the Enlightenment gesture of a total legislative emancipation from law was carried through in practice. With the abolition of policing by the former National Administration of the Book Trade, piracy flourished; with the abolition of the formality of compulsory registration of works in print, disorderly competition ensued to the disadvantage of the public. It is a salutary lesson for anyone who binds her or himself too tightly to the star of cultural enlightenment and adopts a posture of blind opposition to any regulation.

In a further discussion, Hesse (1990: 130) recognises the irreducibility of legal purposes and norms to theoretical grounds of knowledge. The revolutionary legislation, she writes, effected 'an epistemologically impure and unstable legal synthesis that combined an instrumentalist notion of the public good with a theory of authorship based on natural rights'. By implication, legal purposes and norms are not susceptible to philosophical rectification, whatever form the latter might take. So far so good. But it is symptomatic of the unfortunate pressure exerted by philosophical discourse on the work of historians of authorship that, at the start of her essay, Hesse opts precisely into that familiar epistemological discourse which demands that we take very seriously such questions as: 'What is the relationship between authorship and the law, between the central mechanism of representation and the dominant system of discipline in the modern period?' (1990: 109). To ask this question is to make three assumptions: that there is a general human 'subject' of which the 'author' is an expression; that there is a general 'linguistic' process called 'representation' or a general activity called 'representing'; and that there is – waiting to be discovered – a general and necessary relation between 'subject' and 'language', of which the relation between 'author' and 'law' is one realisation.

Of course Hesse's question is constantly being asked and answered. Yet it makes no difference what the answer is. In dealing with the law we are dealing with an apparatus whose purpose is not to 'know' and to judge in the name of universal truths but to settle disputes by means that depend on a practical mastery of correct procedures, not on the prior establishment of some fundamental ground. It might help if these questions were formulated in a more historical and pluralist manner. We might then ask what have actually been the relationships between forms of authorial activity and different legal systems. And we might be less diverted into speculating on how a set of complementary totalities – subject and language, the self and its determinations – might constitute a general ground for all relations of authorship and law.

V

If we followed the doyen of French theorists, Henri Desbois, we would be left in no doubt as to the philosophically unified nature of French law on authors' rights. In his view, this is a law which 'has given place of honour to the *"droit moral"* by means of which is expressed the relation that exists between the author and the work, the mirror of his personality' (Desbois 1978: viii). The *droit moral*, he writes, comprises

> two orders of concerns, which can affect the author outside the area of pecuniary interests: preoccupations, scruples, regrets of a purely intellectual sort come first, in the circumstance where the work, which the author has conceived and executed, betrays his ideal, does not adequately express his ideas or aesthetic tendencies; there then follow considerations of a strictly moral character, in the circumstance where the work, whose form continues to please him, contravenes the author's conscience, his political or religious convictions, because a conversion drives him to burn today what yesterday he loved.
>
> (Desbois 1978: 276)

This highly charged Romantic disposition synthesises the two sets of attributes – paternal or moral and patrimonial or pecuniary – which constitute the modern *droit d'auteur*. It comes as no surprise when from this lofty vantage point Desbois rewrites the history of French law into an ideal tradition centred on the author.

On the ground, things are somewhat more diverse and contested. The notion of a French tradition of protecting the personal or non-proprietorial interests of authors receives short shrift in Pierre Recht's (1969) *Le Droit d'auteur, une nouvelle forme de propriété*. Written in the firm conviction that 'the ground of a right is not created, it is recognised', Recht seeks to displace 'the famous invention of over-juristic jurists, known as the theory of the *droit moral*' (1969: 5, 6). Instead, he proposes his own elaboration on the theme of property, one which rejects any hypothesis of a separate and fundamental right of authorial personality, whether in a unified form or in the form of a dual right synthesising personal and proprietorial prerogatives. Imagining a three-stage history – knowingly or not, this follows the usual three-part dialectical scheme of unity, division and synthesis – Recht proposes 1793 to 1878 as the period of the 'avatars of the notion of property', 1878 to 1902 as the period of the profound 'conflict of doctrines', and 1902 onwards as the period of return to a coherence based on property. The purpose of Recht's theoretical and historical project is to extend the notion of property such that the authorial personality can be relocated well and truly within its boundaries. In this way, his history involves a series of rebuttals of the several nineteenth-century French theorists who, for different reasons, queried whether 'property' was an adequate or even proper category to serve as the rationale of the specific rights attaching to the status of author.

Augustin Charles Renouard (1838–9), for instance, substituted the term *droit d'auteur* for that of 'property', since he favoured a social-contractual rationale that took the author's right to be a fit reward for a valuable social service. His endorsement of this public policy conception was strengthened by his dissatisfaction with the concept of a 'property' that was not perpetual. Renouard's preference was to argue that the writer was not a proprietor but an inventor, one with interests and rights that are personal but non-proprietorial. It is notable, then, that with the law of 14 July 1866 on authors' rights 'property' was dropped by the French legislature too, as the government spokesperson explained in *Le Moniteur* of 2 June 1866:

> We have been faithful to the principle informing our past laws. . . . The Bill does not refer to 'property' but it could have have done so. The Laws of 1793 and 1810 which do refer to 'property' use the word in relation to a right that they designed to be temporary, and because in literary matters 'property' means 'temporary', it would have been no great risk to include it in the title of the present Bill. However, we chose not to do so. Why? The reason is that the word 'property', once quite inoffensive, has in recent times been considerably abused. It is because from 'property' has emerged, fully armed, the theory under whose influence many people believed themselves to be invincible logicians in declaring: since it is a property, let us treat it like any other property.
>
> (in Recht 1969: 55–6)

And indeed, in a congress on authors' and artists' rights held in Brussels in 1858, as Recht describes, a letter from the writer and orator, Montalambert, was read urging the Congress not to allow the 'industrial spirit' to prevail such that literary culture would degenerate into an 'industrial property' in the hands of the speculators. In this fashion those who defended authors' rights sought both to save and extend the sphere of protection by abandoning the notion of property.

In the place of 'property', according to Recht's critical view, there arose in

the work of writers such as Berthauld and Morillot 'personalist theories ...
which derive all authorial prerogatives from a so-called *droit moral*' (1969: 56)
– precisely Desbois' position. Noting that some of these theories go to the
length of including in the *droit moral* a 'right' to create, Recht responds by
denying that this 'right' – as an act of human freedom – falls within the limits
of law. As he puts it: 'Such theories seem to have been invented solely to
contradict the system of property' (1969: 57). In his 1878 *De la protection
accordée aux œuvres d'art en Allemagne*, Morillot in particular argued that
the author's right rested on a purely 'moral' ground: respect for the human
personality in its integrity. Notwithstanding such principled claims, Recht
regards the *droit moral* as a 'juridical heresy', a modernistic invention
imposed on an evolving French tradition of protecting authorial property. In
support of this judgement he cites the argument advanced by Eugène Pouillet
(1879) in relation to the notion of 'intellectual property':

> Accustomed to seeing property only in a more or less tangible and material
> form, we have difficulty in recognising it in this new and wholly non-
> material form; we are drawn to deny it, because we no longer see it in its
> ordinary appearance. But if we resist this initial impression, if we look for
> property in terms of its origins, we soon discover that the author's right
> derives from the same source: labour. Indeed, we recognise that the
> author's property is even more sure and less deniable; for in its ordinary
> origin, property involves the appropriation of an already existing thing in
> the form in which the possessor appropriates it; here, however, the
> property consists of a creation, that is, the production of something that
> was not already in existence, something that is so personal to the author as
> to form part of himself. After that, what does it matter if legislators have
> had or believed they had to apply some special rules? ... It is none the less
> a property.
>
> (in Recht 1969: 62–3)

And yet the fact remains – in France the notion of property as the source of
the authorial right was to recede before the advance of the *droit moral*.

A perhaps less principled but more descriptive approach to the emergence
of the *droit moral* – as something other than a 'heresy' – is via the path mapped
by Stromholm who can admit the 'more confused and diverse realities'
that present themselves at the 'level of practical applications' (1966: 34),
realities that include the mundane facts of chronology. Unlike English
copyright, the *droit moral* was not instituted too soon to be shaped by the
preoccupations of Romantic aesthetics. True, as Stromholm shows, ideas do
not necessarily become legal norms – 'before asking the courts to protect
one's alexandrines, it must doubtless be possible to ask for the protection of
one's name and honour' (1966: 39) – but in this particular case there was an
influence of aesthetic ideas on a regime of positive law. This influence was not
inevitable. After all, the notion that the individual lives in his or her

intellectual works is one that Stromholm terms 'a somewhat elaborate refinement' and 'a fairly extreme prolongation' of more generalised natural law notions that had circulated – as we have seen in relation to the right freely to print – in discourses such as the *Declaration of the Rights of Man and of the Citizen*.

Stromholm also directs our attention to the field of literary criticism and theory where certain aesthetic notions gained an institutional circulation. By the turn of the eighteenth century the concept of 'originality' was 'so generally adopted in cultivated milieus that its translation into legal principles called only for the occasion to manifest itself'(Stromholm 1966: 102). However, the emphasis upon the individual's contribution as the determining element of the work did not of itself generate legal rules 'in all respects favourable to the creation of an effective juridical protection of authors' non-patrimonial interests' (1966: 102). It is therefore not the idea of 'originality' that served as the ground of the legal norm whereby French law came to recognise in literary works this element that demanded protection as a non-proprietorial personal attribute. Rather, the establishment of the *droit moral* depended on the dissemination of the notion that the author's personality 'has an absolute intrinsic value and that, in consequence, the presence in a literary and artistic work of a trace of personality is worth more than the most accomplished technical virtuosity' (1966: 37). It is a matter of a novel theme not some pre-existing notion. Hence Stromholm's observation that the conception of a work as an expression of personality

> translated into terms such as 'an emanation of the spirit' or 'a spiritual bond' is not necessarily very old. It is entirely possible that in a given society very elevated ideas can be entertained concerning art even though that art is conceived as an art of imitation in which technical virtuosity, indeed erudition, constitutes the preponderant element, and not as an expression of the authorial personality.
>
> (Stromholm 1966: 37)

The components of the *droit moral* also acquired their social gravity through association with existing ethical practices. Stromholm correlates the prerogative of publishing or not publishing one's work with the notion that, from the viewpoint of a traditional ethic, indiscretion – unthinking or inappropriate disclosure of a personal secret or confidence – constituted blameworthy conduct. The prerogative of having the fact of one's authorship recognised – the right of attribution or paternity – is correlated with ethical notions condemning the usurping of another's reputation. However, for the prerogative of having the integrity of one's work respected there is, he says, no pre-existing ethical referent in the form of a specified mode of public conduct. We can speculate on why this is so. Is it perhaps because the aesthetic persona – as envisaged in Schiller's design for an 'aesthetic education of man' – was not yet sufficiently disseminated and established on the social scene? Only when this particular persona was more generally in place would the theme of the work as integral to the author's person acquire the cultural gravity to become a possible legal norm in certain jurisdictions.

A historical example will show what is at stake. The history of the recognition of photographers and cinematographers under the French law on authors' rights is recounted in Edelman's (1979) reconstruction of the 'juridical birth' of photography. He tells the story as a play in two Acts. In Act One,

> [the] law recognised only 'manual' art – the paintbrush, the chisel – or 'abstract' art – writing. The irruption of modern techniques of the (re)production of the real – photographic apparatuses, cameras – surprises the law in the quietude of its categories. A photographer who is satisfied with the pressing of a button, a film-maker with the turning of a crankhandle – are they creators? Is their (re)production equivalent to the over-appropriation of the real?
>
> The law is surprised by the question and its first answer is in 'resistance'. The man who moves the crankhandle or the man who works a hand-lever is not a creator. The law's resistance first passes through the *denegation* of the subject in law. The labour of this individual is a *soulless labour. That is the first act.*
>
> *The second act* is *the transition from soulless labour to the soul of the labour.* The time of the resistance was not *economically neutral*. It was the time of craft production. The fact that industry takes the techniques of cinema and photography into account produces a radical reversal. Photographer and film-maker must become creators, or the industry will lose the benefit of legal protection.
>
> (Edelman 1979: 44)

And become creators they did, but not because the law finally 'corrected' its perception and saw that photographers really had been artists all the time. Rather, photographers became creators with the law's decision to re-classify them as creative subjects, such that their labour and its product were reclassified as integral to their person.

The initial personality-less and pre-aesthetic representation of photographic labour is exemplified in an 1862 opinion of a judge of the Court of Cassation (the supreme judicial jurisdiction in France):

> A painter is not just a copyist; he is a creator. In the same way that a musician would not be an artist if with the aid of an orchestra he restricted himself to imitating the noise of a cauldron on the firedog or the noise of a hammer on an anvil, so a painter would not be a creator if he restricted himself to tracing nature without choice, without feeling, without embellishment. It is because of the servility of photography that I am fundamentally contemptuous of this chance invention which will never be an art

but which plagiarises nature by means of optics. Is the reflection of a glass on paper an art? No, it is a sunbeam caught in the instant by a *manoeuvre*. But where is the conception of man? Where is the choice? In the crystal, perhaps. But, one thing for sure, it is not in man.

(in Edelman 1979: 45)

That labour which is classified as mechanical cannot qualify for protection as intellectual, creative, aesthetic. The subject, Edelman writes, 'must always be present in the creation. Once he disappears, then, quick as a flash, his absence will designate his nature – he was mechanical' (1979: 46). But then photography was reclassified as art and the photographer became an author, a process that Edelman characterises as determined by an economic imperative – the new importance of the photographic industry to capital – that the law could not fail to reproduce within itself. The discursive move involved investing the notion of the 'imprint of personality' in the law's representation of photographic technique. Once aestheticised in this way, the working of the machine which previously marked the limit of legally protected subjectivity became an integral extension of the complete mode of being of the subject:

[T]echnique permits the subject's self-affirmation, and in this way the subject can have self-affirmation only through the *mediation of a technique* which permits his investing himself in the real and making it his private domain . . . . One might say that the machine loses its 'being' and that it becomes the means of the subject's being.

(Edelman 1979: 51)

What was a mechanical reproduction of reality – light alone, Daguerre said, produced the photographic image – is now a mode of aesthetic being (or of being aesthetic) protected by a right that is personal as well as proprietorial. This little drama properly concludes when the 3 July 1985 law on author's right drops the requirement – in article 3 of the law of 11 March 1957 – that photographic works could be protected only if they were 'of an artistic or documentary nature'.

It is only to be expected that aesthetic criticism – whether in its Romantic historicist or post-structuralist versions – will claim to see through any positive law. The 1985 French law has been the object of sustained conceptual and practical critique by Edelman (1987a), as we shall see in chapter 8. It has also served as a pretext for post-structuralist speculations on the nature of authorship. In so far as this law opens the authorial status to new categories – performers, writers of software – it has been said that the French definition of the author has 'gone vague'. By this, Molly Nesbit (1987: 229) means that a once sharp boundary between culture and industry has been blurred. It is worth pausing on Nesbit's argumentation to see, yet again, how the dialectical account of authorship always returns us to the same aesthetic schema, albeit now decked out as the post-structuralist game of transgressing the boundaries.

Although her essay is a welter of different phenomena – commentary on

Foucault, report on the American aesthetic avant-garde, biography of a French photographer of the *belle époque*, legal history, French post-structuralist theory and a new 'politics of culture', Nesbit like Edelman has economic forces move the law along. Thus, if in the nineteenth century makers of technical drawings were not protected as authors, this was because 'industry' – here depicted as functionally bound to that other conveniently unspecified but all-explanatory subject of power, 'bourgeois culture' – 'did not want authors in its ranks; it wanted control over every phase of production' (Nesbit 1987: 234). Unlike Edelman, however, Nesbit does not accord the legal order a significant autonomy. At the same time, she overestimates the power of the law of copyright, as if the legal definition of 'author' completely determined the definitions of 'author' that prevail in all other spheres of existence. When there is a breach of an established legal definition – thanks to the rising forces of economy (and culture) – there is said to be a general rupture with the bad old legal-cultural order. This occurs when the old law is caught out by the historical march of cultural development in the form of new post-literary media and their personnel – the 'new stage in industrial production, late capitalism'. However, when these new 'authors' arisen from the ranks of the previously excluded industrial and 'proletarian' producers demanded admission to the legal sphere as authors (we are not told why they should want such a thing – it seems to be assumed that the human subject just wants to be and will become an author), they discovered that the 'law, for all its apparent elasticity, could not handle such a result overnight' (1987: 236). A double dialectical negative is in play: the law, it is implied, is neither the master of the market nor is it equal to new cultural demands from the previously excluded to be admitted as authors.

Another familiar historicist theme now enters on cue: the critique of the law as complicit with that culture which is elitist not popular, individualist not collective. True, the 'law played a critical, though largely unrecognized, role in the definition of modern culture' (1987: 235) by demarcating the zone of 'culture' (and literary authors) from the zone of 'industry' (and producers). But, it seems, this was not in step with history's demands, as embodied in the call by the newly ex-industrial class to be legally recognised and protected as authors, that is, as full (aesthetic) subjects. In other words, now that culture has advanced, copyright law is confronted by the inadequacy of the boundaries and statuses that it had itself previously constructed. The law can no longer 'control' positions that it 'had helped to generate and to consolidate' (1987: 243). While this supposed 'transgression' of legal norms is predictably a moment of excitement for the literary intellectual in *Yale French Studies*, Nesbit in the end herself goes vague. She welcomes the emergence of the cultural industries as a dual subversion: first, of the old elite order of a literary and aesthetic culture that 'could not be expected to accommodate uninvited guests' (1987: 235) in the form of industrial interests and, second, of the legal order that had aligned itself with this archaic and restricted notion of culture as literary, aesthetic and individualistic (1987: 256). Yet she wavers between viewing this circumstance as the necessary victory of a more authentic and complete culture over a legally buttressed cultural boundedness, and a traditional aesthetic concern at the industrial emphasis of the new cultural forms.

The best Nesbit can do is to canonise an ambiguously aesthetic-industrial figure, the previously unheard-of Parisian photographer Eugène Atget who termed himself 'an author or, more precisely, an *auteur-éditeur*' and who referred oxymoronically to his photographs as *documents artistiques* (245). This idiosyncratic Parisian act of self-classification – two persons in one individual – is then read as the sign of a profound and necessary historical rupture achieved by the usual mix of linguistic theory and aesthetic credentials, the unknown Atget being set into the post-modern galaxy of signatures name-dropped in the essay: Foucault and Barthes – here conscripted together into the death (of the author) squad, Mallarmé, Robbe-Grillet, Butor, Cage, Beckett, Moholy-Nagy, Lyotard, Derrida and so on, all this in the new and unbounded space that has emerged now that the old law has been so thoroughly confounded. Nesbit concludes with a confident announcement of 'new critical spaces' and the global assurance – but really to whom can it be intelligible? – that '[i]t is possible to plot a politics of culture and possible to imagine a collective of authors, individuals who do not lose themselves when working with others' (1987: 257). There is, of course, not the slightest hint of how the new politics will be organised nor of whether or how the law should actually deal with new communications technologies.

A final point concerns Nesbit's recourse to the dialectical imperative to classify all phenomena into the complementary totalities of ideal and material. We should ask the question: is the French law of the *droit d'auteur* an ideal phenomenon, a pure conception, or is it a material force? If we say it is an ideal, then what of its material components – the specificity of its jurisdiction, its trained personnel, the technical procedures, its architecture? If we say it is a material force, then what of the law's ideals, its language, its ideology and fictions? The fact is that this law, like the legal system of which it is a part, is too complex and heterogeneous a phenomenon for there to be much point in the question. Historicism flaunts the dialectic of the ideal and the material as the necessary condition of cultural development – their initial division and their ultimate reconciliation and synthesis – but this is no reason to organise the history of law and authorship in the same way.

VI

The positive history of French law concerning the rights of authors reveals a diverse and shifting set of cultural, commercial and legal factors. The *droit moral*, now a distinctive feature of that law, was not a necessary outcome of those factors, driven inevitably author-ward by some underlying process of cultural development. While in retrospect it can be depicted as a most principled legal form, the *droit moral* in fact emerged uncertainly, not from grand legislative initiatives – the Acts of 1844, 1854 and 1866 were concerned with questions of literary property and its administration – but from a patchwork of case law. On a variety of grounds and without any uniform rationale or general theory, case by case the French courts began to develop a jurisprudence on interests and rights relating to authorial personality not property, a jurisprudence resting in part on article 1382 of the *Code civil* (the general rule of liability for civil wrongs). Nor was there one great threshold, a peak change at which authorial personality was all at once recognised by law. In fact, even the right of property was still in the process of consolidation. At mid-century, in his study of 'literary property' law in France and in England, Laboulaye (1858) opens his treatise by observing the novelty and the uncertainty of the new category: 'What is called in France: *la propriété littéraire* and in England: "copyright", is a right whose recognition is of recent date and whose character is not clearly determined'. Two decades later, the textbooks are still recording the view that *la propriété littéraire* can be deemed a 'very modern expression' (Worms 1878: 2).

Rather than a breakthrough to a new categorial order, then, French law concerning the extra-patrimonial rights of authors emerged piecemeal, in a characteristically unplanned accumulation of decisions in the courts.[11] For instance, in its 11 January 1828 judgment the Cour de Paris found that a work comes into being only with the author's decision to release it for publication. A better known case is that of *Lacordaire*, one that concerned an unauthorised publication of lectures. Here, the Tribunal Correctionnel de Lyon on 17 July 1845 judged that 'from the viewpoint of his moral personality and in the interests of his thought, the author must always retain the right to inspect and revise his work, to ensure that it has been faithfully reproduced, and to decide the moment and mode of its publication'. The nineteenth-century courts also recognised that the author of a publication should not have the fact of his or her authorship obscured. The Cour de Paris in a 17 December 1838 decision held that a publisher could not use a periphrasis in place of the author's name. In a similar manner, on 10 August 1858 the Cour de Lyon judged a publisher liable for having published a new edition of a work under a name other than the author's. These cases suggest, however, that it was as much a fault of the publisher as a positive right of the author that was at issue.

A different lapse on the part of a publisher was the concern of the Tribunal de Commerce de Paris on 29 December 1842 when the court found that Auguste Comte's publisher had failed in his professional duties by not observing book trade practice when he put in press a work containing changes that the author had not cleared (*bon à tirer*). With regard to the problem of the publisher's unauthorised modification of a work, some decisions rested on the civil law doctrine of usufruct: that is, the right of enjoying advantages derived from the use of that which is owned by another goes only as far as is compatible with the substance of the thing used not being damaged or destroyed. It was found that the purchase of a manuscript did not give the buyer a right to amend it for publication. This would have damaged the substance of that in which the author's honour and reputation inhered. Thus, in its judgment of 17 June 1852, the Chambre Civile of the Tribunal de la Seine found that '[n]o publisher can be recognised as having the right to make essential changes to the work of the author whose signature it bears. . . . Were such an act to be tolerated, it could lead to nothing less than putting the reputation and good standing of the author at the mercy of publishers.' Similarly, on 24 February 1863, the Cour de Bordeaux found that 'the author cannot be presumed to have alienated the incalculable hope of repute that, in such a case as this, publicity can bring him'. Later that same year, on 24 August, the same Bordeaux court found against a publisher whose 'editing' of a work had had the effect of 'more or less profoundly denaturing the authors' thought and opinions, in consequence exposing them to a public judgement which might be other than that which they would have been expected to receive'.

These decisions are indicative of a treatment of authors not as proprietors but as civil personalities with an emerging legal capacity to restrain the exercise – by its owner, whoever it may be – of a proprietorial right in the work. The decisions are patchy and scattered, having in common only what can retrospectively be characterised as a concern to protect various attributes of personality which are independent of the attributes attaching to a property right. Nevertheless, these decisions suggest that in the French courts of the nineteenth century a legal arrangement was emerging that was to prove amenable to the entry of aesthetic themes and to the later theorisation and synthesis that we now know as the *droit moral*.

Only with the *Lecocq* case, heard first in the Tribunal de la Seine on 21 May 1898, then in the Cour de Paris on 1 February 1900 and finally in the Cour de Cassation on 25 June 1902 is anything resembling a theory of the personal right of authors enunciated. Charles Lecocq was a composer who had been granted a divorce from his partner. In the divorce settlement, the composer's works were treated as property held in common and therefore to be distributed following the divorce. Lecocq appealed, claiming that under the Revolutionary legislation literary and artistic works were not subject to the ordinary law of property, and the Cour de Paris concurred, judging that the author's right in his creation could not be calculated in pecuniary terms and that to do so would raise practical difficulties. Moreover, if his former partner were to have an exclusive right over his works, it would mean that she would appropriate the composer's 'most sacred and personal rights':

The composer, whose moral rights in the work (even if this is ceded) are not contested, would find himself unable to rework his creation, to embellish it by further work or, his talent developing, to destroy it in the circumstance that he judged it to fall below the ideal to which he now aspires.

With Lecocq winning the second round, the case proceeded to the Cour de Cassation. Here, in 1902, the Civil Chamber declared that literary and artistic property published by either partner during their life together was susceptible to distribution in the divorce settlement; however, this *mise en commun* should not constrain 'the author's capacity, inherent in his very personality, to make subsequent modifications to his creation, or even to withdraw it, provided that this does not constitute a vexatious action towards his partner or her representatives'.

The final court of appeal thus recognised the concept of a capacity 'inherent in [the author's] very personality', even though this theme was not yet specified in terms of a right having precise contents. While it has the air of a statement of legal principle concerning the nature of the authorial personality, the proposition was contingent on the fact that divorce had been restored in 1884; when the occasion arose, as it did with the *Lecocq* case, the juridical nature of the right attaching to the status of author had to be defined – for the purposes of the divorce settlement. It is the sort of situation that Stromholm describes:

> The manner in which legal problems are posed depends very much on circumstances. It is rare that jurists address an issue solely for the purposes of pure theoretical analysis without the impulsion to do so being given by a particular dispute. Thus, while they might sometimes be the inevitable result of certain juridical or social facts, disputes for the most part arise from the capriciousness of chance.
>
> (Stromholm 1966: 271)

Resisting the lure of invisible trans-historical processes and structures and remaining instead with the actual legal-cultural arrangements of the times, the most striking feature of the nineteenth-century environment that we observe in France is the late arrival of the *droit moral*, that radical extension of the personalist model into the domain of extra-patrimonial prerogatives. We see that the *droit moral* is the artefact of a specific legal-cultural environment, not a long-delayed codification of a universal truth about the subjectivity of writers, a subjectivity that law had somehow previously missed. Although the tendency of literary thought is to treat it as a matter of high principle, the authorial persona protected by the *droit moral* in fact emerged from a miscellany of lessons taught by concrete instances in French case law.

Chapter 4

German theory: rights of personality

I

At this point, for both descriptive and polemical purposes, let us take a different tack. In chapters 2 and 3 the object was to establish the historical particularity and diversity of arrangements concerning the legal existence of authors in early modern England and in France. In turning now to the German context, the emphasis will fall on philosophy and jurisprudential theory. These were the German specialities – and for good reason: for long there was no national territory to administer, the modern German state being created only with the unification of the territorial states in 1870. Yet the fact of a common language and literary culture made piracy profitable. And because there was no practical legal policing of the book market on a national scale, German publishers and writers were confronted by a particularly difficult problem in controlling levels of book piracy which, in the German territories, were less a matter of legal theory's lack of recognition of authors' property rights than the practical consequence of geopolitical circumstance.

As a practical problem, *Büchernachdruck* – the piracy or counterfeiting of books – was a predominant feature of a market to all effects without regulation. At a 'national' level, something like the French conditions of 1791–4 obtained into the 1840s in Germany. Unlike in France, however, where the deregulation of the book trade involved a legislative intervention in the name of the Enlightenment ideal of universal access to all published knowledge, in Germany the persisting phenomenon of piracy flowed from an absence of legislative interventions and effective agreements on and enforcement of trade regulation across the different states. While political and legal initiatives such as the Prussian Civil Code of 1794 and the Prussian Copyright Act of 1837 offered a prospect of order, the technical capacity of producers – pirates or otherwise – to produce and distribute books continued to outstrip the regulatory abilities of the states, whether unilaterally or bilaterally exercised. As printing itself once had been, now book piracy was a specifically German phenomenon, not thanks to the *Geist* but by virtue of the circumstance whereby books enjoyed a 'national' or trans-border circulation while the multiple jurisdictions of the various states remained local.

To illustrate the situation, we can note that thirty-eight German states agreed on 8 June 1815 to article 18 of the Act of the Germanic Confederation: 'The Diet shall take into consideration, at its first meeting, some plan for uniform legislation on the liberty of the press, and also what steps are necessary to be taken to secure authors and publishers from invasion of their copyrights.' But nothing happened for seventeen years. Then on 6 September 1832 the Diet issued a decree beginning: 'In conformity to the 18th article of the Act of the Germanic Confederation, and to preserve the rights of authors, publishers and booksellers from piracy of works of literature or objects of art, the Sovereign Princes and Free Cities of Germany have resolved to establish as a fundamental principle, that for the future, all distinction with regard to penalties and legal remedies against piracy, between the subjects of one State and the subjects of another, being parties to the Confederation, shall be respectively abolished.' There was still no action. On 2 April 1835, however, another decree was issued: 'The most high governments have agreed to prohibit piracy throughout the whole extent of the Confederation, and to establish and secure literary property on uniform principles.' Further resolutions were passed in 1837 but, to cut the story short, we might note that at the end of the nineteenth century Augustine Birrell could observe that Germany had no law of copyright until 1870.

There was, however, no shortage of theories. At the turn of the eighteenth century '[t]he theory of literary property dominated the doctrine, but its influence on juridical realities was not great' (Stromholm 1966: 184). Indeed, contemporary opinion held that in the German territories 'so thoroughly had it been proved that piracy was forbidden that there was no need for laws against it' (1966: 184). And in the absence of a national administration, the struggle to secure the book market against piracy was pursued into the 1840s in an environment where 'states having modern [legal] texts adjoin neighbouring territories which lack any legislation; the case law remains largely unknown and inevitably lacks unity; the most divergent theories are formulated on authors' rights, often without any relation to positive law' (1966: 182). Market practices, it would seem, were relatively untouched by legislation and not at all by legal doctrine. 'Regional variation' does scant justice to the diversity flowing from the existence of some three hundred independent German states, a diversity which prevented uniform legislation and case law but not theoretical speculation on the ideal nature of rights attaching to literary property and, most importantly, to authorial personality. The division of Germany into independent states such as Austria, Prussia, Baden, Bavaria and Saxony thus saw a minimal body of case law but an explosion of doctrine in 'writings expressing every possible idea and theory about the rights of authors, including their personal or non-pecuniary interests' (1966: 219).

As the German literature of ideas shows, it was in these particular circumstances that claims were made to see beyond particulars and to speak in the name of universals. Like Kant's philosopher 'independent of the orders of government', von Humboldt proposed an ideal safeguarding of disinterested knowledge from interests that would instrumentalise it for particular ends. Was this an ideal for all of humankind and its history or a sign of the divorce of German intellectuals from praxis? A response is appropriate in the style of Weber's commitment never to use the term 'natural law' without quotation marks in order to indicate his rejection of a notion which – along with 'human rights' – threatened to detach itself from actual conflicts. For Weber, these were examples of 'intellectualist fanaticism', artefacts 'merely conceived in thought' (Hennis 1988: 181). Yet, as if they had developed a capacity to live among such artefacts, Enlightenment and Romantic intellectuals in Germany perfected the activity of looking beyond any actual legal or governmental circumstance, aspiring to a universalism of thought in a regionalism of institutions.

The solution to book piracy, we might want to suggest, lay not in the dialectical reconciliation of authorial consciousness and material conditions through a new conception of literary writing but in a better regulation of the territory. Discursive literacy rates were rising and demand for books was growing but the 'national' book trade market remained without effective legal policing. Piracy of profitable books was an attractive activity for entrepreneurs. Unauthorised reprinting might be unethical but it was not illegal. Indeed, as Robert Darnton (1987: 34) has noted, '[w]e do not even have a clear idea of how contemporaries understood and practised piracy (or counterfeiting)'. Certainly there were 'justifications' of piracy – as there usually are of profit – which typically rested on an argument against any exclusive right of property in 'ideas' or in published works. The following, from 1783, makes the familiar claim that an idea once divulged cannot be counted a private property:

> Once expressed, it is impossible for [the idea] to remain the author's property. ... It is precisely for the purpose of using the ideas that most people buy books – pepper dealers, fishwives, and the like, and literary pirates excepted. ... Over and over again it comes back to the same question: I can read the contents of a book, learn, abridge, expand, teach, and translate it, write about it, laugh over it, find fault with it, deride it, use it poorly or well – in short, do with it whatever I will. But the one thing I should be prohibited from doing is copying or reprinting it? ... A published book is a secret divulged. With what justification would a preacher forbid the printing of his homilies, since he cannot prevent any one of his listeners from transcribing his sermons? Would it not be just as ludicrous for a professor to demand that his students refrain from using some new proposition he had taught them as for him to demand the same of book dealers with regard to a new book? No, no, it is too obvious that the

concept of intellectual property is useless. My property must be exclusively mine; I must be able to dispose of it and retrieve it unconditionally. Let someone explain to me how that is possible in the present case. Just let someone try taking back the ideas he has originated once they have been communicated so that they are, as before, nowhere to be found.

(in Woodmansee 1984: 443–4)

Such arguments helped to perpetuate an environment in which the problem of generalised piracy remained unresolved. In this environment the author and the publisher could stand as partners in alliance against the pirates. Once an orderly book market was secured, however, the alliance of author and publisher became subject to internal ruptures as the interests of these two parties – no longer united against a common enemy – were more sharply defined as in potential conflict one with the other.

II

In response to the dog-eat-dog regime of unregulated publishing, philosophical intellectuals of the stamp of Fichte and Kant made their interventions. Under the rubric 'Proof of the illegality of reprinting: a rationale and a parable' (1793), Fichte constructs a set of distinctions and thresholds as the ground of a rational critique of piracy and a defence of the principle of literary property:

[E]ach writer must give his thoughts a certain form, and he can give them no other form than his own, because he has no other. But neither can he be willing to hand over this form in making his thoughts public, for no one can *appropriate* his thoughts without thereby *altering their form*. The latter thus remains forever his exclusive property.

(in Woodmansee 1984: 445)

Fichte's concern is to locate an incontestable ground for a claim of authorial property. This is the purpose of the distinction that he draws between the book which can be owned by anyone who buys or otherwise acquires it, and the form that the author gives to his thought which, though published, 'remains forever his exclusive property'. It is the familiar argument for a property right based on the distinctiveness or originality of the author's contribution. A distinction between ideal form and material object, between the author's discourse and its material support was elaborated also by Immanuel Kant, but not simply with the purpose of justifying a property right. In 1785, he published the essay 'Von der Unrechtmässigkeit des Büchernachdruckes' (by 1798 it had been published in English as 'Of the injustice of counterfeiting books'). A further discussion of publishing rights was to appear under the title 'Was ist ein Büch?' in section 31 of the 1797 treatise *Metaphysische Anfangsgründe der Rechtslehre* (or *The Metaphysical Elements of Justice*).

It is fitting to set Kant's discussion of piracy and the book trade into his broader project for establishing the transcendental condition of moral action, knowledge and judgement. For Kant, to explain 'good behaviour' it is not enough that individuals should have learned how to conduct themselves in ways that do not harm others; truly 'good behaviour' is achieved only to the extent that 'man's' moral nature as a human being is given untrammelled expression. There has to be something deeper, a transcendental condition of possibility; to refer to the fact of an actual ability and its technical conditions is an insufficient explanation, since any actual ability presumes a universal condition of possibility. Kant's discussion of authorial attributes and the publishing process is conducted in terms of a transcendental reason that works at a level higher than empirical realities of commerce and positive law. The Kantian 'kingdom of reason' is thus a jurisdiction of a quite different order (although doubtless having its definite relationship to the circumstances of the absolutist state). It is that realm which 'man' intuits in aesthetic judgement where he glimpses a domain of being that is cleansed of all local features and distinctions. Here, according to *The Critique of Judgement*, he transcends the boundedness of individual experience and judgements of taste: 'The delight which determines the judgement of taste is independent of all interests' (Kant 1957: 43). What follows is logical but somewhat unexpected. If aesthetic judgement is independent of all interests, then it is independent of all actual individuals, whether they know it or not. Thus when someone finds something to be beautiful

> it is not as if he counted on others agreeing in his judgement of liking owing to his having found them in such agreement on a number of occasions, but he *demands* this agreement of them. He blames them if they judge differently, and denies them taste, which he still requires of them as something they ought to have; and to this extent it is not open to men to say: Every one has his own taste. This would be equivalent to saying that there is no such thing as taste, i.e. no aesthetic judgement capable of making a rightful claim upon the assent of all men.
>
> (Kant 1957: 52)

The Kantian imperative is normative rather than positive. 'The assertion', says Kant, 'is not that everyone *will* fall in with our judgement, but rather that everyone ought to agree with it' (1957: 84). It is worth observing that in this space between what is and what ought to be, we find different accounts of how the universal form of being will be achieved, whether by a Schillerian or Marxist dialectic that demands historical intervention to construct the necessary harmony among all, or by a Kantian rationality which sees in every human individual already the common core of reason that transcends all social norms. In other words, the Kantian project is directed not at individual attributes but at what is purported to be anterior to them, the universal condition of all possible attributes. Of course, by definition, the universal cannot be known or experienced because it is what makes knowledge and experience possible. At most, aesthetic judgement provides an intuition of this other order of being that is absolutely free, a law to itself, independent of circumstances and interests, purposes and means. In chapter 2, in referring to *The Conflict of the Faculties*, we noted Kant's proposition that only the philosopher can speak in his own person, disinterestedly, as the voice of reason in the world; this is something lawyers and judges – in the offices and ownership of 'government' – cannot do. The 'person', in this sense, is that which cannot be alienated or owned by another. And to speak in one's own person, or to publish in that guise, is to be the (authorial) subject beyond all actual circumstances, an autonomous end in itself, not the means or instrument of another's interests.[1]

When Kant contemplates the division of labour in the book trade, it is in this dualistic and rationalist key. In a real *tour de force*, he treats the 'author' and the 'book' in terms of the fundamental division of being between the transcendental and the empirical, a dividing-line that is said to bisect both author and book, subject and object. The 'author' becomes a formal subject, the necessary prolegomenon to the legal rights that would organise an actual publishing process and book trade. In this way, a study of book-piracy becomes a transcendental reflection on the ideal freedom and integrity of the author as one who speaks in his own person, not just another pamphlet advocating the individual writer's right of literary property.

In *The Metaphysical Elements of Justice*, Kant discusses these questions in the section entitled: 'Was ist ein Büch?' ('What is a book?'). It would, however, be impossible for the reader of John Ladd's (1965) English transla-tion to know this, since the philosopher-translator omits the sections that include this discussion, commenting that they 'are mainly concerned with technical concepts belonging to eighteenth-century German law. These concepts are derived from Roman law and do not have any exact counterparts in Anglo-American law. Hence they are of little interest except to the specialist' (in Kant 1965: 57). As if philosophical discourse spoke to everyone. Let us restore Kant's voice:

> [T]he book, on the one hand, is a *material product* (*opus mecanicum*) which can be imitated (by he who legitimately possesses a copy of it) and, consequently, there is a right *in rem*; on the other hand, the book is a discourse from publisher to public, and this no one can reproduce publicly, without first having from the author the authority to do so, such that it is a matter of a personal right. The error consists in confusing these two rights.
> (Kant 1907: 240)

Through its existence as a material commodity, the book is thus joined on one side to the book market (and hence to the system of property relations and piracy); but on the other side it is joined – through the *person* of the author and the consensus or agreement between author and publisher – to universal reason. In this latter mode of its being, the book is a non-appropriable ideal entity. The logic of this dual mode of being projects on to the book Kant's view of the material world more generally: on the one hand it is the only locus for the individual's material existence, but on the other it is the place where one might intuit the ideal freedom and totality of perfect being. The rigour of the concept – and the discipline of the ethos of mental disengagement that it accompanies – lies in having the book (and 'man') encompass these two incommensurable orders of being at the same time. The book can be possessed as the material vehicle of beauty in the material realm; yet in so far as it is the discourse of an ideally disinterested person – the author – the book also partakes of the non-material and the non-possessable.

This separability of personal discourse from material form – or of the 'idea' from its material 'support' – does not apply to paintings. While the literary work can always be distinguished from the copies in which it is embodied, in the work of art the idea or intellectual element cannot be separated from the material object, and for this reason Kant excludes paintings from the class of works protected by a personal right. The reasoning is clear: the work of art cannot be distinguished from its embodiment in a particular material and sensory object in the way that the literary 'work' (and with it the person of the author) can be distinguished from its embodiment in the material object that is a book. In this sense, the literary 'work' is a transcendental entity that cannot be confused with the published copy. This distinction carries the principal consequence. Given his extraordinary faculty of abstraction and unbending pursuit of its logic, Kant's interest did not extend to the physical particular but remained with the metaphysical means of standing aside from it. We can understand why Kant made his transcendental cut where he did. But where would he make it today? There is, for once, a reason for putting a counterfactual query. Today, argument on the legal status of the visual artwork seems almost to run in the reverse direction: because there is no mental entity (or 'work') separable from the physical entity of the original artwork, this physical object is taken to be invested with its creator's very 'personality' in a manner that no copy or facsimile of the artwork can match. On this ground a case is argued for legislation in the copyright countries to protect the moral right of integrity specifically with relation to visual artworks.[2]

The rights of authors and legitimate publishers are defined likewise, a distinction being drawn between the book as material object to which there attaches a property right (a right *in rem*), and the book as immaterial discourse, the author's in-person address to the public. But this address can be made only *via* the publisher and the published book (there being in this world no other means of communicating the discourse). The book is the publisher's authorised address to the public (*Rede des Verlegers ans Publikum*), one which cannot be repeated in public by another without the authorisation of the author. Here Kant's concern is to distinguish between the legitimate publisher and the pirate, both of whom convey the author's discourse to the public in the name of the author. What distinguishes the legitimate publisher from the pirate is the former's personal right (*ein persönliches Recht*) to reproduce the work. Piracy constitutes an illegitimate use (*furtum usus*) of the author's discourse, one which harms the legitimate publisher's valid personal right to address the public in the author's name. So it is the publisher whose right Kant describes as personal. Publication – the rendering material of the immaterial discourse and its communication to the public – can be done only *via* the publisher who, unlike the pirate, is authorised by the author and enjoys an affirmative personal right (*persönliches bejahendes Recht*) to speak and publish in the name of the author. The publisher's right is affirmative in so far as it allows him to oblige another party – the author – to answer for what he publishes in the other's name.

Respecting the status of the author in Kant's analysis, Stromholm (1966: 190) offers an important observation: 'The remarks Kant devotes to the right and to the juridical construction of the *author* have a subsidiary and incidental character. It is the right of the publisher that he describes as a "personal right". This term is nowhere used in relation to the rights of the author.' On the other hand, Kant argues that the author cannot be obliged to address the public in spite of himself. Nor can anyone else – in the author's name – address to the public that discourse which constitutes the work, because this discourse is one which only the author can decide to publish and disseminate. However, the 1785 essay 'On the injustice of counterfeiting books' specifies three factors that define the nature of the inalienable right (*unveräusserliches Recht*) that Kant ascribes to the author. First, a work is the exercise of the author's individual faculties and, as such, cannot be alienated, it being impossible to cede the exercise of one's faculties to another. Second, the intellectual activity of composing one's thoughts exists only in the person of the author and as such is the basis of the inalienable right to refuse to publish the composition. Third, the right of the author is a right innate to his or her person. By innate right, Kant refers to a right which, as he explains in *The Metaphysical Elements of Justice*, 'belongs to anyone by nature independently of any juridical act' (1965: 43). Such a right is distinguished from an acquired right, that is, from a right which depends on a positive juridical act. Innate rights consist of the unconstrained exercise of freedom, the 'one sole and original right that belongs to every human being by virtue of his humanity' (1965: 44). The right of the writer as author of the work is thus differentiated in a manner characteristic of natural law thinking from rights established in positive law. The 'personal right' of the publisher belongs in this second (lower) category, being in effect a mandate by the author for the publisher to administer.

So what were the consequences of all this momentous philosophical reflection on the book trade and its law? The question is fair; as Kant (1963: 57–8) himself put it, '[t]his capacity for facing up in the present to the often very distant future, instead of being wholly absorbed by the enjoyment of the present, is the most decisive mark of the human's advantage'. Of course no theory-led reform produced immediate and effective regulation of the German book trade; however, there have been some interesting discursive reactions. Indeed, two centuries later – in what can be read as an ironic riposte to 'Was ist ein Büch?' – Michel Foucault (1969) asked 'Qu'est-ce qu'un auteur?'. For Kant, the book is the regrettably necessary sign that a material medium is needed for humankind to realise its potential freedom and achieve aesthetic intuition of the ideal totality of being. The book's author – as the one who already speaks in the freedom and integrity of his person – is both within and without this material sphere. Denizen of the moral high ground of Kantian reason, the philosopher-author – as person – is the transcendental a priori to there being an actual book trade, and a pointer to what we shall all be in that other sphere of perfect beings. Foucault withdraws 'the author' from this transcendental ground with a vengeance. Far from the necessary unity of a formal prolegomenon, the author – and with it the Kantian subject – is dispersed and multiplied across a miscellany of perfectly material and historically contingent 'author-functions' that have no necessity about them.[3] These functions have included the linking of texts to authors to form an œuvre, linking texts to texts to form a canon or tradition, and other such classificatory or indexing procedures. Perhaps the reversal can be taken further: does Foucault treat 'the book' – in the linguistic figure of 'discourse' – as the (historical) a priori of the author-functions? His essay on the author was, after all, composed at the same time as *The Archaeology of Knowledge* with its ill-conceived speculation on the possibility of excavating the system of formal rules of discourse governing all possible 'statements'.

On a less speculative note, Kant has been accorded the privilege of being 'the first to attach the author's right as a whole to the concept of "fundamental rights" which, in the course of the nineteenth century, became – through laborious detours and through intermediaries other than Kant – what are now called "rights of personality"' (Stromholm 1966: 192). Kant's theoretical originality was to propose an identity between the rights of authors and the category of innate rights. However, given the widespread acceptance from the eighteenth century onwards of the notion of innate rights, when nineteenth-century jurists began to place authorial rights into the category of rights of personality, they might well have been acting independently of any direct influence by Kant. Perhaps the slow emergence of a concept of a 'right of personality' owes something to Kant's treatment of the author as the locus of the higher right of personality or *ius personalissimum* conceived in terms of an 'innate right' – and thus, in *The Metaphysical Elements of Justice*, set among the formal prolegomena to the 'acquired rights' that exist in the domain of statutory or positive law. For us, Kantianism persists as a powerful mode of sceptical and anti-positive argumentation and its claims are therefore not unfamiliar ones. From that lofty perspective, any instituted regime of rights, authorial or otherwise, can be depicted as inadequate and restrictive when set against the ideal of absolute Freedom. The present book, of course, stands outside and even against this particular high theoretical tradition in not treating the legal personality of authors in terms of 'the individual', 'the person' or 'the subject'.

What, then, of the terms in which Kant addresses the issue of publishing in his elaborate discussion of the differential rights of author and publisher? Kant's scheme allowed for the possibility of differentiating between the authorial *ius personalissimum* and the publisher's 'personal right' to publish once the authorial mandate has been given. As long as authors and publishers were engaged in their joint struggle against pirates and for an orderly market, this difference could remain purely a matter of theoretical clarification. However, once that pact was no longer needed – with the regulation of the market and the suppression of large-scale illegal reprinting – attention turned to the relations of publishers and authors, for instance to the issue of authorial interests such as might subsist even after the reproduction and exploitation rights had been assigned to the publisher. And what began to emerge was a notion that the author had inalienable non-economic personal rights that constituted his or her continuing interest in the treatment of the work.

III

We are dealing with a tilting of the axis of authorial legal personality – by German aesthetico-legal theory – away from rights of property and towards the purportedly more fundamental notion of 'rights of personality'. The object of protection was no longer to be just a property (albeit immaterial) but the wholeness and integrity of the human person. Rights of personality represent a logic for establishing and protecting rights of authors that is quite different to the Lockean notion of 'man's' natural right as possessor of himself and thus holder of a natural property right to the fruits of his labour. They are also expressive of something more concrete than Kant's depiction of the authorial person among the prolegomena to all actual positive rights and legal obligations.

In his descriptive bibliographical survey, Kase (1967) classifies the heterogeneous schemes of continental copyright doctrines along a spectrum. One pole is that of 'reflection theory' – where the so-called 'rights' of the author merely reflect the administrative norms of anti-piracy measures; at the other pole are theories in which authorial personality rights are accorded a fully autonomous substance. It was in Germany that these latter theories emerged, but not without a struggle (just as in England there had been a struggle over literary property). With a characteristic 'reflectionist' denial of any independent juridical ground for a specific right protecting an author's personal or non-economic interest, Julius Jolly argued that modification of a printed work was no more a personal harm than those modifications we make to an oral message when we repeat it in conversation. By contrast, for Otto von Gierke the theorist of private law, the property right of an author has its source and ground in a right whose object is precisely the protection of the author's personality, since the right of literary property can in the first instance derive from nowhere but the author's capacity as creator of the work to determine and control its divulgation, reproduction and modification. Seen in this light, the author's 'personality' – of which his or her intellectual works are an exemplary emanation – becomes the locus of protection of a fundamental right, the very foundation and source of a mode of legal being quite distinct from that of property ownership.

Two principal lines of argument were pursued in the elaboration of this new style of right. On the one hand, a catalogue of specific attributes of personality – the right to life, freedom, honour – emerged as new rights were defined; these attributes and prerogatives were related, but they were not taken to depend or rest on a final point of synthesis. Followed by Carl Gareis, this line of argument was content to define a 'family' of relatively discrete rights without presuming a foundational and unified right of personality. On the other hand, von Gierke and Josef Kohler argued that the different personal rights were nothing less than so many different manifestations of the one general right of personality (*allgemeines Persönlichkeitsrecht*). The specific right attaching to one's intellectual creations was thus conceptualised as one of the particular expressions (*Ausladungen*) of a fundamental right whose object was the whole or integral personality. In this German concern to locate the fundamental condition that made the author's right possible – a condition in no sense satisfied by the notion that a given right is simply the positive creation of an enacted statute or an adjudicated case – there were, however, important variations. Kohler's approach was to pair the personality and property interests of authors, thus constituting what has become known as the *dualist* theory. By contrast, the *unitary* theory propounded by von Gierke found that the essence of the right lies in the personality alone, of which the property interest remains a subordinate and derivative expression.

Both approaches can be termed aesthetic. Von Gierke's emphasis is on the whole and thus inviolate personality, taken as the point where the manifold attributes of the human person find their locus of unity and reconciliation. Kohler's emphasis is on the dialectical harmonising of the antinomies – the material and the spiritual – that constitute the author's right as a *sui generis* dual prerogative or *Doppelrecht*. The author's right of personality exists independently of yet in synthesis with the author's right of property in the work, the latter itself being a right in an incorporeal property or *Immaterialgüterrecht*. As Kohler (1888: 114) puts it: 'The authors of an intellectual production and of a material product are as different as Homer's poems and the Jacquard loom. But each have the same right: the right of requiring absolute protection of their creative personality.' An authorial right of personality (*Urheberpersönlichkeitsrecht*) is thus synthesised with patrimonial rights which, however, differ from conventional property rights in that they are rights in immaterial objects. For Stromholm (1966: 327) '[i]t is not necessary to insist on the importance of Kohler for the evolution of authorial rights.... The work of this jurist achieves the synthesis of the elements which were available in German doctrine by 1880 and of the practical experience available in French case law.... After Kohler there can be no further doubt: there exists a German theory of personal rights.'

For Kohler (1892: 587) 'the right of personality, that is to say the right for every man to be recognised as a personality of full value, morally and spiritually, is expressed in different ways'. Among these different ways are the material and the moral or personal interests in one's intellectual works. It is, however, one thing to posit a general right of personality but another to specify that right in relation to the creation of intellectual works. To define precisely what is to be protected as the object of the right, normative calculations have to be made. In this sense the limits of the personality have to be decided, something that can be done only by specifying the component parts of the literary 'work' so as to differentiate those which embody the author's personality from those which do not. This distinction cannot be read off from the work in any objective fashion in advance of decisions on what is to be counted as the 'personality' and on how far it should extend. For the law to be actionable not everything can be 'personality'.

In effect, Kohler has no alternative than to propose a set of aesthetic norms to define the process of literary and artistic composition and thus delimit the personality's zone of protected being. To do this he must select an existing scheme of literary composition or analysis and generalise it as the ground of the proposed legal norm. In the event, his recourse is to the traditional rhetoric that subdivides composition into a phase of 'selecting' from the stock of existing ideas or themes – the *inventio* of classical rhetoric – and a phase of 'arranging' those ideas or themes chosen and then 'wording' them – the *dispositio* and *elocutio*. At first sight, this looks like 'having an idea' and 'giving that idea one's personal expression'. However, in advance of the decision as to where to set the limits of the personality, it must remain unclear whether 'having an idea' will fall within or beyond the compass of the (right of) personality. Having thus stipulated two distinct stages in the act of creating a work, Kohler establishes a threshold prior to which there is no imprinting or expression of the personality because it is a matter of something entirely pre-given: the stock idea and theme (*Weltschöpfungsidee*). This is discovered or selected by the author, not created. There would be no surprise for classical rhetoricians in finding a boundary drawn here, between 'idea' and 'expression', *inventio* and *dispositio/elocutio*. However, Kohler's next stage cuts across the familiar assumption that the subjective distinction between idea and expression coincides with the objective distinction between imperceptible and perceptible, immaterial and material. Here the empire of personality is expanded. From the inventory of stock ideas and themes the author forms an ideal notion, a preliminary mental image of the future work. This Kohler terms the mind picture or 'imaginary representation' (*imaginäres Bild*), conceptualising it as a distinct mental form, independent of both the stock ideas and themes and of any perceptible expression or actual material-isation. Kohler (1892: 33) describes it as a 'floating ideal', and counts it as part of the creative intention personal to the author. Being of the personality, this 'imaginary representation' or 'floating ideal' is a proper object of protection by a right of personality. In practical terms, this means that for Kohler the integrity of the personality extends to 'feelings' for the shape of a plot, impressions and intuitions of the future work's structure and argument. The 'imaginary representation' is said to move next through an 'inner form' (*innere Form*). As a further ordering of elements, this provides the plot or skeleton of the work. The 'inner Form' is that which, according to Kohler's schema, will be reproduced in any translation of the original work. Finally, having advanced into the 'inner form', the 'floating ideal' receives its concrete materialisation or expression in an 'outer form' (*äussere Form*); this constitutes the work in its perceptible form of existence.

The extent of protection is decided in accordance with what is taken to be the extension of authorial personality in the 'work'. By including not only the 'inner form' but also the 'floating ideal' or 'imaginary representation', Kohler extends the protective zone beyond the limit of the form in which the work is actually perceptible to others. And granting protection to non-perceptible entities as part of the domain of individual personality could scarcely avoid becoming a matter of contention. Thus the Swiss jurist Ivan Cherpillod (1985) criticises Kohler's approach to the definition of what it is that authors' rights should protect. For Cherpillod, whose analysis informs the foregoing account of Kohler, the problem lies in the German theorist's drift beyond a concern with the concrete work and its objective attributes and into the imponderables of an irredeemably subjective entity: the authorial personality. Cherpillod's 'objectivist' criticism is centred on the notion that the purpose of the law is to protect the work as object (later – in relation to the importing of the *droit moral* into Anglo-American copyright systems – I refer to the perceived risks in basing legal provisions on such 'subjective' grounds and thus requiring courts to determine on aesthetic matters). He thus takes exception to Kohler's proposal – appropriate enough with the latter's aesthetic concern for the protection of the whole personality – to protect the 'imaginary representa-tion', that set of impressions, images and ideal expectations which only the author could know.

Cherpillod is perhaps too rapid in his rejection of the possibility that aesthetics has exercised an influence on the juridical domain. True, he finds evidence in doctrinal and judicial opinions that – in an etymological sense – 'aesthetics' as the science of sensory perception defined by Baumgarten in the mid-eighteenth century might hold a small significance for law on authors' right, but this admission apart, his judgement is dismissive:

In general, aesthetics offers little help to the law on authors' right. Contemporary [aesthetic] philosophy has rejected objective conceptions of aesthetics and subjectivist arguments are dominant. Aesthetics cannot help to define the work given that its object of inquiry is no longer the objective conditions producing aesthetic responses: its analyses are no longer directed at the work. Moreover, the fact of philosophical disputes over aesthetics should be enough to raise doubt in the mind of jurists as to the well-foundedness of references to aesthetics. Since aesthetics divides into divergent currents, it is not clear that it can offer legal science any measure of certainty, unless the law adopts an unquestioning allegiance to a given theory. But this is not what has happened. Besides, legal protection is granted regardless of the beauty of the work in question; by contrast, in aesthetics and in the science of art [*Kunstwissenschaft*], the notion of beauty plays an essential role. Philosophical reflection thus bears on an object which is not that of the law on author's rights. Recourse to aesthetics must therefore be subject to caution.

(Cherpillod 1985: 23–4)

In one sense, the object of philosophical aesthetics is indeed particular to that field, and legal categories do not depend on philosophical discourse. And it is true that just because the law refers to 'literary and artistic' works, there is no reason to refer the law to the philosophical discourse of aesthetics. However, from the historical viewpoint, this doctrinal separation is too neat by half. Cherpillod treats the law as directed to the protection of a particular object – the literary work – and not a particular subject – the authorial personality. Given this stance, it is not surprising that he finds a considerable problem with Kohler's extension of the personality of the author to include non-perceptible elements of the work.

It is, however, in connection with a personality right which finds its exemplary instance in the ethical integrity of the aesthetic persona that the tradition of aesthetics is best recalled. Cherpillod takes the lack of an agreed theory as reason to dismiss aesthetics. His error is to take the object of the law as the protection of the work. We get a different picture of the relevance of aesthetics to the legal sphere when we recognise that the object of protection is the integrity of an exemplary personality, that of the writer as creator of original literary and artistic works.

IV

In the late nineteenth century, as already noted, there occurred an unforeseen but consequential union of French case law and German doctrine relating to the moral or personal rights of authors. From this convergence in the 1880s emerged the theorised concept of the *droit moral* which, by the late 1920s, was to provide the substance of article 6*bis* of the Berne Convention for the

Protection of Literary and Artistic Works. To judge from Kohler's reactions at the time, the intersection of German theory and French judicial decisions on the non-patrimonial interests and rights of authors was less an inevitable harmonisation than a contingent historical overlap of two relatively independent and competitive national tendencies:

> French authors and conference speakers now talk a great deal about a 'moral right' of the author, as if this was a new invention and not what it really is, an inexact expression used to designate the individual right or right of personality which we have proclaimed and recommended for the last quarter of a century.
>
> (Kohler 1906–7: 439)

A theorist such as Kohler could develop the principles of an authorial right of personality with a purity simply not available to courts confronted with the piecemeal factualities of specific disputes. From the French side, however, the view was somewhat different, as is evident when Plaisant and Pichot (1934: 27) commend their nineteenth-century compatriot Morillot for the 'fine study of the protection of works of art, [in which he] succeeded in distilling the concept of *"droit moral"* from the nebulous Hegelianism of German doctrine'. Recht (1969) too regrets the influence on French law of German doctrine concerning the right of personality, Kohler's dualism in particular, for which he takes the *Lecocq* case (see p. 104) as something of an unfortunate triumph. In part this is because Recht wants to establish a continuous and autonomous national tradition for French law on authors' rights, evolving since the eighteenth century. What he gains in continuity, however, he loses in historical specificity: the impact of aesthetic theories and categories and the discontinuity they introduced into legal thinking on authors' rights are muted if those rights are treated as essentially or potentially there from the very start.

As a Scandinavian observer, Stromholm is well placed to arbitrate; he provides a less partisan accounting, characterising the doctrinal achievement of the Germans as an 'empty frame in search of a content' and the corpus of decisions of the French courts as a 'content in search of a frame' (1966: 254). The synthesis of theoretical and applied accomplishments achieved by Kohler in Germany and Morillot in France was clearly not the inevitable unfolding of an exemplary dialectical reconciliation. Matters were more contingent and opportunistic, Kohler drawing on French case law for concrete illustrations of a theory and Morillot drawing on German theory as a guide for the conceptual ordering and theorisation of French practice. What is beyond doubt is that in European legal writing by the end of the nineteenth century a ground had been laid for the recognition of authors' non-patrimonial rights either as 'rights of personality' or as constituting the *droit moral*. The latter term – in the form of 'moral personality' – had first arisen in the *Lacordaire* case – in the 10 June 1845 finding of the Tribunal Correctionnel de Lyon – and was subsequently elaborated in Morillot's (1878: 108–11) study of the legal treatment of artistic works in Germany and France. Building on the contrast between a *droit moral* and the property right, Morillot defined the fundamental right of the author as a 'complete moral sovereignty' over the decision to publish, the attribution of the work to its author, and the protection of the work against unauthorised representation. In international law, and specifically in the Berne Convention, the term *droit moral* became pre-eminent, perhaps because it seems to echo an Enlightenment appeal to respect an essential human attribute and natural right. By contrast, the German development of a category of 'rights of personality' seems more complicit with the tradition of *Bildung*, as a legal part in the great historical task of completing the human subject beyond its present limitations.

Chapter 5

English copyright in the nineteenth century: the missing person

I

At the end of the nineteenth century in England there was no Josef Kohler or *Urheberpersönlichkeitsrecht* elaborated in the sphere of legal doctrine, no Morillot or *droit moral* emerging from a corpus of judicial decisions. This does not mean that the legal existence of authors in England was without complexities. On the contrary, as we shall see in now returning to the sphere of the English law of copyright, an array of legal, commercial and cultural issues exercised legislators, lawyers, publishers and authors alike: the reform of the copyright laws, the role of copyright protection in determining the price of books, the duration of that protection, the growing urgency of protection for British copyright owners in foreign markets – particularly in the United States, the nature of British publishing trade practices and the treatment of authors, for instance in relation to rights and remuneration. Such issues are reviewed in this chapter. However, to plunge into the thick of things, let us turn immediately to a set of comments dating from the time of the report of the Parliamentary Royal Commission on Copyright in 1878. In Matthew Arnold's essay on 'Copyright', the issues that focus the critic's attention are clear enough:

> The three-shilling book is our great want – the book at three shillings or half-a-crown, like the books of the *format Lévy*, shapely and seemly, and as acceptable to the eye as the far dearer books which we have now. The price proposed will perfectly allow of this. The French books of the *format Lévy*, and the French books in octavo, are as shapely and seemly, as acceptable to the eye, as the corresponding English books at double and treble their price. . . . A cheap literature, hideous and ignoble of aspect, like the tawdry novels which flare in the book-shelves of our railway stations, and which seem designed, as so much else that is produced for the use of our middle class seems designed, for people with a low standard of life, is not what is wanted. A sense of beauty and fitness ought to be satisfied in the form and aspect of the books we read, as well as by their contents . . . . For reforming [our book-trade], the signal innovation necessary, as in France, is the three-

shilling book; although of course the price of our new works in octavo at sixteen or eighteen shillings a volume would also have to be reduced in proportion. If nothing of this kind is done, if the system of our book-trade remains as it is, dissatisfaction, not loud and active at present ... will grow and stir more and more, and will certainly end by menacing, in spite of whatever conclusion the Royal Commission may now adopt and proclaim, the proprietary right of the author.

(Arnold 1904: 254–5)

And the author of *Culture and Anarchy* (1869), who was also Her Majesty's Inspector of Schools, continues:

[A] finely touched nature, in men or nations, will respect in itself the sense of delicacy not less than the sense of honesty. The Latin nations, the French and Italians, have that instinctive recognition of the charm of art and letters, which disposes them, as a community, to care for the interests of artists and authors, and to treat them with delicacy. In Germany learning is very highly esteemed, and both the government and the community are inclined to treat the interests of authors considerately and delicately. Aristocracies, again, are brought up in elegance and refinement, and are taught to believe that art and letters go for much in making the beauty and grace of human life, and perhaps they do believe it. At any rate they feel bound to show the disposition to treat the interests of artists and authors with delicacy; and shown it the aristocratic government and parliament of England have. We must not indeed expect them to take the trouble for art and letters which the government of France will take. We must not expect of them the zeal that procured for French authors the Belgian Copyright Treaty of 1854, and stopped those Brussels reprints which drove poor Balzac to despair. Neither in India, nor in Canada, nor yet in the United States has our aristocratic government interposed on behalf of the author with this energy. They do not think him and his concerns of importance enough to deserve it.

(Arnold 1904: 263–4)

There is no doubting the passion of Arnold's critique of the existing English book-trade; he refers to it as 'our highly eccentric, artificial and unsatisfactory system' (1904: 268).

Here is not only a literary author, an authoritative critic of culture and an educational bureaucrat, but also one who is far from ignorant of developments in France and Germany. Indeed, Arnold's essay starts with a reference to George Sand's testimony to the achievement of the Parisian publisher, Michel Lévy, in extending access to good new books at low prices: the *format Lévy*. This commercial initiative Arnold sees as offering the cultural advantage of making available for purchase and possession books of a quality that is simply lacking in the print materials distributed through 'Lending-Libraries'.

These institutions encourage the habit of 'reading imperfectly and without discrimination, . . . glancing at books and not going through them, or rather, . . . going through, for the most part, a quantity of the least profitable sort of books only, – novels, – and of but glancing at whatever is more serious' (1904: 252). If Arnold recommends that English publishers follow Lévy and the French example by introducing cheap books, the recommendation is thus accompanied by a concern for the quality of book – in form and content – to be offered to the mass of purchasers.

What is the relation between Arnold's cultural politics and the nineteenth-century English copyright environment? How does he envisage the impact of copyright law upon cultural activity in general and upon an author's personal relation to his or her own work – to recall the themes of the *droit moral* and the 'right of personality' – in particular? Arnold identifies the essential problem as a system whose 'eccentricity' lies in its being a 'machinery for the multiplication and protection of bad literature, and for keeping good books dear' (1904: 252). Yet he does not directly attribute the lack of inexpensive books to the existence of copyright. This, of course, is precisely what Macaulay had done in the parliamentary debate on the Copyright Amendment Act of 1842 with his celebrated *boutade* that copyright was a 'tax on readers for the purpose of giving a bounty to writers' (Macaulay 1914: 25). We might note that Macaulay considered himself 'one of the richest men of my acquaintance', and this before he reaped the benefit of his best-selling *History of England from the Accession of James II* (1849) and, to a lesser degree, his *Lays of Ancient Rome* (1842), one of the most popular Victorian publications (Gray 1984). Macaulay's target was neither his publisher's (Longmans) nor the English book trade's general high-pricing policy but the copyright concept of an exclusive statutory right of property over what should be a public asset. Arnold, on the contrary, attacks the norms and practices of the trade, not the law and its statutory provisions. Indeed, he suggests that failure to reform English publishing and to reduce the price of books will end by menacing 'the proprietary right of the author'.

Arnold treats the author's right solely in terms of a proprietary and pecuniary interest. And it is in this connection that the constant themes of the times recur: the need to protect the income of English authors and publishers against depradations by foreign 'pirates', specifically the Americans, and – in a section of the essay not quoted above – the further extension of the *post mortem* term of copyright protection (here Arnold shows himself conversant with the provisions made in French and German law). True, while recognising 'that natural instinct in man which makes him seek to enjoy ownership in what he produces, acquires or has', he expresses scepticism as to the author's production being 'really property', both because 'property is the creation of law' and because of the difficulty in giving more than limited legal effect to this 'instinct of ownership' – spoken words cannot be made the exclusive property of their speaker (Arnold 1904: 244–5). Nor is there a suggestion that as a matter of public policy copyright should be a means of promoting the availability of intellectual works to the public through an equitable social contract and exchange between the public interest and the author, in the form of a temporary right of exclusivity to the copyright owner. Arnold is committed to the project of having as many people as possible own 'shapely and seemly' books – the activity of book owning is accorded a civilising power – and read 'more serious' literature. Copyright is not a mechanism that he recognises as contributing to this end. His overriding concern is how to manage the increased access to literate pursuits without exposing 'good books' – the very material of legitimate national culture – to the degenerative and even pathological immoral forces of mass cultural production. It is the school inspector-aesthete's proper concern with establishing and protecting literary taste and cultural competence in that public which has to live with the 'tawdry novels which flare' in railway book-shelves or in the lending-libraries. In these circumstances the possibility of adding to the flood of mass-produced rubbish seems to render the notion of increased access through lower book prices impossibly ambivalent.

There is no suggestion – despite his acquaintance with French and German cultural and legal circumstances – that Arnold has any conception of an author's personal rights or 'dignitary' and non-pecuniary interests. He does not specify those 'interests of artists and authors' which are treated 'delicately' both by the Latin nations with their 'instinctive recognition of the charm of art and letters' and by the Germans with their esteem of learning. Indeed, the fact that his example of such treatment is the bilateral agreement whereby the French and Belgian governments curtailed the Brussels pirates suggests Matthew Arnold had no inkling of the personal rights that Kohler and Morillot were theorising precisely at this time. Yet no English critic was more committed to establishing as a public ideal the profoundly individualistic pursuit of aesthetic cultivation of one's personal and moral faculties, as *Culture and Anarchy* (1869) demonstrates.

The proprietary right and the *droit moral* might well be simultaneous late nineteenth-century phenomena but, on the evidence of Arnold's essay, they are not contemporary or co-present elements within the English cultural-legal environment. Even in 1899, in his *Seven Lectures on the Law and History of Copyright in Books*, the jurist, parliamentarian and man of letters Augustine Birrell, like Arnold, displays a cosmopolitan acquaintance with continental arrangements but with no sign whatsoever of recognising the emergence in France and Germany of an authorial right of personality, either in substance or in name; nor does he register the absence of such a right where English law and authors are concerned.[1] On the contrary, Birrell (1899: 197–8) takes a certain pleasure in documenting his conviction that '[i]ndifference to the money honestly produced by the sale of books has never been a general characteristic of the British author, who for the most part has always taken whatever he could get'. There follows a list of money-minded authors from

Shakespeare and Milton to Pope and Gibbon, Johnson and Goldsmith, Scott, Byron and Macaulay with his 'famous cheque'. And the list continues: 'Carlyle, Dickens, Thackeray, Miss Bronte, George Eliot, Tennyson and Browning were honest men and women who, though they did not exactly write for money, took as much money as they thought they could get for what they had written.'

At one point only might there be the hint of interests of a different order. Contrasting the relations between a publisher and the author of an illustrated trade catalogue with those between a publisher and a book 'of a literary complexion', Birrell observes that 'the negotiation does become a little delicate':

> After all, sneer as you may at the vanity of human wishes, all authors, even the humblest write for fame as well as for money. The author falls in love with his own phrases, however clumsy, with his own generalizations, however hasty, with the puppets of his own fancy, however ungainly – even his epigrams sparkle – and when he goes to a publisher with his 'copy' under his arm, he is in no mood for petty huxtering.
>
> (Birrell 1899: 199)

Despite the drift towards notions of reputation and 'fame', and his mention of what 'all authors' do, what Birrell proceeds to argue is itself more like 'huxtering' than like some embryonic British *droit moral*. The discussion of the relations of authors and publishers is just the pretext for depicting the former in all their commercial and legal illiteracy: 'never was there a set of men so ignorant of the conditions of the trade on which they largely depended as authors' (1899: 201). Birrell does comment on the practical contribution of the Society of Authors, incorporated in 1884, and on the publishers' move to design a 'model agreement between a publisher and an intending author' (1899: 204), but of anything like an author's non-economic 'right of personality' there is no trace. It is not that Birrell had failed to see the true form of authorial personality; he was seeing in all clarity the particular manner of being an author within the nineteenth-century English legal-cultural environment.

II

In the century following the 1774 decision in *Donaldson* v. *Beckett*, the legal conditions of being an author publishing in England went anything but unchanged. The changes, however, were not in the direction of the aesthetic norms of personality emerging in French and German law by the late nineteenth century. In English legislation and case law, the interests of private literary property continued to hold centre-stage. Remedies against acts of unfair competition and restrictive practices grew more elaborate, as did provisions to protect the territorial and imperial interests of British copyright holders. It is not that nineteenth-century English copyright law was ethically or aesthetically deficient; it was simply not an ethical or aesthetic device.

There was no shortage of new domestic legislation. In the Copyright Act of 1814, the fourteen years' protection for new publications provided by the Statute of Anne in 1710 (with possible renewal for a further fourteen years) became a standard term of twenty-eight years or the life span of the author, whichever was greater. This legislation thereby embedded into English law the principle of authorial creation of copyright and can thus be read as if it shifted the emphasis from publisher to author. But there was no notion whatsoever of an author 'controlling' a work once the copyright had been assigned to the publisher. The preoccupations remained with property and the definition of the terms of its recognition and protection, the persisting issue of debate being the duration of the exclusive right both *pre-* and *post-mortem*, and the continuing tendency being to extend the period of protection. These are matters of management. They do not depend on the law developing or recognising a general theory as to the nature of authorship.

In 1814 the principle of authorial creation of a literary property might have been admitted for the specific purpose of calculating the term of copyright protection. However, the ideal of a perpetual property remained – as already noted, there were contemporary reports to the government that Shakespeare's 'copyrights' were still being traded among the publishers and investors. Indeed, certain living authors responded critically to the fact that a time limit – however extended – was established by the new Act. In the pages of the *Quarterly Review* Robert Southey (1819: 212–13) asked 'upon what principle, with what justice, or under what pretext of public good, are men of letters deprived of a perpetual property in the produce of their own labours, when all other persons enjoy it as their indefeasable right – a right beyond the power of any earthly authority to take away?' The answer, for Southey, was not in doubt: 'The decision which time pronounces upon the reputation of authors, and upon the permanent rank which they are to hold, is unerring and final. Restore to them that perpetuity in the copyright of their works, of which the law has deprived them, and the reward of literary labour will ultimately be in just proportion to its desserts.' Personal literary reputation, it would seem, was inseparable from an improved pecuniary reward and a copyright of unlimited duration.

Nevertheless, towards the mid-century, the view of the law of copyright as it stood shifted from that of an exemplary instance of action on the statute sustained by the finding in *Donaldson* v. *Beckett* to that of a grossly inadequate and inequitable provision, the latter judgment itself coming to be seen as an unsound construction. In part this was due to the agitations of literary authors themselves, from Southey and Wordsworth to Carlyle and Dickens (Barnes 1974: 120–6). However, the central player in this drama was one who, 'free from the taint of party, might stand forth conspicuous on other grounds – on grounds of public esteem for public merit; who might advocate the claims of the great and the noble with a kindred spirit'. In these terms – not the characteristic discourse of legal writing today – John Lowndes (1840: 79) records in his treatise on the law of copyright a widely held view of the 'advocate and poet', Thomas Noon Talfourd. Man of letters, friend of authors, parliamentarian and Serjeant at Law, Talfourd's mission was to reform that law, a mission he pursued from the late 1830s with his Bill for the Amendment of Copyright, debated in tandem with the International Copyright Bill that became law in 1838. Arguing that authors from Milton to Coleridge are now 'published for the gain of others than [their] children', Talfourd rejected the lifespan time limit imposed upon an author's exclusive right – 'your law', he proclaimed, 'declares that his works should become your property':

> Surely the mere outlay of him who has perilled his fortune to instruct mankind, may claim some regard. Or is the interest itself so refined – so ethereal – that you cannot regard it properly, because it is not palpable to sense or to feeling? Is there any justice in this? If so, why do you protect moral character as a man's most precious possession, and compensate the party who suffers in that character unjustly by damages? Has this possession any existence itself half so palpable as the author's right in the printed creation of his brain?
>
> (in Lowndes 1840: 95–6)

Yet there were objections to this appeal to a spirit 'beyond the dead level of a utilitarian philosophy'.

The publishers' lobby resisted the notion that the legal assignee of an author's copyright – the one who sustained the risk of loss in its publication – should have the benefit of an exclusive right only for the lifetime of the author while, if Talfourd's proposal were accepted, the right would revert to the author's heirs for sixty years *post-mortem*. In his *Remarks on the Speech of Serjeant Talfourd*, Thomas Tegg (1837: 19–20) argued that the 'expense of making a book known is much greater than the public, and perhaps, than members of the House of Commons have any idea of; and this all falls on the bookseller, who knows the connexion he forms with the book survives the term of the monopoly, and that he retains a sort of good-will property, after the expiration of the copyright, and generally the principal share of the subsequent sale'. Talfourd's response was clear: 'On what principle is Mr. Tegg to retain what is denied to Sir Walter Scott?' On behalf of the publishers Mr Warburton put the matter more bluntly still:

> The object of the author, as of the publisher, is to obtain immediate advances; and is it possible, by any arrangements we can make under this Bill, to prevent authors, first from receiving their advances, and then

parting with the work altogether? Is the author likely, in that case, to make a much better bargain than he does at present?

(in Lowndes 1840: 98)

Talfourd was immune to such utilitarian reasoning, insisting that the question was not one of reward, but one of justice.

Despite the heat generated on both sides, the Bill was repeatedly deferred. And before an amending Bill to the copyright law was passed, Talfourd had lost his seat in the Parliament. Writing in the year of the Copyright Amendment Act of 1842 – known as Talfourd's Act but in fact carried through the House by Lord Mahon – Peter Burke referred to laws which 'tend to the perfection of the copyright law', adding that the new Act

> has a still prouder aim, 'the affording', to borrow its own words, 'of greater encouragement to the production of literary works of lasting benefit to the world'. That labour of the brain, which in general estimation stands the most eminent, has security there; and genius finds a shield which is to guard it from even its own proverbial improvidence. May the statute have the desired effect, and realize, in some measure at least, the great and good intentions of the poet-statesman, and his brother legislators, whose eloquence and exertions, during so long a struggle, led to its enactment. The change in the law of copyright, at any rate, does one thing; it places the nation on an equal footing with other countries in preserving the just rights of manufacturers and authors. There will no longer attach to us the blame, that superior to foreigners in so much, we are inferior to them in that; since our boast may be for the future 'sunt hic etiam sua praemia laudi'.
>
> (Burke 1842: vi-vii)

The theme of English literary culture in its international standing and the theme of Talfourd's campaigning here stand side by side. And indeed, if we were to judge from the fact that Edouard Laboulaye includes three of Talfourd's parliamentary speeches – he is termed 'le plus éloquent, celui qui a pris la chose de plus haut' among the defenders of the rights of authors – in his 1858 treatise on literary property in France and England, or if we were to note that Talfourd's *Speeches on the Law of Copyright* was published in Philadelphia in 1848, we too might fall under the sway of the 'advocate and poet'.

In fact Talfourd's efforts produced little change. Perhaps this is a further instance of the distance between the aesthetic stance and the business of dealing on the floor of the House, where legislative details are actually decided. Not only did the Act of 1842 not restore the author's perpetual copyright, but the legislature rejected the somewhat shorter term of sixty years post-publication that Talfourd had argued for, settling instead on forty-two years or death plus seven. In the case of posthumous publication, a simple period of forty-two years applied. This latter provision Birrell (1899) deems 'highly irrational', since to correlate the grant of copyright with the date of first publication makes 'an author's intellectual output become common property in driblets'. Thus early works could become available for reprinting while later and improved editions of those works are still protected. This was the case with Hallam's *Middle Ages*, first published in 1818 but amended and augmented until 1848, prior to the death of the author in 1859. Under the forty-two year rule, the copyright of the first edition expired in 1860; under the *post-mortem* plus seven years rule, the date of expiration of copyright in the work would have been 1866. 'What', asks Birrell, 'did the cheap booksellers do? One of them, whose surname happened to be the same as Hallam's authorised publisher, reprinted in the interval between 1866 and 1890 the first edition of 1818, and held it out to the world as Hallam's *Middle Ages*.' And he continues: 'This is a grievous injustice to the reputation of a serious and painstaking author. It is an insult to the memory of a man like Hallam that the law of his country should permit so shameful a treatment of his well-considered writings after his death'(1899: 146–7). To remedy this irrationality Birrell recommends the author's life span as the sole basis for calculating, 'for, lottery though it be, it is a lottery in which all have shares' (1899: 149). We should note the date when Birrell was writing. Despite calls for its reform throughout the second half of the nineteenth century from authors' societies and bodies such as the Copyright Association (founded in 1872), it would not be until the Copyright Act of 1911 – which repealed some seventeen previous acts absolutely and others in part – that the Act of 1842 was updated. By then the sphere of copyright law had been altered by the emergence of the Berne Convention in 1887 and the Chace Act of 1891, the latter marking agreement on an Anglo-American regime of bilateral copyright protection.

Beyond the walls of the legislature, the norms of the law were being decided and elaborated by the courts and other review or policy-making bodies. Lord Campbell stirred the literary profession and trade less by his 1857 Act to regulate obscene publication than by the recommendation from his 1852 *ad hoc* committee of inquiry that retail price maintenance in the book trade, being contrary to the freedom which ought to prevail in commercial transaction, should be abolished. The committee had been established as a result of protests against the attempt in 1848 by the Booksellers' Association to fix the price for books. Following the finding of Lord Campbell's committee, the 'trade broke ranks, and the growing number of booksellers who openly defended free trade in books won the day, not least by recruiting the help of a number of authors who supported their case. These included Dickens, Carlyle, who was always a fervent advocate of cheap books and an enemy of the trade, and Tennyson' (Feather 1988a: 146).

It was also Lord Campbell who, in the Court of Exchequer in *Boosey* v. *Purday* (1849), had ruled on whether the protection of English copyright could extend to a work written by a foreigner beyond the shores of England but first published in England. Was the author to be deemed an 'alien ami' and the published work itself to be considered as 'domiciled' in England even though the foreign author was not? The case turned on whether nine of ten arias from Bellini's *La Sonnambula* could be deemed to have enjoyed 'contemporaneous' publication, having appeared in Milan in 1831 at 9 a.m. (or 8.20 a.m. Greenwich mean time) but in London at noon. The court did not in the event have to decide whether, in determining what constituted 'contemporaneity of publication', account had to be taken of fractions of a day. Finding against the plaintiff on the grounds that Queen Anne legislated for her own subjects, the court was of the view that the intention of the copyright statute was to promote the cultivation of the intellect of the Queen's subjects, not to encourage the importation of foreign works and their first publication in Britain.

If *Boosey* v. *Purday* seemed to close access by foreigners to the protection of British copyright, a case decided in 1851 – *Ollendorf* v. *Black* – pointed in the opposite direction. Heard in the Court of Equity by Vice Chancellor Knight Bruce, the case concerned a French language textbook written by a Parisian professor, Henri Ollendorf, and published by Whittaker during the professor's visit to England in 1843. As the assign of an alien author, Whittaker sued Black for importing a 'pirate' copy from Germany for sale at half the price of the 1843 edition. On the ground of the author's residence in Britain, the court granted Whittaker's suit and, rejecting the decision in *Boosey* v. *Purday*, advanced a broader plea: 'Surely literature is of no country, and the object of an act of parliament must be to promote learning generally. That decision is an unfortunate one for literature in this country; for is it not a benefit that the learned men of other countries should publish their works here?' It thus became a rule of English law that irrespective of the place of residence of a foreign author, first publication in Britain made him or her an author within the meaning of the statutes for the encouragement of learning. The issue remained contentious, however, and arose in other cases, until in 1853 the House of Lords judged that while Queen Anne had indeed legislated for her own subjects – that is, for all who were within the British dominium – provided the author was within the Queen's dominions at the instant of British publication, his or her English copyright was secured. Such was the English way of determining the legal personality of authors.

There is no surprise in the fact that the law was the object of criticism. That criticism came not from dialectically informed cultural critique, but from bodies such as the Society of Authors and the Royal Commission on Copyright which, charged in 1875 with bringing order to the tangle of statutes and judicial rulings, in 1878 published its Report on domestic, imperial and international copyright arrangements. We must recognise that the agencies of government have the capacity not only to be critical but to be critical to a definite end:

The law of England, as to copyright . . . consists partly of the provisions of fourteen Acts of Parliament, which relate in whole or in part to the different branches of the subject, and partly of common law principles, nowhere stated in any definite or authoritative way, but implied in a considerable number of reported cases scattered over the law reports.

(1878 Report: para. 5)

The statutes are 'drawn in different styles, and some are drawn so as to be hardly intelligible', but '[t]heir arrangement is often worse than their style' (para. 9). The state of the law was neither rational nor orderly in any practical sense. The Commissioners remark on the irrationality of having different terms and conditions for different copyrights. For instance, the copyright in a lecture that was neither printed nor published was of an uncertain duration, possibly perpetual, but in printed or published form the lecture attracted a protection for twenty-eight years or the lifetime of the author, whichever was the greater (para. 10). Similar incongruities marked the formalities of copyright registration. The owner of copyright in a book could – but the owner of copyright in a painting could not – sue the infringer of his or her copyright prior to registration. And so on. The piecemeal nature of the legislation is evident in the motley of thirteen statutes promulgated between 1838 and 1886. Six of these addressed problems of international copyright (1838, 1844, 1852, 1875 – two statutes, one on international and one on Canadian copyright – and 1886). Four of the remaining seven dealt with customs and excise arrangements (1845, 1853, 1855 and 1876). The other three included the Copyright Amendment Act of 1842 (in which, as noted, the central issue was the duration of protection), the Act of 1847 dealing with foreign reprints, and – the only legislation of interest from the perspective of the non-pecuniary rights of authors and artists – the Fine Arts Copyright Act of 1862. This statute created a copyright in paintings, drawings and photographs, but also included a provision to protect against unauthorised alteration of art works. No comparable provision emerged in relation to literary works and their authors; nor does anything in the 1878 Report point in this direction.

As to the common-law component of the law of copyright at this time, the Commissioners found that '[the] principles which lie at the root of the law have never been settled. The well-known cases of *Millar* v. *Taylor*, *Donaldson* v. *Beckett* and *Jefferys* v. *Boosey* ended in a difference of opinion amongst many of the most eminent judges who have ever sat upon the Bench' (para. 8).[2] And the publishers, it would seem, were no less perplexed by the tangle of rules than the Commissioners:

[W]as [the publisher] aware of the implications for copyright of a subsection in an act concerning customs and excise or merchandise marks, or of a judicial interpretation of a phrase in an act concerning patents? Were his contracts with authors still valid, or did they need revision, when a new act was passed? Were they invalidated by the terms of an injunction in the court of chancery, or a judgment in the court of Queen's bench or common pleas, or on a writ of error in the exchequer chamber, or in the House of Lords? Did he keep abreast of the legislation and the legal decisions of other countries? Did he even, perhaps knowingly, ignore the provisions which his own legislature had devised for his own protection?

(Nowell-Smith 1968: 14)

The Commissioners had to bring a Victorian governmental rationality and reformist administrative skill to bear on the many accidents of the past. Even basic issues remained unsettled. Regardless of *Donaldson* v. *Beckett*, the 'question of whether there is such a thing as copyright at common law, apart from statute, has never been decided, and has several times led to litigation' (para. 12). Noting that some sort of copyright was recognised in newspapers even though 'it is impossible to say what it is', the Commissioners continue: '[i]t has been decided on the one hand that a newspaper is not a "work" within the meaning of the Copyright Act of 1842, and on the other hand that there is some sort of copyright in newspapers, yet the courts have always lent to the opinion that there is no copyright independent of statute; – at all events, they have never positively decided that there is' (para. 12).

Given these circumstances, the Commissioners came down in favour of a proposal to codify the law of copyright:

[W]e recommend that the law on the subject be reduced to an intelligible and systematic form. This may be effected by codifying the law, either in the shape in which it appears in Sir James Stephen's Digest [which accompanies the 1878 Report], or in any other way which may be preferred, and, we think, one of our most important recommendations is that this should be done. Such a process would, amongst other things, afford an opportunity for making such amendments in the substance of the law as may be required.

(para. 13)

As to the nature of the right of copyright, the Commissioners concluded that copyright should continue to be treated as a 'proprietary right' (para. 16). In fact the alternative they considered lay not between a proprietary right and a 'right of personality' but between the former and a 'royalty' system that – had it been adopted – would have displaced the existing law of copyright. As the Commissioners describe it, under this royalty system 'the author of a work of literature or art, or his assignee, would not have the exclusive right of publication, but any person would be entitled to copy or republish the work on paying or securing to the owner a remuneration, taking the form of a royalty or definite sum prescribed by law, payable to the owner for each copy published' (para. 8). The rationale of this 'royalty' system was put to the Commissioners in terms of public benefit – the 'early publication of cheap editions'. They rejected the proposal, though they recognised the cultural and political problems posed by the traditional practice of the English book trade: first the publication of an expensive and relatively small edition, then – but only when the costs are recouped – a medium-priced edition and, finally, 'often a good many years later ... what are called popular editions at low prices' (para. 19).

III

Donaldson v. *Beckett* notwithstanding, there had been no new age of cheap books. The London trade continued in its old ways well into the nineteenth century, giving up little or nothing of its monopoly on the trade in copyrights that existed – as an autonomous concern – alongside the writing and publication of new works. Following one particular instance, Amory (1984) reconstructs the system of *de facto* perpetual copyright that operated – as if regardless of the letter of the law – in relation to an edition of Fielding's *Works* from its first publication in 1762 to its demise in 1821. In tracing this particular bibliographical history, Amory reveals how a tight partnership of booksellers with shares in the Fielding copyright let their competitors produce the separate editions while they themselves concentrated on an expensive but steadily profitable limited subscription edition of the collected *Works*, the latter format being made attractive to purchasers by the use of engraved plates or royal paper (Amory 1984: 467–8). By keeping the private sale of shares in the copyright within their own number, the partnership cornered the upper end of the market and was able to achieve the same profit at lower volume. It was an echo of the 'conger' or cartel developed by the group of London trading booksellers, numbering some fifteen to twenty, which reached its peak in the early eighteenth century as a device to keep ownership of copyright within the trade and to protect the property of copyright holders.[3] In fact the conger – the term was first used in print by John Dunton as a pejorative reference to the cartel from which he had been excluded – was less a partnership than a mode of commercial collaboration. As in the case of the Fielding collected *Works*, the device operated by controlling the private sales of copyrights and parts therein, a single copyright coming to be divided into as many as sixty-four part-shares (Feather 1988a: 69–71).

Although legal conditions alone do not explain the orientation of the English trade towards a low volume but high profit economy, they played their part. Indeed, *Donaldson* v. *Beckett* is said to have 'fostered the emergence of the nineteenth-century publisher in two ways: negatively, by encouraging booksellers with surplus capital to take over defunct copyrights; positively, by directing new money into new properties' (Amory 1984: 468). With the persistence of trade practices such as this, there was no inevitable advance towards a regime of inexpensive books, one in which new fiction was less a luxury commodity than a staple item of cultural consumption and taste. At the time of the 1774 decision of the House of Lords, the cost of novels was around three shillings; following the fiscal demands of the Napoleonic wars in the first decades of the nineteenth century that price rose seven-fold to the figure of half-a-guinea or ten shillings and sixpence. The three-volume or 'triple-decker' that became the standard format for new fiction thus sold normally at a price of a guinea and a half. By and large, pressures for reform of the copyright laws were directed at extending the term of copyright for authors and their assignees, not at reducing the high price of English books.

Yet by mid-century, original fiction had passed from a luxury to become a 'household word', the Shakespearian formula that Dickens adopted as the title of his weekly magazine. Dickens was the exemplary denizen of the mid-century legal-cultural environment, disposed not only to governmental and social reform but also to commercial profit. He was actively concerned with the legal norms and practices bearing on authors and publishers, and on the relations between them. This level of concern can be gauged by the stark contrast between Milton's conveyance of the manuscript of *Paradise Lost* to his publisher (cited in chapter 2) and an 1863 book proposal from Dickens to a publisher:

> In reference to a new work in 20 monthly Nos. as of old, I have carefully considered past figures and future reasonable possibilities. You have the means of doing the like in the main and no doubt will do so before replying to this letter.
>
> I propose you to pay me £6000 for the half copyright throughout and outright at the times mentioned in your last letter to me on the subject. For that consideration I am ready to enter into articles of agreement with you securing you the publication of the work when I shall be ready to begin publishing and the half share.
>
> As I must be rid of the Xmas No. here [the Christmas issue of *All the Year Round*] and the *Uncommercial Traveller* before I can work to any great purpose, and as I must be well on before the first No. is published, I cannot bind myself to time of commencement as yet. But I am really anxious to get into the field before next spring is out; and our interests cannot fail to be alike as to all such points, if we become partners in the story.
>
> Of course, you will understand that I do not press you to give the sum I have here mentioned, and that you will not in the least inconvenience or offend me by preferring me to make other arrangements. If you should have any misgiving on this head, let my assurance that you need have none set it at rest.
>
> (in Sutherland 1976: 79)

In the event, the novelist did not have to make other arrangements, the contract agreed between Dickens and his 'partners in the story' – the publishing house of Chapman and Hall – meeting all his demands. This order of confidence indicates a practical mastery of the legal relations of authorship, not their denial or transcendence. It was a function of Dickens' proven record in satisfying the conditions and routines of large-scale publication for the habitual consumption of new fiction, and of his cultural demographic sense.

The definition of authors' rights by means of the contracts they entered into with publishers was increasingly important. The Act of 1842 enhanced the practice of contract-making by tightening the relevant definitions (Sutherland 1976: 94–5), encouraging the use of contracts to define the author's interests and obligations and to clarify whether – with the agreement between author and publisher – the copyright was to become an exclusive property of the publisher or whether the agreement assigned only the limited right to print and publish the manuscript.[4] In the decade before 1842, however, even major publishers did not necessarily bother with written contracts. In the early 1830s Bentley published Leigh Hunt's *Sir Ralph Esher* without there being any written agreement – the author was simply paid each Saturday on delivery of copy (Sutherland 1976: 231). Given that it remained established practice for authors unconditionally to sign over the interest in the copyright to the publisher, in this quasi-Grub Street style the relationship between the creator of the copyright and his or her trading partner was quite uneven.

Ideally, a written contract spells out the mutual obligations and duties of publisher and author, their mutual expectations being made explicit and their preparedness to enter into a written contract being a token of good intention. From the viewpoint of legal-cultural history, the publishing contract is a surface on which the relations of authors and publishers are defined and specified. In addition, as Sutherland puts it, 'they are uniquely honest documents which record, better than any amount of discursive commentary, the exact state of play between author, publisher and public' (1976: 53). The legal device of the contract – the making of an offer by the publisher, the acceptance of that offer by the author, the detailing of the ways in which the parties will provide consideration or specify what each asks of the other in return for entering into the agreement – can in principle provide a protection of any personal interest that can gain the agreement of the parties. In the world of the 1830s book trade, however, written contracts could still seem an affront to 'word of gentlemen' agreements; moreover, where written contracts were adopted, the powers of the parties were anything but even. Uneven powers do not of themselves constitute duress or deceit such as would render a contract invalid, it being a matter purely for the individual author whether the contract entered into was over-harsh or over-generous. Yet, in practice, the record of nineteenth-century publishing contracts in providing protection for personal or non-pecuniary rights is indeed as uneven as the powers of those entering into the contracts.

Whether or not gentlemanly honour was involved, publication sometimes proceeded without written agreements establishing the mutual rights and obligations of publisher and author. Such a practice was not inappropriate to the circumstance where, having made an outright sale and signed over the manuscript, an author would have no further legal interest in or control over the publishing and dissemination of the work. Where written contracts were employed, they ranged in form from standard pre-printed agreements for non-established authors to contracts tailor-made for those authors with negotiating power enough to give them a contractual presence and personality of the sort that Dickens or Bulwer Lytton pre-eminently achieved. Thus, in 1847, the latter engaged as follows with Chapman and Hall for a cheap collected edition of his works:

It is hereby agreed that the said Edward Chapman shall publish the works of Sir Edward E.G.L. Bulwer Lytton in the form and manner and upon the terms and conditions hereinafter mentioned – that is to say – the said (Chapman) doth hereby promise and agree with the said (Lytton) to print and publish such of the works of the said (Lytton) as the said (Lytton) shall from time to time direct in weekly numbers in the same form as the last edition of the work called 'Pickwick' – but in type a little larger – and that each such number shall sell for the price of three half-pence and no more or less and the expenses of publishing the said numbers shall not exceed in price to be charged to the said (Lytton) the estimate set forth in the first schedule hereinunder written and the account of sales shall be made on the basis of one shilling per every dozen numbers as set forth in the second schedule, hereinunder written as the trade price thereof without any other deduction whatsoever save and except a commission of Ten per cent as appears in the said second schedule and an additional Ten per cent to such country agents as may be appointed subject to the approbation and consent of the said (Lytton) and shall bear and pay all and every expense charge or outgoing whatsoever – save and except the charges set against the proceeds of the work in the first schedule and the expenses of advertising and bear and suffer all bad debts defalcations and lapses of whatsoever nature or kind the same may be and from time to time and at all reasonable times produce and shew forth all and every account accounts memorandum and agreements relating in anywise to the said publication in order the better to evidence the number published being published and sold and the stock unsold and shall pay over to the said (Lytton) the profits of the said works half yearly upon accounts to be settled each and every half year such half yearly accounts to be made up to the Christmas and Midsummer of each year.

(in Sutherland 1976: 58)

The contract maps in detail the relation agreed between author and publisher, but the personal concerns defined in the document relate to an accounting of the property; they do not specify non-economic interests or rights that the author could exercise in relation to his continuing control over the publication of his work.

A similarly entrepreneurial orientation and equal detail mark the contract signed by Mrs Gaskell in 1855, again with Chapman and Hall, for the publication in volume form of her novel *Cranford*:

> Memorandum of Agreement between the Revd. William Gaskell and Messrs. Chapman and Hall for the publication in a cheap form (at two shillings) of 'Cranford' and a Volume of selected tales both by Mrs Gaskell.
>
> Messrs. Chapman and Hall to be at the entire cost of printing, binding and advertising the two books, and to pay Mrs Gaskell a Royalty of Threepence on each copy sold.
>
> This agreement to be binding for two years from the date of publication after which time either party to be at liberty to put an end to it by giving three months notice.
>
> The Accounts to be made up at Midsummer and Christmas and the Royalty due to be paid by the end of February for the Christmas account and the end of August for the Midsummer account.
>
> (in Sutherland 1976: 97)

An authorial personality – a specified set of legally recognised capacities and attributes – is defined in formal terms in a contract whose purpose is to establish certain conditions of authorship. The writing, printing, publication, advertising and distribution of the work become matters of legal business and management, and the writer becomes a properly legal-professional agent. Such developments cannot be explained in terms of some power purportedly inherent in human subjectivity or in literary writing; they reflect in part the results of the campaign by the first Society of British Authors to instruct writers in the importance and forms of contract-making. However, the fact that even these detailed mid-century publishing contracts do not envisage an author's non-commercial interests should not be taken as evidence of the commodification of literature or the repression of subjectivity or any such thing. Too much is happening in these documents to justify such global and undiscriminating judgements. For instance, as Sutherland (1976: 60) describes it, the Bulwer Lytton contract offered 'a steady and supportive income, a *cadeau de saison* every Christmas and midsummer for years to come. An author living on such income was more likely to work consistently than one who was given a lump sum on delivery.' Here we glimpse the emergence of a definite authorial capacity – consistency in production and delivery – which is both a private moral character and the attribute of a professional conduct bound by legal conditions. Consistency of conduct on the part of writers becomes crucial to the system of literary production and distribution developed for the purposes of periodical publications such as *Household Words* and the appropriately titled *All the Year Round*.

Regularising effects might also be associated with the royalty system whereby the author agrees to a remuneration calculated as a fixed proportion of the retail price of the work. By comparison with outright sale and assignment of copyright, the royalty constitutes a continuing connection between the author and the fortune of his or her work after publication. The *OED* gives 1880 as the earliest example of 'royalty' in the sense of a payment made to an author, editor or composer for each copy of a book or piece of music or for a play performed (*Scribener's Magazine* in May 1880 referring to 'Houses which ... paid no royalty to authors'). However, Sutherland (1976: 236) describes Mrs Gaskell's 8 May 1855 contract with Chapman and Hall as the earliest royalty agreement he has located, with the 'Royalty of Threepence on each copy sold' being specified. It is also in 1855 that Charles Reade indicated to the American publisher Fields his preference for the American royalty system over the standard English joint-profit agreement: 'I have proposed to you to treat me ... as a Boston Author, i.e. allow me what you consider just upon each volume sold. I think no arrangement can be so just or wise as this. By it the Author is paid according to his deserts: and is encouraged to write his very best; and we all need this encouragement' (in Sutherland 1976: 89). The American payment system was recommended also in James Spedding's 1867 *Publishers and Authors*, which describes how the Hurd and Houghton company in New York determine the percentage royalty and inform the author accordingly. The author, knowing his probable return, can then explore what other publishers might offer. As Spedding argues, any publisher aiming to make an unjustified profit at authors' expense would soon become a marked man. Yet it remained for the Society of Authors – under the slogan 'No Secret Profits' – to campaign for justice for authors that would flow from proper disclosure of publishers' financial affairs and from the establishment of royalty agreements as normal trade practice.[5] In mid-century English publishing, however, the part-share in profits – if such existed and were declared – continued as the standard practice, as instanced in Dickens' proposal to Chapman and Hall for half-profits in the proposed novel. With time, however, the part-share system became restricted to hack writers.[6] It was, after all, yet another device that helped the trade minimise the risk of loss.

IV

Despite the Statute of Anne and despite *Donaldson* v. *Beckett*, in 1829 a novelist could still contractually engage with a publisher in terms whereby 'On consideration of ... payment ... [the author] binds himself to assign said novel to [Bentley and Co.] and their heirs *for ever*' (in Sutherland 1976: 94; emphasis added). Written contracts did not mean an end to the practice of full assignment of copyright from author to publisher. On the contrary, copyrights remained a form of speculative investment commodity with an existence independent of the work and its author. It was a convoluted trade. Take the case of Bulwer Lytton's copyright in his *The Last Days of Pompei*. In an agreement of 2 April 1833 the author had contracted with Bentley 'that the said Edward Bulwer Lytton Esq. will write a novel in three volumes post 8vo. of the usual number of pages to be published by the said Richard Bentley, who is to pay for the entire copyright of the same the sum of Eleven Hundred Pounds' (in Sutherland 1976: 54). Upon the payment being made, Bentley became sole holder of the copyright that the author had unconditionally assigned to him, thereby relinquishing all say in and control over the treatment of the work from that point. The work was now in principle quite detached from its author and anything but an integral and inalienable part of its author's person. This was merely the beginning of the copyright history of *The Last Days of Pompei*. The book's extraordinary market success enhanced the value of the copyright property which was now entirely Bentley's. When in 1840 the author sought to re-purchase his original copyright, the publisher demanded and received £750 for its partial return, thus recovering most of the £1,100 that he had paid for the copyright in the first place, along with several thousand pounds' profit derived from the novel while sole owner of the copyright. Lytton was not the only 'victim' of what was, after all, a normal trading practice; Dickens, Wilkie Collins and Reade all had similar dealings with Bentley. On the other hand, the author of *Illustrations of Political Economy*, Harriet Martineau, snubbed Bentley's attempt to buy her book on her visit to America. Despite his 'most extravagant terms', she placed the work with Saunders and Otley, on the grounds that her transactions with them 'were always very satisfactory' (Martineau 1983 [1877]: 96–9). Indeed, she refers to Bentley as 'the London speculator'. As to the 'book merchants themselves, who talk of a book as an "article" – as the mercer talks of a shawl or dress' (1983 [1877]: 94), Martineau's views echo those of Matthew Arnold. Publishers traded the copyrights of living novelists without the latter's gain, just as today, in the absence of a re-sale royalty or *droit de suite*, visual artists enjoy no right to share in the increased values realised in re-sales of their works.

As speculative commodities, copyrights had an existence independent of the author, moving from owner to owner for diverse durations depending on investors' calculations of advantage and return. George Routledge made a fortune through purchasing copyrights which others thought worn out. His most famous coup was the ten-year purchase of nineteen of Lytton's copyrights for £20,000, which he started to exercise in 1854 with thirty-five separate volumes, including a twenty-volume 'complete' Lytton for £3.11s.6d. The risk was real and the traditionalists of the trade were not displeased that some years later Routledge was still ten thousand pounds out of pocket. Not even the author believed Routledge would succeed, but he was wrong. By exploiting new channels of distribution – W.H. Smith's railway bookstands – Routledge saturated the market with his Railway Library editions, achieving outstanding returns on what had seemed a dead investment.

If the 1842 Act and campaigns by the Society of Authors encouraged authors not to alienate their copyright entirely or for ever, the reason can be illustrated by the relations between Reade and Bentley. In 1852 Reade signed a half-profits agreement with Bentley for *Peg Woffington*. The agreement was binding 'for every edition' of the work. As an unknown author, Reade did not resist this condition. The edition of 500 copies yielded £10.12s.8d. of half-profit to the author. By 1857, when Reade was an established and increasingly litigious author, he sued Bentley – unsuccessfully – on the grounds that the publisher had issued multiple 'editions' of *Peg Woffington* although the original agreement was for one edition only. The suit confronted the court with having to decide precisely what for the purposes of the law constituted an 'edition', it being decided that an 'edition' means a quantity of books put forth to the bookselling trade and to the world at one time. An impression set up from new type was not deemed a prerequisite for there being an edition. His lesson learned, in 1855 Reade took care to limit Bentley's sole ownership of the copyright in *It's Never too Late to Mend* to a period of just two years. Yet the publisher was more than equal to this challenge. Before this period expired, Bentley printed three-volume editions in August and September 1856, cheap editions in January, February, March and May 1857, a seventh and even cheaper edition in June, and an 'illustrated edition' in the same month. As the publisher wrote to Reade on 11 June 1857: 'I have the copyright for two years only. After that period the property will revert to you, when it will have been planted before the public so carefully that what I have done will be only like sowing the seeds of a rich annual harvest to you and yours for nearly the third of a century.' In responding, the author took a different view: 'Since . . . to have made honestly £3000 from a book for which the author has received £300 is nothing to you unless you can also squeeze one more miserable hundred pounds out and ruin the property to your benefactor, suck the orange dry by all means' (in Sutherland 1976: 87).

In an increasingly differentiated market for books, the right of literary property was itself dispersed, whether into fractions alienated for shorter or longer periods of time to different publishers, or into forms appropriate to new marketing and distribution mechanisms which produced the possibility of multiplying 'subsidiary' rights above and beyond the primary right of reproduction in volume form. Publication of new fiction in parts and magazine publication in serialised form are the familiar examples of this tendency, the model being Dickens' *Pickwick Papers*, a work designed from the start to be divided into packages as an ongoing series of parts delivered to the reader 'warm from the brain'. Only two of Dickens' full-length works did not appear in this format. The emergence in the 1850s and 1860s of large-circulation magazines carrying serialised fiction is also a familiar event in English publishing history. These magazines disseminated new fiction to popular readers in a form which did not require the purchaser to enter a bookshop and be confronted by the questions of the bookseller. *Blackwood's*

Magazine, the *Cornhill* and Dickens' *Household Words* and *All the Year Round* signal a new set of print-literate relations; they also indicate – yet again – that the definition and handling of authors' interests and rights cannot be separated off from the systems of distribution of printed works.

Dickens' proven capacity to sell allowed him to deal with the division of labour between authors and publishers by occupying both their domains himself. For a period from the 1850s to the 1860s, he was both author in and publisher of the fiction-carrying weekly *All the Year Round*. His claim was that there is 'no publisher whatsoever associated with *All the Year Round*' (Dickens 1938: 194), as though the commercial intermediary or interloper – the publisher – had been removed from the scene. Yet as publisher of fellow authors' works, Dickens displayed no particular sensitivity towards their putative 'right of integrity'. On the contrary, as Sutherland (1976: 169) argues, Dickens adopted an editorial stance that 'allowed him not only to hire a novelist but also, if he felt it necessary, to interfere with the course of a story during publication'. Notwithstanding this, Sutherland takes Dickens' dual venture to offer 'a glimpse of the ideal in publisher-novelist relationships' as a 'judicious application of authority and sympathetic intervention make the frequent appeal to "fellowship in labour" something more than a rhetorical flourish on Dickens's part' (Sutherland 1976: 170). In fact, the actual working practices of this supposedly non-alienated 'writing community' suggest that where respect for the integrity of an individual author's work was concerned *All the Year Round* was on a par with Hollywood. Both enterprises have a genius for industrial productivity and the regular creation and reliable distribution of cultural works; however, neither could be considered a haven for the 'right of integrity'.

On the other hand, the array of property rights and related agreements became increasingly complex and difficult to manage. In order to contract an author as contributor to his magazine, Dickens had to operate a four-signature agreement: his own for the serial rights, the author's, his associate's and – for the publication of the work in volume form – that of a major publisher. The separately negotiated rights included the primary right to print and publish the full price volume, the cheap edition rights, the serial rights, the American rights and the European translation rights. These were the legal-cultural circumstances which saw the further mutation of the division of literary labour from which emerged the figure of the literary agent (Hepburn 1968).

An enterprise somewhat less familiar than Dickens' magazines – Tillotson's Fiction Bureau – provides an instance of how new literary property rights emerged, circumstantially, as new uses of copyright material were developed through new modes of distribution.[7] Tillotson's Fiction Bureau developed the syndication of new fiction in Britain and internationally, applying to works of fiction the distribution mechanism used for news in the newspaper publishing system. In the early 1870s, not in London but in the northern

England industrial city of Bolton, Messrs Tillotson and Sons began to purchase the serial rights for new fiction for weekly part publication in their newspaper, *The Bolton Weekly Journal*. As a cost-sharing measure, Tillotson's began to supply the same material in weekly instalments to other regional newspapers, along with an exclusive right of simultaneous publication in the latter's particular territory. This was the start of the Fiction Bureau. A first round of customers for Tillotson's syndicated stories was generated by the opportunity of territorial exclusivity in respect of a cultural commodity with the habit-forming powers of fiction purchased from author-suppliers including Charles Reade, Thomas Hardy, Walter Besant, Rider Haggard and, later, Bennett and Wells – and therefore the opportunity of an audience building and retaining capacity attractive to the shareholders and to advertisers. When the term of the exclusive right within the given territory was ended, Tillotson's would resell the right at a lower price to less prosperous newspapers in yet other districts. By this chain of sales of rights, the Fiction Bureau 'almost certainly furnished newspaper offices in every town of the British Isles' (Turner 1978:67).[8] Eventually, the Tillotson network extended to the British Colonial territories, the United States – a branch was established in New York in the late 1880s – and continental Europe. The latter territory was serviced by a Berlin agent, while the Bolton head office housed translators and foreign compositors able to meet the continental demand for serialised fiction in English and other languages. The Fiction Bureau was one effect of the demographically expanding disposition towards a regular consumption of new fiction, a small foretaste of the situation which obtains today in Europe where some 125,000 hours of television fiction are consumed annually by the populations of the European community.

Tillotson's syndication process had its consequences for the nature and management of literary property rights. The syndicate's concern was to have exclusive control over the serial rights that they then sold to other newspapers. Where authors assigned these rights in exchange for money, the price was calculated per thousand words – in a fashion later echoed, albeit with a different ideological colouring, in Soviet copyright law (Newcity 1978: 84). At £40 per thousand words, Tillotson's highest-paid author was Conan Doyle. Simple payment, not royalties, was appropriate to the serial form of publication. Authors did not, however, always make an outright sale agreement; sometimes they either leased or merely allowed Tillotson's to use the work for a limited time or for a particular occasion (Turner 1978: 63–4). It was thus possible for authors to sell their serial rights to the Bureau while themselves reserving the right to publish in volume form. Nevertheless, through the purchase of entire copyrights, Tillotson's acquired many volume publication rights although they themselves undertook volume publication only in a very limited fashion (1978: 70).[9] The use to which these rights were put is therefore something of a mystery; in some cases they were returned to authors in part payment for later purchases. Along with serial and volume rights, there were also translation rights, as well as rights specified according to the form of publication and the territory in question, such as British and colonial serial rights, continental English language rights, or rights to supply advance sheets to the United States market for serial and volume publication. As Turner (1978: 72) observes of this 'parcelling', Tillotson's marketing of fiction 'helped to establish the trend towards the division of literary property into different types of publishing rights'.

The Fiction Bureau's practice did not involve the division of a unified right in the manner of the eighteenth-century London book cartel which would divide a single copyright into many shares as a means of risk-spreading. Rather, the Bureau developed new uses of copyright subject-matter and, as a consequence, new subsidiary rights; these were contingent upon the particular technology of distribution, the investors' commercial acumen and – of course – the establishment of a readership now predisposed to a more or less constant consumption of new fictional works. While the literary works that were serialised 'may have left a lot to be desired from the literary point of view, there can be no doubt that [they] did at least establish the habit of reading in many thousands, and possibly some hundreds went on to more worthwhile things' (Turner 1978: 72). Through the increasingly ramified channels of the Fiction Bureau the limits of the literate population were reached.[10] However, being contingent upon the opportunities arising from unforeseen forms of print distribution, these diverse tributary rights of copyright are not amenable to explanation in terms of subjectivity in some general philosophical sense.

V

Although there is good reason not to assume that the same forms of law and legal personality inevitably develop in all jurisdictions, it is allowable to ask why a *droit moral* or right of personality did not emerge as an object of protection in late nineteenth-century English law of copyright. It had been in England that the first statutory base was laid for the copyright protection of literary works, yet neither in subsequent copyright legislation and case law nor in doctrine did there emerge a specific notion of protectable non-pecuniary interests attaching to the authorial status. This was the case even though English models of individual self-fashioning were among the essential sources of Schiller's 'aesthetic education', and even though the complex phenomenon of English Romantic culture sometimes displayed a markedly individualistic bent, coloured in part by the profound influence of German ideas on key figures such as Samuel Taylor Coleridge. Nor did the law of copyright remain entirely closed to the influence of literary culture. As Kaplan (1967: 24) suggests, '[i]n placing a high value on originality, the new [Romantic] literary criticism ... tended to justify strong protection of intellectual structures in some respect "new", to encourage a more suspicious search for appropriations even of the less obvious types, and to condemn these more roundly when found'. The simplest explanation of the non-emergence of an authorial right of personality in England is chronological: first, the law of copyright was an established and familiar working system in the British territories long before aesthetics arrived on the cultural scene purporting to be general theory of 'man's' individual and social development, and long before the theory and practice of the *droit moral* had established itself in certain continental jurisdictions. In these conditions, even if it had been sought, a transplant of the continental norm was difficult. Second, there were existing common-law remedies – albeit not part of the copyright law – to which an author could have recourse to gain redress against 'personal' injuries to honour and reputation and against misrepresentation. In this sense, it might be argued that a separate 'right of personality' was redundant in Britain. And third, we should perhaps question the assumption that an idea circulating in the sphere of literary philosophy – the Romantic ideal of an authorial subjectivity unfolding into its completion – could necessarily play a directive role in relation to shifts within the legal sphere.

It is therefore less surprising that the body of English authors – though neither small nor pusillanimous – failed to pursue in the English courts the protection of their specifically non-pecuniary interests. From Wordsworth to Dickens and Arnold, copyright was a proprietary matter, and personal only in this sense. Hence Wordsworth's 1838 *Plea for Authors*:

> Failing impartial measures to dispense
> To every suitor, Equity is lame;
> And Social Justice, stript of reverence
> For natural rights, a mockery and a shame;
>   Law but a servile dupe of false pretence
> If guarding grossest things from common claim
> Now and forever, she, to works that came
> From mind and spirit, grudge a short-lived fence.
>   'What! Lengthened privilege, a lineal tie
> For *books*!' Yes, heartless ones, or be it proved
> That 'tis a fault in us to have lived and loved
> Like others, with like temporal hopes, to die;
>   No public harm that genius from her course
> Be turned; and streams of truth dried up, even at their source!

Works might come 'from mind and spirit', but the Lakeland poet's sense of authorial rights extended no further than strengthening the family inheritance. However, Eilenberg (1989: 369) has argued that 'the real object of Wordsworth's efforts to reform copyright was to secure a refuge from oblivion, a means to enable writing to transcend itself'. Perhaps so, but she also points out that when his literary politics turned to the matter of copyright, he had not even read the law – although, predictably, Wordsworth regarded the common-law right as the ground of authors' claim to a property in copyright.

And yet there are signs that English arrangements could have been other than so single-mindedly pecuniary. It is not just a matter of there being alternative common-law routes – the law of contract, actions for libel, passing-off and such – to the protection of personal interests. Rather, it is the sort of possibility suggested in the letter written by the political economist and novelist, Harriet Martineau, to the Secretary of the Society of British Authors, a year after passage of the Copyright Amendment Act of 1842:[11]

> Perfect copyright laws would aid us to a certain extent: but what we want more in relation to the price of our books, is mutual assistance to extricate us from the transition between old patronage, and that free communication between speaker and hearers – writers and readers – which must be arrived at sooner or later.
>
> (in Bonham-Carter 1978: 87)

'Perfect' copyright, it seems, could contribute to a transformation of the relations of writer and reader. In the figure and career of Dickens, this idea of a more direct – and thus more personal – communication between author and reader found a material realisation on a considerable scale, it being estimated that at one point his readers made up half the population of metropolitan London (Sutherland 1976: 168). Dickens' magazine *All the Year Round* based its appeal on the running serial publication of new long fictions that occupied five or more of the twelve pages of the two-penny weekly publication. Not only did the authors have to master the technique of advancing the narrative while closing each episode with an adequate charge of suspense and anticipation; the readers' capacities too were trained up into this rhythm of literary distribution:

> Weekly intervals meant that a reader came to every installment primed, which was not the case with monthly serialisation where the plot had that much longer to fade in the memory. Readers became very sharp indeed, bringing to the mystery stories *All the Year Round* favoured the keenness of amateur detectives. Wilkie Collins was pulled up for some slight contradictions in the time setting of *The Woman in White*, Lytton for the solecism of having a man tried *in absentia* in an English court. *All the Year Round* came to specialise in fiction that wasted no time in making an impact on the reader. Hence its preference for autobiographical narrative (four out of the first six full-length novels had 'I' narrators).
>
> (Sutherland 1976: 172–3)

Regularity of consumption and pleasure, recognisable modes of address, satisfaction of generic preferences and fidelities all produced particular relations between Dickens' journal and its readers. These technical factors are important. The identification and involvement of the broadening population of readers depended on their mastering of new literate techniques and acquiring new literate abilities – a new reading persona.

As for the writers, to participate in this exchange they had to produce thirty thousand words per month for more than six months without break. Failure to master the particular writing techniques appropriate to serial publication meant the potential loss of any readership. Dickens' directives to his authors are stark and clear: to Charles Lever he reports that 'we drop, rapidly and continuously, with *The Day's Ride*', while to Wilkie Collins concerning *The Woman in White* Dickens writes that he seems 'to have noticed, here and there, that the great pains you take express themselves a trifle too much, and you know that I always contest your disposition to give an audience credit for nothing, which necessarily involves the forcing of points upon their attention, and which I have always observed them to resent when they find it out – as they always will and do' (in Sutherland 1976: 177–82). With his enormous readership, Dickens as editor specifies the authorial techniques of the new print intimacy. In this intensification of personal relations *via* print, he was not by any means the sole practitioner, Mayhew too having built up a reliable relation with his readers through the correspondence columns of the *Morning Chronicle* and later on the wrappers of the parts of *London Labour and the London Poor*. There were also the 'slum publishers' such as Reynolds and Lloyd, with their penny publications. In the pre-history of these nineteenth-century arrangements lie print experiments such as John Dunton's question and answer technique (see p. 47), itself appropriated from religious casuistry as the selling-point of his *Athenian Mercury*. Just as the casuist enjoyed a special relation with the one who sought direction on a case of conscience, so Dunton's format generated a quasi-casuistical relation of exchange between his 'Athenians' and the eager 'querists', although a reader entered into an imaginary relationship with Dunton's materials for a personal end which was not always that of grace.

By the mid-nineteenth century the capacity existed for a specific exchange between the writers and readers of what can be termed 'educative' fiction, resting on a close didactic relationship of author to reader. Such fiction – identified with the signatures of Dickens and George Eliot, Thackeray and Trollope – disseminated norms of moral self-discipline and capacities for taste more directly and intimately than did popular schooling. The cultivated sense of proximity of author to reader helped make these lessons sought after and familiar as 'household words'. In these circumstances, through the personal proximity with his or her readers, an author might acquire an elaborate authorial persona, but was it one to be fully and specifically recognised in the sphere of an author's legal existence? Copyright law – in doctrine and in application – remained immune to any such personalising or extra-proprietary development. Its object remained that of a trade regulation statute: the printed book as a traded commodity. Indeed, whatever might be the assumptions of literary and aesthetic critics, the fact is that among the cases of copyright infringement actually litigated *literary* publications did not show up as a specific category of protected works calling for a special form of treatment.

This was a matter of regret to Birrell, in 1899, reviewing the reported cases from the previous one hundred years:

> You cannot overlook the literary insignificance of the contending volumes. The big authors and big books stand majestically on one side – the combatants are all small fry. The question of literary larceny is chiefly illustrated by disputes between book-makers and rival proprietors of works of reference, sea charts, Patterson's 'Roads', the antiquities of *Magna Graecia,* rival encyclopedias, gazetteers, guide books, cookery books, law reports, post office and trade directories, illustrated catalogues of furniture, statistical returns, French and German dictionaries, Poole's farce, 'Who's Who?', Brewer's 'Guide to Science'. This is not by any means an exhaustive list but it accurately shows the nature of the proceedings.
>
> (Birrell 1899: 170–1)

As a gentleman of letters and a barrister concerned with copyright matters, Birrell shows dismay at the absence of literary names and cases, complaining that the 'question of copyright has, in these latter days, with so many other things, descended into the market-place, and joined the wrangle of contending interests and rival greedinesses' (1899: 195). These high tones imply – wrongly – that copyright had started somewhere other than the marketplace. For its cultivated users literary fiction could well become the privileged index to the personality of author and reader; within the sphere of English copyright law, however, developments in the cultural department of existence have no necessary purchase.

Nevertheless, in the mid-nineteenth century, a personality rationale for the grant of a property in copyright emerged alongside the Lockean labour model. Although not concerned with rights other than the economic, it was a view that saw copyright as rewarding the author's unique and individual contribution, the work's originality consisting in a distinctive execution that in turn rests on an authorial exercise of subjective judgement. In 1854, in *Jefferys* v. *Boosey*, Lord Justice Erle thus based a grant of protection on the analogy between the work and its author's physiognomy: 'in ordinary life no two descriptions of the same fact will be in the same words. . . . The order of each man's words is as singular as his countenance.' As Ginsburg (1990b: 1874) observes, it is evidence that in English law there were now two different views of what made a work of authorship original.

Chapter 6

The USA: a legal republic and a literary industry

I

Legal circumstances in late nineteenth-century Britain and the United States posed a dilemma for Henry James. In 1879 the novelist was arranging for *A Portrait of a Lady* to be serialised in Britain in *Macmillan's Magazine*, having already contracted for it to be published in the United States in William Dean Howells' *Atlantic Monthly* (Nowell-Smith 1968: 80–4). However, Howells was not well disposed to the prospect of the serial publication in his Boston magazine appearing at the same time as the London serialisation in *Macmillan's*, since imported copies of the British magazine competed with the *Atlantic* in the American market. With James' help, Howells was seeking to publish one of his own novels simultaneously in the *Atlantic* and in the *Cornhill Magazine* in London. The two magazine editors and James agreed that *A Portrait of a Lady* would start in *Macmillan's* in London in October 1880 and in the *Atlantic* in Boston one month later, thus meeting the requirement of British copyright law for prior publication in Britain. But the result of this arrangement was that copies of *Macmillan's* reached America and reviews of James' new novel appeared in American newspapers before American subscribers to the *Atlantic* received the issues that carried those instalments. Had the instalments been published in both magazines in the same monthly issue, James would have risked his British copyright because the publication date of the *Atlantic* was the fifteenth day of the previous month.

To occupy the status of copyright holder in both British and United States territories an author based in Britain was thus confronted by disparate requirements. In the case of the serial publication of *A Portrait of a Lady* it was necessary to observe the British law's requirement of prior publication in Britain if protection was to be secured there. It was convenient for James that American copyright could be secured by meeting the formal condition of registration with the Copyright Office before publication. This legal series – registration in Washington, publication in London and publication in Boston – was complicated, however, by the commercial fact that copies and reviews of the English publication were circulating in Boston before the Boston publication was available to American subscribers eager for James' latest fiction.

Not that it was plain sailing in the eastward direction. Under British law, while copyright was created by the act of publication, it was necessary for the author to be within Queen Victoria's dominions at the instant of publication, even if only for the purpose of securing copyright. United States authors – Nathaniel Hawthorne and Oliver Wendell Holmes, Mrs Stowe and Louisa Alcott included – visited Britain, Canada or the West Indies on publication days. This juridico-touristic practice was to end only with the 1891 Anglo-American copyright agreement.

II

A century earlier, other contingencies had marked the framing of the clause in article 1, section 8 of the Constitution that confers on the Congress of the United States the power to 'promote the Progress of Science and useful Arts, by securing for limited times to Authors and Inventors the exclusive Right to their respective Writings and Discoveries'. The relation of this constitutional provision to English common-law copyright is much debated; this question too is coloured by certain accidents of chronology. It has been argued by Whicher (1962: 133) that the fourth edition of Blackstone's *Commentaries on the Laws of England* exercised a determining influence on copyright legislation in late eighteenth-century America at state and federal levels. This edition of the *Commentaries* was published in England after *Millar* v. *Taylor* (1769) but before *Donaldson* v. *Beckett* (1774), a circumstance that allowed Blackstone's natural right theory of common-law copyright to find its seemingly definitive confirmation in the 1769 decision, with no hint whatsoever of the imminent reversal of that decision in 1774. In pre-revolutionary America, the *Commentaries* were published only in Robert Bell's 1770–1 Philadelphia edition – reprinted precisely in 1774 – of the fourth English edition. The issue of whether under English law an author's common-law right outlived the statutory copyright had an evident bearing on whether Congress' federal Copyright Act of 1790 would pre-empt any state common-law right in works after publication. Yet the determination of this matter was contingent upon which edition of Blackstone's *Commentaries* was available in the United States.

There is also the issue of whether James Madison – one of the framers of the Constitution – might or might not have known of *Donaldson* v. *Beckett* from the fourth volume of *Burrow's Reports*. This volume appeared in England in 1776 and carried a combined report of the recognition of authors' common-law right in *Millar* and the 1774 reversal of that decision in *Donaldson*. Whicher admits that Burrow's fourth volume is cited in American decisions in 1781, although he notes that '[p]robably some Tory lawyer left the book behind when the British evacuated Philadelphia in 1778':

> Nor is it as strange as it may at first blush appear that a whole continent of English-speaking people, many of them able lawyers, were unaware of the House of Lords' decision in *Donaldson* v. *Beckett* nearly fifteen years after it had been rendered. Other more important matters had, after all, been occupying their attention in that interval: a long and arduous war of independence, the establishment of new forms of government, and the severe post-war economic trials which had led, in New England, to actual armed insurrection. Surely, with all these difficulties and dangers on their minds, Americans of that era may well be pardoned for their provincial ignorance of Grub Street's *cause célèbre*.
>
> (Whicher 1962: 136–7)

Added to this is a further chronological factor concerning the status of *Donaldson* as legal authority in United States territory. Because it was published after the American Revolution, Burrow's fourth volume and the English decisions it contains were no longer evidence of American common law (Whicher 1962: 138). According to Whicher, the earliest reported American reference to *Donaldson* v. *Beckett* dates from 1808, more than twenty years after the Constitution had been written. It is possible to appreciate Whicher's historical sense without acceding to his argument that alongside the statutory copyright there existed and indeed exists a common-law author's right before and after publication, a position contested by Abrams (1983) who insists on public benefit as the fundamental value underpinning the copyright clause.

Wheaton v. *Peters* (1834) is the American counterpart of *Donaldson* v. *Beckett*. In the third volume of the *Condensed Reports* Richard Peters, the Supreme Court reporter, included certain cases previously reported and published by Henry Wheaton, his predecessor in office. Wheaton and his publisher injunctioned Peters, claiming infringement of copyright under both statute and common-law provisions. In response the defendant argued that Wheaton had not complied with the prerequisites for statutory protection, that there was no common-law copyright and that the material in question was not eligible for copyright protection (Patterson 1968: 203–12). Where Wheaton's claim of common-law protection was concerned, the court accepted an earlier ruling to the effect that the United States as a federal government had no common law. While the individual states followed English common law, this had not been wholly or uniformly adopted by every state. Moreover, common-law copyright was not judicially recognised in England until *Millar* v. *Taylor* in 1769, by which time a state such as Pennsylvania had developed law and customs of its own (*Wheaton* v. *Peters*: 659–60). And not only that, the English cases had left it unclear whether a common-law copyright continued to exist upon the adoption of a statute. For these and other reasons, the court declined to grant the injunction, but advised Wheaton to try his claim as to the existence of a perpetual common-law right in a court of law, rather than in equity.

Instead Wheaton went directly to the Supreme Court which, in a majority verdict, also found against him. Among the dissenting views, Mr Justice Thompson held that there was a common-law right of property, founded upon the individual author's intellectual labour:

> The great principle on which the author's right rests, is, that it is the fruit or production of his own labour, and which may, by the labour of the faculties of the mind, establish a right of property, as well as by the faculties of the body; and it is difficult to perceive any well-founded objection to such a claim of right. It is founded upon the soundest principles of justice, equity and public policy.
>
> (*Wheaton* v. *Peters*: 669–70)

This alignment of public policy with a Lockean natural right of the author to perpetual copyright supposes that copyright was a 'right unlimited by passage of time, transfer of ownership, distribution of copies or any other consideration' (Abrams 1983: 1181). The purpose of the federal copyright statute was not to curtail the common-law right but to confer a definite remedy to authors whose common-law right had been infringed. This view, however, did not prevail in *Wheaton* v. *Peters*. In their consideration of the nature of copyright, the Supreme Court majority found that the interests of the author should not be protected beyond a point in time at which the public benefit suffers. The court thus drew a limit to the copyright owner's exclusive right, confirming it as a right created by the statute. The author's interest might be absolute prior to publication and protected as such by the common law, but with publication the social contract between author and public comes into play:

> A book is valuable on account of the matter it contains, the ideas it communicates, the instruction or entertainment it affords. Does the author hold a perpetual copyright in these? Is there an implied contract by every purchaser of his book, that he may realize whatever instruction or entertainment which the reading of it shall give, but shall not write out or print its contents?
>
> (*Wheaton* v. *Peters*: 657)

In the opinion of the majority, the rationale of copyright rested on the usefulness of the book to the general interests of American society, not on a perpetual protection of the author's property.

The differences of judicial opinion as to the underlying principles of copyright is a sign of the persisting uncertainty of the early American cultural-legal environment as to the precise legal status of authors. Although through *Burrow's Reports* the Supreme Court had access to both *Millar* v.

Taylor and *Donaldson* v. *Beckett*, what the judges took from the reports was less the vote of the House of Lords than the opinions of the eleven Law Lords. Burrow did not record the arguments and opinions of the Lords in reaching their decision, only the views of the judges, as if these were the essence of the matter. Among the judges, as we have observed in chapter 2, opinions tended against the Lords' final decision, six of the eleven advising that a perpetual copyright existed at common law but had been 'impeached' or 'taken away' by the Statute of Anne. As Abrams (1983: 1170) remarks, this confusion between the judges' opinions and the decision of the House was compounded by Burrow's error in summarising those votes. Yet it was on *Burrow's Reports* that *Wheaton* v. *Peters* was in part decided. Not that historical contingencies went entirely unnoticed at the time. As Mr Justice McLean observed, copyright had been a method of enforcing censorship and was not based on any concept of protecting the rights of authors.

In practice, the historical alternatives of public benefit or authorial right were never quite so neat, nor the priority of the former so blindingly clear. The division of judicial opinion in *Wheaton* demonstrates how the argument for copyright as protecting the personal interest of authors and the argument for copyright as protecting the public interest of society in general co-existed in America in the early nineteenth century. Indeed, these two rationales – one personalist and the other grounded in public interest – are already co-present in pre-Constitution sources such as Noah Webster's 'Origin of the copyright laws in the United States', where the author recounts his attempts to raise the level of American education in 1782 by publishing two textbooks – including his American spelling book – and his efforts to get state legislatures to protect such publications. His 1783 petition to the New York legislature sought 'to secure to your petitioner the benefits of his own labours to which he considers himself solely entitled but which are not protected by the laws which protect every other species of property'. The legislatures of New Jersey and Pennsylvania were not in session, so Webster approached professors at Princeton and the University of Pennsylvania who endorsed his efforts, attesting that 'it is by such attempts that systems of education are gradually perfected in every country, and the elements of knowledge rendered more easy to be acquired'; therefore 'Men of industry or of talents in any way, have a right to the property of their productions; and it encourages invention and improvement to secure it to them by certain laws, as has been practised in European countries with advantage and success' (in Ginsburg 1990a: 1000). Nor should we therefore be surprised if some early American state copyright laws 'set forth author-oriented rationales of which any [post-Revolution] Frenchman would be proud', as Jane Ginsburg (1990a: 995) has argued. In support she cites the authorial orientation of the preamble to the Massachusetts Act of 1783 which, in relation to promoting learning and encouraging writers 'to make great and beneficial exertions', refers to their capacity to have the 'legal security of the fruits of their study and industry to themselves', adding that 'such security is one of the natural rights of all men, there being no property more peculiarly a man's own than that which is procured by the labor of his mind'.[1] Such exchanges were materially possible in the Franco-American networks of the Enlightenment, where a figure of integrity such as Benjamin Franklin could become an exemplar for the ideal and future form of life.[2]

III

Given our usual Romantic habits of mind, there is reason to be as historically stringent as possible in approaching any pre-Romantic cultural milieu such as that in which the early American copyright statutes were enacted. It is a matter of recognising the historical specificity of the turn-of-the-century environment and thus avoiding the anachronism that consists in viewing that environment in terms of a configuration of the law – as guarantor of authorial personality – that was in part to emerge in Romantic aesthetics. In fact 'literature' had not yet taken on the aesthetic attributes which we now recognise when distinguishing between 'literary' and 'non-literary' types of writing and reading. This distinction is perfectly intelligible for us; however, in the late eighteenth century, 'literature' still referred to written or printed matter of any kind, the restricted aesthetic sense of the term being, as the *OED* states, 'of very recent emergence in both English and French'. This is another of those historical differences that we should not flatten by imposing our category distinctions on to another pattern of cultural organisation and activity.

In the eighth volume of the *American Bibliography* Evans (1941) shows that under the first United States copyright statute the years 1790–2 saw the publication of 441 works of political science, history and social science, but only 43 'novels'.[3] The bulk of the novels were reprints of works by English authors, including three editions of Defoe's *Robinson Crusoe*. But what was *Robinson Crusoe*? More particularly, was it read in a way which placed it clearly outside the category of 'instructive' and 'devotional' publications? Recent studies recontextualise Defoe's 'novel' into the complex of Puritan ethical practices for forming a devout and conscientious personality; in other words, the 'novel' rejoins a specific set of Puritan literary genres: spiritual autobiography, spiritual diaries, casuistry, providence literature, conduct books (Starr 1965, 1971; Slights 1981; Hunter 1966 and 1990). The text of *Robinson Crusoe* records an array of model techniques of devotion and moral self-examination, of advice on how to read the signs of Providence which might restore a life of backsliding to a more devout course. Moreover, it contains detailed examples of how to use the literate means – diary keeping, spiritual autobiography, casuistical questioning – that helped produce the quality of human being needed for the Puritan regime and, perhaps, for the civic life of the new American republic. As Weber (1930: 119) puts it, '[t]he

Puritan, like every rational type of asceticism, tried to enable a man to maintain and act upon his constant motives, especially those which it taught him itself, against the emotions. In this formal psychological sense of the term it tried to make him a personality.' Given this historical connection between didactic writing and reading for an ethical and person-forming purpose and what later came to be called 'novels', we must be alert to the possibility that in its contemporary milieu a 'novel' such as *Robinson Crusoe* was bought and read because it played a useful and instructive role.

As in the English cultural-legal environment, 'literature' in the restricted aesthetic sense did not loom large in the field of copyright, in either doctrine or litigation. The federal Act of 1790 – 'for the encouragement of learning by securing copies of maps, charts and books, to the authors and proprietors of such copies' – treats copyright as being a protection for works that are 'useful'. Yet the principle was one thing, the historical practice another. In his history of book publishing in the United States, Tebbel (1972: 142) observes that from 1790 to the turn of the century only 556 books were registered for copyright protection out of the 13,000 published, commenting that '[o]bviously the idea and opportunity of copyright were not grasped by everyone overnight'. In fact a rather different observation can be made on this discrepancy between the protection made available by the federal Copyright Act in 1790 and the actual pattern of activities of American publishers. In the years of the establishment of American publishing as a mass-production industry, copyright was not materially necessary to profitability, however attractive the idea of it might have been. The 1790 Act was both a republican ideal and an instrument of governmental 'policing', aimed at enhancing the levels of national education. The commercial fact of the matter, however, was that in the United States – unlike in Revolutionary France or the German territorial states in the period of piracy – the book market was less than regulated not because the legislative apparatus was lacking but because the publishing industry worked profitably largely to one side of the legal principle and provisions of copyright. This was possible in that particular circumstance where American publishers could draw without statutory risk or financial cost on the copyright products of British authors and publishers, reprinting works that had no protection in the United States. As noted in another connection, such reprinting was not illegal, even though it might be deemed unethical.

There were pragmatic public policy reasons for the United States to desist from regulating the reprint industry – the 1790 copyright statute allowed the free importation, vending, reprinting and publishing of any book written or published abroad by any person not being a citizen of the United States and in this way provided affordable English-language reading matter for the growing population. Yet there were also protectionist and anti-British objectives in US publishing policy. The great American reprinters thus add a further geopolitical variant to the history of law and authorship. In American territory, the absence of international copyright protection meant that the works of foreign publishers or authors were in the public domain. Unauthorised reprinting in these circumstances was not piracy; it allowed and accustomed American readers to buy books at a price which was lower to the extent that it did not include remuneration to the proprietor of the English copyright. Pricing benefits also flowed from the ethos of competition between American reprinters of this unprotected literary raw material.

Geographical and technological factors were involved too. Given continental spaces, the emergence of a national economy, a system of mass production and distribution in the new cylinder press and railroads, population growth and urbanisation, American publishing tended to disperse in a number of cities rather than concentrate in one metropolitan site. As in Germany, semi-annual book trade fairs channelled books to their markets, assisted by the network of railways, commercial travellers and mail order. Books, as noted above, do not disseminate themselves. With a population smaller than Britain's but a reading public that was larger – the white adult population was over 90 per cent literate by mid-century when the United States represented the largest literate public there had ever been (Tebbel 1972: 257–9) – larger editions and lower per-volume price were the rule. For instance, in the United States ten thousand copies of *The Mill on the Floss* at one dollar apiece were sold within four days of its launch. In Britain, Blackwood's were satisfied to wait to clear just 6,500 copies of the novel at a guinea and a half (or $5.50). As a rule of thumb, the Americans operated at four times the size of edition and a quarter of the cost of the British publishers. The biggest American firms grew to dwarf their transatlantic counterparts. There was nothing in London to rival Harper Brothers who, by mid-century, occupied seven five-storey buildings and turned out over 2,000,000 volumes a year.

And yet, in the absence of an agreement on international copyright, the huge and technologically sophisticated American industry drew largely on English materials: devotional texts, dictionaries, technical writings, histories and fiction. Harpers' first catalogue contained 234 titles of which 90 per cent were English reprints, the same pattern being true for Wiley and for Putnam. As non-citizen authors of works published outside the United States, English writers from Wordsworth to Dickens could only be indignant at the use of their works to subsidise the profits of American reprinters and the literary consumption of American readers. In fact, either directly or through their agents, British publishers could market their British-produced works in the United States but without copyright protection. If a British author or publisher had authorised an American publisher to reproduce their works for the American market, in some instances they received *ex gratia* payments from the latter. To complicate matters, however, the contracts drawn up between the authorised 'pirate' and the author would contain a clause 'to the effect that in the event of an unauthorised reprint appearing [on the US market] the royalty would cease' (Nowell-Smith 1968: 74), given the consequent threat to profitability. Despite competition for market share, the American publishers established a certain level of self-regulation through 'courtesy of trade' agreements whereby one publisher would not reprint a British book to which another had a prior 'claim', at least until that particular edition was sold out. In this way the supply of British fiction was shared. As to whether this irregular situation should be regularised, there was no consensus among American publishers. Harpers, the largest printer-publishers in the United States, maintained a resolute opposition to any copyright agreement with Britain, while Putnam was for the principle of such regulation.

It was in this circumstance that 'The Game' emerged. This was a form of self-regulation in which English sources and American publishers found a measure of mutual benefit. As Sheila McVey (1976: 191) has described, '[s]uccess in The Game hinged on being the first to put a popular British reprint in the hands of the American public'. Because any publisher could reprint unprotected British works, it seems that rival American publishing houses went as far as bribing publishers' clerks and printers in England so as to obtain advance sheets of imminent British publications. Granted the irregular circumstance of its source of supply, this unregulated market demonstrated remarkable capacities. Harpers is said to have had one of Scott's longest works, *Peveril of the Peak*, on the bookstore shelves less than a day after the advance sheets were landed in the United States. But, as Kaser (1957) tells it, when Harpers failed to observe the 'courtesy of trade' in relation to an English novel published by Carey and Lea, the latter printed and distributed Harpers' next novel – Bulwer Lytton's *Rienzi* – so quickly that it 'was for sale in all the New York bookstores one day earlier than Harpers' edition of the same work'.

From this competition over lead time, British publishers and authors could derive a more than useful supplement to their legal income by selling the early proofs of a new work to an American reprinter. As the 1878 British Commissioners on Copyright were told, the latter would often pay a substantial sum for such proofs, sometimes more than was earned from the copyright royalties on English sales. In fact, although the British were willing to sell advance sheets to American publishers and make an unearned profit, at the same time they protected their domestic market, the Booksellers' Association in Britain having threatened 'to ruin any dealer who retailed an American book on a cost plus small commission basis' (McVey 1976: 193). There was thus a certain complicity on both sides of the Atlantic. In the United States, these irregular agreements could be represented as if in accord with the political principle that the public good would be harmed if the price of books were to rise as a consequence of giving foreign authors a capacity to fix their prices in the United States as well as abroad. As in the German states, however, price undercutting by pirates constantly threatened an orderly market in books, especially in the context of a regime based on mass sales at low price. The 'reputable' publishers were without legal power to halt the cheap book trade. Harpers, for example, paid £6,000 for the advance proofs of a new novel by Wilkie Collins only to have the cheap book trade pirate it for sale at 10 or 20 cents a copy. And newspapers began publishing weekly fiction in parts, 'pirated' from American reprinters who had already pirated the material from the British.

The figure of Charles Dickens reappears here. In 1842, the year of the United Kingdom Copyright Amendment Act, Dickens was making his first reading tour in the United States. From there on 1 May he wrote complaining to his brother-in-law:

> Is it not a horrible thing that scoundrel-booksellers should grow rich here from publishing books, the authors of which do not reap one farthing from their issue, by scores of thousands? And that every vile, blackguard and detestable newspaper, – so filthy and so bestial that no honest man would admit one into his house, for a water-closet doormat – should be able to publish those same writings, side by side, cheek by jowl, with the coarsest and most obscene companions?
>
> (in Moss 1984: 1)

We recognise co-present the pecuniary and the moral or dignitary interests that ground the history of authors' rights. However, before sympathising with Dickens as victim of the American pirate reprinters – to the Mayor of Boston he wrote in February 1842 referring to himself as 'the greatest loser by the existing Law, alive' (Dickens 1965: 76–7) – we should picture the historical circumstances. As Sidney Moss (1984: 82) reminds us, relations between Britain and the United States in the 1830s and 1840s were marked by tensions that went beyond the dispute over copyright protection for British authors and publishers. In addition to the British attack on the institution of slavery as practised in the Republic, disputes over national boundaries and the repercussions of the repudiation of their public debt by state legislatures defaulting on bond repayments soured Anglo-American relations. What is more, the early 1840s was a time of recession in the United States economy, a fact that made Dickens' campaign to have Americans recognise and pay for use of British copyright material singularly ill-timed, given that such recognition was alleged to threaten the American industry with much higher costs (Barnes 1974: 75–6).

None the less there was some political support for Dickens, for instance from the Senator from Kentucky, Henry Clay, who as early as 1837 had presented to the United States Senate a petition by fifty-six British authors seeking to secure copyrights for their works in the United States – Dickens' views were anti-northern and anti-black (Moss 1984: 192). An organisation was formed to work for international copyright.[4] And, even if less from principle than by *force majeure*, some American publishers – but not the great reprinters – did petition Congress to legislate for international copyright, they were themselves being undercut by cut-price publishing (Moss 1984: 43). But this was not enough to prevent Dickens from using *Martin Chuzzlewit* as a vehicle for his anti-Americanism, knowing that the American pirates and 'bookaneers' would distribute it.

By the 1860s, however, matters were different, although there was still no agreement on Anglo-American copyright. In its absence there was a network of quasi-legal *de facto* arrangements. Moss describes how, in 1866, Ticknor and Fields of Boston made Dickens a proposal which their rivals – Harpers, and Petersons of Philadelphia – did not better: 'Instead of offering Dickens a one-time lump sum for advance sheets of his novels, as Harpers had done since 1852, [Fields] would pay him and his publisher [Chapman and Hall] a royalty on the retail price of every Dickens volume sold under his imprint – namely, those in a Diamond Edition, plain and illustrated' (Moss 1984: 213–14). This was not all. In addition, Fields undertook to sell Chapman and Hall's Illustrated Library Edition and to publish 'simultaneously with Chapman and Hall, their new Charles Dickens Edition, from the sale of which editions Dickens would draw his usual substantial royalties from Edward Chapman, as well as royalties from Ticknor and Fields' (1984: 214). In return, the author was to recognise the latter as his sole authorised publishers in America, with exclusive American rights in any book he wrote in the next five years. With Dickens' acceptance of these terms, Ticknor and Fields advertised theirs as being 'the only editions in which Mr. Dickens is pecuniarily interested'! But matters were not quite so straightforward, given the complexity of Dickens' financial manoeuvres. In relation to the serialisation of his works, he had dealt with Harpers since the early 1850s; Petersons had regularly purchased Dickens' advance sheets for volume publication and, on this ground, found that Ticknor and Fields had broken the courtesy of trade agreement among publishers. Petersons issued press advertisements to this effect. And then, in 1869 – just three years after granting Ticknor and Fields exclusive American rights to all his books until 1871 – Dickens accepted £2,000 from Harpers for the sheets of *The Mystery of Edwin Drood*, creating yet another wrangle. It was solved by directing the serial rights to Harpers and the book rights to Ticknor and Fields.

Given such conduct, it is no surprise that the Americans' practice had its home defenders. Indeed, the year after Senator Clay presented the petition from 'certain Authors of Great Britain' to the Senate, Philip H. Nicklin (1838) propounded the reasons against granting the requested international copyright. In the petition, the authors alleged their long exposure to 'injury in their reputation and property'; the third paragraph argued

That, from the circumstance of the English language being common to both nations, the works of British authors are extensively read throughout the United States of America, while the profits arising from the sale of their works may be wholly appropriated by American booksellers, not only without the consent of the authors, but even contrary to their express desire – a grievance under which your petitioners have, at present, no redress.

Nicklin's response is to ask how their 'reputation' can be injured if these authors are as widely read as they claim to be, and he suggests that 'their American fame is echoed back across the ocean, and increases the value of their copyrights at home' (1838: 14–15). Indeed, if a 'copyright tax' were introduced and the price of books raised, the sales would fall 'from two thousand to five hundred, or to nought'. The fourth and fifth paragraphs of the petition had complained that 'the works thus appropriated are liable to be mutilated and altered, at the pleasure of the said booksellers . . . and that, the names of the authors being retained, they may be made responsible for works which they no longer regard as their own'. Such actions, it was claimed, had 'been of late actually perpetrated by citizens of the United States'. Again Nicklin is equal to the challenge: he rejects the charge, referring to the 'prejudices of the petitioners' and wondering if it was British opinion on the slavery question that was in mind when the 'mutilation' of works was invoked. Yet most reprinting goes on, he argues, in the middle and northern states, where the anti-slavery argument is endorsed. More generally, as he points out, there is 'not the least inducement to mutilate English books, or to alter them in any way without distinct acknowledgement; for they come here with reputation already gained, and it is an exact copy which the reader requires, and which the publisher is obliged to furnish' (1838: 16). Thus the intense competition between reprinters militates against mutilation.

Indeed, Nicklin makes play with the fact that in America publishing is not a monopoly, unlike in Britain where the 'spirit of the ancient guilds, a spirit of ferocious monopoly' stands in the way of competition. It was the achievement of the American industry regularly to have an edition out within forty-eight hours of the landing of the advance sheets, with the expectation of a rival edition forty-eight hours later, as a result of which 'the public are furnished with an abundant supply at reasonable prices' (1838: 43). The same commercial factualism leads to the comment that in American book-publishing companies – estimated to employ 200,000 people including 50,000 women and children – it is 'probable that one fourth of the business done is in reprinting foreign books, and this large proportion of their business would be reduced perhaps by as much as nine-tenths, certainly as much as three-fourths, if copyright be granted to foreign books at present' (1838: 40). So much for the property; as for the principle, Nicklin responds to the petitioners' call for 'justice' by asking 'where was justice when parliament took from British authors the perpetual right to their own productions?' (1838: 24). If the tones of Talfourd seem to echo here, it is no mistake; Nicklin explicitly endorses the 'poet–statesman's' efforts to recover justice for British authors and cites five pages of 'elegant extracts' of Talfourd's speeches. And on a further issue of principle, Nicklin's resistance to an Anglo-American copyright agreement is grounded also on the cultural imbalance – the American reception of British authors and critics is not reciprocated in Britain. 'Therefore', he argues, 'the works of *our* authors must obtain the approbation of *their* critics, before they can be available for purposes of profit in the Britannic market' (1838: 42).

Nevertheless, initiatives related to bilateral agreements between the United States and Britain generated as many as eleven copyright bills in Congress. In 1854 an Anglo-American copyright treaty was signed but failed at the last hurdle to gain confirmation in the Senate. But until the 1891 Chace Act, no legislative move was successful.

It was against this background of American protectionism, advanced production and distribution techniques and an absence of agreement on an Anglo-American copyright that Henry James had to develop a fine sense of timing concerning the magazine publication of *A Portrait of a Lady* in the *Atlantic Monthly* and in *Macmillan's Magazine*. A firm such as Tillotson's, however, used an American agent to manage their supplying of advance sheets of new English works to the United States market for both volume and serial production, opening their own New York office in 1889, just before the Anglo-American copyright agreement of 1891. In these circumstances – lower cost, larger production, broader distribution and a higher literacy rate – the relations between readers, books and authors were precisely those which, for Matthew Arnold, posed a fundamental threat to moral and aesthetic culture. Yet Arnold's American contemporary, the publisher John B. Alden, could declare in the *Publishers' Weekly* of 21 March 1885 that 'the best literature of the world has by my efforts been placed within the reach of millions to whom it was before unattainable' (in Stern 1980: 6).

IV

Given these distinctive legal and commercial circumstances, what configuration did the American literary field assume? Private patronage had never taken root in America, *belles-lettres* remaining a patrician pursuit of the few. In this refined milieu, authors hired publishers, paying them either outright or by a percentage of the profits; as a result, authors exercised control over the work. For publishers this particular division of labour offered no material reason to encourage a native American 'literature', especially when the lack of international copyright allowed the reprinting of foreign books on which profits did not have to be shared. Indeed, this private sphere of literary and ethical exchange became marginal to the main enterprise of American publishing as a mass market emerged for books, a market supplied by highly competitive publishing houses. While this allowed publishers to make a profit on works written by American authors, aesthetic-minded literary historians have treated this market-oriented and publisher-directed system as little more than a commodification of culture, a system sustained by publicity where 'cultural entrepreneurs devised sophisticated techniques for merchandising art, treating the writer's biography and even his [or her] appearance as important factors in the selling of the books' (Gilmore 1985: 4).

The major publishing lists were dominated by the 'pirated' reprints of English fiction, published without copyright protection. What were the consequences? According to McVey (1976: 193), 'through carefully contrived extralegal devices designed to protect their excessive profits from British books without undue cost, American publishers, with the full cooperation of British publishers interested in maintaining their own high domestic prices, prolonged American dependence on British culture'. The American market was thus saturated with works which had proven commercially successful according to English tastes, while indigenous American writing was devalued both culturally and commercially.[5] This situation persisted until the late 1860s when arguments for an international copyright agreement began to turn not only on the injustices done to British authors, but also on the possible advantages for American cultural independence (196). But there were also the 'scribbling women':

> In the decade before the Civil War, a succession of unprecedented bestsellers overwhelmed the American publishing scene. At a time when Hawthorne [who polemicised against the 'scribbling women'] could hope to appeal to five or perhaps six thousand readers, a first novel by one of the female authors, Susan B. Warner's *The Wide, Wide World* (1850), amazed and delighted its publishers by selling over forty thousand copies in less than a year. The book went into its fourteenth printing by 1852 and eventually attracted more than a million buyers. Comparable levels of popularity were attained by 'Fanny Fern' (the pen name of Sara Parton), Mary Virginia Terhune, E.D.E.N. Southworth, Maria Cummins and other women novelists. *The Lamplighter* (1854), Cummins' first book, recorded forty thousand in sales after only eight weeks and exceeded seventy thousand by the end of a year.
>
> (Gilmore 1985: 7)

Not for nothing was there talk of the 'feminine fifties'. The union of these successful women writers and the American system of mass production and marketing throws into relief the caste-like nature of those American Romantics – Hawthorne, Emerson, Melville – later canonised by literary criticism. The women writers were a key part of the process whereby improved manufacture, distribution and publicity allowed new fiction to become a regular article of commerce, something sought and bought by a broad audience that was acquiring a habitual interest in and thus a demand for fiction. For all his competence in the exacting pursuits of ethical and aesthetic self-fashioning and social critique, the gentleman author writing for a coterie of like-minded persons here gave way to the women professionals whose works actually sold to a general public.

By contrast, an author such as Hawthorne followed a regime of intensely private ethical and aesthetic ascesis. He began his 'literary vocation' by 'retiring to a room in his mother's house and serving a self-imposed apprenticeship of a dozen years' (Gilmore 1985: 4). Unlike the scribbling women, the conduct of the man of letters is the response of an aesthetic caste to the new technical, cultural, commercial and legal circumstances. However 'modern' and 'anticipatory' the postures and dispositions of the American Romantics have subsequently come to seem – Emerson's concern at the emerging market economy, Thoreau's at the alienation of man from his labour, Hawthorne's at the commodification of the literary artist, Melville's at the dissolution of humanity into the commodity form – from the contemporary marketing perspective they were rather the *confrères* of patri-archal federalists such as Noah Webster and the denizens of guild or familial economies. They were more in place in the early nineteenth-century English publishing house – or the late twentieth-century literary and aesthetic seminar – than in a mass-production publishing economy whose object was to make, distribute and sell as many books as possible to as many people as possible. According to the publisher Robert Sterling Yard, writing in the later 1800s, ' the minimum turnover [for a publishing venture] should be 200,000 dollars to give a profit and 400,000 are necessary for prosperity' (in Gedin 1977:37). For a house such as Harpers, this meant a production rate of twenty-five books per minute, ten hours per day all the year round, together with a system of distribution able to disseminate the books to the widely dispersed and culturally non-specialist readerships making up the large literate popu-lation. This is not the scene for that 'heroic reader', pictured by Thoreau for a book which, like the waters at Walden, was 'too pure to have a market value' (Thoreau 1971: 199).

A century of industrialisation transformed the United States. An economy of production and distribution emerged appropriate to the national circum-stances, as did a set of dispositions and bits of taste on the basis of which definite readerships would form. The relation of the mid-nineteenth-century American reader to work and author was a relation of potential consumer to a desirable commodity, produced by an industrially efficient production and distribution process. Confronted with the usual aesthetic denunciation of large-scale production and uniformity, it is worth making two observations. First, for us the cultural phenomenon of literary writing and reading – including the person-forming uses made of such writing – has become inseparable from the system of mass distribution. Second, this is not neces-sarily a cause for regret. To this end we should recall thatwhat might be termed statistical enthusiasm was a historical alternative to aesthetic worry as a response to the new technological circumstance in which unlimited numbers of perfect copies could be produced. The English mathematician Charles Babbage greeted this new order of things with wonder: 'Nothing is more remarkable, and yet less unexpected, than the perfect identity of things manufactured by the same tool' (in Welsh 1984: 41). Perhaps Babbage's immunity to aesthetic worry still does not come easily to us. He treats the printed word – with not a mention of the specific instance of the literary printed word – as just one of the techniques for producing copies by printing from surfaces, along with cotton handkerchiefs, casts in plaster, umbrella handles, forged bank notes and lasts for shoe making. A general history of the law of copyright would give consideration to all the forms of copying by 'printing from surfaces': maps and charts, engravings and patterns for linen.[6] The purchase of the notion of literary authorship on such activities as these is, to say the least, uncertain.

The industrial capacity to produce and distribute standardised copies in multiples was most completely pursued and realised in the American system.[7] Unhampered by guild dispositions like that of the London book trade whose guiding principle was avoidance of risk, and encouraged by an increasingly affluent urban and rural citizenry willing to purchase books, American publishers established the mass market for large editions at low prices. An English cultural critic such as Matthew Arnold remained suspicious towards low-priced books and the 'double-entry' approaches to literary culture with which he associated them. Arnold's view of American publishers – who, as he put it, 'deal with authors much as Manchester might be disposed, if left to itself, to deal with them' – was that of one schooled in a developed form of sensibility that detested industrial mass-production and took a craft-based and communitarian view of literary culture. Perhaps it is the case that American success in the industrial production and mass marketing of books was accompanied by the formation of a taste for a homogenised and formula product which lacked the uniqueness demanded by an aesthetic critic for whom cultural distinction is more of a value than high price is a disadvantage. Yet if we recall what life was actually like in chaotic nineteenth-century urban populations and how specialised was the aesthetic concern with achieving completeness of being, then we might discern in the standardisation of taste based on a broadly disseminated discursive literate ability not merely a regrettable short-circuiting of human cultural development but a remarkable cultural achievement, one that rested on the industrialisation of publishing in America.[8] No comment is needed on the remark of the London publisher, John Murray, to Gladstone in 1851 that 'it must be borne in mind that books are a *luxury*; when a time of distress comes the first expense to be curtailed is the purchase of books. That is done (without any outward display of economy) rather than laying down a carriage or dismissing servants' (in Barnes 1985: 232).

V

It was not entirely an international legal vacuum. With the passage of the British Act of 1838 on international copyright, American publishers who had been not illegally reprinting subject matter protected by copyright in other countries became pirates.[9] Yet, despite the earlier attempts at legislation, only in 1886 did the major US publishers begin to organise as a corporate group whose collective interests might be better served by having Congress agree to an international accord on copyright between the Americans and the British. In fact, by this time, the latter were perturbed at the rise of German influence in Europe and all too ready to reach some accommodation with their English-language fellows.

With the Act of 1891 the principle of international copyright was finally admitted under American law, even though reciprocity of protection extended only to countries with which the United States had made specific treaties. Under the Act, in order to secure a copyright foreign authors had to register and deposit their works. Moreover, as a concession to the American printing lobby, copies of books with foreign copyright proprietors had to be manufactured in the United States. Whatever might be thought of this protectionist leaning, a singular shift occurred in the ratio of American authors in the total of American publication. No longer was it the case that 'copy for copy American publishers vastly outproduced English; title for title English novelists vastly outproduced American' (Sutherland 1976: 17). According to McVey (1976: 198): 'Before 1891, 70 per cent of the books published in the United States were of foreign origin; after 1891, the figure was reversed, and 70 per cent were by native authors.' In the last decade of the nineteenth century, with Jack London and Upton Sinclair, William Dean Howells and Henry James, the American novel came into its own in its home territory.

If it had taken 'a century of American independence for there to be as many American as British authors published in the United States' (McVey 1976: 187), this was in part a material effect of the copyright legislation of 1891 which put an end to the profitable option – for American publishers – of drawing on the free supply of British works. The Act established new legal-cultural conditions in which, for instance, American publishers could now print and export to Britain. As always there were contingencies: because the British reading public was accustomed to a heavier grade of paper than was used in the American presses, an unforeseen trade opportunity arose for British paper manufacturers to set up US agencies to supply American printers with paper for editions destined for re-export to Britain.

Unlike the British and the French, the American book industry was not linked to an international cultural project or ethos of world ascendancy in literature and the arts. Geographically and philosophically remote, the Americans' success at home in a market large enough, rich enough and literate enough to allow economies of scale made the exporting of books no more than an incidental addition to domestic strategy. However, a broader movement for international copyright protection was under way, one that in 1887 achieved the Convention for the Protection of Literary and Artistic works enacted at Berne. The Convention provided for international copyright protection on the simple creation of an original work, no formalities of registration being necessary. Having delayed for 102 years, the United States finally signed the Berne Convention in 1989.

Chapter 7

The internationalisation of copyright and authorship

I

To this point it has been a matter of underscoring the fact of national variations in the legal conception and execution of authors' rights. Such rights flowed neither from authorial consciousness nor from the unconscious determination of language. Rather, they were the outcome of decisions to adopt certain legal norms defined by particular criteria – the nationality or citizenship or domicile of an author; the place of publication of a work or, in the case where the national law protected only a work first published on the national territory, the place and time of publication. Some nations adopted territoriality as the criterion defining the threshold of protection of authors' rights – for instance Britain, the Netherlands, Italy and Mexico; others opted for the citizenship or nationality criterion – the United States and, for instance, Greece, Portugal, Spain, Sweden and Finland. In Germany the law protected the unpublished or published works of nationals, that is, the nationality criterion was operative; it also protected foreign authors' works that were published in Germany by a German publisher. A similar position existed in Norway. In Switzerland and Hungary place of residence, not nationality, was the condition of protection. The preceding chapters have shown something of this diversity of circumstances, and the tactics adopted by writers who sought to occupy the status of protected author in one or more national jurisdictions. We recall Henry James (see p. 149), manoeuvring to ensure his protection across different legal environments where he had to meet the British law's criteria of territoriality and first publication, while to gain protection in the United States he had to meet the registration requirement and satisfy the citizenship criterion, under the American law the works of foreigners being unprotected even if published locally. It is ill-conceived to ask in which jurisdiction, British or American, Henry James was most fully himself as author. We can express a preference one way or another, for the British or the American regime of protection. But that is a practical decision, without theoretical importance. The question is ill-conceived because this choice cannot be resolved by reference to some independent knowledge of what authorship really is, knowledge against which a given form of law might be assessed. What counts as 'authorship' cannot be defined in advance of the positive legal criteria deployed within one or another jurisdiction.

Although it has thus far been a matter of describing how legal norms relating to the rights of authors achieved nationwide scope, some international factors have been glimpsed: the Franco-German exchanges from which emerged the *droit moral*, the importing of *Millar* v. *Taylor* and *Donaldson* v. *Beckett* into the United States, the struggle over Anglo-American copyright. In this chapter the focus moves to the historical achievement of a properly international law of copyright. Trans-border movement of copyright works raised different issues in different circumstances. Unlike the importing of foreign (especially Belgian) printed French-language materials into France which damaged the French publishers' domestic market, the unauthorised reprinting of British works in the United States constituted a loss of potential income to British copyright holders from the use of their property in a non-British territory. But from this diverse set of circumstances emerged the Berne Convention for the Protection of Literary and Artistic Works, ratified and carried into force in 1887. The Convention is evidence that in the latter decades of the nineteenth century a coherent internationalisation of such rights was achieved, its primary purpose being to overcome the problem of international piracy of literary property.[1] Internationalisation could mean the harmonisation of existing regimes of protection of literary property; more radically, it could mean the elaboration of entirely new norms for the universal codification of the rights of authors regardless of nationality, residence, place or time of publication.

It is best to treat the British nation as an exception in so far as its centuries-old national legal-administrative system – the common law – long pre-dated the processes of internationalisation. More generally, the modern nation state was 'born within an international framework ... its forms and functions developed internationally' (Picciotto 1988: 59). National literary-property regimes were themselves in the process of formation even as an international order was crystallising. It will therefore be no surprise if the emergence of the Berne Union – whatever the metaphysical ideals that inspired the goal of universal rights for authors – was marked by contingencies, circumstantial arrangements and compromises. Moreover, the new international legal order which found expression in the Berne Convention was just one element in a further set of internationalising processes. The proliferation of international organisations was such that already by 1910 a 'meta-organisation' was founded: the Union of International Associations.[2] By 1914, established international governmental and non-governmental organisations numbered 50 and 300 respectively, while by 1980 the totals had increased to 600 and 6,000. In practical and logistical terms, these organisations depend on formal and informal contacts, discussions, committees and memoranda from which emerge not only organisational norms and practices but also a set of international habits of mind.[3]

In 1887 ten nations ratified the Berne Convention, thus instituting the principle of a universal regime of authors' rights. This was one outcome of the later nineteenth-century practice of organising international gatherings for the purpose of dealing with specific problems. Unlike the territorial focus of many eighteenth-century treaties between nations, the nineteenth-century international order was extended to economic, legal and cultural interests, including those relating to literary and artistic property. It can be argued that the foundations of modern international laws – as distinct from the older Law of Nations – were laid down from the 1860s. The formal elaboration of rules for civilized conduct in war begins with the first Geneva Convention on Warfare in 1864, when the International Red Cross was founded. Reliable trans-border communications were pursued through the International Telegraph Union (1865) and the Universal Postal Union (1874), agreements which pointed the way towards further schemes of international cooperation.

Private or non-governmental bodies were active participants. In the sphere of intellectual property these included the Association Littéraire et Artistique Internationale (ALAI), founded in 1878 and forerunner of the International Bureau of Literary and Artistic Property. The ALAI now finds itself alongside the Confédération Internationale des Sociétés des Auteurs et des Compositeurs (CISAC) and the International Federation of Producers of Phonograms and Videograms (IFPI), not to mention the International Federation of Inventors' Associations (IFIA) – of which Phillips (1986: 292) remarks that 'it is difficult to think of a smaller or less effective body'. Given their historical particularity and diversity, the emergence of these international organisations cannot sensibly be considered in terms of a general singular process of cultural development. Yet the fact is that since the last decades of the nineteenth century these organisations have been effective agents of the literary field: the representatives of authorial interests, the decision-makers, the lobbyists, the determiners of the future shape of legal regulation and protection and of the legal conditions of authorial existence. It is uninformative to approach the history of an organisation such as the ALAI by invoking the necessary evolution of the human consciousness or the subversive force of writing. A more concrete historical observation provides a better starting point: the formation of the ALAI was contingent upon the existence of a novel cultural institution – the international exposition or world fair. This institutional account need not be boring. What other institution, it might be asked, succeeded in establishing a committee whose members included Dostoevsky and Tolstoy, Tennyson and Trollope, Emerson, the Emperor of Brazil and Ferdinand de Lesseps, engineer of that other internationalising opening, the Suez Canal?

The world fairs or international exhibitions held from 1851 occasioned 'the largest gatherings of people . . . of all time' (Greenhalgh 1988: 1). The British staged the first international exhibition – the Great Exhibition of the Industry of All Nations in London. However, the idea had previously been debated in France. Starting with the 1855 Exposition Universelle in Paris, French governments set out to seize world leadership of the exhibition medium.[4] It was a French initiative in 1867 to use an international exposition not only as a trade and industry display but also as a stage for international conferences. Subsequently, at the 1878 Exposition Universelle in Paris, the Société des Gens de Lettres staged an international literary conference under the presidency of Victor Hugo. Distinguished authors, publishers and prominent public figures from three continents were present, including Turgenev from Russia, Bancroft from the United States, Löwenthal from Germany and Jerrold from the UK. The Association Littéraire Internationale was founded at this 1878 Congress, and opened to writers and writers' organisations of all countries. Its aims were to protect the principles of literary property; to establish a basis for regular international exchanges between the literary societies and writers; and to initiate enterprises having an international character. Like the Congress, the Association was under the presidency of Hugo. It was here that the Committee of Honour, including Dostoevsky and de Lesseps, Tolstoy and the Emperor of Brazil, was appointed.

In 1883, the membership of the Association was expanded to include visual artists, and its name was changed to the Association Littéraire et Artistique Internationale (ALAI). Given its brief to deal with all matters of concern to authors and artists, questions of copyright have regularly arisen at the ALAI congresses. From the start there was a call for effective and comprehensive international copyright, the 1878 Congress resolving that: 'The right of the author in his work constitutes, not a concession by the law, but one of the forms of property which the legislature must protect'; and 'the right of the author, his beneficiaries and legal representatives is perpetual'. Ricketson (1987) identifies these as 'universalist' views that envisage a single global standard. The call for a truly international protection of literary and artistic property would be met only by a union analogous to the International Postal Union. Being the site of previous international meetings and of the head-quarters of the Postal and Telegraph Unions, the Swiss city of Berne was chosen as the venue for the work of developing a future world copyright Union.

II

Considerable economic and territorial interests were in play. At the opening session of the diplomatic conference in Berne in 1886, the Swiss chairperson, Numa Droz, observed that the accession of Britain and its colonies would bring 300 million people into the Union, doubling the combined populations covered by the other original signatories. Despite the scale of the undertaking, the Berne Convention emerged in an unpredictable manner, due not least to the persisting tension between international 'universalists' and 'absolutists' on the one hand, and national 'pragmatists' on the other. For the former, a copyright Union implied an absolute uniformity of treatment of literary and artistic property; for the latter, insistence on this principle was seen as likely to deter from membership of the Union those nations whose laws did not meet the criteria advocated by the universalists. On occasions the division between universalists and pragmatists corresponded to that between civilian and common-law countries; but on any given issue it also demarcated French from German positions. And so it was from a diversity of goals and means that the finished Convention emerged in 1887 as a mode of using international law to enhance a diversity of rights attaching to the profession of publishing and the practice of authorship.

Viewed from prior historical circumstances – the times of Irish, Scottish and American pirating of works published in England, or Dutch, Belgian and Swiss pirating of French publications, or the unregulated pirating that occurred in the German territorial states – the idea of such a Convention must have seemed utopian. According to Ricketson (1987: 19), the main aim of copyright agreements between nations in the nineteenth century was the elimination of trans-national piracy. From the 1838 Act deriving from inter-governmental discussions between Britain, France and Prussia to the legis-lative measures of 1844, 1852 and 1875, the British government explored the possibility of forming conventions with other countries to secure copyright protection in those foreign territories for British copyright holders. The French government had gone further, the decree of 28 March 1852 according the protection of French law to all works regardless of their place of publication. The motives were both material and ideal. By unilaterally according protection in France to the works of foreign nationals, it was hoped that other states would be moved to offer reciprocal protection to the works of French authors. At the same time, it was argued that if authors' rights were natural rights of property, they must transcend nationality and territorial boundaries; in this light, the decree of 1852 did no more than express a pre-existing natural right. At the other end of the spectrum were countries such as Belgium and the German states; these tolerated international piracy because, on balance, it was to their advantage.

However, as in America in the 1880s, at a certain point the creations of indigenous producers seem to have acquired importance as an exportable product and as a source of cultural legitimacy. For Ricketson (1987: 20–1) this threshold was reached by most European countries by the mid-nineteenth century. But a measure of caution is appropriate. As well as being evidence of 'progress', the French decree of 1852 was not only a ringing statement of Enlightenment principle; it was also the legal instrument of a specific international cultural politics of which the world fairs were another spec-tacular manifestation. How might a nation take on a universal role? An answer is hinted at in Victor Hugo's apostrophe to France in the *Guide* to the 1867 Exposition Universelle:

> O France, adieu! You are too great to be merely a country. . . . . You will cease to be France, you will be Humanity; you will cease to be a nation, you will be ubiquity. You are destined to dissolve into radiance and nothing of this is so majestic as the visible obliteration of your frontier. Resign yourself to your immensity. Goodbye, people! Hail man!
>
> (in Greenhalgh 1988: 16)

If not quite in the same luminous key as the *mère des arts*, Britain too was on the world highway. Thus the press columnist 'Helix' had proclaimed *à propos* of the 1851 Great Exhibition in London: 'magnificent was the conception of this gathering together of the commercial travellers of the universal world' (in Greenhalgh 1988: 23).

Three types of legal initiative were available to nations pursuing international protection for literary property: unilateral national laws providing for all foreign authors; bilateral agreements between nations defining the treatment each will accord to the other's authors; and multilateral agreements – in the style of the Berne Convention or the Universal Copyright Convention – which seek to establish either an absolute uniformity of treatment across all nations party to the agreement or, more pragmatically, a scheme that allows each nation to meet the agreed standards in a manner possible under the local metropolitan law. Each of these options found concrete expression in different nineteenth-century arrangements of authors' rights.

Despite the exceptional character of the unilateral French law of 1852, a contemporary French authority such as Alcide Darras could view the provision not as assimilating all authors to the status enjoyed by French nationals but as simply allowing a foreign author to enjoy in France the rights given to him under the laws of his or her own country (Ricketson 1987: 22). In the period prior to Berne, unilateral action faced evident problems. A decision to accord foreign nationals as much protection as they would have received in their own countries presumed that a court could know the state of the law in the other country. It was therefore better for countries to make bilateral agreements under which, as Ricketson observes, the terms and conditions of the reciprocal provisions were more precisely determined. And agreements at a bilateral level began to be made 'almost as soon as countries acknowledged the need to obtain international protection for their authors' (1987: 25). The picture of the emerging network of bilateral conventions was complicated by there being a plurality of German and Italian states not yet organised under unitary national regimes but – as the bearers of cultural interests – already entering into the international cultural-legal environment. By 1886, the year prior to the ratification of the Berne Convention for the Protection of Literary and Artistic Works, France was engaged in thirteen bilateral agreements on authors' rights, Belgium nine, Italy and Spain eight, and Britain five. Their concern to enter into bilateral copyright agreements serves to classify these nations, along with the German states, as the major *producers* of literary property.[5]

Yet there were limits to the success of attempts to negotiate piracy out of existence through bilateral accords. In 1852 France was able to reach an agreement with Belgium – the major site of pirate reprinting of French publications. However, with respect to the United States whose publishers were causing British authors and copyright owners most injury, the United Kingdom failed to reach any agreement (although, as we have seen in chapter 6, there were efforts to this end on both sides of the Atlantic). The United States resisted any international copyright commitment, despite the scale of its literate population and book market and despite the fact that from 1876 a series of international exhibitions across the United States helped shape a world view for Americans (Rydell 1984: 235). Nor were the United States alone; the Scandinavian countries and Holland remained in the posture of *users* of copyright subject matter, and though Holland signed a convention with the German Empire in 1884 – it remained unratified – pirating of German works continued.

The operation of the bilateral system was cumbersome and uncertain. The content of bilateral accords was variable, with no common set of criteria to harmonise the whole. Some conventions limited protection to authors who were nationals of the contracting states (France, Sweden and Norway); others gave protection on the basis of territoriality to authors of works published in the territories of the contracting states, regardless of nationality (France and Portugal). Some conventions, for instance the Franco-German agreement of 1883, adopted the criterion of nationality but also protected works of authors who were nationals of other states if published in the territory of the contracting states. Similar variations characterised definitions of the object protected.[6] Some early bilateral conventions protected only 'works of the intellect and of art', dramatic works and musical works being excluded; later conventions were directed at 'literary and artistic works', to which 'scientific' works were sometimes added (Ricketson 1987: 31). Lacking in uniformity it might have been, yet the bilateral network represented a definite regulatory environment for authorship.

Across the latter half of the nineteenth century, a third and more comprehensive type of legal arrangement emerged to define the rights and attributes attaching to authorship at an international level: the multilateral agreement. The multilateralist approach to authors' rights rested on the competing lines of argument already noted. On the one hand there was the *universalist* argument that would have every nation adopt uniform provisions for all authors and rights holders. As Ricketson (1987: 40) describes it, this universal law of copyright would 'accord directly with the conception of the author's natural right of property in his work, existing independently of, and prior to, the formal rules and sanctions of positive law, and admitting no artificial restrictions such as a limited term of protection or national boundaries'. This is a grand Enlightenment view, committed to principle but relatively disinterested in the means whereby the principle could be put into practice. On the other hand, the *pragmatic* view held that the universalist idea was unrealisable in that it presumed every nation would recognise and protect to an equal degree the rights claimed by authors. But in practice, would all nations agree that protection is justified by the author's natural right of property in his or her work? As Ladas (1938) and Kase (1967) have shown, even among the major civil-law systems, there are differing approaches to this matter.

In assessing the universalist argument and the call for a universal codification, Ricketson (1987: 41) finds that its proponents have 'often been uncompromising in their advocacy, invariably convinced of their correctness, and, at times, apparently prepared to sacrifice all for the integrity of their beliefs'. Against this Kantian stance, the pragmatists have been prepared to 'sacrifice high principle in order to gain the widest possible adherence to a particular proposition'. Thus if the universalists can claim credit for the progressive expansion in the scope of protection afforded by the Berne Convention, the pragmatists' caution has allowed this expansion to be achieved without losing broad-based support.

Against the background of this persisting tension – in general France and Germany held to the universalist persuasion while the common-law countries have been pragmatists – let us follow the main stages in the formation of the Berne Convention. There had certainly been false starts. The earliest call for a universal law protecting authors' rights was made by the 1858 Brussels congress on authors' and artists' rights to which reference has already been made (see p. 96). Endorsed by an 1861 Antwerp congress on the arts, the call was echoed in an 1877 meeting, again at Antwerp, where the Institute of International Law was requested to draft a universal law on artistic works. The Institute agreed to this request later that year in Zurich, and a study group was appointed consisting of legal and artistic representatives from Belgium, the United Kingdom, Italy, the Netherlands and France. Despite the Institute's initial response and a proposal to extend its terms of reference to include literary works, the working party was not formally constituted until 1882. But nothing came of this groundwork; indeed, by 1878, the role of the Institute had been taken over by the International Literary Association, whose formation has already been described. The line from the 1858 Brussels Congress on Literary and Artistic Property to the Institute of International Law might have petered out in the 1880s; however, the Brussels call for global protection of rights set the tone for the long campaign that ensued. With its mix of representatives from the major European countries and the United States, together with the diversity of participants – writers, journalists and artists, publishers and printers, academics, economists, lawyers and politicians

– the 1858 Congress serves as a reminder that only through such organisations, with their committees, agendas and resolutions do ideas acquire social existence and become actionable. In the initial maximalist formulation the resolutions were high-principled and dogmatic. The Congress asserted, for instance, that the 'principle of international recognition of the property of authors in their literary and artistic works should be enshrined in the legislation of all civilised peoples' and that no distinctions whatsoever should be drawn between foreign and national authors.

The campaign leading from the foundation of the International Literary Association in 1878 was altogether more consequential. In a series of congresses – Lisbon 1880, Vienna 1881 and Rome 1882 – a path was beaten towards concrete governmental action on the international protection of literary property. But still there were setbacks. Perhaps in view of its positive historical stance on the issue since the unilateral provisions of 1852, the French government was invited by the Association to summon an international conference with the aim of formulating a set of standards for such protection. In the event the French declined, and it fell to the Swiss to take up the initiative. It was therefore less the dialectical resolution of consciousness and its material determinations than the diplomatic enterprise of the Swiss government that generated the international framework for the legal management of literary and artistic works that the Berne Convention was to provide. Meeting yearly in Berne from 1883 to 1887 the commissioners proceeded from a set of five draft propositions circulated by the ALAI (for a 'Universal Literary Convention') prior to the first Berne Conference in 1883; the Convention came into force in December 1887, ratified agreements having been exchanged by the member states in September of that year. The ten articles drafted in 1883 received a more universalist and less pragmatic reformulation in 1884, before being reworked into a more balanced compromise in 1885 and polished in 1886. This achievement depended not least on the Swiss government's selection of personnel for the task in hand. Prior to the 1883 Conference, it nominated Numa Droz, a distinguished Swiss jurist, member of the Federal Council and head of the Department of Agriculture and Commerce, to act as its representative in the projected proceedings. Droz had a strong interest in copyright matters; in an article published shortly after the Rome Congress, he had declared his commitment to an international convention on literary and artistic property.

The first Berne Conference, in 1883, set the business-like tone for the whole operation. Before the meeting, a French, German and English commission previewed the questions for consideration at the conference. A set of five draft proposals was circulated by the ALAI as the basis of discussion. Headed 'Universal Literary Convention', these proposals were of limited scope. The first was that authors of literary or artistic works appearing or performed in one of the contracting states should receive automatic national treatment in all other contracting states. The second, according to Ricketson, was the most radical, calling for complete assimilation of translation rights to rights of reproduction. The next two proposals concerned procedures whereby foreign authors could enforce their rights through national courts, and the distinction between the right of reproduction and the right of property in the object in the case of artistic works. The fifth proposal envisaged the establishment of a central office as a depository of the laws of the contracting states, and the publication of a regular review to disseminate relevant documents and information. This is a further reminder that ideas (and ideals) rely for their social implementation on definite organisational arrangements, just as they rely on the contributions of competent individuals and personnel. In the latter respect, the Berne conferences were able to draw on contributions from jurists such as Eugène Pouillet – who, writes Ricketson, provided 'a more radical perspective' – and Josef Kohler.

The 1883 Conference produced a draft convention of ten articles that were to form the basis of the final 1886 text. They included proposals to make territoriality, not nationality, the determining criterion for protection of literary property; to assimilate translation rights completely to rights in original works; and to allow contracting states to enter into separate bilateral arrangements, provided these met the minimum levels of protection required by the Convention. By December 1883, the Swiss government was able to extend 'to all civilised nations' an invitation to a further international conference, couched in the following terms:

> The protection of the rights of authors in their literary and artistic works (literary and artistic property) is becoming more and more the object of International Conventions. It is, in fact, in the nature of things that the work of man's genius, once it has seen the light, can no longer be restricted to one country and to one nationality. If it possesses any value, it is not long in spreading itself in all countries, under forms which may vary more or less, but which, however, leave in its essence and its principal manifestations the creative idea. This is why, after all civilized States have recognised and guaranteed by their domestic legislation the right of writer and of artist over his work, the imperative necessity has been shown of protecting this right in international relations, which multiply and grow daily. This need has been responded to by the numerous [bilateral] conventions entered into between the principal States during the last few years.
>
> (in Ricketson 1987: 54)

The purpose of this amalgam of natural law, Romantic Hugolian world vision and reportage on the current state of literary property was to establish that bilateral arrangements are inadequate for a proper international protection of literary property. The Swiss document thus continued:

> But regardless of the advantages presented by these [bilateral] conventions it must first be recognised that they are far from protecting the author's

rights in a uniform, efficacious, and complete manner. This insufficiency results, without doubt, from the diversity of national laws, which the conventional regimes must necessarily take into account. The inequalities, and even the grave omissions, in the present international law cannot fail to affect deeply those concerned, authors, publishers and other interested parties. We therefore see great efforts on their part to secure, on the one hand, universal recognition of the rights of authors without distinction of nationality, and on the other, the desirable uniformity in the principles which govern this matter.

(in Ricketson 1987: 54)

This circular also recognised the measure of the task involved in achieving a general understanding of the principle at stake: that no matter what may be his or her nationality, the author of a literary or artistic work ought to be protected everywhere on a par with the nationals of each state. A general Union based on this principle would remove existing differences between levels of protection and institute a definite and more uniform regime of law for authors and their representatives where internationally traded literary publications were concerned.

The Swiss approach succeeded. The 1884 Conference followed positive responses by Germany, France, Britain, Sweden, Norway, Italy, Luxembourg, Argentina, Colombia, Guatemala and Salvador. The United States remained apart, giving no commitment to participate in the 1884 meeting. Notwithstanding this negative disposition, the text of the American response is interesting in that it represents very much an industrial and commercial view of publishing, stressing the collective nature of the publishing process rather than the individualistic nature of literary authorship:

Differences in tariffs, and the fact that, apart from the author or artist, several industries have an interest in the production or the reproduction of a book or a work of art should be taken into account when considering whether to accord to the author of a work the right to have it reproduced or to prevent its reproduction in all countries. There is a distinction between the painter or the sculptor, whose work is saleable as made by his hands, and the literary author, to whose work the paper manufacturer, the type-setter, the printer, the bookbinder and many other persons in commerce contribute.

(in Ricketson 1987: 56)

We are reminded that there is no intrinsic necessity to draw the division of literary labour such that the writer is distinguished from the agents of all other stages of the publishing process. It is also interesting to recall that in the Woman's Pavilion at the Philadelphia Centennial Exhibition of 1876, alongside working machinery operated by women engineers, '[w]riters were given a high profile, celebrating the fact that some of America's most popular novelists were women. Indeed the first American book to sell a million copies was Susan Bogart Warner's *Wide, Wide World,* a statistic proudly flaunted in the literature section' (Greenhalgh 1988: 176). As to the Swiss initiative, the United States was in fact represented at each of the Berne Conferences, even though – as we have noted – American adherence did not eventuate until 102 years after the Convention came into force.

The 1884 Conference drew twenty delegates from thirteen countries. Given the exploratory character of a first meeting, together with the fact that uniform international protection of literary property was uncharted territory, the resolutions were predictably universalist. Compromises were deferred while favourite principles were enunciated:

> Instead of concluding a convention based on the principle of national treatment, would it not be preferable to aim for a codification, in the framework of a convention, regulating in a uniform manner for the whole projected Union, and in the framework of a convention, the totality of dispositions relating to the protection of copyright?
>
> (in Ricketson 1987: 59)

This question was put to the Conference by the German delegation. In the face of this universalism, even the French adopted a pragmatic posture, seeing in the fact of current national variations a reason for anticipating that such universalism would limit rather than enhance the appeal of the proposed Union. The diversity of positions resisted any single logic. If France and Germany could disagree on the question of the feasibility of codification, they could none the less agree – as 'producer' countries – on a general norm for the protection of translations. While France and Germany favoured complete assimilation, the Swedes would accept only a much shorter term of protection; indeed, they made this matter decisive for their participation in the Union. Diplomacy and negotiating skills were at a premium in such circumstances, particularly when on a further issue we find Germany opposing protection of non-nationals, while France and Sweden hold that such protection was essential to encourage other states to join the Union. Yet from these exchanges emerged the documents containing what Ricketson (1987: 62) terms 'the first formal proposals, at a governmental level, for a full multilateral copyright convention'.

The persuasive and performative aspects of these documents were anything but trivial. Proposals were adopted or rejected by delegates who had to calculate the probable effects of the article in question on the future capacity of the proposed Union to attract members. These calculations were unavoidably complex. Thus Switzerland's proposal that foreign residents be assimilated to nationals was rejected in favour of an article according national treatment to the publishers of literary and artistic works published in one of the countries of the Union and of which the author was a national of a non-Union country. The contingencies and circumstantial pressures show through, as in the decision to exclude photographs from protection – they were not protected under German law – unless they were photographs of protected works. The same is true of translation rights as addressed in article 6; this embodied the German and Swedish proposal for a limited period of protection, on condition that the translation was done within a certain period following publication of the original work, an approach opposed by France which favoured complete assimilation of translations to original works. The more restrictive view prevailed because Sweden insisted that readily available translations were crucial to the Scandinavian countries with their small dispersed populations and limited resources to meet educational needs. Here the requirement was that each Union country accord to authors of other Union countries an exclusive translation right of ten years' duration, to date from first publication of the work in any Union country. To enjoy the benefits of this provision, however, an authorised and complete translation had to appear within three years of the date of publication of the original, the exclusive right thereby conferred being limited to the language (or languages) of the authorised translation. In general terms, as Ricketson observes, significant differences emerged between producer nations such as France and Germany that were net exporters of literary and artistic products, and user nations such as the Scandinavians, net importers of these products.

Resting on the conviction that an 'international codification is in the nature of things and will be effected sooner or later', the 1884 Conference produced a draft convention for consideration by the participating nations. Although the draft convention was more coloured by universalist views than might have been expected, authors' and artists' organisations were disappointed that their claims had not been fully recognised. Yet material advances had been made, thanks largely to the questions prepared by the German delegation that provided a focus for debate. In the words of the British delegate F.O. Adams – the British minister to Switzerland and a member of the Society of Authors founded by Walter Besant in 1884 – the Germans 'succeeded in transforming a moderate programme into a draft Convention of considerable dimensions'. Ricketson (1987: 70–1) comments that the French, usually the leaders in the field, had been overshadowed by the Germans, several French proposals having failed to persuade the Conference. But this was merely an initial meeting, and a number of delegates had been given only a watching brief. Indeed, to the British, at this stage just four nations – France, Germany, Switzerland and Sweden – looked certain to join the proposed Union.

It remained to finalise matters at a working conference in 1885, again organised in Berne by the Swiss government. An unexpected aspect of the 1885 proceedings was the effective contribution of the British who, according to Ricketson (1987: 73) 'stepped out decisively from their role of silent observer at the first conference to become the most persuasive advocates of the principle of national treatment "pure and simple"'. In short, wherever the principle of global uniformity provoked disagreement, the British proposed that the matter be handled through the local law. For instance, the British won agreement that those nations whose law required the source of newspaper articles to be indicated should be able to keep this requirement without a reciprocal obligation being imposed on those nations whose law did not require such indication to be given. This sort of compromise marks the international legal order emerging from the 1885 discussion of the 1884 draft convention. As Ricketson describes it: 'If the 1884 draft was like a tree that had had an unexpected spurt of spring growth, the work of the 1885 Conference was similar to that of the gardener who does the pruning before the next spring' (1987: 73). Not that the predictable dose of Gallic fertiliser was not applied: the French pursued their usual advocacy of a more complete and uniform international protection of authors' rights. As prepared for the 1886 Conference, however, the 1885 draft was thus less absolutist and more pragmatic, partly through British influence but also reflecting a general wish that the Convention should not discourage countries whose law provided a lower level of copyright protection from joining the Union. Delegates were nevertheless uncertain whether their governments would approve the 1885 text. In the case of the Scandinavians, legislative changes would be necessary before accession could be agreed to, and Belgium's domestic law was in the process of revision. For France, on the other hand, the proposed text fell short, for instance in relation to translation rights. The French thus endorsed the text only to ensure the adherence of states such as the UK, not as their last word on the form that international protection for authors should take.

Twelve countries were represented at the 1886 Conference – Switzerland, Germany, France, the UK, Belgium, Spain, Italy, Tunisia, Liberia, Haiti, the USA and Japan, the last two as observers. The Berne Convention came into force on 5 December 1887. Not until 1989 did the United States Congress calculate that its citizens' copyright interests would be best served by joining the international copyright Union. By contrast, since 1887, the British law of copyright has been that of the Berne Convention, the two major common-law regimes thus diverging in this important formal respect. Of course, to the extent that the American cultural and copyright industries have come to dominate the international market, it is not clear that the reluctance to accede to Berne has locked the United States out of the international circuit.

IV

Three sets of remarks complete this historical sketch of the formation of the first multilateral Union of literary property: they relate to the heterogeneity of interests and legal norms embraced by the Berne Convention; the decision at the 1928 Rome Revision of the Convention to institute international protection of the *droit moral*; and a reflection on the Berne Convention in the light of a recent critique of international law.

The diverse interests that found common ground at Berne obeyed no single logic. The Convention ratified in 1887 by nine countries was the outcome of unforeseeable interactions between a variety of geopolitical interests, legal traditions, cultural politics, commercial calculations, literary and artistic professional pressures and governmental concerns with trade economics, foreign-policy priorities and national cultural distinction. In this uncertain amalgam, acceptance of compromise in the present was balanced by provision for regular revision of the treaty. The national give and take described in the preceding paragraphs is evidence that in the late nineteenth-century cultural-legal domain there was not so much one national hegemonic force as a balance of powers with respect to what might be desirable yet feasible legal norms to manage and protect the international circulation of literary property.

It is unhelpful to view the Berne Convention as the inevitable consequence of the logic of capitalism. This stance is adopted by the Soviet jurist Boguslavsky (1979: 190) in arguing that the Convention was established 'in the interests of capitalist enterprises and . . . continues to serve the interests of publishing and other companies', although 'this does not mean that they cannot be used also for the distribution in other countries of works of socialist culture'. The Marxian perspective equates a company with a capitalist while the dialectic ensures that an author equates with the proletariat. That publishers and booksellers were among the interests which generated the Berne Conferences suffices to establish the multilateral agreement as flawed. Indifferent to the complexity of the division of labour in the publishing process, the Marxian theory of labour – like the Romantic image of creation – holds fast to the dogmatic dichotomy of capitalist and creator. Boguslavsky thus declares that the treaty's drafting was 'conducted in such a way as to satisfy the said interests [of capital], and not the interests of the creators of the work' (1979: 55). The fact that the Berne Convention emerged from a motley of governmental and non-governmental initiatives contradicts the jurist's assertion that the national interests of states were incidental to those of private publishing capital. It is unhelpful to imagine the private and the public interests as perfectly complementary opposites, each with a unified mission and the technical means to attain it. If Ricketson is correct in identifying the emergence of international copyright primarily as a response to the pirating of German publishers and authors by the Dutch, of French publishers and authors by the Belgians, and of English publishers and authors by the Americans, it is not easy to see publishing capital as a unified interest. The international regime of law which emerged from compromises and conces-sions as the Berne Convention was anything but a historically inevitable monopoly. It was rather a typical creature of a nineteenth century that at one and the same time pursued ideals of universalism – a natural law notion that all are equal – and of imperialist (or Darwinist) differentiation.[7] This inter-national milieu was not the transparent expression of a universal logic of development; it marked an occasion of mixing, not only of different national legal regimes but also of cultural ideals and styles of calculation.

My second set of remarks concerns the appearance – with the 1928 Rome Revision of the Convention – of the provision for protecting the *droit moral*. The logic, if not the sole purpose of the *droit moral*, is to curtail the capacity of the market to interfere with a complex legal, ethical and aesthetic attribute: the right of personality attaching to the status of author that an individual writer might occupy or bear. The delegates to the first Berne Conferences did not have to consider the standing of this attribute which, in the 1880s, was still under construction in the laws of France and Germany. By 1928, however, it had acquired the status of a founding principle and, by the end of the Conference, it had also become an international legal norm providing for the protection of the *droit moral*. The principle is enunciated in article 6*bis* (1) of the revised Convention:

> Independently of the author's economic rights, and even after the transfer of the said rights, the author shall have the right to claim authorship of the work and to object to any distortion, mutilation or other modification of, or other derogatory action in relation to, the said work, which would be prejudicial to his honour or reputation.

In retrospect, given the subsequent dissemination of the aesthetic personality as the image of 'wholeness' of being, this revision might seem to mark a proper realignment of the legal provision. At the time, however, matters were somewhat less certain.

As is normal prior to a diplomatic conference, proposals for consideration had been circulated in advance to delegates to the 1928 Rome Conference by the host Italian government and the Bureau of the Berne Union. These proposals made no mention of the *droit moral*. Only when the Conference began did the Italian delegation propose that the right of attribution, the right of integrity and the right of disclosure be adopted as part of the Convention. Given the Italians' leading role at the 1928 Rome Conference, it is appropriate to consider the exposition of the *droit moral* by the Italian jurist and delegate to the Conference, Eduardo Piola-Caselli, who considers the matter in his 1927 *Trattato del diritto di autore e del contratto di edizione* and again in his 1943 *Codice del diritto di autore*. In the latter work – a commentary on the Italian legislation of 22 April 1941 – Piola-Caselli looks back to his part in the 1928 Conference. He depicts the 1925 Italian law on authors' rights – the so-called Rocco Law – as one of the first to sanction the recognition and protection of an author's right to defend his personality. With reference to the 1928 Conference, he credits the Italian delegation with having introduced an equivalent provision into international law (Piola-Caselli 1943: 16).[8] The *droit moral* is discussed in that section of the commentary concerned with articles 20–4 of the 1941 law respecting the protection of the author's personality. Following observations on the different approaches to this issue in French, Belgian, English and German law – Kant, von Gierke and Kohler are mentioned – Piola-Caselli expresses his distaste for the notion of a general 'right of personality' whose object is also its subject and, in particular, for Kohler's 'dualist' theory of authorial right as comprising two distinct sets of prerogatives, pecuniary and moral or personal. As for the author, Piola-Caselli (1943: 326) writes that 'he *lives in the work* to the extent that society identifies the nature of the work with the personal gifts and merits of the author, such that the personality of the latter grows in stature through the work he has created, just as it can equally be diminished'. In this sense the work is *'representative* of the personality of the author in its social relations'.

Piola-Caselli then recalls his intervention in the reforms leading up to the Italian law of 7 November 1925 and his 'virtually single-handed' resistance to the Kohlerian dualism 'threatening' the outcome. In relation to the protection of an author's non-pecuniary rights, Piola-Caselli's considered formulation was as follows:

> Independently of the exclusive patrimonial rights recognised in the preceding articles [of the proposed law], the author will have at all times the right to bring an action to prevent the paternity of the work from being unrecognised, to prevent the work from being modified, altered or mutilated in such a way as to cause serious and unjust prejudice to his personal interests.

> (Piola-Caselli 1943: 323)

Noting that the Minister of Justice Rocco had adopted his suggestion for article 16 of the 1925 Italian law on authors' rights (albeit substituting 'moral' for 'personal' interests), Piola-Caselli claims that the text of article 6*bis* adopted at the 1928 Revision Conference derives directly from his original formulation.

To the common-law delegates at Rome in 1928 the notion of a *droit moral* was quite new. Given the national treatment approach, however, they could assume that it was left to each member of the Union to determine how to give effect to the requirement that an author's 'personal interest' be protected. The common-law delegates seem to have believed that the personal interests protected by the *droit moral* were in essence identical to those protected not by copyright but by common-law remedies against breach of confidence (for the right of divulgation), defamation and libel (for the 'right of integrity') or against misrepresentation (for the 'right of attribution'). 'Honour' and 'reputation' – familiar categories to lawyers of common law otherwise ill at ease with continental notions of the 'moral' or 'spiritual' or 'intellectual' rights of personality – allowed this style of compromise (Ricketson 1987: 459–63). Article 6*bis* was taken to require no change to existing English law.

Now to my third and final remark. As already noted, the Berne Convention was one among other multilateral conventions achieved in the cultural environment of the later nineteenth century, sitting between the Paris Convention for the Protection of Industrial Property of 1883 and the Madrid Agreement on the International Registration of Trademarks of 1891.[9] These three treaties established the international coordinates of the field of intellectual property. They are now simply one element of the web of international agreements that includes the UNESCO Convention for the Protection of World Cultural and Natural Heritage, together with agencies such as WIPO (World Intellectual Property Organisation) and UNCTAD (United Nations Committee on Trade and Development). The latter's concerns extend to the devising of norms for an international regulation of intellectual property meeting the specific interests of the developed ('producer') and the developing ('user') nations.[10] These agencies work under the terms of the Paris Convention (revised in the 1967 Stockholm text), the Berne Convention (revised in the 1971 Paris text), the Universal Copyright Convention of 1952 and the Patent Cooperation Treaty of 1970. Copyright and patent matters are now admitted to the GATT (General Agreement on Tariffs and Trade), designed to be one of the three elements of the International Trade Organisation, alongside the International Monetary Fund and the World Bank. To grasp the international cultural-legal environment as it now is, we would also need to know about the 1957 Nice Agreement on the Classification of Goods and Services (on the international categorisation of registrable trademarks), the 1961 Rome Convention for the Protection of Performers, Producers of Phonograms and Broadcasting Organisations, the International Patent Classification Agreement (on the categorising of scientific knowledge for the purpose of ordering the field of patentable ideas), the 1971 Geneva Convention for the Protection of Producers of Phonograms Against Unauthorised Duplication of their Phonograms, the 1973 Vienna Agreement for the Protection of Typefaces and their International Deposit, and the 1980 Brussels Convention on the Protection of Satellite Transmissions and the Guidelines of the Protection of Privacy and Transborder Flows of Personal Data. Leaffer (1990) has gathered together no fewer than twenty-two international treaties on intellectual property now in force, not including regional agreements such as the Benelux Designs Convention or the Pan American Union.

Confronted by this deep layering of international agreements and by the evidence that, despite those occasions of conflict where states act in disregard of international norms, such agreements are usually observed, what do we make of critical claims that international law is a pseudo-rational enterprise? In *The Decay of International Law? A Reappraisal of the Limits of Legal Imagination in International Affairs*, Anthony Carty (1986) depicts a legal discipline which, he claims, has failed to reflect upon its own theoretical grounds of possibility, thus putting itself out of contention for consideration as a historically self-conscious knowledge. International law and lawyers, he argues, remain closed within a formal-technical discourse that hides its lack of rational foundations by an imaginary projection of the private law of individuals on to the domain of activity of states. Sheltering behind this projection and the doctrine of *pacta sunt servanda*, the pseudo-rationality of international law is said to allow its practitioners to avoid confronting the real political and epistemological conditions of their discipline. It also provides a deceptively objective and neutral cover for the interests of the modern capitalist state which, argues Carty, are pursued regardless of the norms established in international law. He thus adduces 'no evidence that the lawyer's perspective is dominant or even particularly significant in either reflective or powerful circles of international relations' (1986: 21).

Such a conclusion might be appropriate in respect of the two instances selected by Carty to support his argument: the Anglo-Argentinian conflict over the Malvinas Islands and the Israeli invasion of Lebanon. But can the same case be argued in respect of the intellectual property field? If the Berne Convention affords an international generality to the authorial attributes protected by the *droit moral* is this not evidence of the effectiveness of international law? And, indeed, evidence of a possibility which Carty prefers not to recognise: that international law may curtail rather than enhance the interests of capital. Like Boguslavsky, Carty (1986: 113) discerns 'an international economic elite for whom the primary goal is to subject nationalist self-interest to a framework of predictable constraints. For this elite the hypothesis of an international legal order may be quite functional.' Perhaps so, but only for some purposes. Where article 6*bis* of the Berne Convention is concerned, the international legal order would seem to function, whether we like it or not, to protect a highly specialised form of legal and aesthetic personality – that of the author – against the interests of the market. Advocates and opponents alike recognise this as the purpose of the *droit moral*.

Chapter 8

Some cultural issues for legal study

I

At the outset I referred to the subtext of the present study: that discussion of
the relations of the law of copyright and authorship is likely to be conducted
across a historical threshold where two different styles of reasoning and two
different manners of intellectual conduct confront one another – the legal-
governmental and the philosophical, the positive and the aesthetic. I am not
sure that mine has quite been the 'cheerful positivism' to which Michel
Foucault alludes, but what is certain is that the object has not been to
reconcile the two contending styles of reasoning. They are too well established in their difference to be levelled in this way. Were this to be doubted,
we would need only to look at two brief definitions, the first of copyright
from a current English handbook of the law of intellectual property, the
second from the writings of a French advocate of the *droit moral*.

Copyright, as Jeremy Phillips (1986: 106) writes, 'has no existence outside
the four walls of the Copyright Act. To put it another way, ownership of
copyright is only a legal right to exercise a legal right, and has no existence
except as a legal right.' Compare this to Bernard Edelman's statement of the
principle of the *droit moral*, where work and creator are one person, such that
to injure the work is to injure the creator:

> If one wishes to understand the deep nature of the French juridical system,
> this fundamental fact must be kept in mind: the work is nothing less than a
> specific *formalisation* of the personality of the author or, better still, it is the
> author's personality *in action*, in the Aristotelian sense of the term.
>
> (Edelman 1987b: 562)

And Edelman goes on to suggest that one of the virtues of the *droit moral* is
that it is open to, admits and protects the 'libidinal relation' between author
and work, a relation that copyright regimes simply cannot recognise.

The first quotation depicts a particular body of law and an associated legal
right as grounded in a specific legislative enactment, a condition of finitude
that neither presupposes nor flows into a fundamental attribute of the human

subject. The second quotation, especially when taken in conjunction with its amplifying comment, depicts a different regime of law, one that is grounded in the attributes of an authorial personality which, in turn, is aligned with the forces of the human psyche. Were we to take these two statements at their face value, we would have to conclude that the French system has about it a profound necessity – a transcendental guarantee which makes the French law's conventionality something more than just historical contingency. No such guarantee is available to the law of copyright.

It need not of course be the libido that serves in the role of guarantor that positive convention is grounded in something deeper than positive convention – consciousness, reason, history, labour and, more recently, language and discourse have all served just as well. And they have served not only in an affirmative mode but also to debunk the claim that positive institutions and knowledge – including positive law – are adequate institutions and knowledge. It has thus been held that a 'critical linguistic methodology can read within the structure of legal discourse the socio-historical and political affinities and conflicts that led to the emergence of the myth of law as a unitary language and as a discrete scientific discipline' (Goodrich 1987: ix). By turning to 'discourse theory' – 'discourse' is used as cognate with 'dialogue' and 'dialectic', and 'theory' is defined as 'openness to context, dialectic or dialogue' (1987: 206) – the law's real determinations, the ones it cannot know itself, are supposedly brought to consciousness. But is this not just another instance of the now familiar assertion that a momentous theoretical breakthrough has been achieved that finally dissolves appearances and grounds the object of knowledge in a revelation of its real determinations? The demonstration takes the form of claiming that a gap has been opened between what the law (or court or judge) does and its understanding of what it does. In this gap the theorist claims to recover the law's 'unconscious', its real conditions of possibility, knowledge of which allows us to measure how far actual law and lawyers fall short of self-understanding. But the suspicion remains: is not this 'unconscious', this gap between the workings of the law and the condition that is said to make them possible, itself a positive construction of the theorist?

To resist such schemata need not land us entirely within the hands of the pragmatists. Nor need it commit us utterly to the purest of legal positivisms, for instance to the view that where explanation is concerned every legal decision is *sui generis* or to the habit of assuming that the law's own materials are the limits of its universe. An extension of positivism – the nineteenth-century theory holding that the proper object of scientific enquiry was restricted to what was given as observable sense experience – legal positivism in this style is rightly criticised as a theoretically impoverished standpoint, a closure to theoretical concerns. However, positivism has been allowed 'at least one healthy effect': 'It directed the attention of lawyers towards their only box of tools – legal language and concepts – which had been somewhat neglected in the high-flown eloquence of rationalistic natural law thinking. It deepened their insight and their interest in the law as a system and a machinery of a special kind' (Stromholm 1985: 276–7).[1]

The law of copyright, it could be said, emerged as a 'machinery of a special kind'. In making this statement, there is no intention to deny the definite regularities – in the form of the jurisdictional traditions described in the foregoing chapters – that mark the history of legal arrangements pertaining to the rights and remedies of authors. Nor has this emphasis on the law of copyright as a positivity, a machinery of a special kind, precluded engagement in theoretical debate. On the contrary, given the various transcendental schemata now circulating – dialectical and discursive, historicist and post-structuralist – the measured positivism endorsed in the present study is a goad to theoretical debate. It is also a means for strengthening our theoretical nerve so that we hold fast to the descriptive brief, rather than succumbing to philosophical scheming. The point of the exercise has been to avoid transforming into philosophically necessary preconditions the varied historical conditions – legal and other – that have determined the contingent forms and attributes of the person of the author. This has been a way to achieve concreteness.

Commitment to defend the historical positivity of the law of copyright has not led to a picture of that law as a purely formal, neutral and self-enclosed system of rules. The legal arrangements described in the foregoing chapters might have been legally efficacious but they can scarcely be said to have been rationally pure. On the contrary, they have been open to a variety of local circumstances, interests and pressures. The law of copyright has been – and is increasingly – aestheticised. In attempting to describe the processes of this aestheticisation – the aim of the following section – it will again be a matter of arguing that the aesthetic is not the general theory of human cultural development that it purports to be. It is, rather, a specific technology of personification or personal formation, a technology now disseminated into and by education and management. This is despite its initially delimited use – in the form envisaged by Schiller in 1795 – as a highly specialised form of self-stylisation designed to achieve a mode of being that would transcend the division in 'man's' existence obtaining since 'the inner unity of human nature was severed ... and a disastrous conflict set its harmonious powers at variance':

> State and Church, laws and customs, were now torn asunder; enjoyment was divorced from labour, the means from the end, the effort from the reward. ... Everlastingly chained to a single little fragment of the whole, man develops into nothing but a fragment ... he never develops the harmony of his being, and instead of putting the stamp of humanity upon his own nature, he becomes nothing more than the imprint of his occupation or of his specialised knowledge.
>
> (Schiller 1967 [1795]: 33, 35)

This powerful image of a divided nature, and its purported resolution through an aesthetic (self-)culture, confronts lawyers and the rest of us with the challenge to complete what is said to be our present incompleteness. It can also play upon a characteristic tension in a contemporary jurisprudence attached on one side to the historical scatter of statutes, case law, procedures and determinate legal personalities and, on the other side, to a philosophically grounded critique which seeks to subject positive law to a rational (or dialectical and aesthetic) rectification.

One manner of responding to the possibility that aesthetic completeness is now the standard by which people will judge one another is to build on the historical anthropology of personhood proposed by Mauss and Weber. It will be recalled that the crucial move in the argument was to differentiate *persons* from *individuals* – the former depend for their delineation and distribution on definite forms of social organisation and cultural technique. Much of the present study has been devoted to tracing how in different legal systems certain legal attributes and statuses have been delineated and distributed to individuals (and non-individuals), attributes and statuses that have helped organise the practical deportment of those individuals (and non-individuals). By not conceptualising the delineation and distribution of authorial personality in terms of consciousness (or its illusion), we have taken seriously the legal conditions that formed the public person of authors. I have also taken care not to treat the aesthetic persona as the complete or fundamental form of human subjectivity. In part this was in order the better to admire it as a truly remarkable and specialised achievement of European Romanticism. Such a notion may be also useful, however, when we confront the claim of aesthetics to critically address positive law in the higher name of the 'whole' person or the 'complete' culture. If the approach of Mauss and Weber is right, the aesthetic persona is neither more nor less fundamental, moral or 'political' than the legal personality of the copyright holder. Attached to their different purposes, the former has arisen in one department of existence – that of 'aesthetic education', and the latter in another – the sphere of law. The former depends on one set of technical conditions – the aesthetic dialectic as a technique of personality formation; the latter depends on another – the specific set of legal categories and procedures whose emergence has been described in the foregoing pages.

II

Ours is a culture at once profoundly juridified and, now, profoundly aestheticised. Given the project – historical description of the role of copyright in the history of authorship – my choice has been to treat the aesthetic persona as a highly specialised artefact incapable of being the ground or anchorage of legal personality. Matters of identity, origin and ownership, on the other hand, I have treated not as ideological crudities that the law of copyright imposes on a purportedly complete development of human capacities but as legal positivities that have defined and administered the legal personality of authors. That said, it remains the case that the legal sphere has been anything but immune to the rise of aesthetic themes. What happens to these themes once they enter the legal sphere and are deployed as legal norms? In their new environment, aesthetic themes behave like any other legal norm. They no longer float in that purportedly unbounded time and space into which aesthetics has projected 'man's' completion. Instead, as legal norms, they reach no further than the limits of the legal sphere or, more concretely, of the particular jurisdiction in which they have been taken up. When the law talks of integrity and the person as a whole, the reference is therefore not to philosophical universals but to forms of legal personality appropriate to particular legal purposes (Wolff 1938).

Along with a juridification of the aesthetic has gone an aestheticisation of the law, a reorienting of certain areas of law towards the magnetic image and ideal of aesthetic personality. To illustrate certain problems attendant on this phenomenon, let us briefly turn to developments in the field of obscenity law. Jurisprudential reasoning has been disabled by its openness to the psycho-aesthetic analysis which has come to dominate discussion of pornography and the regulation of obscene publications.[2] In the mid-twentieth century, English and American obscenity law began to look away from the medical norms which for nearly a century had shaped and guided the legal policing of pornography, particularly through the delineation of vulnerable categories of person and the elaboration of the doctrine of 'variable obscenity' (what is not socially harmful in one circumstance is so in another). The new regime of regulation (and deregulation) was based on the aesthetic norm of personality. Obscenity law and aesthetics joined forces. Obscene publication was re-defined from a socially harmful conduct to a display of immature personality, and pornography was reclassified from a social pathology in need of legal prevention to a 'failed' art in which sexual imagery and moral seriousness do not achieve aesthetic balance. Within the discourse of aesthetics, the boundary is drawn in this manner whether the work in question is Victorian por-nography distinguished by its being 'dissociated from itself, from experience, from literature' (Marcus 1966: 228) or twentieth-century pornography – 'daydream material, divorced from reality, whose main purpose is to nourish erotic fantasies or, as the psychiatrists say, psychic autoeroticism' (Lockhart and McClure 1960: 65). Thus redefined, pornography is said to appeal to those persons who, as incomplete (and immature) as it, are unable to balance the sexual and the moral elements in an integral response.[3] This diagnosis is intelligible only by reference to the aesthetic norm of the complete (or integrated) personality, defined as one in which sexual excitement or desire are successfully balanced against moral responsibility. To take this persona as the image of human emancipation and potentiality fulfilled is completely to miss the fact that is the opposite of universal. In historical and cultural terms, this persona is the highly specialised – and still unevenly distributed – artefact of aesthetic education.

The emergence of this figure displaced the nineteenth-century medical and moral norm which gave English and American criminal law its longstanding test of obscenity as that which has a tendency to deprave and corrupt those types of person – the morally vulnerable – into whose hands such material might fall or, more likely, be distributed. The penetration of aesthetics into the legal sphere is registered in the United Kingdom Obscene Publications Act of 1959. The Act retained its older medical component of harm but at the same time provided a 'literary merit' defence based on the testimony of literary experts. In American law, a Supreme Court majority agreed in 1957 in *Roth* v. *United States* on a standard to define obscenity: to be obscene a publication had to 'appeal to the prurient interest of the average person', and 'be utterly without redeeming social value'. The 'prurience' test makes sense only by the implied reference to the integrated personality as one that can reconcile the excitation of the erotic with an appreciation of the work as a whole.[4]

Supporting the shift from a medical to an aesthetic regulation of pornography is the looming presence of the dialectically 'complete' person. It is here that the integrity of the work joins up with the integrity of an authorial persona which, in turn, aligns with the imagery of the fully developed individual and society. These coordinates persist from the first formulations of the aesthetic personality by Schiller in the late eighteenth century, for instance where he expounds on the use of the work of art for fashioning a distinctively complete social persona in which the balance of intellect and emotion, content and form, is achieved. Having observed that it is 'by no means always a proof of formlessness in the work of art itself if it makes its effect solely through its contents', Schiller diagnoses a failure of aesthetic education in the reader: 'this may just as often be evidence of a lack of form in him who judges it':

> If he is either too tensed or too relaxed, if he is used to apprehending either exclusively with the intellect or exclusively with the senses, he will, even in the case of the most successfully realised whole, attend only to the parts, and in the presence of the most beauteous form respond only to the matter.
> (Schiller 1967 [1795]: 157)

This mode of conducting oneself towards the work of art will re-emerge one and a half centuries later and with only a slight alternation of vocabulary as the newly discovered 'psychological' truth about pornography and its consumers, a truth which Anglo-American law of obscenity has adopted as a fundamental norm. In the meantime, this personally formative technique has been taken up and widely disseminated through the apparatus of literary education.[5] The most influential psychological account of pornography in the 1960s depicts an ideal human sexual development that must meet 'the natural and desirable interest in sex, without turning it into morbid channels, confusing and linking it with violence, or keeping it antiseptically detached from the physical sensations which should accompany it, and by connecting the sexual impulse with those love feelings which are its highest perfection' (Kronhausen and Kronhausen 1959: 260). Psychologised and sexualised it might be, but there is no mistaking the aesthetic lineage of this psychology in that ideal of the aesthetic 'man' who had differentiated himself from those lesser persons whose interest in a work of art was 'quite simply either a moral or a material interest; but what precisely it ought to be, namely aesthetic, that it certainly is not' (Schiller 1967 [1795]: 157). The American Law Institute's proposal for a new obscenity statute could thus state that its primary aim was to 'prevent exploitation of the psychosexual tension created by the conflict between the individual's normal sexual curiosity and drive, and the powerful social and legal inhibitions that restrain overt sexual behaviour' (Lockhart and McClure 1960: 56). Pornography and its consumers alike are specified in terms of a dialectical schema in which failure to balance desire and norm, sex and seriousness, is assumed to constitute failure to achieve wholeness of being. Under this sort of aesthetic pressure, even the procedures and conduct of obscenity law were affected. For instance, expert literary witnesses in obscenity trials were supposedly there to give an objective statement of the work's standing as serious literature. In practice, what they gave were often brilliant demonstrations of their own wholeness as aesthetic personalities, showing how to face up to sex while all the time directing it to higher moral ends. To cite just one example from a rich gallery, in *Reg.* v. *Penguin Books Ltd.* in 1960 – the trial of *Lady Chatterley's Lover* – Dame Rebecca West demonstrated how to read thirteen detailed descriptions of sex as so many moments in 'a return of the soul to the more intense life'. This capacity to weigh the content of the work against its form, to balance sexual descriptions against moral messages, has become the norm for judging what counts as the 'mature' or 'integrated' way of relating oneself to erotica.

Let us take the case of the British government's 1979 *Report of the Committee on Obscenity and Film Censorship* (the Williams Report). There is no mistaking the style in which a distinction is constructed between the supposedly mechanical coerciveness of photographic works and the cooling passage through a consciousness which the act of reading print works is said to involve. At least in some minimum way all written works are thus taken to participate in an act of consciousness and thereby to achieve the balancing of physical and mental needed to meet what we should now recognise as the aesthetic criterion, not the universal truth about 'mature' humanity. Hence the *Report's* proposal to deregulate all erotica that consist solely of the written word.

But why should the aesthetic image of 'man' as 'whole' person be a problem? It is indeed a matter of mistaking a particular for a universal, a cult practice for a general truth of culture. Historicising the aesthetic persona (and its dialectical technique of self-fashioning) relativises it as a specialised but increasingly widely distributed cultural attribute and activity. This promises a better chance of grasping the diversity of forms of personality, including those that have emerged within the legal sphere, without subordinating them to the image of the aesthetically 'whole' person, however prestigious the latter has become.

Reference to the phenomenon of privacy as a legal right provides a further example.[6] Discussing the origins of the right of privacy and the concept of the 'rights of the personality', Stromholm (1967) reviews developments in Anglo-American common law on the one hand and German and French civilian jurisdictions on the other. He contrasts the invention by the American jurists Warren and Brandeis (1890) of a 'right to privacy' that protected an 'inviolate personality' (as noted in chapter 1) and the researches of their French and above all their German contemporaries Gareis, von Gierke and Kohler directed at defining the fundamental 'right of the personality' (*Persönlichkeitsrechte*). British writers remained disinterested in the concepts of privacy and personality, although there had in fact been a British connection, one that Stromholm (1967: 31) characterises as a 'remarkable coincidence'. In both Kohler's theorisation of a basic 'right of personality' and in Warren and Brandeis' outline of a 'right to privacy', the case of *Prince Albert* v. *Strange* (1849) played a role. This well-known case extended the tort of breach of confidence to include the obligation not to publish information that was not generally available to the public, in this instance copies of and information concerning etchings by Prince Albert and Queen Victoria (Phillips 1984). The issue was not argued on the grounds of a copyright infringement, although some etchings had been reproduced without authorisation in the catalogue of an exhibition that Strange proposed to stage (and although the plaintiff was represented by Serjeant Talfourd). In his judgment Vice Chancellor Knight Bruce referred to such information as a 'property of a private nature, which the owner, without infringing on the right of any other, may and does retain in a state of privacy'. The Prince's pursuit of litigation did anything but achieve the 'privacy' he sought.

From this and from other decisions related to the common-law right of copyright Warren and Brandeis (1890: 200–1) drew a distinction between a concern to protect one's property (albeit literary) and a concern to protect one's self, that is, one's 'privacy'. As they described the circumstance obtaining at common law, 'the value of the production is found not in the right to take profits arising from its publication, but in the peace of mind or the relief afforded by the ability to prevent any publication whatsoever'. This dignitary aspect of common-law copyright was clearly not what the London booksellers had once thought to matter.

The American and German researches need not be considered as so many different lines tracing a common origin to the 'whole' person. For Warren and Brandeis it was a matter of extending a liberal conception of the individual's right to independence from interference by government and law to cover the encroachment of 'yellow press' gossip upon the consecrated private space of the American home and family. The German development rested on quite different grounds. Drawing on natural law and early nineteenth-century Romantic themes, the German writers elaborated a general 'right of personality' from an array of rights 'recognised by positive law or postulated by writers which had often little more in common than the name' (Stromholm 1967: 29–30). These included rights to one's body, life and liberty, honour and social reputation, freedom, name and likeness (or image), as well as what Kohler (1880) termed a right to a 'sphere of intimacy' and a 'right of secrecy' against unauthorised publication of private correspondence and against the exploitation of real individuals as recognisable models for fictional characters. Stromholm (1967: 44) speculates that the right to privacy and the right of personality arise from 'a common core' but he does not specify what this core consisted of. Noting his comment that it was in the sphere of copyright that the concept of a right of personality proved most resilient, in this urge to unity we might suspect the aesthetic imperative at work, the figure of the Romantic author and the aesthetic persona being exemplary for the integrated right of personality that the writers wished to establish.

III

The *droit moral* arguably entails an equivalence of the writer's legal and aesthetic personalities. In this, it does more than differentiate from the law of copyright and thus demonstrate the latter's historical particularity; it also provides a limiting case for my argument on the historical and theoretical relation between law and aesthetics. In fact, as I shall argue, the particular construction and distribution of rights achieved in the regime of the *droit moral* represents one solution to a regulatory problem that, in other circumstances, might have been solved in other ways. However, in order to set the *droit moral* into its broader intellectual context, let us follow at some length the path of one particular advocate of this particular right.

   Unlike the law of copyright, European law has constructed a definite personality for the writer as author, a personality or status grounded in natural law and in aesthetic notions of the inviolability and the ideal wholeness of the individual's 'person' and of the expressive embodiment of the integrity of that person in the integrity of their creative work. These provisions are not part of the law of copyright, which emerged in a pre-aesthetic common-law environment as a means of assigning and regulating an economic right to the mechanical copying of works. By contrast, the *droit moral* takes its name from a term meaning 'non-economic' or 'non-material'.[7] It refers to a specific set of non-economic attributes that constitutes the legal status of the writer as creator. The French jurist, Bernard Edelman, our advocate of the doctrine of the *droit moral* in its purest form, defines a prime consequence of this particular arrangement:

> [A]ny attempt on the work is construed as an attempt on the *identity* of its creator. In other words, there is a complete homology between the two, and to interfere with the one is to interfere with the other. It follows that, just as one cannot commit one's labour for life – at the risk of being deemed a slave – so one cannot abandon one's work to another, without alienating one's own self. In short, the work is of the same juridical nature as the human person, with the one reservation that the work enjoys an undeniable advantage: it is perpetual.
>
> (Edelman 1987b: 562)

Within the copyright system matters are quite different. There, says Edelman, 'the work is radically detached from the person of the author, and acquires an absolute juridical autonomy.... [T]he work can lead a free economic existence.' As a result of this freedom which he regrets, '[i]n the copyright system, one cannot talk in the strong sense of authors' rights but only of *rights in the work*. In other words, the author, as person, disappears in favour of his creation and, in this way, the relation of belonging is broken' (1987b: 567–8).

But before the 'relation of belonging' can be broken it must first be established, something that has never been done in copyright jurisdictions. It is necessary therefore to temper Edelman's powerful statement of the contrast between the two systems and to qualify his picture of the *droit moral* as an organic attribute of the creative subject. Under the *droit moral* the work is conceived of as an embodiment of the writer's authorial personality, one in which an inscription, investment or placement of subjectivity seems necessary. However, we need to see that as a legal construction this conception goes no further than the instituted ensemble of tributary rights that comprise the *droit moral*: the right to publish; the right to retract one's publication; the right to have one's authorship attributed; the right to have the integrity of one's literary or artistic creation respected, in other words, the right to object to distortions. Unlike a copyright which can be sold, assigned or otherwise alienated, the elements of the *droit moral* are by legal definition perpetual, unassignable and inalienable. But the point is this: for all its use of natural law and aesthetic terms, in relation to copyright the *droit moral* is neither more nor less than an alternative legal means of regulating a system of literary production. It simply proceeds through a different (but similarly distinct and limited) legal delineation and distribution of rights.

For students of copyright the great lesson of the *droit moral* is its reminder that the delineation and distribution of rights could have been otherwise than they have happened to be in Anglo-American jurisdictions. The relation between the writer's legal and aesthetic personalities is historically and geopolitically specific. That copyright should have taken the form of a commercially transferable 'right in the work' is not the sign of a failure to recognise the integral aesthetic subject. It is simply that this is the form of right constructed when the instruments of juridification available within a particular legal system were used to address a historically specific problem of legal regulation. As we have noted, before any system of law could distinguish literary writing from the manifold other forms of human labour and classify that writing as part of its producer's person, literary writers had to *acquire* a capacity for an aesthetic relation to the work, and literary writing had to *become* an aesthetic activity. Thus the law of copyright and the *droit moral* have each come to deploy their particular categories, procedures and forms of personhood.

Neither of them, however, can support a universal judgement. This is because their means of judging – their procedures, categories and norms (including the legal persons that they construct) – and thus their practical validity reach no further than the limits of their deployment. If for the *droit moral* the author 'lives in his work' (Piola-Caselli 1943: 326; Ricketson 1987: 462), it is within the specified conditions of a particular legal framework that this living is done. Thus, for instance, the right of integrity specified in Article 6*bis* of the Berne Convention is subject to the qualification that at issue are only those distortions, mutilations, modifications or other derogatory actions in relation to the said work which are prejudicial to the honour and reputation of the author. As noted in chapter 7, adoption of the terms 'honour and reputation' at the 1928 Rome revision of the text of the treaty was contingent upon their being intelligible to the common-law delegates to the Conference; the technical understanding of honour and reputation deployed in the context of common-law defamation proceedings was thus taken to be broadly commensurate with what the Europeans understood as injuries to 'moral' interests.

This example suggests why the emergence of the *droit moral*, like that of copyright, cannot be adequately understood through a history or theory centred on a universal subject. But it also suggests why – as a legal mechanism – the *droit moral* conception of the work as embodying the writer's authorial personality is by no means entirely identical to the parallel conception found in the sphere of aesthetics. What, then, of the notion that – in recognising and protecting the author's whole person as present in the work and in balancing the author's 'moral' and material attributes – the *droit moral* achieves an equivalence of the writer's legal and aesthetic personalities? Kain (1982) and others have shown why we should not take the aesthetic persona as the necessary and universal form of complete human being. We might still admire the imagery of an existence beyond present division, alienation and commodification, but this is no reason to concede to the pressure to reconcile the complex and contingent relations that have obtained between legal and aesthetic personalities.

Yet how does the issue look from the aesthetic side? Let us now follow Bernard Edelman's writings across a range of matters in order to set his advocacy of the *droit moral* into its broader conditions of intelligibility. In his account of the recognition of authors' rights under French law, Edelman identifies a 'logic' whereby – over the course of the nineteenth century – the 'human person' emerged as the 'public' translation of the principles of the Declaration of the Rights of Man that found a particular expression in the domain of authors' rights (Edelman 1989: 35–6). This 'person' was the key to a dual reconciliation of the ideal and the material – the resolution of how an author can be more than just an owner and how a work can be more than just a property:

> As long as the author appeared as the owner of his work, he could not be assimilated to it. The right of property in fact presumes an *extrinsic relation* between the possessor and the object possessed: the owner of a house does not confuse himself with his property. Thus, to break free from the property right and to imagine on the one hand that the author was more than the owner of the work and, on the other hand, that the work was more than a property, a thing, this *extrinsic relation* had to be broken; the work had to become part of the total activity of the person.
>
> (Edelman 1989: 35)

Once established as the integrating entity, 'the person' provided the anchorage for author's right, 'affirming not only that the work was the expression of creator's personality but also that the linkage of author and work was of the same nature as the linkage of the person to his or her voice, image, privacy and so on' (1989: 37). As does Recht (1969: 69–75), Edelman credits the Belgian jurist Edmond Picard with having conceptualised a relation of right between incorporeal goods (*biens immatériels*) and the person's action as expressed in his or her 'legal being'. He also notes that by the early twentieth century French courts were confirming the new relation of personal right and incorporeal good. However, this relation received its statutory formulation only with the law of 11 March 1957. Edelman (1987a: 9) finds this statute exemplary in its vision – he describes it approvingly as 'totally permeated by individualism' – and in its provision in article 1 that '[t]he author of an intellectual work shall, by the mere fact of its creation, enjoy an exclusive incorporeal property right in the work, effective against all persons. This right includes attributes of an intellectual or moral nature as well as attributes of an economic nature, as determined by this law.'[8]

The cornerstone of Edelman's approach is a radically personalist conception of the relation of work and author. For him, the *droit moral* is the supreme form of law that, unlike a mere property right (or copyright), does justice to this integral and unbreakable relation. The 'personality' of the author is treated as the exemplary expression of the free universal subject. Notwithstanding this, a degree of concern with historical circumstance is admitted, even if – predictably in such an approach – the role of circumstance is negative. In other words, when circumstance is admitted to the picture, it is because it constitutes a threat to this authorial person and its law. One such threat – occasioned by new communications technologies and by the new cultural policy with its 'industrial vision of creation' (Edelman 1989: 121) – is said to have found statutory expression in the more recent French legislation on Authors' Rights and Neighbouring Rights:

> The law of 3 July 1985 breaks new ground. Indeed, it innovates to the point where there is reason to fear that the 1957 law, which the new legislation was supposedly to modify, has in fact been radically denatured, or, worse still, condemned to become purely residual, along with those whom it has traditionally protected. The writer alone in the study, the artist at the easel, the composer poring over the score, all risk being transformed into the pale survivors of a bygone age. At the very least, we are now in the presence of two laws, that of 11 March 1957 and that of 3 July 1985. These two laws organise two regimes: one regime is that of the individual creator, the other is that of the mass creator. This amounts to saying that these two laws, merged into one – the 'modified' law of 11 March 1957 – promise us conflicts, doctrinal disputes and tortuous cases. The law of 3 July 1985 brutally dumps us into a cultural era where the creator becomes the indispensable yet secondary cog in an enterprise – that of the audiovisual work – of which he is no longer in control. Whether we welcome it or deplore it, the fact is clear: Balzac is a diplodocus, and Marguerite Duras a consoling exception for suffering spirits.
>
> (Edelman 1987a: 1)

This statement opens a commentary on the 1985 law where, 'for the first time in French legislative history, the rights of authors are envisaged from an essentially economic perspective' (1987a: 9). To characterise what he takes to be the retrograde provisions emerging in the new law, Edelman coins an oxymoron – 'copyright à la française'. The principles underpinning the *droit moral* are, he says, seriously diluted.[9]

In viewing authors' rights 'from an essentially economic perspective', the legislators' aim was in fact to help French film and television products competing in an international environment in which even France risks becoming a losing player. As does, in Edelman's view, the individual author traditionally the subject and beneficiary of the *droit moral*. In the new scale of operations in the cultural industries, 'no matter how fertile a Balzac, a Dumas or a Dostoevsky might have been, they could never have produced the 125,000 hours of televised fiction which the European Community will soon be consuming annually' (1987a: 5). Grounded in the imperatives of cultural production and marketing on this scale, the 1985 law is said to favour enterprises and investors, not individual creators. In debate on the Bill in the National Assembly, the sacred primacy of individual right was proclaimed. However, what eventuated were mechanisms such as article 19(3) providing for the remuneration of performers to be determined – if not otherwise specified by contract or collective agreement – 'by reference to the schedules established under the specific agreements concluded in each sector between the employees' and the employers' organisations'. Edelman seizes on the term 'employee' (*salarié*) to argue that there is a fundamental contradiction between recognising an 'author's right' in all its individuality and imposing 'the collective status of employees'. The traditional individual right, he argues, has been displaced by norms drawn from labour law, 'a law with a strongly collective connotation and which, *a priori*, appears antithetical to the author's *droit moral*' (1987a: 5). Another new mechanism (article 13) extends in the producer-investor's favour a presumption that the audiovisual author has assigned the exclusive exploitation rights in their work. This is taken as evidence that 'we are no longer very far from the system of *copyright*' (1987a: 6). With such measures, the 1985 law opens a 'hiatus ... between a *droit moral* which is necessarily subjective and individual, and patrimonial rights which are collectively determined and administered' (1987a: 13). As a result, '[w]e are no longer in the "purity" of the *droit moral*, but heading towards a "*copyright à la française*"' (1987a: 18).

The new law was thus a perturbation both of the principle and of the practical defence of individual authorial personality and the rights and attributes attaching to it under French law. From the columns of the *Recueil Dalloz Sirey*, Edelman has since the late 1960s elaborated his own not always orthodox analysis and defence of these rights and attributes. From early theoretical discussions (1970) on the nature of the legal subject – one that exists in its representations as these are 'thought' by a law which is at once an independent structure and a system tied to the dominant relations of property – the emphasis has shifted to the precise manner in which authorial personality has been treated by the specific norms of French law on authors' rights: the legal life of an author's fictional characters and the 'right' of parody in 'Le personnage et son double' (1980), the treatment of original ideas and banality in 'Création et banalité' (1983) and the limits of the freedom to appropriate a private life for fictional purposes in a comment on 'Fiction et vie privée' (1985a). However, as the discussion of the 1985 law shows, a profound rupture is taken to have occurred in the legal tradition and more broadly. It is not only a matter of French legislators' action. Commenting on three 1986 Cour de Cassation findings on lower court decisions concerning the applicability of author's right protection to video games and software, Edelman (1986: 414) observes that 'prior to the law of 3 July 1985, judges freely sought to establish the *artistic character* of photographs. This exception [to the rule that aesthetic merit was not a precondition of originality and thus of protection] derived from a mistrust of machines; these, it was suspected, were incapable of producing art! Other times, other manners! *Today technical requirements are at the basis of the intellectual effort.*' The last phrase requires explanation. 'Intellectual effort' does not, at first glance, belong in the same category as 'imprint of personality', the traditional requirement for recognition of an authorial presence in the work. Yet, Edelman continues, 'for a considerable time the courts have privileged, in the notion of an intellectual work, not a *creative will* but intellectual work or effort. This evolution is due to a dual phenomenon: on the one hand the pressure of a *market* which tended to seek protection for all those products that did not fall within the provisions of specific laws (patents, designs, models); on the other hand, the interpretation accorded to the notion of *merit*.' Equating 'merit' with 'beauty' but knowing that aesthetic merit had been expressly excluded as a criterion for determining whether or not a work was protected, French judges have proceeded to avoid the matter of an author's 'will' to produce a work of art. As a result, the courts behave as though 'artistic and literary productions could not be envisaged from a perspective that was . . . literary and artistic'. By this approach – even in France – the 'author's right was emptied of all its aesthetic substance: creative will was displaced by "intellectual effort" and the product obtained became the result of this effort'.

This judicial shift made it plausible to argue that an item of software could bear the imprint of an individual author's subjectivity. Edelman reconstructs the argument as follows. First, the originality of a program derives from the freedom of its developer in relation to certain choices; second, exercising this freedom by making a choice constitutes what the law now counts as a 'personalised effort' that gives rise to an 'individualised structure' that carries the 'imprint of [one's] intellectual work'. It is enough to fan a sardonic response:

> Is it certain that every *freedom of choice* is original? If so, then the whole of daily life will be marked by this imprint, for every action – eating, drinking, reading, etc. – implies a choice. The Cour de Cassation, in deciding that a 'personalised effort' followed from the mere fact that a choice was to be made, and that the individualised structure in which the choice materialised possessed an original character, determined in favour of an ideology of intellectual *effort* to the detriment of the very concept of *creation*.
>
> (Edelman 1986: 416)

But there is more. By equating an intellectual work with the making of a choice and the making of a choice with the originality that the program requires if it is to be recognised and protected as the work of an author, the court has merely drawn a vicious circle: the same concept – choice – is used in two quite different forms, as freedom and as 'personalised effort'. As Edelman puts it: 'once a program is a work of the mind, it is *de jure* original.' The power to discriminate between an original and a non-original work is lost.

The historical reality of this shift is correlated with a deeper reorientation in modern culture. Recalling the traditional philosophical distinction between human actions on the natural world (technology) and reflexive actions on oneself (philosophy, religion, art), Edelman draws out the juridical distinction between a patent law concerned with human actions on nature that have an 'industrial result' and a law of literary or artistic property concerned with something else entirely:

> Indifferent to human action on nature or, more generally, on the material world, its sole pretension was to demonstrate the superiority of mind over matter, of the immutable over the mutable, of eternity over the historical, of Shakespeare over Watt, or of Plato over manufacturers' trade secrets. Unlike the inventor, the artist reveals that which has always – already – existed.
>
> (1986: 415)

This was the reason why a *droit moral* existed, 'perpetual and unwaivable, needing no formalities of registration'. But things have changed:

> Now, this ideal division of the world is in the process of collapse. Not only are we seeing the emergence of new intellectual properties . . . that relate at one and the same time to intellectual speculation and to industrial applications, but also and above all we are witnessing a significant detaching of the author from the work. Insofar as the market propels all production as an economic value, organising its circulation, the author is becoming a producer of his own works. Henceforth, from being a creator, he is transformed into a worker.
>
> (1986: 415)

From this, it seems, we can observe a 'redistribution of human activities which transgresses the traditional boundaries between the industrial world and the world of mind and which, moreover, goes hand in hand with an upheaval in our relation to nature'.

Even as Edelman was expressing his concern at matters such as the transplanting of copyright norms into French law in France, so in Anglo-American jurisdictions there were expressions of concern at a possible transplanting of *droit moral* norms into copyright systems. I return to this coincidence presently. First, however, let us set this defence of the *droit moral* into the larger philosophical and political picture by tracing certain themes that Edelman has developed from *Le droit saisi par la photographie* (1973) to *La propriété littéraire et artistique* (1989). These dates mark the passage from a Marxian project for a science of law to an aesthetic defence of the *droit moral* and an ecological plea for the respect of the integrity of species. It will therefore be a case of moving some apparent distance beyond that authorial personality which, for Edelman, had once found sanctuary in the French law of 1957 but is now an 'endangered species'. Yet, as we have noted, Marxism and aesthetics are coming to be seen as having a profound historical identity – the Schillerian aesthetic having been embodied not only in the image of 'man's' non-estranged labour under communism but also in that of non-estranged authorial creation under the *droit moral*.

An aesthetically grounded jurisprudence such as Edelman's takes it to be possible, indeed necessary, to contemplate the state of human history and culture as a whole. As might be expected from the foregoing paragraphs, the view is sombre:

> For if we look at what is happening to us, I believe, we run the risk of being shocked. On the one hand, in the sphere of private law, we see a Nature that is finally mastered now being transformed into an industrial product, together with a human subject that is subordinated to a commercial logic. On the other hand, in the sphere of international public law, we see Nature in its most recent manifestation as the 'common patrimony of Humanity' becoming an object of management, while Humanity becomes a managerial subject.
>
> (Edelman 1985b: 125)

It is less the jurist than the aesthetic critic of culture who here looks beyond the legal sphere to see a nature commodified and a human subject alienated by commerce, law and government – on a scale hitherto unknown. In such an optic, a single world-historical truth can embrace not only the endangered integrity of the aesthetic work and that of the person of its author, but also the integrity of the subject in law, the integrity of the nation, the integrity of the universal human subject and the integrity of the human species. Such is the scope of aesthetic vision.

In *Ownership of the Image*, Edelman (1979) argued in his distinctively oblique manner both the autonomy of law and its complicity with the prevailing capitalist system of production and circulation. Were the law not independent, it could not persuasively furnish individuals with the means to imagine themselves as legal subjects in a form appropriate to the circulation of commodities entailed in the system of production, that is, in a form in which as a legal subject he or she is recognised by the law as having the capacity of a proprietor – whether or not an individual actually holds property and seeks to be so recognised. In this formal sense, the individual is recognised to have a legal property in his or her own attributes – reputation, body and labour – which he or she alone can choose to dispose of or put into circulation through the exercise of a free and equitable contract whereby a property in the fruits of one's labour is legally exchanged against a wage. In *Ownership of the Image* Edelman did not dwell on the specifics of Anglo-American copyright. However, he provided the terms – a formally non-coercive and equitable contract, a 'freedom' to alienate the property in the fruits of one's intellectual labour consonant with the needs of commodity circulation – that are taken up in his later writings (1987a; 1987b; 1989) to depict copyright as an independent legal form yet one structurally complicit with the market.

The less interesting aspect of such propositions is their claim, as theory, to open up that familiar gap between what the law does and its understanding of what it does, the gap that is so convenient for the critical theorist's posture of recovering the purportedly tacit powers, meanings, interests, fictions and contradictions normally kept hidden but which, to the 'critical and reflexive' gaze, are always symptomatically visible. Edelman as theorist lays bare the tautology whereby in recognising individuals as free subjects in law, the law in fact merely obeys historical necessity by establishing them as subjects in the form appropriate to the capitalist system of production. In the last instance, but only then, law obeys the economy. Hence the play of the French title – *Le droit saisi par la photographie* – the law caught (in its appearance) but also caught out (in its real workings) by photography. This title – its wit obliterated in the English *Ownership of the Image* – points to the more interesting aspect of Edelman's approach: its focus on those definite historical and institutional sites where, as a result of technological, cultural or commercial conditions, the established law is interrupted in its routines and its contradictions and aporia made visible. At the end of chapter 3, I referred to Edelman's discussion of the treatment of photography and cinematography under French law and the shift in legal opinion whereby these 'soulless' technologies were aestheticised, thereby acquiring the capacity to have a subject, that is, an author. In this shift a dual problem had to be resolved. First, photography could not be protected under author's right since, as the product of the interaction of a natural process (light) and a mechanical device (the camera), a photograph involved no admixing of subjectivity and therefore no author. Second, it was not clear how to treat ownership of the photographic image in so far as it is the image of a 'real' that was already the property of other proprietary subjects. This problem was resolved procedurally not epistemologically, since '[l]iterary and artistic property has the strange, unique, original characteristic of being acquired through superposition on an already established property' (Edelman 1979: 38). The solution was also circumstantial or, in the Marxian perspective, necessary in so far as the level of capital investment in the growing film industry – the one now protected in the law of 3 July 1985 – was the real determinant of its acquiring the legal buttress of author's right. Thus was the photographic machine reclassified as a man-machine.

The shift of legal opinion contingent upon new circumstances is the topic of 'Nature et sujet de droit' (Edelman 1985b), the source of the quotation concerning a Nature that has been transformed into an industrial product and object of government and a Humanity that – subordinated to a commercial logic – has become a governmental or managerial subject.[10] This modern disaster – embracing manifestations ranging from the excesses of unrestrained genetic engineering, biotechnology and birth technology to a trans-national managerial administration whose object is the exploitation of a once inappropriable Antarctica and extra-terrestrial space – has occasioned a variety of shifts in different spheres of law – from private law and contract to international public law. Summary cannot do justice to this style of syncretistic scepticism which aligns so many different problems and serious policy issues – personal, national, international and of the species – as if they met in the one figure: that of the integrity of being or, since we seem to be in dialectical history's middle phase of division, the fragmentation and objectification which precedes the future recovery of our unified and finally decommodified being.

It is as though the one fundamental historical process was at work in the application of a 'copyright French style' to the integrity of the authorial person once protected under the *droit moral* and in the application of new birth technologies to the integrity of the act of sex:

> We now witness the deconstructing of the integral act of procreation into a temporal series, since the desire to procreate is separated from the act of fertilisation. By virtue of this fact, desire is substituted by a legal intention and fertilisation is reduced to a technical manipulation. In other words, the decomposing of the act of procreation transforms it into legal *artifice* and technique.
>
> (Edelman 1985b: 134)

This non-aesthetic splitting of (sexual) desire and (legal) norm is not all. The same (aesthetic) schema is applied in considering the integrity of terrestrial and sub-ocean space now threatened by environmental 'management'. As an ethical dilemma, the issue is none the less profound for being familiar: at the level of principle, how does one reconcile the exercise of technology as the expression and achievement of the human will with the human subject as the object of that exercise of technology?

Whatever the answer may be, the concern to divide and regulate is here identified as the sign and consequence of a technology and a 'western reason' no longer tempered by Nature. Schiller would not have disagreed. Yet Edelman now rejects Hegelian and Marxian conceptions of history and labour as the means whereby history's divisions will be healed and global integrity restored. Indeed, along with 'Hegel's dialectic liberty', 'Marx's industrial demiurge' (Edelman 1985b: 130) is castigated as the cause of the modern division, not its resolution. The figure of Hegel 'or the intoxication of reason' (1985b: 126) becomes the sign of the disembodied and abstracted forces of fragmentation, while the chilling formula of the *Philosophy of Right* is cited as the essence of unfreedom: 'A person has as his substantive end the right of putting his will into any and every thing and thereby making it his, because it has no such end in itself and derives its destiny and soul from his will. This is the absolute right of appropriation which man has over all "things"' (Hegel 1952: 41). We shall encounter this formula again, in chapter 9, but there it will be used to justify the practice of artistic appropriation as unconstrained aesthetic speech. Edelman's intention is clear enough and – in the ecological domain – the reality of the problems cannot be denied. Yet the question remains: is a general adjudication of the law in these terms possible when, like the Hegelian and Marxian conceptions he now rejects, Edelman's own means of judgement are so indebted to the self-same aesthetic conception of a whole and self-realising being, necessarily and dialectically achieved?[11]

The answer to this question illuminates just what it is in the *droit moral* tradition that this radical advocate holds so valuable. The problem, says Edelman, is that with the full support of law we are 'rushing towards a transparency which would be the reign of thought that has no mystery' (Edelman 1985b: 125). The dialectical balancing of rational transparency and mystery, intellect and body, finds a further expression in the observation that – in the new and totally administered world – what we call our 'common patrimony' or 'world heritage' is no longer constituted by an inalienable 'nature'. There is no denying that these are difficult political and ethical issues: Edelman is charging that in the regulation of entities such as the world environment, contemporary law has abandoned a boundary it once guarded, the boundary that protected 'a mysterious domain shrouded by an interdiction' (1985b: 141). This was the domain of the legally non-appropriable. It included natural species and processes, the act of sex, the person of the author – in other words what have been deemed fundamental human and natural integrities. This abandonment is, moreover, double: not only is a once protected domain now made open for exploitation, but the subject in whose name that protective legal boundary was once drawn is emptied too. The 'Humanity' of which the Universe is now the 'Common Property' is a vacuous administrative fiction and the human subject a sort of general management board. Along with this nostalgia for an old taboo there is regret at the loss of a species of pleasure: 'Nature no longer presents itself in a concrete form, suitable for appropriation and evoking a certain libidinal relation that gives "pleasure" to the subject. Instead, it comes in the totally abstract form of a market. This presupposes a different "enjoyment", it too perfectly abstract' (1985b: 141).

Elsewhere we might debate whether the notion of this former unity of ecological being corresponds to a fact of history or constitutes the most recent avatar of that original phase of human cultural development that dialectical history imagines as the necessary preliminary to the 'modern' division of 'man'. What is not in doubt, however, is that legal boundaries and industrial property rights have shown marked instability in the uncertain field of biotechnological processes. But does this justify the tragic global view of modern law elaborated in 'The de-juridification of the fact of law'? Here Edelman (1984: 290) addresses the paradox of a simultaneous proliferation of legislation and a decline of law, a circumstance where 'our modern laws [*lois*] no longer have as their objective a society organised by right [*droit*], but are limited to giving a normative force to other [non-legal] systems'. The claim that we have more laws but less right has both a Kantian ring and a mundane familiarity. For Edelman, these 'laws' are a point of profound disavowal, and a sort of melancholy. Again a matter of circumstances has interrupted legal principle, causing it to change; this time – with the phenomenon of 'de-juridification' – the mutation involves 'an abandoning of right [*droit*] by law [*loi*]'. And Edelman continues: 'This perverse phenomenon, which creates the illusion that right exists by mere virtue of the fact that law exists, this silent work of law against right, feeds, it seems to me, on an ideology of transparency which is nothing but a reprise of the golden age or of paradise lost!' (1984: 294–5). One can still joke, however, and Edelman enjoys himself at the expense of those Enlightenment progressives still blindly and unknowingly committed to an ideal of total transparency and social management whom he likens to characters bound map in hand for Treasure Island.

The more serious point, however, is indeed Kantian: saying that 'the law orders is not enough to guarantee that what it orders is necessarily in accord with right' (Edelman 1984: 294). As a consequence of observing the present inflation of law-making, we should, it seems, abandon 'the persistent and tenacious belief that law inevitably produces right, a belief at once sacred and otiose, inherited from a purely formal conception of the sources of right' (1984: 294). Only then will the issue become clear:

> Where has right [*droit*] gone? If we consider the legal subject, then right has gone into norms whose content is technical and economic and not, strictly speaking, legal. This has meant neglecting not only the prerogatives of the legal subject but also his or her legal relations which presuppose an individualised will and capacity.

> (1984: 294)

Confronted again by what appears to be yet another modern failure to achieve the dialectical balance, the jurist commits himself to the defence of this organic legal subject and his or her 'right of privacy, right over his or her image, and right to anonymity' (1984: 292). He appeals to a domain of inalienable right, calling for respect for the right of 'opacity', 'intimacy' and, above all, the 'right of caprice' – this last being 'the sworn enemy of transparency' (1984: 292–3). These attributes are the essence of the subject of law. We can recognise their filiation with the *droit moral* and the rights of divulgation and integrity. What is more, they underscore what is distinctive in the attributes that constitute the *droit moral*: the manner in which their recognition and protection by the law sets limits to the capacity of the market to intrude upon the person of the author – as this has been defined in that particular jurisdiction.

IV

Under the combined pressure of the increasingly international market in intellectual property and the existing body of international law relating to such property and to the protection of the rights of authors, the United States Congress has now approved the Berne Convention Implementation Act of

1989. Forms of *droit moral* protection have also been provided in the United Kingdom Copyright, Designs and Patents Act of 1988 and the Canadian Copyright Amendment Act of the same year.[12] It is true that no consensus exists as to the desirability or the quality of these legislative innovations. On the one hand, welcoming the convergence of British and European law, Cornish (1989: 452) regrets the provision allowing an author to waive the moral rights granted by the 1988 British Act, deeming it a 'highly significant difference' from those European legal systems which 'seek to protect authors as persons whose special creative abilities may lie alongside an uncalculating naivety in commercial matters' and which 'understand, as part of a broad concept of "inalienability", that an author should only have to decide finally whether or not he wants to assert a moral claim *at the time of the particular exploitation of his work in question'*. The point is that there should be no compelling an author to surrender this protection in advance.

On the other hand, precisely those values for which its European advocates defend the *droit moral* its common-law critics identify as flaws, at least with respect to a legislative transplanting of the *droit moral* into American, English, Canadian or Australian copyright jurisdictions. Indeed, an American copyright jurist happens on Edelman's very term – caprice – in polemically proposing that the *droit moral* would be better termed a *droit caprice*, the better to signal both its subjective character and what are said to be its practical disadvantages.[13] Thus only the author of a work – not a court of law – could assess whether a modification of a work is an 'objectionable' interference with that particular author's right of integrity. This is not the case in relation to existing common-law torts of defamation or negligence where, rather than depending on the plaintiff's own sense of injury, an objective standard is provided by the judgement of a reasonable person or the known community standard. What is more, say its common-law opponents, the exercise of this subjective right to block another publication would introduce profound uncertainty into the law since that exercise is by its nature unpredictable, particularly when the right (of integrity) can be exercised *post-mortem*.[14] Who, they might say, could predict with certainty which performances of his works Samuel Beckett would have objected to and therefore blocked? Concern is also voiced at the inappropriateness of so profoundly individualistic a device as the *droit moral* to the complex collaborative modes of authorship that have emerged in magazine and newspaper publishing, with their centralised coordination of the diverse work of writers, photographers and layout designers, just as in educational publishing – in compiling textbooks and readers – the publisher exercises overall control over content and style. A historical corollary of these modes of authorship has been the development of collectively negotiated contracts and appropriate regulatory mechanisms for handling employee-employer relationships.

It is also charged that to institute the *droit moral* within a functioning copyright system would inhibit creativity. In part this perhaps surprising objection is related to the economic fear that investment in the production of new works would cease if, to protect a right of integrity, an author could at any time prevent the publication to which that investment was directed. The exercise of the right of integrity arises less with the original edition of a work than with subsequent versions. Since profitability has come to depend increasingly on subsidiary uses of works, a potentially objectionable alteration or mutilation would occur in revised editions, editions for subsidiary markets, serialisations, translations, abridgements and excerpts for educational textbook purposes, film and television versions and audiotapes. There is no denying that French case law offers stunning examples of what can happen. In 1966, for instance, the Caisse Nationale des Lettres – a body established by the law of 11 October 1946 to ensure among other things that literary works are respected after their author's death – sought an injunction against a publishing house that, said the Caisse, had published a 'scandalous deformation' of a classic work: *Les Misérables*. The new version, it was claimed, 'not only amputated the work from political and social developments, but also altered events, changed phrases and syntax, such that the work, although presented as the work of Victor Hugo, is deprived of its social and political character and loses its poetry and style' (Tribunal de Grande Instance, Seine, 15 April 1964). The Caisse had standing as the agent competent to protect the *droit moral* of Victor Hugo – a task carried out, in the event, by the author's heirs. Perhaps the very existence of a body such as the Caisse Nationale des Lettres is a sign that a society values its authors enough to give them this specific protection under the law. Nevertheless, it is the logic of the *droit moral* to furnish the original author (and his or her legal representative) with a power of 'aesthetic veto'.[15] In principle, this power to protect oneself by preventing the publication of the work of others could be used by an author whose sensibility was sufficiently stung by a criticism or parody of his or her work that he or she took action against them as an objectionable distortion or derogation. In addition, this preventive power institutes an aesthetic orthodoxy – the power to decide what is and what is not the 'social and political character' of Hugo's work – no less objectionable were a living author to exercise it. It is a telling reminder of how what looks like an extension of the domain of personal rights can lead to more rather than less regulation.

An argument of a different sort against legislating a *droit moral* into a copyright regime rests on the proposition that these different rights are too well-adapted to their different environments to be transplanted. Thus it is said that European legal systems have less respect for the security of contract. Copyright advocates hold the contract to be the best and proper means for protecting the personal rights of authors, a view advanced also by some common-law libertarians. Palmer (1989) thus regards the rights created by statutes as illegitimate impositions by government, not as natural emanations or an exercise of a traditional liberty of the common law by natural subjects who, directly responsive to the market, enter into agreements subsequently ratified by legal forms.[16] To this the European lawyer has a response: 'True, by means of contractual arrangements, the author can stipulate that some link should remain between the work and himself, but this is merely a matter of contractual obligation and in no way a relation of natural right' (Edelman 1987b: 567–8). Of course, if Edelman is right, the French law too in no way rests on a statutory 'social contract' imposed by government to balance public access and reward to the copyright owner. Rather, 'not only is the author's monopoly a "natural right" (which sets it apart from any notion of "social contract"), but the relation of author to public is envisaged in terms of a "gift". Everything is arranged as if the creator made a gift of his work to the collectivity which, in return, paid him its respects and thanks' (1987b: 575).

Confronted with the alien threat of the *droit moral*, the defenders of copyright have had to state what copyright is and in the process, perhaps unfortunately, they have tended to discover 'principles': promotion of learning and the arts, enhancement of literary creativity and so on.[17] In such a principled debate the temptation is to assert that the adversary is as absolutely wrong as we are absolutely right. In practice, as case law, the *droit moral* is anything but immune to circumstances. On the one hand, the historicity of its principles is demonstrated by the fact that these principles have acquired different inflections at different times; for instance, 1940s accounts (Roeder 1940) can be found which represent the *droit moral* as a protection of the authorial personality against the threats of authoritarian ideologies – concentration camps are mentioned – a theme not pursued today (although it echoes obliquely in Edelman's (1984) resistance to 'transparency'). On the other hand, a purposive and adaptive capacity is introduced into the administration of the doctrine of the *droit moral* by the relative freedom of European judges – less bound by a strong doctrine of *stare decisis* or consistent precedent – to invoke *droit moral* provisions in one case but not in another (for instance where they might have undesirable consequences). Practical calculations – a sense of how to play the game intelligently – can thus determine any particular decision according to the circumstances of the case while the general principle remains intact.

There are, indeed, judgments that threaten to disturb the principle. In the Microfor case of 30 October 1987, the full Cour de Cassation ruled on a dispute between *Le Monde* and Microfor. The latter was a publishing company which, since 1977, had produced an electronically compiled index to the French press, drawing without authorisation on articles in *Le Monde* and *Le Monde diplomatique*. The Index was published in an analytical section giving the title and bibliographical details of the articles indexed and a section reproducing brief extracts from those articles. In the earlier trial court *Le Monde* had claimed that its authorial right of integrity had not been respected by this selective quotation which failed to give a full and proper idea of the content. But whatever was a *corporation* doing claiming infringement of its *droit moral*? And whatever was the Cour de Cassation doing when it entertained the possibility that a non-individual could occupy the status and have the standing of a *droit moral* holder? As a corporation, *Le Monde* scarcely met the traditional criterion whereby only a *personne physique* (human individual) could claim an injury to his or her personality as present in the work.[18] The court in fact found against *Le Monde*; yet, in so doing, it treated Microfor's electronically compiled index as an original intellectual work despite its lack of 'author' and authorial 'personality'. As Edelman (1989: 93–4) puts it: '[A] database, which is an enterprise like any other and whose social object is defined by a commercial activity that consists of organising a certain body of information more or less reworked, can now be considered ... an author.' The Microfor case does not suggest doctrinal purity, but a spirit of compromise and accommodation that, even in France, may in practice be less the exception than the rule.

V

As we have seen, it has been claimed that the *droit moral* is the necessary form of law with respect to the recognition and protection of the rights of authors, in so far as it alone admits the libidinal domain. In responding to such a claim, we might argue that any reference to the libidinal in the course of a debate on jurisprudence cannot be other than a metaphorical gesture, one whereby a contingent – and now perhaps precarious – legal conventionality seeks to be represented as a historical necessity, the form that the law must assume when it is brought into line with the fullness of the human person as manifest in the exemplary figure of the literary author. Copyright, by contrast, was said to rest on nothing deeper than the power, 'pulsions' and interests of the market.

Nevertheless, a certain pressure on the boundaries and norms of copyright is there, and not only as a consequence of the internationalising of the cultural market and the presence of the Berne Convention. From the generalising of the Romantic expressivist conception of the author has emerged what Brown (1985) terms an 'exaltation of authorship'. Although dealing primarily with the issue of the criteria of eligibility for protection of semiconductor devices, Brown argues that this 'feeling' – 'whatever its emotional appeal' – does not of itself justify the extension of existing rights: 'It is easy for proponents of this "exaltation of authorship" approach to slip into bathos about the lofty and lonely position of the author'; however, he adds, these 'lonely authors are often in fact the well-paid henchmen of monster multi-national conglomerates that grind out – whatever the cynic despises' (1985: 589–91). An 'exaltation' of this sort exerts its pressure on the manner in which the grounds and purposes of the law of copyright are conceptualised. At first glance, the temptation is to assume no connection between this pressure and such notions as libido. After all, terms like 'libido' and 'pleasure' trouble Anglo-American lawyers – much as terms like 'law' and 'regulation' trouble literary critics. And yet, if the references to the libido are evidence of a particular and ascendant ethic – that of the whole or aesthetic personality – we are left less than certain that the apparatus of the law of copyright is simply immune. Certainly, copyright's literary historians have not been immune to dialectical history's unremitting pressure to have us vault over the complex and shifting relations between legal and aesthetic personalities in favour of the notion that they find their necessary synthesis in the human subject.

For critical intellectuals and perhaps more generally, as aesthetic interests and capacities are disseminated and implanted as private and public ideals, this metaphorics of integrity becomes increasingly powerful, as does its dialectical counterpart, the aesthetic imagery of 'man' (or woman), labour and culture as profoundly fragmented, alienated, divided. The polemic of this study is therefore directed against the ambition of philosophical histories centred on the formation of the subject – in whatever version – to integrate in a single sweep everything from the integrity of the author in the work to the integrity of the species in the universe.

Chapter 9

Some legal lessons for literary and cultural studies

I

In describing a number of different legal-cultural environments, one of my objects has been to avoid imposing a general synthesis on the history of law and authorship, in particular the style of synthesis that would have the legal and cultural personalities converging in the figure of the human subject. Working its way towards copyright, the legal system would then have appeared as a more or – more probably – less successful attempt to recognise the truth of subjectivity, as if the proper object of the law of copyright was the presence of the writer's personality in the work. As for a law whose object was limited to the regulation of the heterogeneous array of commercial, technical and cultural activities that constituted the book market, it would have appeared an incomplete realisation of what the law of copyright should have become. It is as though such a law failed history, culture and the human subject in a fundamental way when it took as its purpose the delineation and assignation of the right to trade in mechanical duplicates of the work. Global assessments in this style are one sign that aesthetics and the aesthetic persona are being taken to constitute the necessary foundation and destiny of the particular forms of legal personality constructed in the sphere of copyright.

To readers who have followed the argument to this stage, it should be clear why this will not do. A lesson of the preceding chapters is that the aesthetic persona – the artefact of a highly specialised form of ethical exercise or way of having a relation to oneself – has not so much directed the emergence of the law of copyright as come to overlap with it in an important but none the less contingent way. That said, it is no easy task to lay aside the intellectual habit of viewing legal attributes as extrinsic to that personality recovered or formed in literary writing and reading, a personality that we have learned to take as the intrinsic self and thus as the necessary goal of the legal form of being. However, by now it should also be clear what damage is done to descriptive history by this philosophical pressure to collapse the contingencies and complexities of the relations of legal and aesthetic personality into the unity of a necessary process or singular direction of cultural development. Hence, to help avoid this tendency to elide differences of personality or status, the refrain of the present study: the object of the law of copyright has been the regulation of printed books as traded commodities. It might have been pleasing to say that the law's object is to practise critical self-consciousness or to generate all possible meanings. But then it would not have been the law of copyright that we were discussing but something else, moral philosophy perhaps or post-structuralism.

II

In a culture as juridified as ours, the phenomenon of authorship cannot be defined independently of or prior to its legal conditions. In the Anglo-American context, these conditions include the provisions and procedures of the law of copyright. The writing, publishing, distributing and consuming of printed books is not imaginable outside the regulatory and protective norms of copyright, that highly specified regime of law in which legislators or courts have decided and defined the concepts of original work, literary work, dramatic work, musical work and artistic work, and established the terms of protection for the multiple forms of derivative works and adaptations. The duration and territorial coverage of copyright have had to be decided too, as have the degree and manner in which the historical norms of copyright first developed for the print publication process can be applied to new communications technologies – photography, film, broadcast, satellite and cable television, video and computer – that have occasioned not only new forms of work but also new and unforeseen uses of existing works. These rights and their conditions of exercise have in some cases been the object of campaigns that have led to reasonably workable agreements. In short, whatever it is that we now count as authorship, it has been determined in part by decisions taken in this regime of law. This is no reason for regret, even if for many literary scholars it is a matter of historical ignorance.

The historical array of decisions on the object and the scope of copyright protection is extensive and disorderly. It includes the familiar rule whereby the law protects as property an original expression or presentation of ideas, not the ideas themselves. Indeed the work is taken to exist in order to put ideas into a circulation – the marketplace of ideas – where they form our common heritage and freely present themselves for comment and criticism, and it is on this ground that the United States Copyright Act of 1976 expressly excludes ideas from protection. The assumption is that ideas cannot be appropriated because they are already common property, like breathing, magnetism or Shakespeare, a notion that leads Posner (1988: 341) to treat 'ideas' found in literature as the necessary 'commonplaces of life, with stock situations, stock characters, stock narratives'. In principle, therefore, protection does not extend beyond the actual formulation that appears on the page. Yet it is difficult to imagine a verbal expression separated from an idea, or an idea from an expression; whenever a wording or verbal formulation is protected, so too, it would seem, is an idea. A distinction of this sort would no doubt provide for unending philosophical and hermeneutic debate; however, the task of copyright law is to provide relatively rapid and predictable judgments in the relatively rare cases where this distinction becomes a matter of legal dispute. In practice, the exclusion of ideas from copyright can pose problems. Copyright law has thus had to deal with the question of how much development a banal idea or a generic formula requires in order to be deemed distinctive and thus protected. Patterns of events are protectable, but only to a certain level of abstraction from the actual wordings:

> Upon any work . . . a great number of patterns of increasing generality will fit equally well as more and more of the incident is left out. The last may perhaps be no more than the most general statement of what [the work] is about, and at times might consist only of its title; but there is a point in this series of abstractions where they are no longer protected, since otherwise [the author] could prevent the use of his 'ideas', to which apart from their expression, his property is never extended. Nobody has ever been able to fix that boundary, and nobody ever can.
>
> (*Nichols* v. *Universal Pictures Corporation*: 121)

This celebrated opinion of Judge Learned Hand does not signal the law's arrival at some ontological and epistemological imponderable. From the copyright perspective, the distinction between a stock idea and an original expression is simply a matter for legal decision. Depending on the judgment of the court and the circumstances of the case, a given formulation will for legal purposes be either the expression of an idea or the idea of an expression, protected in one case but not in the other.

The legal status of fictional characters and their conditions of existence and use offer a further instance of the juridification of aesthetic culture, perhaps especially important in those sectors of the publishing trade where the identification between work and reader, commodity and consumer, operates through the reader's acquired capacity to recognise and to identify with the character. Studies of the legal status of characters, as well as defining what it is in the character that qualifies for protection – distinctive name, appearance, actions – have even suggested that 'once it is taken up by the law, a character achieves the secret objective of every creator: it comes to life, just like a real person; it bears a name, it possesses a right to its image, a right to privacy and, under certain conditions, it can even defend its honour and its reputation' (Edelman 1980: 225). The constant extension of an exclusive right to the use of characters has provoked counter-defences of the 'rights' of the public domain of non-appropriable language or imagery on which all can freely draw to make new works. Lange (1981: 160) asks 'why a property of any kind ought to be recognized in characters like the ones created by the Marx brothers'. He cites the 1981 action brought by Groucho Marx Productions Inc. – holder of the rights in the names and likenesses of the characters created by the brothers – against the theatre company responsible for the New York production of Richard Vosburgh's *A Day in Hollywood, A Night in the Ukraine*. The Ukraine half of the play represented Chekhov's *The Bear* as the Marx brothers might have played it. In this instance parodic distance from the original did not prevent the court deciding that valid rights had been infringed by an unauthorised use of protected characters. In other words, Vosburgh's work was deemed insufficiently distinct to be legally considered a work in its own right. This and a set of other similar judgments provoke scepticism on three grounds: first, a doubt as to the degree of originality of the protected characters; second, a sense that it is unreasonable to grant exclusive rights to merely legal owners of the characters, for instance to an estate, the author or authors being deceased; third, the conviction that an unjustified impediment is laid in the way of creating new works.[1]

The relatively familiar instances considered in the foregoing paragraphs – ideas and their expression, generic forms, literary characters – in no way exhaust the repertoire of elements of literary works that are administered by the law of copyright. Other instances – rare but historically real – include the set of circumstances constituted by the civil (or non-criminal) doctrine of obscenity, that is, where copyright protection is withheld from works deemed obscene or immoral, even though this obscenity or immorality is not proven in a criminal sense. The ownership of copyright has thus observed the particular principle of equity known as the 'clean hands' doctrine to which Chief Justice Best gestured in *Poplett* v. *Stockdale* (1825): 'The person who lends himself to the violation of the public morals and laws of the country, shall not have the assistance of the laws to carry into effect such a purpose. It would be strange if a man could be fined and imprisoned for doing that for which he could maintain an action at law' (in Phillips 1977: 145). The printer Poplett sued the publisher John Joseph Stockdale to recover the costs of materials and labour incurred in printing the *Memoirs of Harriet Wilson*, an autobiographical money-making venture in which a celebrated Regency courtesan published her recollections by instalments, sending her past associates pre-publication copies of the index of names cited, together with a chance to buy their way out of the book. It seems many paid up; one who did not was the Duke of Wellington who returned Wilson's text with the instruction 'Publish and be damned!' (McFarlane 1986: 183). Harriet Wilson apart, in *Shelley* v. *Clark* (1821) and *Murray* v. *Benbow* (1823) the publishers of Shelley's *Queen Mab* and Byron's *Cain* sought by means of Chancery injunctions against pirate publishers of the works to assert their status as proper owners of the copyrights. However, they were constrained from doing so by their status as persons liable for an immoral publication in which a claim of property would not have been protected by the common law. This civil doctrine of obscenity raises the question of what happens to the status of author when, as in this particular contingency, individuals are rendered incapable of exercising the rights that the law invests in them when constituting them as authors with the capacity to own (and to assign) copyright.

In such circumstances we see that the authorial personality has no essential unity. Three incommensurate statuses are involved: the bearing of an ownership right in a copyable commodity; the locus of criminal (as distinct from moral) responsibility for the publication of an obscene or immoral matter; and the cultural standing afforded to an exemplary being made whole in and by his or her works. The right of copyright attaches only to the first of these statuses, but is cancelled by occupancy of the second. However, because ownership is a legal status, it is in no sense derivable from the third status, that of the aesthetic personality, however 'whole' this latter claims to be. This is an instance that shows the complexity of the phenomenon of authorship as a phenomenon in the domain of copyright law – and, of course, the present study does not begin to address those other conditions of authorial conduct defined by the law of libel concerning the defamation of private persons by fiction,[2] or the limits set to publishable fiction by the law of privacy[3] and the law of obscenity.[4] No single theory or history lies behind these diverse sets of legal conditions, nor can these different bodies of law be aggregated in such a way that generalities about 'the law' – for instance in its purportedly repressive relation to literature or life – can lay claim to any great descriptive value (whatever uses they might find in moral discourse).

III

Historical caution has not on the whole appealed to recent literary historians of copyright – Kernan and Rose, Woodmansee and Nesbit – whose writings constitute the corpus to which passing references have been made in the preceding chapters. On the contrary, these writings demonstrate that an aesthetic historiography of authorship will always claim to recover the necessary origin and goal for the legal personality in that other form of personality that I have been calling aesthetic. This is equally true for both of the main strategies or templates for conceptualising the birth (or death) of the author in terms of the formation of the subject – the Romantic historicist and the post-structuralist. These 'adversaries', however, are better seen as variations on the one philosophical theme. Accounts of authorship written from a Romantic historicist position elevate the expressive author and authorial consciousness to the philosophical status of the subject of universal history. Whatever might be the form of legal personality constructed in the copyright field, it cannot but be treated in relation to this underlying subject. This means that in practice, in the Romantic historicist model, it was always to be the role of copyright law to support the authorial personality required and enshrined by Romanticism. The account of authorship written from a post-structuralist position rejects the expressive author and authorial consciousness as an illusion of discourse, anything but the true and unconstrained form of the subject. The post-structuralist model none the less retains the figure of the author but as the necessary preliminary to the action of non-conscious (linguistic) determinations. In this second account it was always to be the role of copyright law to support the illusion of the authorial personality, for instance as proprietor of copyright.

The recent work of Alvin Kernan (1987) demonstrates the Romantic historicist approach to the law of copyright and the history of authorship. *Printing Technology, Letters and Samuel Johnson* depicts the necessary movement of history as grasped in its profoundly dialectical tensions by the exemplary authorial consciousness of Johnson. As we might predict, through his reflexive consciousness of historical determination and through his writing, the author gives history its necessary direction:

> [Johnson's] struggle to create dignity for himself and his writing in new economic conditions that tended to make the writer only a paid worker in the print factory, and his work only a commodity – a struggle that has extended on into the romantic and modernist resistance to capitalist reality – shows in the most immediate terms the power of technology over life and belief, even as it dramatizes human resistance to absolute mechanical determinism. Furthermore, Johnson, as Carlyle (also a professional writer) saw and said, was a 'culture hero', which means that his responses to the new situation of being a paid worker for the printing press, accepting print as the fact of writing but still actively shaping its tendencies to satisfy at least some part of his own needs for a worthwhile and meaningful life, are paradigmatic of the way in which people use culture to meet technological and other types of disruptive change.
>
> (Kernan 1987: 6)

This is Romantic historicism in full dialectical flush. It is no surprise when Kernan represents the development of copyright as the necessary outcome of the author's struggle to reclaim the product of his labour – his writing, though printed, is conceptualised as the vehicle for the inalienable expression of the human self through literary art. For Kernan, Samuel Johnson becomes the first 'modern', the necessary author-subject who conceives of his work both as the expression of his self and as his economic (and legal) property. In doing this, of course, Johnson takes on the very attributes habitually attributed to that other subject of history, the proletariat, destined to reclaim – on 'man's' behalf – the presently alienated and commodified products of its labour. From this high point the critic then looks back – as noted at the outset of chapter 2 – to the times when 'legalized piracy' seems to have troubled virtually no one. The absence of an effective (author-centric) copyright law in the early eighteenth century becomes the sign that the product of the writer's labour was already alienated by a commodifying capitalism (the book trade) and a de-individualising technology (printing). But is the fact that the Statute of Anne concerned itself with a print commodity evidence of the law's acquiescence and complicity in the alienation of the authorial subject in commodity production? This is not the lesson of the preceding chapters. On the contrary, it makes no historical sense to treat copyright in terms of the necessary working out of a grand dialectic whereby economic interests and human subjectivity move into a general relation, first of alienation and division, then of reconciliation and synthesis in and through the authorial consciousness.

The Romantic historicist account, by contrast, depicts the writer's access to copyright as the necessary recovery – in consciousness and in cash, the ideal and the material – of the inalienable product of the authorial subject's labour: his self as expressed in his literary work. In fact it might be more appropriate to invert Kernan's approach and ask whether it would have been possible even to conceive of the author in this way if print technology and the book market had not first allowed the work to appear *as a commodity* and copyright had not allowed the author a legal existence *as a proprietor* of that commodity. Committed to its all-embracing dialectic, Romantic historicism is finally indifferent to the details and contingencies of actual legal arrangements, preferring an account that rests on grander Hegelian and Marxian postulates – the labour form as the universal principle of all human cultural development. The historicist account is therefore open to the criticisms increasingly addressed to the claims of Hegelianism and Marxism as general theories of labour. It will be recalled from chapter 1 that – as Philip Kain (1982) argues – these Hegelian and Marxian theories of labour as the necessary process of 'man's' self-realisation are themselves neither more nor less than versions of the aesthetic conception of art as a self-realising activity that have been projected on to 'history' and the 'proletariat'. As such, they are too indebted to the aesthetic concept of authorship to be able to assess the latter's relation to the legal domain.

To explore another instance of the historicist scheme, let us leave Kernan's Johnson and the English cultural-legal environment and turn to Martha Woodmansee's (1984) 'The genius and the copyright', an account of the emergence of professional writers in late eighteenth-century Germany. It will be of no great consequence that quite different geopolitical and cultural contexts are involved – the scheme remains the same. Woodmansee's object is idealist and aesthetic: to align the legal and economic conditions of authorship with a new theorisation by German writers of what it was to write 'literature'. To support her claim that in this reconciliation of law and literature these writers 'gave the concept of authorship its modern form' (1984: 426), Woodmansee depicts the advance of three generations of German literary intellectuals. First, as an emergent phenomenon of culture, the generation of Lessing tries but fails to achieve the balance between a material freedom – living by the pen – and fidelity to an aesthetic ideal of personal integrity. Second, advancing towards the watershed, the middle generation of Burger,

Moritz and Friedrich Schiller makes more ground. However, as a transitional phenomenon of culture, this generation fails to achieve the dialectical balance of material self-sufficiency and ideal self-realisation in a Germany which 'found itself in a transitional phase between the limited patronage of an aristocratic society and democratic patronage of the marketplace' and where 'the requisite legal, economic and political arrangements were not yet in place to support the large number of writers who came forward. What they encountered were the remnants of an earlier social order' (Woodmansee 1984: 433). Like the first wave, the writers of this middle generation were in advance of a 'fully developed concept of literary property'. Confronted by an incomplete law and an economy inadequate to their new historical self-consciousness as aesthetic authors, they become appropriately alienated subjects. To survive as writers, they have to take the 'step backwards' (1984: 431) and accept patronage of princes. As for the law, the best it can offer at this stage are the archaic devices of the *honorarium*, the princely privilege and *ex gratia* patronal payments, the 'remnants of an earlier social order'. But, with the law of 'copyright', the third and final stage of legal and cultural development is achieved – the synthesis in which material and ideal, 'the legal and the aesthetic discourses' are reconciled.

At the heart of this Romantic fable is the claim that German writers 'set about redefining the nature of writing' (Woodmansee 1984: 426), adopting Edward Young's notion that the literary work was the organic expression of a unique personality. The aesthetic conception of the work as the expression of its author's personality is held to have emerged as the means of pursuing the writer's economic interest in ownership. As evidence Woodmansee (1984: 441) cites Goethe who – following Klopstock's campaign in support of literary property – had alleged that the time was now ripe 'for genius to become self-conscious, create for itself its own conditions, and understand how to lay the foundations for an independent dignity'. Living by the pen is thus said to have caused – but also to have been caused by – an aesthetic reconceptualisation of the act of writing. At the same time, the puzzle of where this new economic interest might have come from is solved by having it derive from the expressive conception of authorship.

The problem is not just a circularity of logic. Accounts like Woodmansee's are signs of philosophical history's unremitting pressure on its devotees to reconcile the dialectical 'opposites', in this case the legal-economic 'real' and the literary-aesthetic 'ideal'. Under this pressure, description suffers. What, for instance, is made of the fact that copyright was nearly always held by printers and booksellers, not by writers? Or the fact that in a cultural milieu where owning and selling one's work was seen by many to be beneath the moral dignity of a calling, writers did not necessarily recognise an economic interest in their writing. But these and other circumstances fall before the greater imperative: accounts in the Romantic historicist manner authors have to be dialectically organised. Depicted on the one hand as the objects of historical determinations – the economic pressures of the German book trade and the legal provisions such as they were – literary authors must also be shown as exemplary subjects who, in redefining the role of literary writing, bring these determinations into consciousness, thus achieving the long-awaited epochal reconciliation of the self and its historical determinations. As for the specific legal attributes enabling the ownership of an exclusive right of property in a work, they lose their positivity and independence and are made to comply, conveniently, with whatever is dialectically necessary for 'man's' history at last to manifest itself in the completing of his subjectivity.

It is as if the historical emergence of a specialised and purposive legal personality such as the copyright holder obeyed the dialectical schemata of subjective and objective, organic and mechanical – the reconciliation of these antinomies being the sign of 'man's' advance to a higher and more complete mode of social and individual being. The same schema exerts its force even on an excellent legal history such as L. Ray Patterson's (1968) *Copyright in Historical Perspective*. While Kernan and Woodmansee want to show the epochal moment when the legal and the aesthetic personalities achieve a necessary reconciliation, Patterson leaves us in no doubt that the law of copyright has been and remains no more than a trade regulation device. His argument is clear – the rights and remedies available under the law of copyright arose in relation to the demands and interests not of authors but of publishers:

> Authorship came of age in eighteenth-century England as a respectable profession, and it would be fitting to think that the first English copyright statute was enacted in 1709 to benefit such authors as Pope, Swift, Addison, Steele and Richardson. Fitting perhaps, but hardly accurate. The Statute of Anne was a trade regulation statute enacted to bring order to the chaos created in the book trade by the final lapse in 1694 of its predecessor, the Licensing Act of 1662, and to prevent a continuation of the booksellers' monopoly.
>
> (Patterson 1968: 146)

Yet throughout his study Patterson insists that copyright should have been what it was not – an authorial right. From the execution of the Statute of Anne, copyright has been a publisher's proprietary instrument inappropriately applied to an interest that is authorial:

> [C]opyright, in short, was to become a concept to embrace all the rights to be had in connection with published works, either by the author or the publisher. As such, it was to prevent a recognition of the different interests of the two, and thus preclude the development of a satisfactory law to protect the interests of the author as author.
>
> (1968: 151)

In the final sentence there are two symptomatic elements on which we should pause. The first is the teleological inference that there could have been a more complete form of law to protect authorship than there has in fact been. Dual historicist assumptions persist here: first, that at some level deeper than the positive law the writer has rights that flow from his or her being an 'author as author', these 'deeper' rights being what the law should have recognised; second, that the publisher's access to these rights has been an alienation, an incomplete realisation of what copyright law should have been and still ought to become. When it failed to recognise 'the author as author', it is as though the positive law of copyright failed in a fundamental way. The second element of note is Patterson's tautology – 'the interests of the author as author'. This might be an uninformative formulation, but it signals the pressure exerted by the discourse of aesthetics on the legal historiography of copyright. If the ideal integrity of 'the author as author' did not find adequate or appropriate expression in a legal personality designed for 'booksellers', then at best – it is implied – the forms achieved by the law of copyright are just a stepping-stone towards the ultimate equivalence of legal personality and aesthetic persona. At worst, they are an institutional impediment to the aesthetic goal.

IV

Historicist accounts of authorship presume that the historical mission of the law of copyright was to recognise and protect the authorial consciousness. They thus identify a problem consisting in an initial *absence* of copyright. What then do we make of a post-structuralist account that depicts the *presence* of copyright precisely as an impediment to the realisation of a finally unconstrained and unbounded subjectivity? In 'The author as proprietor', Mark Rose (1988) discards authorial consciousness as a discursive illusion and the proprietary author as a delusional subject, an alien nature sustained by an archaic but legally buttressed ideology of individual 'originality' and private property.[5] That impediment and that illusion, however, have now been swept away by a post-structuralist theory of 'writing' which, among other things, promises to rectify the error of the law of copyright:

> 'Originality', the necessary and enabling concept that underlies the [legal] notion of the proprietary author, is at best a problematic term in current thought, which stresses rather the various ways in which, as it is often put, language speaks through man. Where does one text end and another begin? What current literary thought emphasizes is that texts permeate and enable each other, and from this point of view the notion of distinct boundaries between texts, a notion crucial to the operation of the modern system of literary property, becomes difficult to sustain.
>
> (Rose 1988: 78)

There is a certain ambivalence here. On the one hand, the claim is to disperse a fixed subjectivity – the legal person of the proprietary author – as an imaginary self called into fictive being by language; on the other hand, the claim is to have recovered the unity of the universe of texts by denying their (merely legal) differentiation into separately ownable and authorially identifiable commodities. Whatever the case, it seems to be assumed that the old order has been dissolved by the critical acid of the 'structuralist and post-structuralist transformation of the intellectual scene' (Rose 1988: 78). 'History' is displaced by 'language' as the dialectical medium responsible for the birth of the author. Eclipsed by the non-conscious force of language that 'speaks through man', authorial consciousness ceases to be a necessary fact of history and becomes just a premature fixing – in part due to the intervention of copyright – of the endless play of text.

This is a characteristic piece of post-structuralist bravura. The break-through of linguistic theory is held to have revealed an ideal truth – the principle of textual indeterminacy – that, in the preceding pages of Rose's essay is made to flow from a particular material history: the struggle over copyright in the years between the Statute of Anne and *Donaldson* v. *Beckett*. Rose is not wrong to say that the 'London booksellers invented the modern proprietary author, constructing him as a weapon in their struggle with the booksellers of the provinces' (1988: 56). However, in the context of this struggle, if the proprietary author has a certain fictive character, this cannot be shown by theories of discourse which posit language as the self-generating reality underpinning the legal construction of authorship. Speaking from the 'gap [which] has appeared between the dominant mode of legal thinking and that of literary thinking' – it is also termed the 'gap between poststructuralist thought and the institution of copyright' (Rose 1988: 78) – such theories treat the legal personality or status that a writer may occupy as no more than a confining illusion of consciousness hung on a system of language capable of producing meanings and subjectivities in unbounded profusion, unless weighed down by legal crudities such as identity, originality and ownership. These theories thus disqualify themselves from attending to the *non-fictive* history of the law of copyright, that is, to the array of positive norms and procedures whose object is not language as universal generator of meaning, but printed books as traded commodities.

If eighteenth-century London booksellers manoeuvred with the notion of a customary and perpetual author's right in the unpublished manuscript, this was in the context of a local campaign whose historical determinations and reality lie elsewhere than in a post-structuralist aesthetic of transgressive writing. Their campaign depended on legal procedures for deciding what was an owner of copyright for the purposes of legal protection; they used the legal instruments available – customary trade practice, common-law precedent, injunctions in the Court of Chancery. These actions are not adequately grasped by a universal logic of subject formation, even if this is expressed in the newer and purportedly more critical post-structuralist style as the dispersal of the subject of consciousness by the deconstructive play of language. To insist on applying such a singular logic ends only in once again subordinating the forms of positive law to a philosophical schema. If I have argued for the historical positivity and independence of the law of copyright and the legal personality it constructs, it is on the ground that they do not fall within the field of philosophical history any more than they fall within the field and determination of literary theory and criticism.

V

When Rose (1988: 78) announces that a critical 'gap has appeared between the dominant mode of legal thinking and that of literary thinking', unfortunately he does not have in mind the Weberian precept that these ways of thinking should be approached as mental activities pursued in different 'departments of existence'. Far from Weber's pluralism, post-structuralism is claiming here to speak with the epochal voice of universal history. It is as if a linguistically rectified theory of authorship – it is now 'language' not the author that makes sense – could debunk the law of copyright as an arbitrary short-circuiting of the infinite possibility of language. But legal procedures and judgments do not have as their purpose the enunciation of endless meanings. Their purpose is to produce decisions that are legally correct and socially binding. For those who insist upon a less short circuit of interpretation and a universally true meaning, a definite place is available – not the court of law but the literary seminar. Here determinate meaning can and, in certain pedagogical and ethical exercises, must be perpetually deferred. Drawing out the task of interpretation is neither less nor more arbitrary than drawing it in; each is an activity appropriate to its particular milieu and purpose.

We begin to see what is wrong with the post-structuralist account of the legal person of the proprietary author as a choking-off of a potential of texts and meanings and subjectivities. It is as though a visit to the library or a drive to the beach was not a successful arrival at a particular and intended destination but a failure to pursue an infinitely long voyage. If it has become possible for some of us to read in a manner that does not separate off one book or author from another, and to defer decisions as to what anything means because we take each text to be continuous with every other one in an endless chain of quotation and pastiche, this is not a sign that we have been liberated by a theoretical breakthrough that has revealed to consciousness the delusional character of the author. It is evidence that individuals can do these things, once they have acquired the appropriate cultural interest and technical competence to read, write, think and conduct themselves in this way. But they must be careful *where* they conduct themselves in this manner.

In an interview in 1975, to the predictable query as to the importance of literature for his work, Michel Foucault responded that 'traditionally literary or philosophical discourses could be made to function ... as a general envelope for all other discourses' and that he had therefore adopted 'a frankly negative position, trying to bring out positively all the non-literary or parallel discourses that were actually produced at a given period, excluding literature itself'. He then asked: '[W]hy is it that a number of [narratives] are sacralized, made to function as "literature"?' Foucault's answer to his own question should be kept in mind when considering any contemporary literary theory or practice, however 'critical' and emancipated they might claim to be. Certain narratives, he says, the ones that function as 'literature', are nowadays

> immediately taken up with an institution that was originally very different: the university institution. Now it is beginning to be identified with the literary institution. There is a very visible slope in our culture. In the nineteenth century, the university was the element within which was constituted a so-called classical literature, and which was valued both as the sole basis of contemporary literature and as a criticism of that literature. Hence a very curious interplay occurs, in the nineteenth century, between literature and the university, between the writer and the professor. And then, little by little, the two institutions, which, despite all their squabbles, were profoundly linked, tended to merge completely. We know perfectly well that today so-called avant-garde literature is read only by university teachers and their students. We know very well that nowadays a writer over thirty is surrounded by students writing their theses on his work.
>
> (Foucault 1988: 308–9)

By the time of this interview in 1975, Foucault had abandoned his leaning towards the notion of 'language' as the autonomous and self-referring system of non-conscious rules that makes all possible statements possible. This chronology helps clarify his remarks. Thus, on the one hand, the new principle of the intransitivity of language and writing had usefully challenged the traditional assumption of the 'expressive character of literature'; however, this 'principle' proved to be an instrument that fell into misuse as 'a kind of exaltation, both ultra-lyrical and ultra-rationalising, of literature as a structure of language capable of being analysed in itself and on its own terms'. This intransitivity Foucault now decisively rejects:

> Some people were even able to say that literature in itself was so eman-cipated from all determinations that the very fact of writing was in itself subversive, that the writer, in the very gesture of writing, had an inalienable right to subversion! The writer was, therefore, a revolutionary and the more writing was writing, the more it sank into intransitivity, the more it produced, by that very fact, the movement of revolution! As you know, such things were, unfortunately, said.
>
> (1988: 309–10)

And not only in France, and not only in the early 1970s. But this lesson in the historical demography of literary theory is valuable: the migration of literature into the university confirms it as one institutional activity among others. As such, the claim to a radically new critical power released by what purports to be an epochal theoretical break – Rose's 'gap' 'between the dominant mode of legal thinking and that of literary thinking' – must be heard with caution.

Yet in that gap so much has been noisily challenged. And the same anti-positive convictions expressed in Rose's claim to have exposed the illusory and alien nature of the proprietary author surface in William Burroughs' claim to have exposed – thanks to broken syntax and material transformations of consciousness – the whole business of copyright. Theorist and novelist both have recourse to non-conscious forces – linguistic for Rose, psychical for Burroughs. Hence Burroughs' (1986: 88) proposition that the authentic creator 'is in fact transcribing from the unconscious'. On this ground he proposes an anti-copyright slogan which also allows him to lay claim to the moral authority attaching to the confessional courage displayed in breaking taboos and prohibitions: 'Let's come out in the open with it and steal freely.'[6] Unlimited appropriation of others' work is the precondition for escaping the fetish of originality:

> I had been conditioned to the idea of words as property – one's 'very own words' – and consequently to a deep repugnance for the black sin of plagiarism. Originality was the great virtue. I recall a boy who was caught out copying an essay from a magazine article and this horrible case discussed in whispers. . . . For the first time the word 'plagiarism' impinged on my consciousness. Why, in a Jack London story a writer shoots himself when he finds out he has, without knowing it, plagiarized another writer's work. He did not have the courage to be a writer. Fortunately, I was made of sterner or at least more adjustable stuff.
>
> (Burroughs 1986: 20)

The point is less to find a logical flaw in the claim that 'Everything belongs to the inspired thief' than to recognise in these portentous avowals the high moralism corresponding to the high theory of post-structuralism. It is in the claim to confront the law with a higher 'morality' that an aesthetic advocacy of what has been termed 'appropriation' as authentic creative practice has posed its challenge to copyright norms. This challenge is not expressed only in the abstraction of post-structuralist speculation or the street-stridency of Burroughs. Within this arc are found now canonical critical-fictional texts such as Roland Barthes' (1977) 'The death of the author' and Jorge Luis Borges' (1966) 'Pierre Menard, author of the Quixote'. I shall return to the former; as to the latter, unlike Jack London's ultra-ethical and suicidal plagiarist, Borges' twentieth-century French author is remorseless in pursuing his 'plagiaristic' intention 'to produce a few pages which would coincide – word for word and line for line – with those of Miguel de Cervantes' (1966: 66). From a legal viewpoint, Borges is too knowing not to have Menard reproduce a source well out of copyright; no legal shadow hangs over

Menard's aesthetic success in reproducing verbatim but independently some two and a half chapters of the original: 'Cervantes' text and Menard's are verbally identical [but] the second is almost infinitely richer. . . . The archaic style of Menard – quite foreign after all – suffers from a certain affectation. Not so that of his forerunner, who handles with ease the current Spanish of his time' (1966: 69).

We make a serious mistake if we underestimate the impact of Roland Barthes' essay title, 'The death of the author', however portentous the content may now seem. Entering English language circulation in 1968, the essay proclaimed a break with the error of the past, attacking 'the image of literature to be found in ordinary culture', propounding in its place a new critical practice grounded on the 'necessity to substitute language itself for the person who until then had been supposed to be its owner. For [Mallarmé], for us too, it is language which speaks, not the author; to write is, through a prerequisite impersonality, . . . to reach the point where only language acts, "performs", and not "me"' (Barthes 1977: 142–3). In its turn, writing is redefined as 'that neutral, composite, oblique space where our subject slips away, the negative where all identity is lost, starting with the identity of the body writing' (1977: 142). How was it possible to read this as anything other than a new asceticism, a claim to withdraw to the higher ground, a disengagement from 'ordinary culture'? The proffered icons for this mode of disavowing identity were figures such as Mallarmé and Thomas De Quincey who, it is claimed, anticipated this new ethic – in fact Barthes explains De Quincey's cultivated capacity to live in an endless web of allusions by referring to the latter's 'internalising' of a massive Greek lexicon! No such austere toil and self-discipline are signalled as the conditions of the new linguistic mode of being: 'literature (it would be better from now on to say *writing*), by refusing to assign a "secret", an ultimate meaning to the text (and to the world as text) liberates what may be called an anti-theological activity, an activity that is truly revolutionary since to refuse to fix meaning is, in the end, to refuse God and his hypostases – reason, science, law!' (1977: 147). And with this claim of liberation comes the long-delayed synthesis, the recovery of a wholeness relocated in that antinomy of the dead author – the re-born reader:

> Thus is revealed the *total existence* of writing: a text is made of multiple writings, drawn from many cultures and entering into *mutual relations of dialogue*, parody, contestation, but there is the reader, not, as was hitherto said, the author. The reader is the space on which all the quotations that make up a writing are inscribed without any of them being lost; a text's *unity* lies not in its origin but in its destination!
>
> (Barthes 1977: 147)

It seems churlish to ask how readers actually acquire the competence to read, let alone to enter into this dialogue with the totality of that which has been written. Unlike De Quincey we shall not all be able to spend some years mastering Greek formulas by the thousand. But the principle is certain: thanks to the epistemological break introduced by the theory of writing's essential intransitivity, the text is now read as a 'tissue of quotations' (Barthes 1977: 146). And to 'give a text an Author is to impose a limit on that text, to furnish it with a final signified, to close the writing' (1977: 147).

Apart from the crash of 'law' announced in 'The death of the author', Barthes' essay in fact makes no mention of actual laws and legal systems. This is not the case in the writings of Jacques Derrida and Michel Foucault (to whom I return presently). Yet it seems to have been the work of Barthes – or at least the title of his essay – that has circulated a little more widely. It is interesting to observe what happens when a copyright lawyer confronts 'appropriation' as a contemporary creative practice – art on art – that challenges the instituted norms of authorship, originality and individual or corporate ownership of copyright by the explicit and unauthorised reproduction – in part or in whole – of protected works. It is not clear that John Carlin (1988) recognises the problem of speaking within the terms of both the discourse of copyright and the discourse of aesthetics. The contours of the problem – and, yet again, of the pressure to subordinate positive law to the direction of aesthetics – are suggested by his comment that the work of Sherrie Levine (in 1981 she began to re-photograph photographs of nudes by Edward Weston) 'may be unjustified within current interpretations of copyright law [but] it can be justified in terms of recent art history' (Carlin 1988: 137). The combination of legal incertitude and aesthetic certitude gives the game away. The unexamined assumption is that copyright law must adapt itself to the new mode of authorship in which 'piracy, with its overtones of infringement and lack of authorization, *was the point*'. For her part, the artist wanted it understood that 'she was flatly questioning – no, flatly undermining – those most hallowed principles of art in the modern era: originality, intention, expression' (1988: 137).

As a first step towards his recommendation that the existing doctrine of fair use be extended to allow 'a limited exception for valid appropriation without granting a broad right to copy protected properties, something which might undermine the incentives that copyright serves to uphold' (1988: 122), Carlin reviews the history and theory of appropriation. In this way, however, the parameters are set by aesthetic necessity. A particular story of art is treated as the general history of human cultural development, the highest stage of which is glimpsed when yesterday's ideals of 'man's' self-realisation are today revealed as so many crudities and confinements that human potentiality will transcend. The aesthetic appropriators, being more fully in step with 'history', are taken to light the way for us all: 'To understand Appropriation as transcending re-use or plagiarism one must accept that our social environment is increasingly determined by simulated signs and that the realm of the "imaginary" has supplanted the "real" in determining our sense of self and nature' (Carlin 1988: 110–11). Once he adopts the grand Romantic antinomies

– the 'imaginary' and the 'real', the 'ideal' and the 'material' – Carlin is no longer describing aesthetics but extending its empire. The historicist account of 'modern' life and 'man's' divided state comes as no surprise: 'Mass reproduction and its dissemination through the media has changed the nature of modern art and life. After almost a century of saturation advertising . . . and ubiquitous television programmes, our collective sense of reality owes as much to the media as it does to a direct, unmediated perception of nature' (1988: 103–4). Necessarily, in this inauthentic life, 'artists often feel compelled to appropriate the popular images that pervade our daily lives and, to some degree, to help us understand the process by which the media has come to monopolise huge chunks of reality' (1988: 104). At this point Carlin cites Emerson citing Goethe: 'What would remain to me if this art of appropriation were derogatory to genius?' (1988: 120) – the essay is headed by Hegel's not undisturbing claim of man's 'absolute right of appropriation over all things', the 'thing' being defined as that which has no 'end in itself and derives its destiny and soul' from the imposition of man's will.

Would there be less of a problem if the aesthetic and the legal were recognised as two independent and comparable spheres of activity? Within the former, it might be that appropriation 'challenges the traditional notions of originality and authorship upon which value in art typically has been judged' and constitutes 'an important and perhaps an inevitable chapter in the evolution of modern art' (Carlin 1988: 108). Yet here art alone – not positive law – is accorded the voice of universal history: 'Throughout the twentieth century, we have looked to art to challenge our assumptions and expectations' and thus, even though it seems superficially to violate copyright law, '[appropriation art] deserves not to be suppressed, or even shaped by the law' (1988: 138). To sustain this historical necessity whereby a highly specialised creative practice is taken as an index of culture in general, an evolutionary canon is culled from art history. It leads from Manet's 'Olympia', Picasso's collages, Duchamp's ready-mades to Warhol's multiples, post-modern theory and music master-mixes, the latter signalling the expansion of appropriation into mainstream cultural life. The notion of appropriation as true creation receives its theoretical support in a reference to Julia Kristeva's account of the displacement of 'representation' by 'signifying practice', and the claim that the 'literal quotation of popular imagery divorced from any natural context or framework has helped shift the basic mode of representation in Western art from a mimetic to a semiotic basis. The rise of semiotic figuration in late twentieth century art and theory must be recognized in order to accept the legitimacy and social value of Appropriation' (Carlin 1988: 110). Although cloaked in contemporary linguistic terms the rationale is classically aesthetic, moral and dialectical: 'society needs artists to comment upon corporate imagery in order to balance its monopoly over our sense of social reality' (1988: 111). And it will fall to appropriation through its endless unauthorised quoting of existing works to achieve the definitive evacuation of the field of meanings frozen by such bounded and bounding institutions as the norms of copyright.

By contrast with this transcendental aesthetic primacy – 'if one values art at all, one must recognise that its intent and result, if successful, is trans-historical' (Carlin 1988: 126) – the legal calculus is made to stand out in its caution and conservatism. The law is depicted as having to differentiate at a much more mundane level. Thus the object of copyright 'is not to give artists absolute license to appropriate whatever they wish, but to argue that *in certain instances* the flexibility of fair use should be construed to allow innovative artistic expression, which may, *for valid conceptual reasons*, involve the superficial copying of a pre-existing image' (1988: 138; emphasis added). Writing as lawyer, Carlin sees that a limited grant of freedom to appropriate is to be balanced – not dialectically, but according to a practical calculation of the consequences – against the exclusive right constitutionally mandated to copyright owners of imagery, a right whose exercise must itself be balanced against the public policy of access to the marketplace of ideas. In precisely this fashion, the law has drawn a protective boundary around parodic or satiric appropriations by granting them 'a limited safe harbour from the general prohibition of copying in a commercial context' (1988: 125).[7] Far from recognising a unified category called 'imagery' – the law has differentiated appropriation of imagery whose purpose is commercial from imagery whose purpose is artistic. As a result, no fair use defence 'explicitly exists in the trademark context' (1988: 114). It is scarcely necessary to point to the contingency of such arrangements. Even if the courts were to recognise a conceptual distinction between appropriation and, on the other hand, false designation of origin, false description and plagiarism, it would still be necessary to decide 'under what [legal] theory they will protect Appropriation' (1988: 133). This is a matter that aesthetics – because it lacks the appropriate tools – cannot begin to address, let alone resolve; it is a matter of the technical capacity of a legal system to make a discrimination fine enough to 'realistically distinguish between commercial exploitation, which if allowed would undermine the creative incentives the law serves to bolster, and valid artistic expression' (1988: 135).

When writing as a copyright lawyer, Carlin proposes a tightly specified and purposive solution to how to handle 'artistic Appropriation', looking to the United States Copyright Act of 1976 where section 107 codifies the long history of fair use 'as a court-created equitable defence that permitted a limited use of a copyrighted work based on public policy grounds' (Carlin 1988: 105). On this statutory and historical basis, he then proposes allowing 'a limited exception for valid appropriation without granting a broad right to copy protected properties, something which might undermine the incentives that copyright serves to uphold' (1988: 122). There is no word here of that 'necessity to substitute language itself for the person who had been supposed to be its owner'. Here – as a copyright lawyer – the writer recognises that if there is a legal problem there can only be a legal answer.

VI

Perhaps we should question the image of a canon of texts – Barthes, Derrida, Foucault – that seemed so clearly to revolutionise our thinking about authorship by signalling the death of the author at the hand of discourse? But was there such a canon? Having reread 'The death of the author', it is salutary to return to Jacques Derrida's (1977) 'Limited Inc abc . . . ', written and published as a response to the American speech act theorist John Searle's 'Reiterating the differences: a reply to Derrida'. Derrida's response to Searle's reply has us reading very slowly and becoming quite observant. Above the title of Searle's text, Derrida tells us, is 'Copyright © by John R. Searle', while attached to the word 'Derrida' in Searle's title is the figure '1', indicating the first of the four footnotes. The note reads: 'I am indebted to H. Dreyfus and D. Searle for discussion of these matters' – an innocent enough academic protocol until we read Derrida:

> If John R. Searle owes a debt to D. Searle concerning this discussion, then the 'true' copyright ought to belong (as is indeed suggested along the frame of this *tableau vivant*) to a Searle who is divided, multiplied, conjugated, shared. What a complicated signature! And one that becomes even more complex when the debt includes my old friend, H. Dreyfus, with whom I myself have worked, discussed, exchanged ideas, so that if it is indeed through him that the Searles have 'read' me, 'understood' me, and 'replied' to me, then I, too, can claim a stake in the 'action' or 'obligation', the stocks and the bonds, of this holding company, the Copyright Trust. And it is true that I have occasionally had the feeling – to which I shall return – of having '*dictated*' this reply. I therefore feel obliged to claim my share of the copyright of the 'Reply'.
> But who, me?
>
> (Derrida 1977: 165)

The response to Searle's 'Reply to Derrida' maintains itself at this level of rhetorical intensity, with Derrida provoked by the American's serenely dogmatic certainty in his ability to handle 'the intention and the origin of an utterance or of a signature'. As to the ©, the 'question of the "copyright", despite or because of its marginal or extra-textual place (but one which is never simply anywhere, since, were the © absolutely detached, it would lose all value), should no longer be evaded, in any of its aspects, be they legal, economical, political, ethical, phantasmatic, or libidinal (*pulsionnel*), etc.' (Derrida 1977: 168). There is no end to preliminary minutiae which, on inspection, turn out to be the visible tip of deep conventionalities that we accept for the most part without questioning. But perhaps there is no general reason to do so, especially if we take to heart the lesson of Derrida's remorseless twin demonstration of the literate condition of philosophical debates and the plurality of origins and destinations for writing. There is always a further qualification to be made. From the start, Derrida tells us,

> I had, first of all, to resist the temptation of contenting myself with a commentary (in the American sense) on the thing. I say thing because I don't know how to name it. What kind of a performance is it, if it is one? The whole debate might boil down to the question: does John R. Searle 'sign' his reply? Does he make use of his right to reply? Of his rights as author? But what makes him think that these rights might be questioned, that someone might try to steal them from him, or that there could be any mistake concerning the attribution of his original production? How would this be possible? Can the thing be expropriated, alienated? Would anyone dream of countersigning or counterfeiting his signature? Why would anyone repeat this gesture and what would such repetition signify? Why should or would it remain outside of the text, above the title or below the 'normal' boundary of the page? What of all the relations involved in the legal and political context of the 'copyright', including the complexity of the system and its history? Why are copyright utterances making a serious claim at truth? Had I asserted a copyright, 'for saying things that are obviously false', there could have been no doubt as to its appropriateness. But that John R. Searle should be so concerned with his copyright, for saying things that are obviously true, gives one pause to reflect upon the truth of the copyright and the copyright of the truth.
>
> (1977: 163–4)

Pause indeed. The object is clearly not descriptive history; but just as clearly Derrida's polemic is not directed at pre-empting historical descriptions – which of course will work within their protocols – of the 'complexity' of the copyright system and its history.

More than once a door is opened to the 'importance of the desires and fantasms that are at stake in a proper name, a copyright, or a signature' (Derrida 1977: 170–1), yet – unlike Barthes' aesthetic slogans – Derrida's essay builds a sense of the gravity, complexity and positivity of the historical and institutional conditions – including copyright – in which 'originality' or 'ownership' might be invoked. In this respect, it shares a common concern with Michel Foucault's 'What is an author?' (1977[1969]), already considered in chapter 4 as an ironic counterpoint to Kant's 'What is a book?'. Foucault too does not pursue Barthes' aim of debunking the 'author' as an ideological error to be displaced by 'language'. Indeed, he explicitly rejects this latter as a 'transcendental anonymity' (Foucault 1977: 120). The proposal is rather to see the 'author' as functional, historically variable, procedural and marking a plurality of forms of person:

[T]he 'author-function' is tied to the legal and institutional systems that circumscribe, determine, and articulate the realm of discourses; it does not operate in a uniform manner in all discourses, at all times, and in any given culture; it is not defined by the spontaneous attribution of a text to its creator, but through a series of precise and complex procedures; it does not refer, purely and simply, to an actual individual insofar as it simultaneously gives rise to a variety of egos and to a series of subjective positions that individuals of any class may come to occupy.

(Foucault 1977: 130–1)

This is a deconstructive stance with which I am in sympathy. Foucault's 'pluralism' might seem to echo Barthes' avant-garde enthusiasms, particularly given the essay's Beckettian closing words – 'What matter who's speaking?'. And indeed the essay has been read in just such a manner. Foucault, however, was proposing that we approach the author as a set of diverse positivities. In a second English version, the conclusion states that it 'would be pure romanticism . . . to imagine a culture in which the fictive would operate in an absolutely free state, in which fiction would be put at the disposal of everyone and would develop without passing through something like a necessary or constraining figure' (Foucault 1979c: 159). In short, it is not a matter of fact being absorbed into the flux of fictions. It is the notion of transgressing all constraints that is the illusion.[8]

'What is an author?' sets out a programme of historical and cultural researches that has little in common with Barthes' proclamation of aesthetic revolution and liberation. Foucault's 'author' is inseparable from definite conditions of finitude. To give its history and anthropology would be a matter of tracing, among other institutional conditions, 'the legal systems that circumscribe, determine and articulate' literary discourses; this is very much the task pursued in the present study, less with the aim of emancipating than of informing and persuading. Having traced these multiple conditions and historical determinations, it would become clear – as Foucault indicates – that the 'author-function' is neither a universal phenomenon of all cultures nor an evenly distributed feature within a given culture. He illustrates this latter point by remarking that 'in our culture, the name of an author is a variable that accompanies only certain texts to the exclusion of others: a private letter may have a signatory, but it does not have an author; a contract can have an underwriter, but not an author; and, similarly, an anonymous poster attached to a wall may have a writer, but he cannot be an author' (1977: 124). It is also suggested, somewhat programmatically, that whereas in the European Middle Ages 'literary' works – stories, folk tales, tragedies – circulated and were valorised in anonymity, in our day 'literary works are totally dominated by the sovereignty of the author' (1977: 126); at the same time, the pattern of treatment of 'scientific' works has shifted in precisely the opposite direction. As to how a text acquires an 'author-function', Foucault contents himself with indicating that 'precise and complex procedures' are involved. A given work might be claimed as 'literary' rather than journalistic and thus enter the aesthetic circuit where – through interviews, biographical notices and authorial interpretation – it becomes an authored aesthetic work, one whose function is – as Kant might put it – to become functionless. Foucault's programme of researches, unlike Barthes' slogan, does not envisage the dissolution of the author but, on the contrary, the careful retracing of this variable figure across a diversity of institutional contexts, forms and functions not organised into the usual polarity of economic and ideal.

What seems to dissolve, however, is the notion of a canon of writings that had rid us once and for all of the author – and this in so epochal a manner that the set of legal norms founded upon individual identity, originality and ownership was rendered henceforth redundant. Not so, it would appear. Indeed, to have believed that a mutation in the literary theory of authorship must produce a corresponding mutation in the law of copyright was perhaps a sign of naivety or aesthetic arrogance.

The forms in which literate attributes have been personified have varied with different technologies of personification, of which the law of copyright is one and aesthetic education another. These technologies belong to spheres of existence – the legal and the literary – that for the most part have operated as independently from one another as their respective personnels still do. This is not surprising, given their different institutional purposes and competences. In accepting the fact of this historical difference, I am evidently non-aligned with the so-called 'Law and Literature' movement, whose object – however historical its aspirations – has been a dialectical and hermeneutic recovery of a unified substrate for the legal and the literary spheres.[9] In so far as 'Law and Literature' pursues a philosophical unity in this style, I concur with Richard Posner's assessment of the movement:

> Although some fine scholarship has appeared, the extent to which law and literature have been mutually illuminated is modest. Some practitioners have exaggerated the commonalities between the two fields, paying insufficient heed to the profound differences between law and literature. In their hands literary theory, or particular works of literature, are contorted to make literature seem relevant to law, and law is contorted to make it seem continuous with literature. At the same time, important opportunities for mutual illumination have been overlooked.
>
> (Posner 1988: 13–14)

While I hope there has been some illumination of the legal and the literary spheres, it has not been in a dialectical sense, where the one is taken to complete the other in a synthesis arising from a necessary reconciliation of opposites. By generalising the notion of interpretation or reading, the literary sensitivity might think to overcome the usual division of academic labour and gain a footing in the real world of material determinations through contact with the legal text, while the law is supposedly redeemed from mechanicity by contact with the ideal of literary imagination, the whole exchange appearing to rest on a unified foundation in that form of language or writing where mutuality is at last recovered. At its most intense, this dialectical reuniting of law and literature becomes post-structuralist and dialogic.

There is no reason why we must be interested in dialectical interpretation of and commentary on legal and literary texts (of which there has been little in the present study) as distinct from the reconstruction of the historical conditions of their production, distribution and deployment. And there is no reason why we must believe that categories such as 'representation' or 'fiction', 'discourse' or 'meaning', 'enunciation' or 'writing' make much more sense than 'consciousness' or 'history' as unifying determinants or common cores of the legal and the literary spheres. As Posner goes on to say, 'the problems of literary and of legal interpretation have little in common except the word "interpretation"' (1988: 17).

Perhaps the point is this: the dialectical application of interpretive grids to literary and to legal texts is not informative concerning legal norms, juris-dictions, litigation and the paraphernalia of positive law. On the contrary – no matter how historical it too aspires to be – it functions primarily as an ethical demonstration of the reader's own aesthetic completeness, of his or her capacity to unbind the bindingness of legal judgment by performing a textual practice that claims to know no 'final word' since, as Ricoeur put it, this would be a 'violence'. Rather than the infinite possibility of meanings and the profusion of subjectivities no longer tightly bound by legal norms, what I have described is a patchwork of contingent but sometimes consequential exchanges between the legal and the literary spheres and the forms of personhood that each of them has shaped.

Chapter 10

Conclusion

Authorship, as has become clear in the course of this study, is not a unified phenomenon of culture. It is a contingent amalgam of diverse attributes, statuses and persons. Authorship and the authorial persona did not emerge in a single historical or theoretical space, directed by a fundamental imperative in human culture, whether the rise of 'man's' historical consciousness or its dispersal by the transgressive powers of language. Nor did it arise in a single legal framework, with a single set of norms and a common object and direction. It is therefore distressing to read the following words at the end of a superb study of the book-privilege system as it emerged in early sixteenth-century France:

> The concept of literary property as we understand it indeed finds no expression in the French documents of the period. Authors and publishers relied on virtually the same arguments in seeking privileges: they might quote such considerations as public usefulness, but their main plea was always the expenditure of time, skill and money involved in producing the new book and the need to recoup themselves before others were allowed to reprint it. But the author's privilege was a step in the right direction.
>
> (Armstrong 1990: 207)

This distress is occasioned by a mere detail, a rhetorical flourish at the end of Armstrong's important study in the early organisational history of print publishing. Yet the detail is symptomatic of the unhelpful pressures exerted on studies of authorship by a subject-centred schema of cultural history. Why this final reference to 'the right direction'? And what is this unexamined assumption of a rightness and directedness in the history of authorship and copyright? The 'right direction', I would argue, signals the historian's failure to avoid that particular anachronism which consists in describing no matter what element of the authorial field from the standpoint of the Romantic author and the aesthetic persona. The particular conditions and local imperatives of the book trade in France in the 1520s take on the part of necessary preconditions of the modern Romantic author. This is how Armstrong succumbs in the last instant to the pressure to connect up her quite particular zone or island of legal-cultural organisation to what is assumed to be the universal history, to a singular but all-embracing master-plan of cultural development. The 'right direction' is the sign that once again the account of authorship has been conceived of and located within the analysis of subjectivity. And this is to impose a 'future' on the contingently developed and differentially distributed attributes – literate, legal, moral, aesthetic – of the sort that I have been describing.

This instance is not exceptional. We have observed L. Ray Patterson – while adamant that copyright has been a right for publishers not authors – persisting in the unexamined assumption that at some level deeper than that of positive law writers have rights which flow from their being an 'author as author'. Publishers' historical access to these rights must therefore be an incomplete realisation of what the law of copyright should have been and will become – by following the 'right direction'. We have observed Carla Hesse – having so powerfully revised the historical record in relation to the state of Revolutionary publishing – exchange her historian's nerve for the philosopher's bad conscience to ask reflexively what is the general relation between subjectivity and language, consciousness and law. What she in fact succeeds in doing is to confront historical investigation with an obstacle: the assumption that authorship and law must at a certain level of abstraction and conceptual profundity form a pair of complementary totalities – the self and its determinations – joined by a universal process – 'representation'. We get an inkling of what could happen if the history of authorship and copyright became the toy of literary and cultural theory. And supposing we could answer the great question of the relation of subjectivity and language, what practical bearing could that answer have on Hesse's proposition that '[b]ooks require protection in order to exist'?

The object of the present study has been to establish a framework for a descriptive history of authorship as it has appeared in the variable jurisdictional optic of positive law. In particular, I have argued against assuming that the history of authorship has been governed by a singular logic or principle of development. For this reason, I have underscored the importance, for instance, of not collapsing the complex and variable relations that have obtained between legal and aesthetic personalities into a single necessary relation of mechanical and organic, material and ideal, object and subject. The framework that I have envisaged, in other words, is fluid enough to admit quite varied historical determinants and forms of authorship.

I have argued that the aesthetic persona – as the historical artefact of the aesthetic education – cannot be the origin, foundation or destiny of writers' legal personality (where they have had some such status). Perhaps it will seem that in removing aesthetics from this role we deprive the law of its direction – the 'right direction' – and ideals. In fact, once we are comfortable with the notion that the aesthetic persona is not the fundamental mode of all forms of personhood, it becomes easier to admit the practical ideals that the law of copyright has embodied. These include the (non-dialectical) balancing of the interests of producers and users of copyright subject matter; the equitable recompensing of copyright holders (whether individuals who write or corporations that invest); the promotion and encouragement of literary and artistic creation by a reasonable reward for labour and investment; the elimination of piracy; the development of an international regime of copyright protection for an incorporeal and mobile literary property. Unless we dogmatically insist that an ideal is an ideal only if it transcends all possible interests, circumstances, means, purposes, time limits and territories, these historical achievements associated with the law of copyright can be counted as ideals that work. It is quite proper to claim an ethics for the tight line too. The posture of openness does not have a monopoly of goodness.

In the event, the object has been less to proclaim ideals than to open a space of description, one in which authors' legal personality is recognised as a positive creation of the legal sphere. In its turn, this has meant recognising the limits of legal personality – it is not as a human being or as the human subject (complete or otherwise) but as a copyright holder that we can actually participate in the copyright system. This system and the aesthetic education are among the different surfaces on which authorship as a cultural phenomenon emerged. However, that first historical rule – chronology – reminds us that the copyright owner is a form of legal personality that emerged prior to and quite independently of the aesthetic persona. The copyright-owning person was formed in an area of law whose object was the regulation of a traded commodity; as a result, this person has overlapped only fortuitously with the sphere of Romantic aesthetics. Where such an overlap has happened, an individual who writes might have come to bear an array of attributes, some legal and some aesthetic, attaching to statuses and standings whose organisational functions and distributions are quite different. Most importantly – as the case of the corporate or non-individual holder of copyright demonstrates – these attributes, statuses and persons do not all fall within the field of a literary or cultural theory organised by the aesthetic figure of the 'whole' human being. Other organisational imperatives are involved.

This pluralist conviction rests not only on the historical differentiation of legal and non-legal spheres but also on the internal differentiation of the former. Three points can be advanced on this theme. First, it is difficult to agree with those who deny the fact of a 'great divide' between the traditions of the law of copyright and the *droit moral* – this is the view of Stewart (1983: 16) who argues that these traditions knew only an 'interval' of divergence, beginning with the French Revolutionary decrees (he is wrong on two scores). It is worth reiterating that for students of the law of copyright the lesson of the *droit moral* is that the delineation and distribution of rights pertaining to authorship could have been other than they are in copyright jurisdictions. No legal personality is independent of the jurisdiction that creates it as such. Second, while the present study has been limited to print authorship and the law relating to that particular communications technology, there are important differences of chronology, content and policy between the various sectors of what are now termed the copyright industries – music and recording, the visual arts, the dramatic and performance arts, the film industry, radio and television, the computer software industry, all have their different histories. Third, even within the sphere of print publishing different rationales or justifications for the grant of copyright protection are now in contention with each other. On the one hand there is an author-centric or personality-based rationale defined in terms of creation not commercial value, personal originality not capital investment, subjective expressivity not objective or factual content; on the other hand there is a rationale or model more appropriate to the fact that the works protected by copyright are not all 'aesthetic' works, but include directories, compilations and like publications where the element of value is constituted by the labour and resources expended, not by a subjectivity expressed.

Against the assumption that copyright must be one and unitary, pragmatic pluralists have argued that 'the sensible response is neither artificially to force such works into a high authorship mold nor to quarantine those decisions protecting the commercial value of low authorship works lest the grander principles of copyright be infected' (Ginsburg 1990b: 1870). In this instance, double negation does not presage dialectical ascent to a higher and more complete form of being; fortunately, the point is to have us return to the fact that the law of copyright too is not a unified phenomenon. It is not a rationally pure scheme derived formally from a unitary logic; it is a contingent assemblage of legal provisions for regulating and protecting various types of commodity. It achieves this end by a particular legal personification. Only in the special circumstance of a theoretical interrogation are the different sectors and different rationales of copyright called upon to account for how they routinely work. In short, the point is that the law of copyright emerged as a device able to regulate and protect more than one form of authorship.

The pluralism that does not impose a unitary theory on a historically differentiated legal apparatus such as the law of copyright is not a pluralism mortgaged to an anti-positive programme promising emancipation from norms and access to meanings and subjectivities in profusion. To justify its adoption, a pluralism in the former style need do no more than recognise the historical diversity of legal arrangements, of the forms of authorship and of the attributes of the authorial personality that have emerged in relation to the print publishing process.

There is a lesson here for any project to shape a field of legal-cultural studies. What are the options? One is a philosophical and theoretical effort to search out a deep level of necessity in legal-cultural arrangements; another is a more practical and historical effort to limit the work to positive description (acknowledging the protocols and conventions of this latter). In the case of authorship as a cultural phenomenon, this could mean choosing to theorise commodification of the human subject and to imagine its de-objectification or, on the other hand, choosing to trace the legal means whereby a printed and traded commodity and its market have been regulated. In the terms used at the outset, the choice is between studying the conditions of all possible forms of personhood or some actual ones.

In making our choice, we almost certainly encounter the pressures of Romantic cultural history's commitment to subject-centrism and the primacy of the aesthetic. These pressures flow in part from two central philosophical assumptions of Romanticism: first, that there must be a fundamental identity to all the different forms of personhood – legal personality included – ascribable to individuals in their passage through social institutions; second, that this identity is most completely realised and developed in the aesthetic persona or 'whole' person. In historicising these assumptions, the aim has not been an elimination of the aesthetic persona as if it were some terrible mistake, but a better acknowledgement of its cultural and historical rarity. By recognising the aesthetic persona as the remarkable artefact of a highly specialised form of ethical self-discipline that has enjoyed a variable distribution since the late eighteenth century, I hope to have opened a way towards the historical description of the authorial personality in its diversity, complexity and contingency.

The good convention is to draw some lessons from history. A first lesson of the present history is one which the field of literary and cultural studies both acknowledges and dismisses: namely, that so much goes on outside literature and culture. However, a second lesson to be drawn from the historical evidence and the theoretical arguments I have presented is more pointed: positive law – for instance the statutory and the case law of copyright – has a great claim on what goes on within the literary and cultural field. Perhaps there is a further lesson here for the future orientation of literary, cultural and legal studies. It will be in this direction – is it the right one? – that I hope to elaborate the subtext of the present book: the cultural and the legal as different spheres of intellectual conduct.

Notes

1 PRELIMINARIES: POSITIVITIES AND POLEMICS

1 On the historical role of the Stationers' Company, see chapter 2 below.
2 On Curll's case, see Hunter, Saunders and Williamson (1992: chapter 3).
3 On Max Weber, see also Lash and Whimster (1987) and Tribe (1989).
4 I am indebted to Ian Hunter for this formulation. It shows how and why to shift the 'subject' from a conceptual to a historical accounting.
5 It is not a matter of reconciling the different rationales or justifications for granting copyright – commercial value and creation – as if they stood in a dialectical relation of real and ideal. It is simply that the law of copyright has had more than one purpose and therefore more than one rationale. This has not prevented aesthetic projections that treat the law in this determinedly dialectical manner.
6 But see Yen (1990), and p. 243n.1, this volume.

2 EARLY MODERN LAW OF COPYRIGHT IN ENGLAND: STATUTES, COURTS AND BOOK CULTURES

1 See p. 67; also see Whicher (1962) and Abrams (1983).
2 Feather here underscores Natalie Zemon Davis' (1975) valuable recommendation that 'we consider a printed book not merely as a source for ideas and images, but as a carrier of relationships', a recommendation that I have attempted to follow in the present study. Feather's studies on the English book trade are usefully accessible in his *History of British Publishing*(1988a).
3 In the following sections, my debt to L. Ray Patterson and John Feather will be clear.
4 On Shakespeare and 'literary property' see Kirschbaum (1955).
5 On this practice, see Kirschbaum (1955: 197–209).
6 See p. 81.
7 On Pope's mode of using the provisions of the Statute of Anne, see Sutherland (1936). Swift too was a best-seller, but displayed less concern with his interests and 'career' as an author. It is also worthy of note that another successful author – Richardson – was himself a printer and bookseller and, in 1754, Master of the Stationers' Company (Bonham-Carter 1978: 19).
8 For the detailed history of the Stationers' Company, see Blagden (1960).
9 On late seventeenth-century press regulation, see Crist (1979). For eighteenth-century arrangements, see Feather (1983).
10 On the 1695 Bill – including an indication of Locke's role and his position on

copyright – see Astbury (1978).

11 On Harley and the press, see Downie (1979).

12 On the other hand, it was to be the financial crash of the expansionist 'cheap book' Edinburgh houses of Constable and Ballantyne – the publishers of Scott and of the *Edinburgh Review* – that, in the 1820s, intensified the traditional caution of the London publishers.

13 On the early history of English publishing and bookselling, the freedom of the press and the struggle for literary property, see the rich collection of contemporary documents reprinted in facsimile in Parks (1974–5). Unfortunately, given the restrictions of space, I have not included detailed discussion of these forty-two volumes of English documents from the period 1660–1853 in the present book. However, let me indicate those which are of particular interest. In the volume entitled *Freedom of the Press and the Literary Property Debate: Six Tracts, 1755–1770* are found James Ralph's (1758) 'The case of authors by profession or trade stated with regard to booksellers, the stage and the public no matter by whom' and Lord Dreghorn's (1767) 'Considerations on the nature and origin of literary property'. In *The Literary Property Debate: Six Tracts, 1764–1774* are included Alexander Donaldson's (1764) 'Some thoughts on the state of literary property' and James Boswell's 'The question of literary property'. Sir James Burrow's (1773) 'The question concerning literary property determined by the Court of King's Bench on 20th April, 1769, in the cause between Andrew Millar and Robert Taylor' is in *The Literary Property Debate: Seven Tracts, 1747–1773*, while Francis Hargrave's (1774) 'An argument in defence of literary property' – the discourse he had prepared as counsel for the defendant in *Donaldson v. Beckett* but which the Lords declined to have him give – forms an independent volume. To complete this selection from Parks' archive, Catherine Macaulay's (1774) 'A modest plea for the property of copyright' is reprinted in *The Literary Property Debate: Eight Tracts, 1774–1775*, these years marking an intense activity by the tract writers. On the battle over perpetual property in copyrights, see Collins (1927: chapter 2) and Walters (1974).

14 The following account is based on Howard (1965). For relevant documents on Thomson, see Thomson (1958).

3   FRANCE: FROM ROYAL PRIVILEGE TO THE *DROIT MORAL*

1 See below p. 198.

2 While a 1723 *règlement* refers in passing to the 'rights of the author in his work', the authorial right was explicitly expounded in the preamble to the 1777 edict.

3 Despite this, Viala identifies Scarron, Corneille, Racine and Molière as big earners in 'the commercial circuit'. These authors appear to have demonstrated the same acumen as Pope in their financial dealings on the publication of their works.

4 The following section draws on the account of the *privilèges en librairie* in Birn (1971).

5 On the long domination of the French book trade by the Parisian guild, see Martin (1984).

6 The distinction was drawn in the fifth *arrêt* of 30 August 1777, which also allowed authors to participate in the sale and distribution of their works without losing their rights. On this edict as a policing measure, see Hesse (1990).

7 On Malesherbes and the pressures for press freedom, see Birn (1990).

8 Hesse (1990: 123–4) refers to the position advocated by the publisher Charles-Joseph Panckoucke, who called for a scheme modelled on the Statute of Anne.

9 There had been a two-theatre monopoly in England: Drury Lane and Covent

Garden, performing under exclusive royal patents, a situation which was progressively flouted in the 1730s, until the monopoly was restored by a new licensing act in 1737 (Taylor 1990: 136).
10 For an extended discussion of this disjunction, see Hesse (1991).
11 On these judgments, see Edelman (1989).

4 GERMAN THEORY: RIGHTS OF PERSONALITY

1 In 'What is Enlightenment?', Kant (1986: 265–6) offers a further formulation of this point; in effect he 'sociologises' and 'desociologises' his own discourse. Having distinguished between a 'public use of one's reason' – it 'must always be free, and it alone can bring about enlightenment among men' – and a 'private use of reason [which] may often be very narrowly restricted without particularly hindering the progress of enlightenment', Kant makes the further distinction: 'By the public use of one's reason I understand the use which a person makes of it as a scholar before the reading public. Private use I call that which one may make of it in a particular civil post or office which is entrusted to him.' In the former status, the writer addresses the public 'as a member of the whole community or of a society of world citizens'. And then, in yet another reformulation of what is clearly a crucial distinction, Kant writes the following:

> The use, therefore, which an appointed teacher makes of his reason before his congregation is merely private, because this congregation is only a domestic one (even if it be a large gathering); with respect to it, as a priest, he is not free, nor can he be free, because he carries out the orders of another. But as a scholar, whose writings speak to his public, the world, the clergyman in the public use of his reason enjoys an unlimited freedom to use his own reason and to speak in his own person.
>
> (1986: 266)

2 See, for instance, the US Visual Artists' Rights Bill (1990).
3 In his *History of Sexuality,* Foucault (1979b) follows a similar rhetorical and genealogical procedure in dealing with the Freudian subject and psyche.

5 ENGLISH COPYRIGHT IN THE NINETEENTH CENTURY: THE MISSING PERSON

1 In one of his collections of literary essays, Birrell (1902: 125–54) devotes a piece to Matthew Arnold as a literary personage.
2 On *Jefferys* v. *Boosey* (1854), see p. 148.
3 The publication of Johnson's *Dictionary* was financed by just such a conger, headed by Robert Dodsley.
4 Sutherland (1976: 94) instances the 1830s trade in living authors' copyrights.
5 See Bonham-Carter (1978).
6 Dickens was able to achieve a 75:25 per cent division in his favour on new books. See Sutherland (1976: 82).
7 On Tillotson's Fiction Bureau, I follow the account in Turner (1978).
8 There was a technological side to this trade. Tillotsons supplied ready-set text in stereotype form, or printed sheets ready for the local typesetter to copy. As a labour- and cost-saving device, this technique of distribution had an evident appeal.

9 In Tillotsons' Shilling Fiction series (1885–7) only seven titles appeared, the works being published by the commercial houses such as Routledge, although sometimes printed by Tillotsons.

10 On the shift from Shelley's intimate coterie of 'five or six readers' of *Prometheus Unbound* to massive anonymous audiences, see Klancher (1987: 14).

11 In this section I draw particularly on Nowell-Smith (1968) and Sutherland (1976).

6 THE USA: A LEGAL REPUBLIC AND A LITERARY INDUSTRY

1 On the Lockean tradition in early American copyright thinking, Yen (1990) argues that the natural law notion of a right of property deriving from one's personal labour was from the start embedded in American law of copyright. On this ground Yen recommends that the economic model of copyright should again be complemented by the recognition that principles beyond the realm of economics are involved.

2 Ginsburg (1990a) cites Recht (1969: 26), for whom the *rapporteur* of the Revolutionary decree of 1791 drew on these very terms. On Franklin as a Revolutionary icon, see Outram (1989).

3 This seems to indicate adherence to Jefferson's (1903: 166) precept: 'A great obstacle to good education is the inordinate passion prevalent for novels, and the time lost in that reading which should be instructively employed.'

4 On the quest for an Anglo-American copyright agreement, see Barnes (1974).

5 On the emergence of specific genres in American writing and literary taste as a result of patterns of British copyright protection that favoured the British writers' monopoly of existing forms, see Griswold (1981).

6 In England, under George III, three statutes were promulgated in relation to the protection of what was printed on linen: 27 Geo. III c.38., 29 Geo. III c.19. and 34 Geo. III c. 23. See Godson (1823: 302).

7 It would be interesting to compare the development of American book manufacture with the armaments and automobile industries, the usual instances studied in economic history of the emergence of large-scale mass-production (Hounshell 1984).

8 The issue of the homogenisation of consumer taste as a cultural achievement deserves a non-aesthetic treatment. There is a start in Rosenberg (1976).

9 On the Act of 1838, which principally concerned relations between Britain, France and Prussia, see Nowell-Smith (1968: 22–3).

7 THE INTERNATIONALISATION OF COPYRIGHT AND AUTHORSHIP

1 In this chapter I rely on Sam Ricketson's (1987) comprehensive treatment of the Berne Convention and its history.

2 The current *Year Book of International Associations* provides evidence of their continuing vitality and diversity.

3 According to Northedge (1986: 16), no fewer than 2,897 formal international gatherings took place between 1840 and 1914 in relation solely to the founding of the League of Nations.

4 'Into the 1880s an atmosphere of megalomania came to surround the exhibitions, as nations struggled to better immediately preceding foreign shows' (Greenhalgh 1988: 15). Even in this sphere of titanic struggle through the medium of commercial and cultural national self-display, there emerged in 1928 the

Convention Relating to International Exhibitions. For Greenhalgh, however, it was not this treaty, signed by ninety-two nations, but the Second World War which brought effective regulation to the international exhibition system.

5 Ricketson (1987: 38) provides a diagrammatic plan of the network of bilateral copyright treaties.

6 Recall from chapter 3, Kohler's mode of defining the object of protection. See Cherpillod (1985).

7 See Rydell (1984), on the extreme ambiguity of the role of physical anthropology in the US world fairs.

8 Piola-Caselli's account is substantially confirmed by Plaisant and Pichot (1934: 26–9), although not without a certain French chauvinism: the 1928 revision of the Berne treaty to include the *droit moral* provision thus becomes 'the final step in the long task of incubation' begun in the nineteenth century in French courts and carried on by French theorists such as Morillot. Plaisant quotes his own discourse at Rome: 'France – who was first to proclaim as early as the eighteenth century the necessity of protecting writers and who ordered this principle to be embodied in the decrees of the Revolution – is pleased to salute in Rome, mother of peoples and cradle of the law, the advent of a new provision at law for the greater glory of literature and the arts, the nursemaids of humanity' (Plaisant and Pichot 1934: 29).

9 Picciotto (1988: 59) argues that historians of inter-state relations have neglected legal institutions such as the 1883 Paris Convention for the Protection of Industrial Property.

10 On the context of copyright in the Third World, see Altbach (1987 chapter 6).

8 SOME CULTURAL ISSUES FOR LEGAL STUDY

1 It is curious that Stromholm (1985: 277) then proceeds to show lawyers behaving and worrying exactly like philosophers. Lawyers are said to have come back, 'bewildered, to the question what is the motor of this well-functioning apparatus?'. But, when the car's engine is running well, do we ask: what is the motor of this motor?

2 The following remarks draw on Hunter, Saunders and Williamson (1992).

3 Feminist initiative has in fact succeeded in restoring the nineteenth-century concept of pornography as an element in a socially harmful conduct (pornography the theory; rape the practice) which discriminates against the right of all women freely to realise their own integral being. The feminist aim of de-objectification is, however, itself drawn from the aesthetic model of the complete personality.

4 A further relativisation follows from the most significant modern problematising of pornography, feminism's account of its consequences for women. Catharine MacKinnon thus argues that the aesthetic 'principle' of the work 'as a whole' is far from transcending particular (masculine) interests:

> Taking the work 'as a whole' ignores that which the victims of pornography have long known: legitimate settings diminish the perception of injury done to those whose trivialisation and objectification they contextualise. Besides, and this is a heavy one, if a woman is subjected, why should it matter that the work has other value? Maybe what redeems the work's value is what enhances its injury to women, not to mention that existing standards of literature, art, science, and politics, examined in a feminist light, are remarkably consistent with pornography's mode, meaning, and message.
> (MacKinnon 1987: 174–5)

5 This theme is elaborated in I. Hunter (1988).

6 On the historical construction of the right of privacy under United States law, see Hixson (1987). The difficulty of attaching a coherent meaning to the notion of privacy is a sign that this increasingly powerful personal attribute is still in the process of formation. An ambivalent notion in the discourse of liberalism, privacy embraces an uneasy dualism: on the one hand there is the moral privacy of one's conscience and thoughts, a moral or philosophical sense of a conduct that is private because inherent in the freely reasoning subject and, as such, beyond the scope of legal or governmental intervention; on the other hand, an architectural sense of a conduct that is private because pursued behind closed doors and drawn curtains (Brown 1980). There is no necessary historical or theoretical identity between these two 'privacies'.

7 Rather than a moral denotation, the *droit moral* refers to rights which are of a non-material nature, just as *dommage moral* refers to the mental apprehension element of an assault, that is, the injury to feelings, loss of full enjoyment of life, damage to reputation.

8 Thus concepts and terms which later appeared in articles 1 and 6 of the law of 11 March 1957 emerged in the findings of courts, as when in 1931 the Cour de Paris ruled on a case involving a painter who, in 1914, cut up and left for garbage certain works with which he was dissatisfied, only to find that the pieces had been recovered, repaired and, in 1925 offered at public auction. The painter Camoin sought and gained their destruction, the Cour de Paris finding that the moral right 'attached to the very personality of the author or artist allows him during his lifetime to divulge his work to the public only in the manner and under conditions which he judges fitting' (Paris, 6 March 1931). For the leading French authority on author's right, '[t]he French law of 11 March 1957 . . . presents a place of honour to the "moral right" by means of which is expressed the relation that exists between the author and his work, the *mirror of his personality'* (Desbois, 1978: vii; emphasis added).

9 The legislative history of the law of 3 July 1985 was marked by a dispute over whether or not to include computer software under the provisions which were aimed primarily at restoring the international competitiveness of French film and television production both by positive initiatives on these industries' administration and funding (including a tape levy to compensate for loss occasioned by private copying) and also by significant curtailments of the *droit moral*. Other commentators agree with André Kerever's (1986: 68) assessment that 'by and large the new law fully respects the humanistic orientation of the law of 1957, in keeping with the French tradition, yet takes the new technological imperatives into account'. Even in the house journal of the French Society of Authors the view is put that 'the law of 11 March 1957 on literary and artistic property remains in force. It was merely modified on 3 July 1985' (Duvillier 1986: 6).

10 These themes are developed in Edelman and Hermitte (1988).

11 One wonders if, after 'the economy', it is not the 'global ecology' that is now becoming the new last instance of determination.

12 In Australia, the Australian Copyright Law Review Committee considered the case for legislating on protection of *droit moral*, but found against by five to four. See *Report on Moral Rights* (1988).

13 See Jon A. Baumgarten (1992).

14 See Ricketson (1987: 468–9) on the extent of the uses which, under article 6*bis* of the Berne Convention, could count as interfering, with an author's right of integrity. They range from paraphrases and abridgements to typographical mistakes and (mis)performances.

15 The phrase is Robert Gorman's, quoted in Baumgarten (1992).

16 On one side of the debate are those who view statutory copyright as an illegitimate interference, in the form of a state-created monopoly, in a market where creativity could flourish perfectly well without such legislative intervention (Palmer 1989) and those who view this arrangement as economically invalid, such as Breyer (1970). Breyer depicts a contradiction between a (US) government causing an artificial scarcity of supply of books via the instituting of copyright rights and then itself – as the agency responsible for stocking the public schooling system with textbooks – buying at the higher price resulting from its own copyright policy. On the other side are jurists such as Posner (1988) and Landes and Posner (1989), for whom the copyright created by statute is both a legitimate and an efficient form of property right.

17 This discovery of the 'principle' of copyright also has a negative version articulated by critics of copyright. Thus Porter (1989) treats the admission of intellectual property to the GATT as confirmation of what he had suspected all along, the 'essence' of copyright is 'capital'. The present book describes the historical variability, complexity and technicality of law, legal systems and customary practices concerning literary and artistic property partly in order to refute approaches – whether of endorsement or critique – which impose a unified essence on copyright, as if it could be either entirely confirmed or transformed.

18 The French terminology might at first glance appear confusing. While *personne physique* unproblematically names a natural or actual human individual, *personne morale* refers to a non-human individual legal person, such as a company or corporation. As noted above (note 7), in phrases such as *droit moral* or *dommage moral*, the term *moral* has the sense of non-physical or mental, conceptual. Hence the corporation is a conceptual not an actual person.

9   SOME LEGAL LESSONS FOR LITERARY AND CULTURAL STUDIES

1 On the legal status of characters, see Marks (1980) and Kurtz (1986), who argue against over-extension of protection as posing a danger to the public domain of freely accessible forms.

2 Among extensive writing on this topic, see Silver (1978), who expresses concern that the mechanical application of defamation law may ignore the writer's craft and constrain his or her artistic freedoms; Wilson (1981) who suggests a standard whereby if the work is worthy of classification as fiction it cannot be found libellous unless there is clear evidence of an intention to defame on the part of the author; Schauer (1985) who explores the roots of the problem which he locates in more general issues of First Amendment and constitutional theory; and LeBel (1985) who raises doubts as to the applicability of defamation theory to a cultural phenomenon such as fiction.

3 See Prosser (1960), Bloustein (1964), and, for a French opinion, Edelman (1985a).

4 See Hunter, Saunders and Williamson (1992).

5 Rose's (1988) argument operates in the same register as that of Molly Nesbit (1987) considered in chapter 3. However, for an entirely more sophisticated treatment of these themes, see Derrida (1977), considered on p. 230, this volume.

6 This is what in a different context Foucault (1979b) disparagingly terms 'the speaker's benefit', seeing it as part of confessional strategy, not as a brave breaching of convention.

7 Parody is discussed in the House of Representatives Report on the US Copyright Act (H. R. Rep. No. 1476 (1976)). See also Wheelwright (1976), Bernstein (1984) and Dorsen (1985). Edelman (1980) has some comments on the French treatment

of parody. However appropriate the distinction between illegal copying and parodic licence seems to us now – as if the law had properly acceded to the greater values of art and aesthetic expression – the historical emergence of a phenomenon such as the 'right' of parody was a much more contingent matter. Under English law, it was the unforeseen outcome of three trials on 17, 18 and 19 December 1817, in which the radical writer and publisher William Hone successfully defended himself against three charges of having published blasphemous libels. In three political parodies – *The Late John Wilkes' Catechism*, *The Political Litany* and *The Sinecurist's Creed* (Hone himself wrote this last work) – he employed the language of the Catechism, the Litany and the Credo for the purposes of political parody. Hone undertook his own defence and won, despite the efforts of the Attorney General and the judge, Lord Ellenborough. His defence turned on his reminding the court of numerous well-known parodies in which biblical or religious language was used for secular purposes, yet which had not provoked the charge of blasphemy. Why, he asks in his account of his three trials (Hone 1876 [1818]), if these earlier parodies had not been made the object of charges, should his now suffer such a fate? Olivia Small (1984) describes Hone in the courtroom, quoting parody after parody and insisting that he had used religious language to criticise the government, not the church. This obliged Lord Ellenborough and the Attorney General to deny the political character of Hone's parodies so as to argue that every parody of Scripture constituted a blasphemous libel, although they were unable to find any supporting precedent in common law. The defendant responded that, if all such parodies were criminal, then so too were several 'official' parodies which the British government had published in five languages for distribution to the armies deployed against Napoleon:

> Oh, Emperor of France! We accuse thee.
> We acknowledge thee to be a tyrant.
> Thou murdering Infidel! All the world detest thee.
> To thee all nations cry aloud,
> BONEY, BONEY, BONEY!

Hone then named the writers of these official parodies, thus challenging the court's claim that only persons of ill repute were capable of such an action; he further recalled that such deeply religious spirits as Martin Luther and Bishop Latimer had written parodies without being suspected of ridiculing religion while Pitt and his cabinet had subsidised parodies published in the *Anti-Jacobin*. This constituted a successful defence.

8 Yet we read that 'it was at the moment when a system of ownership and strict copyright rules were established (toward the end of the eighteenth and beginning of the nineteenth century) that the transgressive properties always intrinsic to the act of writing became the forceful imperative of literature. It is as if the author, at the moment he was accepted into the social order of property which governs our culture, was compensating for his new status by reviving the older bipolar field of discourse and by restoring the danger of writing which, on another side, had been conferred the benefits of property' (Foucault 1977: 124–5). Here the treatment of the author in terms of the historical positivity of an institution is balanced by Romantic leanings towards a notion of the transgressivity of literary writing. Perhaps Foucault is having things both ways: the argument that discourses are historically formed and bounded by their material conditions and deployments appears side by side with the notion of a dangerous transgressivity intrinsic to writing. It is thus an essay that can be cited in support of quite divergent arguments.

9 The founding contributor to 'Law and Literature' was White (1973); elaborations
   have typically come in the form of interpretive commentary and hermeneutic
   theorising, as in Levinson and Mailloux (1988). Like any other 'movement', Law
   and Literature now has its institutional apparatus, including the symposia
   published in 1976 in the *Rutgers Law Review* 29 and in 1982 in the *Texas Law
   Review* 60. To give one instance of the profoundly dialectical style of such work,
   Brook Thomas' (1987) 'Opening statement' provides the rationale for his use of
   selected literary texts of the American Renaissance to define the legal ideology of
   the period of Cooper, Hawthorne, Stowe and Melville. Adopting a 'rhetorical'
   orientation does not in this instance curb a dialectical urge: 'If law, like literature,
   is related to the narratives a culture tells about itself, so literature, like law,
   responds to its historical situation by seeking ways to resolve social contradictions.
   Whereas legal discourse is conscious of its effort to resolve social contradictions
   but often unconscious of its narrative basis, literature is conscious of its narrativity
   while often unconscious of how its narratives are generated as a response to social
   contradiction' (Thomas 1987: 6). Law thus becomes associated with 'social
   cohesion' and literature with 'utopian projections and possibilities'. Schiller would
   not be ill at ease in reading the 'history' of the American literate field that flows
   from this dialectical vision: 'one result of the specialization and professionalization
   of knowledge that contributed to the breakup of the [former] law-and-letters
   configuration was the establishment of disciplines each with its own criteria for
   legitimate knowledge. Although professional specialization led to important
   advances in knowledge, it also led to the production of categories that excluded
   certain types of questions. The separation of law and literature is a case in point. In
   rejoining the two ...' (Thomas 1987: 15). In fact, Thomas is scrupulous in
   recognising that 'the law and literature of the time were shaped by many more
   factors than one another' (1987: 16). For current surveys of the Law and Literature
   landscape, see Weisberg (1988) and Thomas (1991).

Bibliography

Unless otherwise indicated, all translations are mine.

Abrams, H.B. (1983) 'The historic foundation of American copyright law: exploding the myth of common law copyright', *Wayne Law Review* 29: 1120–91.

Allen, C.K. (1964) *Law in the Making*, Oxford: Clarendon Press.

Altbach, P.G. (1987) *The Knowledge Context: Comparative Perspectives on the Distribution of Knowledge*, Albany, NY: State University of New York Press.

Amory, H. (1984) '"De facto copyright"? Fielding's *Works* in partnership, 1769–1821', *Eighteenth-Century Studies* 17: 449–76.

Armstrong, E. (1990) *Before Copyright. The French Book-Privilege System 1498–1526*, Cambridge: Cambridge University Press.

Arnold, M. (1904) 'Copyright', in *Irish Essays and Others*, London: Macmillan & Co. Ltd; Smith, Elder & Co.

Arnold, M. (1932 [1869]) *Culture and Anarchy*, Cambridge: Cambridge University Press.

Astbury, R. (1978) 'The renewal of the Licensing Act in 1693 and its lapse in 1695', *The Library* 33: 296–322.

Baker, J.H. (ed.) (1978) 'Introduction', in *Legal Records and the Historian. Papers Presented to the Cambridge Legal History Conference, 7–10 July 1975*, London: Royal Historical Society.

Baldwin, T.W. (1944) *William Shakspere's Small Latine and Lesse Greeke*, Urbana, IL: University of Illinois Press.

Barnes J.J. (1974) *Authors, Publishers and Politicians. The Quest for an Anglo-American Copyright Agreement 1815–1854*, Columbus: Ohio State University Press.

Barnes J.J. (1985) 'Depression and innovation in the British and American book trades, 1819–1939', in K.E. Carpenter (ed.) *Books and Society in History*, New York and London: R.R. Bowker.

Barthes, R. (1977) 'The death of the author', in *Image, Music, Text*, trans. and ed. S. Heath, Glasgow: Fontana-Collins.

Baumgarten, J.A. (1992) 'The case against moral rights', in P. Anderson and D. Saunders (eds) *Moral Rights Protection in a Copyright Regime*, Brisbane: Griffith University Institute for Cultural Policy Studies.

Belanger, T. (1975) 'Booksellers' trade sales, 1718–1768', *The Library* 30: 281–302.

Bennett, H.S. (1970) *English Books and Readers 1603–1640: Being a Study in the History of the Book Trade in the Reigns of James I and Charles I*, Cambridge: Cambridge University Press.

Bernstein, R.A. (1984) 'Parody and fair use in copyright law', *Copyright Law Symposium (ASCAP)* 31: 1–44.

Birn, R. (1971) 'The profit in ideas: *privilèges en librairie* in eighteenth-century France', *Eighteenth-Century Studies* 4: 131–68.

Birn, R. (1989) 'Malesherbes and the call for a free press', in R. Darnton and D. Roche (eds) *Revolution in Print. The Press in France, 1775–1800*, Berkeley, CA: University of California Press.

Birrell, A. (1899) *Seven Lectures on the Law and History of Copyright in Books*, London: Cassell & Co.

Birrell, A. (1902) *Collected Essays*, vol. 2, London: Elliot Stock.

Blackstone, Sir W. (1766) *Commentaries on the Laws of England*, vol. 2, Oxford: Clarendon Press.

Blagden, C. (1960) *The Stationers' Company: A History, 1403–1959*, London: Allen & Unwin.

Bloustein, E.J. (1964) 'Privacy as an aspect of dignity: an answer to Dean Prosser', *New York University Law Review* 39: 962–1007.

Boguslavsky, M.M. (1979) *Copyright in International Relations: International Protection of Literary and Scientific Works*, trans. N. Poulet, ed. D. Catterns, Sydney: Copyright Council Ltd.

Bonham-Carter, V. (1978) *Authors by Profession*, vol. 1, London: The Society of Authors.

Borges, J.L. (1966) *Labyrinths*, Harmondsworth: Penguin.

Bourdieu, P. (1984) *Distinction. A Social Critique of the Judgement of Taste*, London and New York: Routledge & Kegan Paul.

Boyle, J. (1988) 'The search for an author: Shakespeare and the Framers', *American University Law Review* 37: 625–43.

Breyer, S. (1970) 'The uneasy case for copyright: a study of copyright in books, photocopies and computer programmes', *Harvard Law Review* 84: 281–351.

Briggs, A. (ed.) (1974) 'Introduction. At the sign of the Ship', in *Essays in the History of Publishing and in Celebration of the 250th Anniversary of the House of Longman, 1724–1974*, London: Longman.

Brooks, C.W. (1986) *Pettyfoggers and Vipers of the Commonwealth. The 'Lower Branch' of the Legal Profession in Early Modern England*, Cambridge: Cambridge University Press.

Brown, B. (1980) 'Private faces in public places', *Ideology and Consciousness* 7: 3–16.

Brown, R.S. (1985) 'Eligibility for copyright protection: a search for principled standards', *Minnesota Law Review* 70: 579–609.

Burke, P. (1842) *A Treatise on the Law of Copyright, in Literature, the Drama, Music, Engraving and Sculpture; and also in Designs for Ornamenting Articles of Manufacture: Including the Recent Statutes on the Subject*, London: John Richards & Co.

Burroughs, W.S. (1986) *The Adding Machine. Selected Essays*, New York: Seaver.

Cairns, J.W. (1984) 'Blackstone, an English Institutionalist: legal literature and the rise of the nation state', *Oxford Journal of Legal Studies* 4: 318–60.

Carlin, J. (1988) 'Culture vultures: artistic appropriation and intellectual property law', *Columbia-VLA Journal of Law and the Arts* 13: 103–43.

Carty, A. (1986) *The Decay of International Law? A Reappraisal of the Limits of Legal Imagination in International Affairs*, Manchester: Manchester University Press.

Carty, A. (ed.) (1990) *Post-modern Law. Enlightenment, Revolution and the Death of Man*, Edinburgh: Edinburgh University Press.

Chambers, E. (ed.) (1741) *Cyclopaedia; or, An Universal Dictionary of Arts and Sciences*, 4th edn, London: Midwinter

Chartier, R. (1987) *The Cultural Uses of Print in Early Modern France*, Princeton, NJ: Princeton University Press.

Cherpillod, I. (1985) *L'objet du droit d'auteur*, Lausanne: Centre du droit de l'entreprise de l'Université de Lausanne (CEDIDAC).

Cobbett, W. (1813) *Parliamentary History of England, from the Earliest Period to the Year 1803*, vol. 17, London: Longman & Co.

Collins, A.S. (1927) *Authorship in the Days of Johnson. Being a Study of the Relation Between Author, Patron, Publisher and Public 1726–1780*, London: Robert Holden.

Colombet, C. (1988) *Propriété littéraire et droits voisins*, 4th edn, Paris: Dalloz.

Copyright Law Review Committee (1988) *Report on Moral Rights*, Canberra: Attorney General's Department.

Cornish, W.R. (1989) 'Moral rights under the 1988 Act', *European Intellectual Property Review* 12: 449–52.

Crist, T. (1979) 'Government control of the press after the expiration of the Printing Act in 1679', *Publishing History* 5: 49–77.

Darnton, R. (1987) 'Histoire du livre, Geschichte des Buchwesens: an agenda for comparative history', *Publishing History* 22: 33–41.

Davis, L.J. (1983) *Factual Fictions. The Origins of the English Novel*, New York: Columbia University Press.

Davis, N.Z. (1975) 'Printing and the people', in *Society and Culture in Early Modern France. Eight Essays*, Stanford, CA: Stanford University Press.

Dawson, J.P. (1968) *The Oracles of the Law*, Ann Arbor: University of Michigan Law School.

Defoe, D. (1948 [1704]) *An Essay on the Regulation of the Press*, Oxford: The Luttrell Society.

[Defoe, D.] The Ages Humble Servant (1704) *The Storm: or, a Collection of the most Remarkable Casualties and Disasters Which Happened in the Late Dreadful Tempest Both by Sea and Land*, London: G. Sawbridge.

Derrida, J. (1977) 'Limited Inc abc . . . ', *Glyph* 2: 162–251.

Desbois, H. (1978) *Le droit d'auteur en France*, 3rd edn, Paris: Dalloz.

Dickens, C. (1938) *The Letters of Charles Dickens*, vol. 3, ed. W. Dexter, London: Nonesuch Press.

Dickens, C. (1965) *The Letters of Charles Dickens*, vol. 3, ed. M. House, Oxford: Clarendon Press.

Dock, M.-C. (1962) *Contribution historique à l'étude des droits d'auteur*, Paris: Librairie générale de droit et de jurisprudence (LGDJ).

Dock, M.-C. (1963) *Etude sur le droit d'auteur*, Paris: Librairie générale de droit et de jurisprudence (LGDJ).

Dorsen, H.K. (1985) 'Satiric appropriation and the law of libel, trademark and copyright: remedies without wrongs', *Boston University Law Review* 65: 923.

Downie, J.A. (1979) *Robert Harley and the Press*, Cambridge: Cambridge University Press.

Duppa, R. (1813) *An Address to the Parliament of Great Britain on the Claims of Authors to their own Copy-Right. By a Member of the University of Cambridge*, London: Longman.

Duvillier, L. (1986) 'Une réforme inachevée: la loi du 3 juillet 1985', *Journal des lettres et de l'audiovisuel* 6: 6–13.

Edelman, B. (1970) 'Esquisse d'une théorie du sujet: l'homme et son image', *Recueil Dalloz Sirey* 26: 119–22.

Edelman, B. (1973) *Le droit saisi par la photographie*, Paris: Maspero.

Edelman, B. (1979) *Ownership of the Image. Elements for a Marxist Theory of Law*, trans. E. Kingdom, London: Routledge & Kegan Paul.

Edelman, B. (1980) 'Le personnage et son double', *Recueil Dalloz Sirey* 30: 225–30.

Edelman, B. (1983) 'Création et banalité', *Recueil Dalloz Sirey* 12: 43–6.

Edelman, B. (1984) 'La déjuridicisation du fait de la loi (regards un peu sombres sur les lois Auroux)', *Droit social* 5: 290–5.

Edelman, B. (1985a) 'Fiction et vie privée', *Recueil Dalloz Sirey* : 489–92.

Edelman, B. (1985b) 'Nature et sujet de droit', *Droits* 1: 125–42.

Edelman, B. (1986) 'Note', *Recueil Dalloz Sirey* 31: 412–17.

Edelman, B. (1987a) *Droits d'auteur et droits voisins*, Paris: Dalloz.

Edelman, B. (1987b) 'Une loi substantiellement internationale. La loi du 3 juillet sur les droits d'auteur et droits voisins', *Journal du droit international* 114: 555–609.

Edelman, B. (1989) *La propriété littéraire et artistique*, Paris: Presses Universitaires de France.

Edelman, B. and Hermitte M.A. (1988) *L'homme, la nature et le droit*, Paris: Bourgois.

Eilenberg, S. (1989) 'Mortal pages: Wordsworth and the reform of copyright', *English Literary History* 56: 351–74.

Eisenstein, E. L. (1979) *The Printing Press as an Agent of Change: Communications and Cultural Transformations in Early-Modern Europe*, vol. 1, Cambridge: Cambridge University Press.

Elias, N. (1983) *The Court Society*, trans. E. Jephcott, Oxford: Blackwell.

Evans, C.T. (1941) *American Bibliography* (vol. 8), Chicago: privately printed.

Feather, J.P. (1980a) 'Cross-channel currents: historical bibliography and *l'histoire du livre*', *The Library* 6, 2, 1: 1–15.

Feather, J.P. (1980b) 'The book trade in politics: the making of the Copyright Act of 1710', *Publishing History* 8: 19–45.

Feather, J.P. (1983) 'From censorship to copyright: aspects of the government's role in the English book trade 1695–1775', in K.E. Carpenter (ed.) *Books and Society in History*, New York and London: R.R. Bowker.

Feather, J.P. (1985) *The Provincial Book Trade in Eighteenth Century England*, Cambridge: Cambridge University Press.

Feather, J.P. (1988a) *A History of British Publishing*, London: Croom Helm.

Feather, J.P. (1988b) 'Authors, publishers and politicians: the history of copyright and the book trade', *European Intellectual Property Review* 12: 377–80.

Feather, J.P. (1988c) 'Publishers and politicians: the remaking of the laws of copyright in Britain 1775–1842', *Publishing History* 24: 49–76.

Febvre, L. and Martin, H.J. (1976) *The Coming of the Book: the Impact of Printing 1450–1800*, trans. D. Gerard, London: New Left Books.

Fifoot, C.H.S. (1936) *Lord Mansfield*, Oxford: Clarendon Press.

Flint, M.F. (1990) *A User's Guide to Copyright*, 3rd edn, London: Butterworth.

Flint, M.F., Thorne C.D., and Williams, A.P. (1989) *Intellectual Property - The New Law. A Guide to the Copyright, Designs and Patents Act 1988*, London: Butterworth.

Forbes-Gray, W. (1926) 'Alexander Donaldson and his fight for cheap books', *Juridical Review* 38: 180–202.

Foucault, M. (1969) 'Qu'est-ce qu'un auteur?', *Bulletin de la Société française de philosophie* 63: 73–104.

Foucault, M. (1977) 'What is an author?', in *Language, Counter-Memory, Practice. Selected Essays and Interviews*, ed. D.F. Bouchard, trans. D.F. Bouchard and S. Simon, Oxford: Blackwell.

Foucault, M. (1979a) 'On governmentality', *Ideology and Consciousness* 6: 5–23.

Foucault, M. (1979b) *The History of Sexuality. Vol. 1: An Introduction*, trans. R. Hurley, London: Allen Lane.

Foucault, M. (1979c) 'What is an author?', in J.V. Harari (ed.) *Textual Strategies. Perspectives in Post-Structuralist Criticism*, Ithaca, NY: Cornell University Press.

Foucault, M. (1980) 'The confession of the flesh', in C. Gordon (ed.) *Power/Knowledge. Selected Interviews and Writings by Michel Foucault 1972–77*, New York: Pantheon Books.

Foucault, M. (1981) '*Omnes et singulatim*: towards a critique of political reason', in S. McMurrin (ed.) *The Tanner Lectures on Human Values*, vol. 2, Salt Lake City: University of Utah Press.

Foucault, M. (1985) *The History of Sexuality. Vol. 2: The Use of Pleasure*, trans. R. Hurley, Harmondsworth: Penguin.

Foucault, M. (1988) 'The functions of literature', in L.D. Kritzman (ed.) *Michel Foucault: Politics, Philosophy, Culture. Interviews and Other Writings 1977–84*, London: Routledge, Chapman & Hall.

Gaukroger, S. (1986) 'Romanticism and decommodification: Marx's conception of socialism', *Economy and Society* 15: 287–333.

Gedin, P. (1977) *Literature in the Marketplace*, trans. G. Bisset, London: Faber.

Gilmore, M.T. (1985) *American Romanticism and the Marketplace*, Chicago: University of Chicago Press.

Ginsburg, J.C. (1990a) 'A tale of two copyrights: literary property in Revolutionary France and America', *Tulane Law Review* 64: 991–1031.

Ginsburg, J.C. (1990b) 'Creation and commercial value: copyright protection of works of information', *Columbia Law Review* 90: 1865–1938.

Godson, R. (1823) *A Practical Treatise on the Law of Patents for Inventions and of Copyright; with an Introductory Book on Monopolies; Illustrated with Notes of the Principal Cases*, London: Joseph Butterworth & Son.

Goodrich, P. (1987) *Legal Discourse: Studies in Linguistics, Rhetoric, and Legal Analysis*, London: Macmillan.

Gray, D.J. (1984) 'Macaulay's *Lays of Ancient Rome* and the publication of nineteenth century British poetry', in J.R. Kincaid and A.J. Kuhn (eds) *Victorian Society and Literature. Essays Presented to Richard D. Altick*, Columbus: Ohio State University Press.

Greenblatt, S. (1980) *Renaissance Self-Fashioning: From More to Shakespeare*, Chicago: University of Chicago Press.

Greenhalgh, P. (1988) *Ephemeral Vistas. A History of the Expositions Universelles, Great Exhibitions and World Fairs*, Manchester: Manchester University Press.

Griswold, W. (1981) 'American character and the American novel', *American Journal of Sociology* 86: 740–765.

Harris, M. (1982) 'Trials and criminal biographies: a case study in distribution', in R. Myers and M. Harris (eds) *Sale and Distribution of Books from 1700*, Oxford: Oxford Polytechnic Press.

Hawkes, T. (1986) *That Shakespearean Rag: Essays on a Critical Process*, London and New York: Methuen.

Hegel, G.W.F. (1952) *Hegel's Philosophy of Right*, trans. T.M. Knox, Oxford: Clarendon Press.

Hennis, W. (1988) *Max Weber. Essays in Reconstruction*, trans. K. Tribe, London: Allen and Unwin.

Hepburn, J. (1968) *The Author's Empty Purse and the Rise of the Literary Agent*, Oxford: Oxford University Press.

Hesse, C. (1989a) 'The dilemmas of Republican publishing, 1793–1799', unpublished paper, Library of Congress Symposium on Publishing and Readership in Revolutionary France and America.

Hesse, C. (1989b) 'Economic upheavals in publishing', in R. Darnton and D. Roche (eds) *Revolution in Print. The Press in France 1775–1800*, Berkeley, CA: University of California Press.

Hesse, C. (1990) 'Enlightenment epistemology and the laws of authorship in

Revolutionary France, 1777–1793', *Representations* 30: 109–137.

Hesse, C. (1991) *Publishing and Cultural Politics in Revolutionary Paris, 1789–1800*, Berkeley, CA: University of California Press.

Hixson, R.F. (1987) *Rights in a Public Society: Human Rights in Conflict*, New York: Oxford University Press.

Hone, W. (1876 [1818]) *The Three Trials of William Hone*, ed. W. Tegg, London and Leeds (no pub.).

Hounshell, D.A. (1984) *From the American System to Mass Production, 1800–1932: the Development of Manufacturing Technology in the United States*, Baltimore, MD: Johns Hopkins University Press.

Howard, J.H. (1965) 'Literature and regulation. A study of the development of literature and literary practice in relation to the laws regulating publication in the first half of the eighteenth century', unpublished Ph.D. thesis, University of Leeds.

Hunter, I. (1988) *Culture and Government. The Emergence of Literary Education*, London: Macmillan.

Hunter, I., Saunders, D., and Williamson, D. (1992) *On Pornography: Literature, Sexuality and Obscenity Law*, London: Macmillan.

Hunter, J.P. (1966) *The Reluctant Pilgrim. Defoe's Emblematic Method and the Quest for Form in Robinson Crusoe*, Baltimore, MD: Johns Hopkins University Press.

Hunter, J.P. (1990) *Before Novels. Cultural Contexts of Eighteenth Century English Fiction*, New York: Norton.

Jefferson, T. (1903) *The Writings of Thomas Jefferson*, vol. 15, ed. A.A. Lipscombe, Washington, DC (no pub.).

Kain, P.J. (1982) *Schiller, Hegel and Marx: State, Society and the Aesthetic Ideal of Ancient Greece*, Kingston and Montreal: McGill-Queens University Press.

Kant, I. (1798) 'Of the injustice of counterfeiting books', in *Essays and Treatises on Moral, Political and Various Philosophical Subjects. From the German by the Translator of the Principles of Critical Philosophy*, vol. 1, London: William Richardson.

Kant, I. (1907) *Metaphysische Anfangsgründe der Rechtslehre, Kants Werke*, vol. 6, Berlin: Drück und Verlag von Georg Reimer.

Kant, I. (1957) *The Critique of Judgement*, trans. J.C. Meredith, Oxford: Clarendon Press.

Kant, I. (1963) *On History*, trans. L.W. Beck, New York: Bobbs-Merrill

Kant, I. (1965) *The Metaphysics of Morals. Part 1: The Metaphysical Elements of Justice*, trans. J. Ladd, New York: Bobbs-Merrill.

Kant, I. (1979) *The Conflict of the Faculties*, New York: Abaris Books.

Kant, I. (1986) 'What is Enlightenment?', in *Philosophical Writings*, ed. V. Sander, New York: Continuum Publishing Co.

Kantorowicz, E.H. (1961) 'The sovereignty of the artist. A note on legal maxims and Renaissance theories of art', in M. Meiss (ed.) *Essays in Honour of Erwin Panofsky*, New York: New York University Press.

Kaplan, B. (1967) *An Unhurried View of Copyright*, New York and London: Columbia University Press.

Kase, F.J. (1967) *Copyright Thought in Continental Europe: its Development, Legal Theories and Philosophy. A Selected and Annotated Bibliography*, South Hackensack, NJ: Fred B. Rothman.

Kaser, D. (1957) *Messrs Carey and Lea of Philadelphia. A Study in the History of the Book Trade*, Philadelphia: University of Pennsylvania Press.

Keeble, N.H. (1987) *The Literary Culture of Nonconformity in Later Seventeenth Century England*, Athens, GA: University of Georgia Press.

Kerever, A. (1986) 'Un aspect de la loi du 3 juillet 1985: la modernisation de la loi de

1957', *Revue internationale du droit d'auteur* 127: 17–69.

Kernan, A. (1987) *Printing Technology, Letters and Samuel Johnson*, Princeton, NJ: Princeton University Press.

Kirschbaum, L. (1955) *Shakespeare and the Stationers*, Columbus, OH: University of Ohio Press.

Klancher, J.P. (1987) *The Making of English Reading Audiences, 1790–1832*, Madison, WN: University of Wisconsin Press.

Kohler, J. (1880) *Das Autorrecht, eine zivilistische Abhandlung. Zugleich ein Beitrag zur Lehre vom Eigenthum, vom Miteigenthum, vom Rechtsgeschäft und vom Individualrecht*, Jena: G. Fischer.

Kohler, J. (1888) *Forschungen aus dem Patentrecht*, Mannheim: J. Bensheimer.

Kohler, J. (1892) *Das literarische und artistische Kunstwerk und sein Autorschutz, eine juridisch-äesthetische studie*, Mannheim: J. Bensheimer.

Kohler, J. (1906–7) *Urheberrecht an Schriftwerken und Verlagsrecht*, Stuttgart: F. Enke.

Koselleck, R. (1988) *Critique and Crisis: Enlightenment and the Pathogenesis of Modern Society*, Oxford: Berg.

Kramer, M.H. (1991) *Legal Theory, Political Theory, and Deconstruction: Against Rhadamanthus*, Bloomington: University of Indiana Press.

Krauss, M. (1989) 'Property, monopoly and intellectual rights', *Hamline Law Review* 12: 305–20.

Kronhausen, E. and Kronhausen, P. (1959) *Pornography and the Law: the Psychology of Erotic Realism and Pornography*, New York: Ballantine Books.

Kurtz, L.A. (1986) 'The independent legal lives of fictional characters', *Wisconsin Law Review* 3: 429–525.

Laboulaye, E. (1858) *Etudes sur la propriété littéraire en France et en Angleterre. Suivies de trois discours prononcés au Parlement d'Angleterre par Sir T. Noon Talfourd*, Paris: Auguste Durand.

Ladas, S.P. (1938) *The International Protection of Literary and Artistic Property*, vol. 1, New York: Macmillan.

Lambert, S. (1971) *Bills and Acts. Legislative Procedure in Eighteenth-Century England*, Cambridge: Cambridge University Press.

Landes, W.M. and Posner, R.A. (1989) 'An economic analysis of copyright law', *The Journal of Legal Studies* 18: 325–63.

Lange, D. (1981) 'Recognizing the public domain', *Law and Contemporary Problems* 44: 149–78.

Lash, S. and Whimster, S. (1987) *Max Weber, Rationality and Modernity*, London: Allen and Unwin.

'Law and Literature: A Symposium' (1976), *Rutgers Law Review* 29: 223–318.

Leaffer, M.A. (ed.) (1990) *International Treaties on Intellectual Property*, Washington, DC: The Bureau of National Affairs.

LeBel, P.A. (1985) 'The infliction of harm through the publication of fiction: fashioning a theory of liability', *Brooklyn Law Review* 51: 281–354.

Lehmann, M. (1985) 'The theory of property rights and the protection of intellectual and industrial property', *International Review of Industrial Property and Copyright Law* 16: 525–40.

Levinson, S. and Mailloux, S. (eds) (1988) *Interpreting Law and Literature: a Hermeneutic Reader*, Evanston, IL: Northwestern University Press.

Locke, J. (1960 [1690]) *Two Treatises of Government; a Critical Edition and Apparatus Criticus*, ed. P. Laslett, Cambridge: Cambridge University Press.

Lockhart, W.B. and McClure, R.C. (1960) 'Censorship of obscenity: the developing constitutional standards', *Minnesota Law Review* 45: 5–121.

Loewenstein, J. (1985) 'The script in the marketplace', *Representations* 12: 101–14.

Lowndes, J.J. (1840) *An Historical Sketch of the Law of Copyright, with Remarks on Sergeant Talfourd's Bill, and an Appendix of the Copyright Laws of Foreign Countries*, London: Saunders & Benning.

Luhmann, N. (1982) *The Differentiation of Society*, trans. S. Holmes and C. Larmore, New York: Columbia University Press.

Lytle, G.F. and Orgel, S. (eds) (1981) *Patronage in the Renaissance*, Princeton, NJ: Princeton University Press.

Macaulay, T. (1914) *Speeches on Copyright*, London: C. Gaston.

McFarlane, G. (1986) *Copyright through the Cases*, London: Waterlow Publishers.

McKeon, M. (1987) *Origins of the English Novel, 1600–1747*, Baltimore, MD: Johns Hopkins University Press.

MacKinnon, C. (1987) *Feminism Unmodified: Discourses on Life and the Law*, Cambridge, MA: Harvard University Press.

McVey, S. (1976) 'Nineteenth century America: publishing in a developing country', in P.G. Altbach and S. McVey (eds) *Perspectives on Publishing*, Lexington, MA: D.C. Heath & Co.

Mann, E.L. (1939) 'The problem of originality in English literary criticism, 1750–1800', *Philological Quarterly* 18: 97–118.

Marcus, S. (1966) *The Other Victorians. A Study of Sexuality and Pornography in Mid-Nineteenth Century England*, London: Weidenfeld & Nicolson.

Marks, M. (1980) 'The legal rights of fictional characters', *Copyright Law Symposium (ASCAP)* 25: 35–92.

Martin, H.J. (1984) 'La prééminence de la librairie parisienne', in R. Chartier and H.J. Martin (eds) *Histoire de l'édition française*, vol. 2, Paris: Promodis.

Martineau, H. (1983 [1877]) *Autobiography*, vol. 2, London: Virago Press.

Mauss, M. (1985) 'A category of the human mind: the notion of person; the notion of self', in M. Carrithers, S. Collins and S. Lukes (eds) *The Category of the Person: Anthropology, Philosophy, History*, Cambridge: Cambridge University Press.

May, S.W. (1980) 'Tudor aristocrats and the mythical stigma of print', *Renaissance Papers*: 11–18.

Mayo, R.D. (1962) *The English Novel in the Magazines 1740–1815*, Evanston, IL: Northwestern University Press; London: Oxford University Press.

Morillot, A. (1878) *De la protection accordée aux œuvres d'art, aux photographies, au dessins et modèles industriels et aux brevets d'invention dans l'empire d'Allemagne*, Paris: Cotillon.

Moss, S.P. (1984) *Charles Dickens' Quarrel with America*, Troy, NY: The Whitson Publishing Co.

Nesbit, M. (1987) 'What was an author?', *Yale French Studies* 73: 229–257.

Newcity, M. (1978) *Copyright Law in the Soviet Union*, New York: Praeger.

Nicklin, P.H. (1838) *Remarks on Literary Property*, Philadelphia: P.H. Nicklin & T. Johnson, Law Booksellers.

Northedge, F.S. (1986) *The League of Nations. Its Life and Times, 1920–46*, Leicester: Leicester University Press.

Nowell-Smith, S. (1968) *International Copyright Law and the Publisher in the Reign of Queen Victoria*, Oxford: Clarendon Press.

Oestreich, G. (1982) *Neostoicism and the Early Modern State*, Cambridge: Cambridge University Press.

Ong, W. (1971) *Rhetoric, Romance and Technology*, London: Cornell University Press.

Orgel, S. (1981) 'The Renaissance artist as plagiarist', *English Literary History* 48: 476–95.

Outram, D. (1989) *The Body and the French Revolution*, New Haven, NJ: Yale University Press.

Palmer, T. (1989) 'Intellectual property: a non-Posnerian law and economics approach', *Hamline Law Review* 12: 261–304.

Parks, S. (ed.) (1974–5) *The English Book Trade 1600–1853. 156 Titles Relating to the Early History of English Publishing, Bookselling, the Struggle for Copyright and the Freedom of the Press*, 42 vols, New York and London: Garland.

Parks, S. (1976) *John Dunton and the English Book Trade: a Study of his Career, with a Checklist of his Publications*, New York and London: Garland.

Patterson, L.R. (1968) *Copyright in Historical Perspective*, Nashville, TN: Vanderbilt University Press.

Peck, L.L. (1981) 'Court patronage and government policy: the Jacobean dilemma', in G.F. Lytle and S. Orgel (eds) *Patronage in the Renaissance*, Princeton, NJ: Princeton University Press.

Phillips, J.J. (1977) 'Copyright in obscene works: some British and American examples', *Anglo-American Law Review* 7: 138–71.

Phillips, J.J. (1984) 'Prince Albert and the etchings', *European Intellectual Property Review* 12: 344–9.

Phillips, J.J. (1986) *Introduction to Intellectual Property Law*, London: Butterworth.

Picciotto, S. (1988) 'The control of transnational capital and the democratisation of the international state', *Journal of Law and Society* 15: 59–76.

Piola-Caselli, E. (1943) *Codice del diritto di autore. Commentario della nuova legge 22 aprile 1941 – XIX, n. 633*, Turin: UTET.

Plaisant, M. and Pichot, O. (1934) *La conférence de Rome. Commentaire pratique de la nouvelle Convention pour la protection internationale de la propriété littéraire et artistique*, Paris: Sirey.

Pollard, A.W. (1920) *Shakespeare's Fight with the Pirates and the Problems of the Transmission of his Text*, Cambridge: Cambridge University Press.

Porter, V. (1989) 'Copyright: the new protectionism', *Intermedia* 17: 10–16.

Posner, R.A. (1988) *Law and Literature. A Misunderstood Relationship*, Cambridge, MA: Harvard University Press.

Pottinger, D.T. (1952) *The French Book Trade in the Ancien Régime, 1500–1791*, Cambridge, MA: Harvard University Press.

Pouillet, E. (1879) *Traité théorique et pratique de la propriété littéraire et artistique et du droit de représentation*, 2nd edn 1894, Paris: Marchal & Billard.

Prescott, P. (1989) 'The origins of copyright. A debunking view', *European Intellectual Property Review* 12: 453–5.

Prosser, W. (1960) 'Privacy', *California Law Review* 48: 382–423.

Recht, P. (1969) *Le droit d'auteur, une nouvelle forme de propriété. Histoire et théorie*, Paris: Librairie générale de droit et de jurisprudence (LGDJ).

Renouard, A.C. (1838–39) *Traité des droits d'auteurs dans la littérature, les sciences et les beaux arts*, Paris: Jules Renouard.

Report on Moral Rights (1988) Attorney General's Department, Copyright Law Review Committee, Canberra; Australian Government Publishing Service.

Richards, I.A. (1949) 'The places and the figures', *Kenyon Review* 11: 17–30.

Ricketson, S. (1987) *The Berne Convention for the Protection of Literary and Artistic Works: 1886–1986*, London: Centre for Commercial Law Studies, Queen Mary College and Kluwer.

Ricoeur, P. (1973) 'The model of the text: meaningful action considered as a text', *New Literary History* 5: 91–117.

Roeder, M.A. (1940) 'The doctrine of moral right: a study in the law of artists, authors and creators', *Harvard Law Review* 53: 554–78.

Rogers, P. (1979) *Robinson Crusoe*, London: Allen & Unwin.

Rose, M. (1988) 'The author as proprietor: *Donaldson* v. *Beckett* and the genealogy of modern authorship', *Representations* 23: 51–85.

Rosenberg, N. (1976) *Perspectives on Technology*, Cambridge: Cambridge University Press.

Royal Commission on Copyright (1878) 'Report on the laws regulating home, colonial and international copyrights', *British Sessional Papers*, vol. 24, London.

Rydell, R.W. (1984) *All the World's a Fair: Visions of Empire at American International Expositions*, 1876–1916, Chicago: University of Chicago Press.

Saunders, D. (1990a) 'Copyright, obscenity and literary history', *English Literary History* 57, Summer: 431–44.

Saunders, D. (1990b) 'Italian fascism, legality and author's right', in J. Milfull (ed.) *The Attractions of Fascism: Social Psychology and Aesthetics of the Triumph of the Right*, New York, Oxford; Munich: Berg.

Saunders, D. and Hunter, I. (1991) 'Lessons from the "Literatory": how to historicise authorship', *Critical Inquiry* 17, 3: 479–509.

Saunders, J.W. (1951) 'The stigma of print: a note on the social bases of Tudor poetry', *Essays in Criticism* 1: 139–64.

Schauer, F. (1985) 'Liars, novelists and the law of defamation', *Brooklyn Law Review* 51: 233–67.

Schiller, J.F.C. (1967 [1795]) *On the Aesthetic Education of Man*, ed., trans. and intro. E. Wilkinson and L.A. Willoughby, Oxford: Clarendon Press.

Silver, I. (1978) 'Libel, the "higher truths" of art, and the First Amendment', *University of Pennsylvania Law Review* 126: 1065–98.

Slights, C.W. (1981) *The Casuistical Tradition*, Princeton, NJ: Princeton University Press.

Small, O. (1984) *The Politics of Language 1791–1819*, Oxford: Clarendon Press.

Southey, R. (1819) 'Inquiry into the Copyright Act', *Quarterly Review* 21: 196–213.

Spedding, J. (1867) *Publishers and Authors*, London (no pub.).

Starkey, D. (1977) 'Representation through intimacy. A study in the symbolism of monarchy and court office in early-modern England', in I. Lewis (ed.) *Symbols and Sentiments: Cross-Cultural Studies in Symbolism*, London and New York: Academic Press.

Starr, G.A. (1965) *Defoe and Spiritual Autobiography*, Princeton, NJ: Princeton University Press.

Starr, G.A. (1971) *Defoe and Casuistry*, Princeton, NJ: Princeton University Press.

Stern, M.B. (ed.) (1980) *Publishers for Mass Entertainment in Nineteenth Century America*, Boston, Mass: G.K. Hall & Co.

Stewart, S.M. (1983) *International Copyright and Neighbouring Rights*, London: Butterworth.

Straus, R. (1970 [1927]) *The Unspeakable Curll. Being Some Account of Edmund Curll, Bookseller, to which is Added a Full List of his Books*, New York: Augustus M. Kelley.

Stromholm, S. (1966) *Le droit moral de l'auteur en droit allemand, français et scandinave, avec un aperçu de l'évolution internationale. Etude de droit comparée. Vol. 1: L'évolution historique et le mouvement international*, Stockholm: P.A. Norstedt and Söners Förlag.

Stromholm, S. (1967) *Right of Privacy and right of Personality. A Comparative Survey*, Stockholm: P.A. Norstedt and Söners Förlag.

Stromholm, S. (1983) 'Droit moral – the international and comparative scene from a Scandinavian viewpoint', *International Review of Industrial Property* 14: 1–42.

Stromholm, S. (1985) *A Short History of Legal Thinking in the West*, Stockholm: Norstedts.

Sutherland, J.A. (1936) 'The "Dunciad" of 1729', *Modern Language Review* 32: 347–53.

Sutherland, J.A. (1976) *Victorian Novelists and Publishers*, London: Athlone Press and the University of London.

'Symposium: Law and Literature'(1982), *Texas Law Review* 60: 373–586.

Taylor, G. (1990) *Reinventing Shakespeare. A Cultural History from the Restoration to the Present*, London: Hogarth Press.

Tebbel, J. (1972) *A History of Book Publishing in the United States: the Creation of an Industry 1630–1865*, New York: R.R. Bowker.

Tegg, T. (1837) *Remarks on the Speech of Serjeant Talfourd, on Moving for Leave to Bring in a Bill to Consolidate the Laws Relating to Copyright and to Extend the Term of its Duration*, London (no pub.).

Thomas, B. (1987) *Cross-Examinations of Law and Literature*, Cambridge: Cambridge University Press.

Thomas, B. (1991) 'Reflections on the Law and Literature revival', *Critical Inquiry* 17, 3: 510–39.

Thomson, J. (1958) *Letters and Documents*, ed. A.D. McKillop, Lawrence: University of Kansas Press.

Thoreau, H.D. (1971) *Walden*, Princeton, NJ: Princeton University Press.

Timperley, C.H. (1977[1842]) *Encyclopedia of Literary and Typographical Anecdote*, vol. 2, T. Belanger (ed.), New York and London: Garland.

Tribe, K. (ed.) (1989) *Reading Weber*, London: Routledge.

Turner, M. (1978) 'Reading for the masses: aspects of the syndication of fiction in Great Britain', in R.G. Landon (ed.) *Book Selling and Book Buying. Aspects of the Nineteenth Century British and North American Book Trade*, Chicago: American Library Association.

Viala, A. (1985) *Naissance de l'écrivain. Sociologie de la littérature à l'âge classique*, Paris: Editions de Minuit.

Walters, G. (1974) 'The booksellers in 1759 and 1774: the battle for literary property', *The Library* 29: 287–311.

Warren, S. and Brandeis, L. (1890) 'The right to privacy', *Harvard Law Review* 4: 193–220.

Watt, I. (1963 [1957]) *The Rise of the Novel. Studies in Defoe, Richardson and Fielding*, Berkeley, CA: University of California Press.

Weber, M. (1930) 'The religious foundations of worldly asceticism', in *The Protestant Ethic and the Spirit of Capitalism*, trans. T. Parsons, London: Allen and Unwin.

Weber, M. (1968) *Economy and Society*, vol. 2, Berkeley: University of California Press.

Weinbrot, H.D. (1978) *Augustus Caesar in 'Augustan' England: the Decline of a Classical Norm*, Princeton, NJ: University of Princeton Press.

Weisberg, R.H. (1984) *The Failure of the Word; the Protagonist as Lawyer in Modern Fiction*, New Haven, CN: Yale University Press.

Weisberg, R.H. (1988) 'The Law-Literature enterprise', *The Yale Journal of Law and the Humanities* 1: 1–67.

Welsh, A. (1984) 'Writing and copying in the Age of Steam', in J.R. Kincaid and A.J. Kuhn (eds) *Victorian Literature and Society. Essays Presented to Richard D. Altick*, Columbus, OH: Ohio State University Press.

Whale, R. and Phillips, J.J. (1983) *Whale on Copyright*, 3rd edn, Oxford: ESC Publishing Ltd.

Wheelwright, K.W. (1976) 'Parody, copyrights and the First Amendment', *University of San Francisco Law Review* 10: 564–85.

Whicher, J.F. (1962) 'The ghost of *Donaldson* v. *Beckett*. An inquiry into the constitutional distribution of powers over the law of literary property in the United

States – Part 1', *Bulletin of the Copyright Society of the USA* 9: 102–51.

White, H.O. (1965) *Plagiarism and Imitation during the English Renaissance: a Study in Critical Distinctions*, New York: Octagon.

White, J.B. (1973) *The Legal Imagination: Studies in the Nature of Legal Thought and Expression*, Boston: Little, Brown.

Wilson, V.D. (1981) 'The law of libel and the art of fiction', *Law and Contemporary Problems* 44: 27–50.

Wimsatt, W.K. and Brooks, C. (1957) *Literary Criticism: A Short History*, New York: Alfred A. Knopf.

Wincor, R. (1962) *From Ritual to Royalties (an Anatomy of Literary Property)*, New York: Walker & Co.

Wolff, M. (1938) 'On the nature of legal persons', *Law Quarterly Review* 54: 494–521.

Woodmansee, M. (1984) 'The genius and the copyright: economic and legal conditions of the emergence of the "author"', *Eighteenth-Century Studies* 17: 425–48.

Worms, L.F. (1878) *Etude sur la propriété littéraire, avec une préface de M. E. Pouillet*, Paris: A. Lemerre.

Yen, A.C. (1990) 'Restoring the natural law: copyright as labor and possession', *Ohio State Law Journal* 51: 517–59.

Yeo, R. (1991) 'Reading encyclopedias. Science and the organisation of knowledge in British dictionaries of arts and sciences, 1730–1850', *Isis* 82: 24–49.

Young, E. (1968[1759]) 'Conjectures on original composition', in J. Nichols (ed.), *The Complete Works: Poetry and Prose*, vol. 2, Hildesheim, W. Germany: G. Olms.

Index of cases

Index

Abrams, H.B. 151–2
abridgments 29, 59, 208
Act of Union 1707 (UK) 52, 55
Adams, F.O. 179
aesthetics 1, 13, 23–4, 33, 78, 83, 91, 100, 110–11, 118–19, 190, 196, 216, 229, 236–7, 239; as complete development of self and 'man' vii, 2, 7, 13, 23–7, 29, 33, 43–4, 73, 101, 114, 118–19, 121, 145, 164, 182, 188–99, 211, 216, 220, 226, 237–9; and copyright 2, 10, 13, 23, 28–9, 188–9, 211, 212, 221, 233; and *droit moral* 7, 28, 78, 97–9, 104, 116, 126, 182, 194–9, 201; as an ethical practice and social skill vii–viii, 13–15, 20, 24–7, 35, 73–4, 79, 98–9, 125, 144, 161–4, 188–93, 211, 212, 236, 239; and law 8, 13–15, 23, 28–9, 32–4, 74, 78, 91, 97–8, 100, 115, 118–20, 126–7, 188–95, 202, 208, 212, 228, 236; and literary composition 71, 100, 117, 154, 219–20; and obscenity law 28, 190–2, 244n; as style of intellectual conduct vii, 9, 33–4, 181, 186, 203, 239; *see also* cultural history; dialectics; Romantic historicism; Romanticism
Alcott, L.M. 150
American Law Institute (Model Penal Code) 192
Amory, H. 134
appropriation, 2, 225, 227–9
Armstrong, E. 33, 80–3, 235–6
Arnold, M. 122–5, 140, 161, 164
Association Littéraire et Artistique Internationale (ALAI) 169, 170, 174–5
Atget, E. 102
attribution, right of 77–9, 98, 116, 121,

182–3, 195; *see also droit moral*
augmentation, as mode of composition 70–2, 86
author: 'birth' of viii, 1–2, 76, 82, 216, 222; 'death' of viii, 2–3, 216, 225–7; definition of for legal purposes 20–1, 56, 189, 194–5
author's right *see droit d'auteur*
authorship: as ethical standing 7, 10, 13, 15–16, 35, 73–4, 79, 95, 98–9, 111–13, 117, 119, 138–9, 147, 161–3, 196, 216, 217–20; legal constructions of 1, 42, 167–8, 189, 213–16, 232, 237; post-structuralist account of viii–ix, 1–9, 28–9, 71, 100–2, 216–17, 221–33, 235; Romantic historicist account of viii, 1–9, 28–9, 35–6, 41–4, 74, 76–9, 82, 89, 91, 95, 100–2, 154, 194, 210, 216–21, 227–8, 235–7

Babbage, C. 163–4
Baker, J.H. 36
Baldwin, T.W. 27
Balzac, H. de 69, 123, 198
Barnes J.J. 127, 164
Barthes, R. 3, 102, 225, 226–7, 230, 231, 232
Bellini, V. 131
Bennett, A. 143
Bennett, H.S. 46
Berne Convention for the Protection of Literary and Artistic Works 17–19, 33, 119, 121, 130, 165–6, 168–85, 196, 210
Berne Convention Implementation Act 1989 (USA) viii, 206–7
Besant, W. 143, 179
Birn, R. 85–9, 90